Making Sense of China's Economy

For years, China's transformation from one of the world's poorest nations was lauded as a triumph that lifted hundreds of millions of people out of poverty. There were always questions about data reliability and growth sustainability, but the general views on China have recently taken a decidedly sour turn. Concerns abound about state interference in the economy, an ageing population and high debt level. *Making Sense of China's Economy* untangles China's complex economic structure, evolving issues and curious contradictions, and explains some key features of this most puzzling of global economic powerhouses.

This book reveals how factors such as demographics, the initial stage of development in 1978, the transition away from full state ownership and central planning, the dual urban-rural society and a decentralised governance structure have combined to shape the economy, its development and its reforms. It shows how the usually pragmatic and adaptive nature of China's policymaking upends familiar perspectives and hinders simple cross-country comparisons. The book also explores crucial topics, including the property market, debt accumulation and environmental challenges.

In this book, Tao Wang innovatively weaves the multiple strands of China's economy into a holistic and organic tapestry that gives us unique insights from both a Chinese and an international perspective.

This book is critical reading for business leaders, investors, policymakers, students and anyone else hoping to understand China's economy and its future evolution and impact, written by a specialist who has studied the country from both inside and out.

Tao Wang, Ph.D., is Chief China Economist at UBS Investment Bank in Hong Kong and formerly an economist at the IMF.

Making Sense of China's Economy

Tao Wang

Routledge
Taylor & Francis Group

LONDON AND NEW YORK

Designed cover image: CHUNYIP WONG/Getty

First published 2023
by Routledge
4 Park Square, Milton Park, Abingdon, Oxon OX14 4RN

and by Routledge
605 Third Avenue, New York, NY 10158

Routledge is an imprint of the Taylor & Francis Group, an informa business

British Library Cataloguing-in-Publication Data
A catalogue record for this book is available from *the* British Library

Library of Congress Cataloging-in-Publication Data
Names: Wang, Tao, author.
Title: Making sense of China's economy / Tao Wang.
Description: 1 Edition. | New York, NY : Routledge, 2023. | Includes bibliographical references and index.
Identifiers: LCCN 2022048507 (print) | LCCN 2022048508 (ebook) | ISBN
9781032317045 (hardback) | ISBN 9781032317069 (paperback) | ISBN
9781003310938 (ebook)
Subjects: LCSH: China--Economic conditions--21st century. | China--Economic
policy--21st century. | China--Social policy--21st century. | China--Politics and government--21st century.
Classification: LCC HC427.95 .W3567 2023 (print) | LCC HC427.95 (ebook) |
DDC 330.951--dc23/eng/20221205
LC record available at https://lccn.loc.gov/2022048507
LC ebook record available at https://lccn.loc.gov/2022048508

ISBN: 978-1-032-31704-5 (hbk)
ISBN: 978-1-032-31706-9 (pbk)
ISBN: 978-1-003-31093-8 (ebk)

DOI: 10.4324/9781003310938

Typeset in Sabon
by SPi Technologies India Pvt Ltd (Straive)

Contents

Figures

Acknowledgement

This book came about after having been a student of China's dynamic economy for over three decades. Over the years, I have benefited greatly from intellectual exchanges with and insights from many other China economists, scholars, policymakers and financial market participants in and outside of China.

I am grateful to my past and present colleagues at UBS Investment Research for their support and encouragement, especially Jon Anderson, whose own excellent research on China has been a constant source of inspiration. My colleagues in the UBS China economics team assisted and collaborated with me throughout my career at the firm, especially Harrison Hu, Ning Zhang and Jennifer Zhong.

People who read various chapters and whose critiques have made the book much better include Jon Anderson, David Dollar, Bert Hofman, Nicholas Lardy, Huang Yiping, Pei Minxin and Yu Yongding. Professor Wang Yong of Peking University shared his insight on China's industrial policy, and I have learned a great deal about China's land policy from Professor Liu Shouying of Renmin University.

I would like to thank Louis Kuijs for his unwavering support. He also read the entire first draft and gave honest and important suggestions. Kristina Abbotts at Routledge encouraged me to undertake this project, on the kind recommendation of Paul, who generously guided me through the process. Poilin Breathnach edited this book, patiently and carefully correcting my grammar errors and ensuring the consistency of style and accurate referencing.

Introduction

Over the past 40-some years, China has developed from one of the poorest nations on earth into a high-middle-income country and the second-largest economy in the world, lifting hundreds of millions of people out of poverty. As the planet's largest exporter and second-largest importer, its fortunes affect nearly every economy and every industry, and matter enormously to international businesses and the global financial markets.

China's remarkable transformation is not just a collection of awe-inspiring numbers or abstract facts to me; I have experienced it personally. Having faced extensive food rationing growing up in China, I witnessed first-hand the blossoming of markets and the growing abundance of goods following reform. As a student of economics in Beijing, I learned from debates and discussions on campus about different development strategies, as the country's leaders were deciding on the dual-track price reform and the maximum size of a private firm. The reform and opening up of China made it possible for me to study and work abroad, gaining a different perspective. And as I continued to study China's economy over the decades, the physical and social transformation around me bore testament to the macro numbers I followed and analysed.

China's economic success has earned it much praise; its economy has sometimes been dubbed a miracle alongside neighbouring economies in East Asia. In recent years, however, the China story has turned more negative in the international arena, with issues such as the state's interference in the economy and high debt featuring prominently. Meanwhile, Beijing's policymakers have grown more concerned about social inequality and the sustainability of growth.

The fact is, China's economy remains a giant puzzle – complex and full of contradictions. Moreover, its economic policies are often hard to read and its data are not always reliable or easy to decipher. This adds to the questions, misunderstandings and debate about China's ever-changing economic landscape. In the past 15 years, working as a China economist in the financial industry, I have been asked questions on every possible subject by people from every part of the world. I have also observed how narratives have evolved both inside and outside the country as China has navigated various challenges.

DOI: 10.4324/9781003310938-1

While the theme of the day or the week has often varied as the market has leapt from one hot topic to another, some questions have never changed. What was the root of China's rapid growth? Was it mainly its demographic dividend, unsustainably high investment levels or, as some claim, its access to foreign markets and capital after joining the World Trade Organization? How fast can China grow in the future and what are the key drivers likely to be? When will consumers start to lead growth? How big is the property bubble and will the country be able to avoid a property-led debt crisis? Can China become more innovative without major state-owned enterprise reform? Can it escape the 'middle-income trap'?

More recently, questions on the impact of deglobalising forces and rising geopolitical tensions have featured more heavily, as have concerns over the potential of domestic regulation to stymie entrepreneurship and innovation.

There are no simple responses to these questions, as one needs to knit together layers of facts, history and contradictions to get the full picture. China is simultaneously a developing country, an economy transitioning from central planning and state-ownership to increased market orientation, and the most populous nation on Earth, with limited natural resources. These factors, combined with its decentralised governance structure and two-track urban-rural society, mean that familiar world views and economic models may often be inadequate to explain its economic trajectory. The pragmatic and adaptive nature of China's policymaking in response to challenges over the years, often successful and sometimes distortive, can also hinder any meaningful extrapolation or simple cross-country comparison.

I feel compelled to share what I have learned with those who may be new to analysing China's economy or interested in a different take on a familiar story. I am fully aware that there are many excellent and well-informed books on the market by experts from whom I have learned a great deal throughout my career. With this book, I hope to offer some new insights from both a Chinese and a western perspective. In bringing to light the changing dynamics of the economy, the influence of key stakeholders, the history of reforms and the evolution of the country's development strategy, I try to explain why China's economy and policies have evolved the way they have. In doing so, I hope to answer many of the questions that persist about this most complex and intriguing of global economies.

1 China's economy
The ever-changing puzzle

China's economy now

For most people, China's economy is a massive puzzle, an incomprehensible behemoth unlike any other. At times, its development seems to mimic that of other economies; at others, it appears to defy logic, not following any familiar pattern. China's economy is a coat of many colours. It is the world's largest economy on some measures, but still underdeveloped compared with the United States, Japan and the western European nations. China's modern cities, with state-of-the-art infrastructure, coexist with very poor inland regions. Its vibrant private firms operate alongside giant state-owned enterprises (SOEs) and are subject to frequent government intervention. It has alarmingly high debt levels, but has not suffered a traditional debt crisis. It is a proud, ancient nation, yet a clumsy newcomer to the international stage. It is only when we knit these contradictions together that we can start to form a more complete picture of the Chinese economy.

The largest economy on some measures, but still an underdeveloped one

China's economic power has been growing since the country surpassed Japan to become the world's second-largest national economy in 2010. In 2019, before the COVID-19 pandemic hit, its gross domestic product (GDP) was USD 14.3 trillion, compared with USD 21.4 trillion for the United States, USD 15.6 trillion for the European Union (EU) and USD 5.1 trillion for Japan. In 2019, the World Bank valued China's economy at USD 23.4 trillion in purchasing power parity (PPP) terms, the measure of what a country's income can buy in comparable goods and services, exceeding that of the United States and the EU (both at USD 21 trillion).[1]

There is plenty of other evidence attesting to the might of China's economy. It is the world's largest exporter; shoppers in developed countries consume products made in China at a dizzying pace – from cheap clothing to high-end smartphones and everything in between. Before the COVID-19 pandemic, the world had grown accustomed to seeing floods of Chinese tourists in global beauty spots, high-end retail outlets and luxury hotels. The Chinese

DOI: 10.4324/9781003310938-2

have become the world's biggest consumers of European luxury goods, from Italian handbags to Swiss watches.

The large size of the Chinese economy and the amount of luxury purchases do not take away the fact that China is still a developing country, as the government continues to insist. Although China's economy may be the second largest globally, its GDP per capita was only 83rd in the world rankings in 2020. At USD 10,550 in 2021, the GDP per capita of China's 1.4 billion people was only about 18% of the US level (and lower than the US level in the 1940s on a comparable basis), and just over a quarter of the Organisation for Economic Co-operation and Development (OECD) country average of about USD 40,000.

Even after President Xi's anti-poverty campaign between 2016 and 2020, which lifted another 50 million people above China's absolute poverty line, there were still 200 million Chinese people living on less than USD 5.20 a day in PPP terms, the World Bank's poverty line for high-middle-income countries such as China.[2] While Shanghai and Shenzhen had an annual per capita disposable income of USD 12,100 in 2021, Guizhou, a province in southwest China, had just USD 3,500.[3] Official data also show that half of rural residents had an annual income of less than USD 2,600 in 2021.

International travellers to Beijing and Shanghai are often dazzled by their state-of-the-art airports, high-speed rail networks and traffic jams dotted with luxury cars. And the modern infrastructure of these cities may, indeed, put New York or London to shame. Some visitors have observed that China, a 'third-world' country, seems to have 'first-world' infrastructure, while 'first-world' countries, such as the USA, have the reverse. China has the most extensive high-speed railway network globally – over 40,000 kilometres

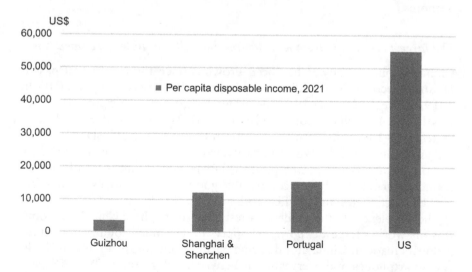

Figure 1.1 Income levels are low in international context and unequal across regions.

Source: CEIC, NBS, Federal Reserve Bank of St. Louis, author's calculation.

of it – connecting all major cities to the capital, Beijing, with a journey time of no more than eight hours.[4]

However, while the 'tier-one' cities of Beijing, Shanghai, Shenzhen and Guangzhou may look impressive, they are home to only a small share of China's population. Very few foreign visitors get to visit smaller cities in inland China or remote, poor rural areas, where public utilities and transport systems are far from first rate, despite the government's massive infrastructure building programme since the global financial crisis. China has almost 100 cities with a population of more than 1 million, but two-thirds of them did not have a subway system in 2020. As much as China has invested in its railway system over the past decade and a half, the total length of its railway system as of 2020 stood at 146,000 kilometres, well shy of about 400,000 kilometres of route the US boasted back in the 1920s.[5] The two countries are about the same size in terms of area.

China's sheer population size and uneven regional development are perhaps two of the key factors complicating the full understanding of the country and the debates as to whether it is a developing country or developed one. Based on its modest stage of development, crudely measured by its GDP per capita, and its less developed market structure and institutions, China looks very much like a developing country and an emerging market. At the same time, the vast size of its economy and financial markets, the number of rich people who can afford European and US-style luxuries, its shiny new infrastructure and the large quantity of sophisticated industrial products it sends to the rest of the world each year make it hard not to view China as a developed economy. While the three largest cities – Shanghai, Beijing and Shenzhen – account for less than 5% of China's total population, they have a combined population of 65 million, almost equivalent to France. These 65 million people had a per capita GDP of more than USD 27,000 in 2021, on a par with the income level of a mid-level European country (such as Portugal or the Czech Republic), and wield sizeable consumer power. Moreover, the number of people who can afford a certain type of high-end product has grown exponentially from a low base, though China's average income is rising just 6–7% a year.

Vibrant private firms operate alongside state-owned behemoths

A common impression of China's economy is that it is by and large state-controlled. In recent trade disputes between the United States and China, a chief complaint of the United States has been that companies in China's state-controlled economy compete unfairly with free-market, private western companies. Following the global financial crisis, when China rolled out large government stimulus for infrastructure, and again after President Xi Jinping emphasised the importance of enhancing Party control across the economy, many China observers believe that China has backtracked on economic reform and become more state-owned than before.[6] Regulatory tightening since 2021 has further enhanced such beliefs.

So, is China a state-controlled or a market economy? The answer is both.

Recent developments notwithstanding, the private sector still accounts for a bigger share of the economy than the state sector. In the agricultural sector, almost all farming is conducted by individual farmers rather than the state, as farmers have user rights to the land, even though the state probably plays a more active role than many others in the procurement of key staples and rural infrastructure.

In the industrial sector, according to data from the fourth economic census in 2018, state-owned and state-controlled companies accounted for 32% of total industrial assets and 25% of industrial sales but less than 12% of industrial employment.[7] Foreign-invested companies and Hong Kong, Macao and Taiwan-invested companies, account for about 20% of total industrial sales and employment. In the services sector, businesses in wholesale and retail, restaurants and catering, daily services and real-estate intermediation are mostly private, while those in telecoms, banking and finance, education and healthcare are mainly state owned.

Weighting the aforementioned sectors by their individual importance to the economy suggests that the state-owned sectors (including majority state-controlled companies and the government sector) account for 30–40% of GDP, though less than 15% of total employment. Both shares have been relatively stable in the past decade, but are significantly lower than at the start of the reform period (Chapters 2 and 4).

In fact, China has a vibrant private sector. Many of the country's largest and best-known companies are private – including listed internet giants Alibaba, Tencent, Baidu and JD. In recent years, other e-commerce and internet companies, such as Meituan and Pinduoduo, have also become very large. Telecom equipment and smartphone giant Huawei is a private company, as is top smartphone producer Xiaomi.

Arguably, some of the most competitive and vibrant private companies are the lesser-known ones in the manufacturing and export sectors, as they have had to compete not only on the domestic market, but with international rivals. In fact, domestic private companies accounted for 56% of China's total exports in 2021 and foreign-invested companies more than a third, while less than 10% of exports were from SOEs.[8] Auto-parts producer Fuyao Glass (featured in the 2019 film *American Factory*), appliance producer Media and sportswear producer Li-Ning are just a few examples. As of 2018, in China, there were about 3.2 million domestic, private industrial companies and almost 13 million private services companies with an annual revenue of more than RMB 20 million (USD 3 million), not to mention the millions of small- and micro-sized firms operating mostly in the services sector.

So, why do people have the impression that China's economy is mostly state-owned or state-controlled? First, the 30–40% state ownership ratio is higher than in most other economies. Also, according to its constitution, China is a socialist country led by the Communist Party of China (CPC).

The '"foundation of the socialist economic system' is 'socialist public ownership of productive factors' and the 'state-owned economy' is a leading economic force.[9] That aside, China observers see many essential services, including utilities, airlines, the railway system and banking, being provided by the state or state-owned companies. The state's dominance of the 'commanding heights' industries,[10] such as energy and financial services, means it wields significant influence over the economy, including private business.

The state's influence stretches beyond ownership, however. For example, while most prices are market determined and free, some key factor prices, most notably those of capital and electricity, are set by the government – or are at least subject to heavy government regulation. Local governments control land allocation in urban areas and can guide state-owned entities or developers in the land auction process.

Another key reason may be that China's government often calls on companies, including private ones, to contribute to national objectives, including through industrial policy. In times of major economic shocks (the global financial crisis, for example) or deep economic downturn, China's government has tended to increase infrastructure spending, mostly through state-owned firms and local government platforms. Such increases in the role of the state have usually happened at a time when the private sector has suffered substantial negative impact from the shock in question, leading to complaints of *guojinmintui* (国进民退) – the advance of the state-owned sector and retreat of the private sector.

A third reason may be that in China, not only are some SOEs still running hotels and bookshops, but the state is also dominant in traditional news media, higher education and research institutions. For western observers, it may be difficult to comprehend that the people they interact with most, their counterparts in China – professors, journalists and researchers – are almost all employees of public institutions.[11] Moreover, most financial-sector employees in China, from security brokers and financial analysts to fund managers, also work for public institutions.

Despite the seeming omnipresence of the state in the business sphere, however, China has had a remarkable lack of state presence in social areas, especially compared with European countries. For example, pension coverage was less than half of the population until about a decade ago and, even now, most people have only very basic coverage. Healthcare coverage used to be solely for urban state employees, though a rudimentary health insurance scheme has now been set up to cover most people, albeit with vastly different benefits to those enjoyed by the state sector. When SOEs got into trouble in the late 1990s, the state effectively defaulted on SOE workers' pensions and healthcare (Chapter 3). Various public events and public administration crises over the past 20 years have also revealed areas lacking government regulation and control, including environmental protection, food and drug safety, consumer protection and market rules (Chapter 10).

Alarmingly high debt levels, but the debt-financed growth model has endured

This past decade, one issue that has dogged the Chinese growth and success story is the country's high level of debt. It first caught international investor attention soon after the global financial crisis, when China embarked on a massive, debt-fuelled government stimulus package.[12] At the onset of the financial crisis, China rolled out its 'RMB 4 trillion' stimulus package to support domestic growth and offset the unprecedented shock. With super-easy monetary and credit policy all round, local governments borrowed extensively to invest in infrastructure. As a result, China's overall debt-to-GDP ratio rose by more than 30 percentage points in 2009 and another 13 percentage points in 2010.

That proved just the beginning of China's long stretch of leveraging up. Exiting this debt-financed growth has been tricky. Construction that began with stimulus needed additional funding to continue; demand created by stimulus led to more corporate investment financed by additional debt; and each time the central government tightened credit, the threat of a sharp growth slowdown dented its resolve. From 2008 to 2016, China's debt as a share of GDP increased by 120 percentage points to 272%. A deleveraging campaign between 2016 and 2018 briefly helped China stabilise its debt levels, but this was interrupted by the US–China trade war in 2019 and the COVID-19 pandemic thereafter. At the end of 2020, China's debt-to-GDP ratio was almost 300%, more than 140 percentage points higher than in 2008, though it dipped by about 8 percentage points in 2021.[13] China's debt level is not only the highest among emerging markets, but also higher than those of many more developed economies (though not yet as high as that of Japan, which stood at more than 400% of GDP in 2021).

With the sharp rise in Chinese debt over the past decade, international investors, China observers and international financial institutions have all raised concerns about the threat of a debt or financial crisis. Globally, periods of rapid credit growth are often followed by financial crises.[14] Naturally, alarms were sounded after the 2009–2010 credit boom. Worries about China's debt burden were ramped up again in 2015–2016, as the country borrowed more to finance its excess capacity industries after the property downturn.[15] Indeed, many observers at the time forecast a serious debt or financial crisis in China that would not only bring a sharp drop in growth, but also the failure of the banking system and the collapse of the renminbi. So far, however, predictions of China's debt demise have not materialised, even as debt levels climb to new heights.

Defying convention, China has had one of the largest and longest credit booms in history. Its financial system has 'high leverage, maturity mismatches, credit risk and opacity' – all the features of an economy 'liable to a crisis', as the *Financial Times*' Martin Wolf wrote in 2018.[16] Yet, its debt-financed growth model appears to have lasted far longer, at much higher debt levels than many thought possible. This is a puzzle we will analyse in greater detail in Chapter 9. One thing to highlight here, however, is China's high domestic savings rate, which has helped it to finance its debt. Government controls on the banking system and limited ways for domestic savings to leave the country have also played a significant role.

A proud, ancient nation, but a clumsy newcomer to the international stage

China is proud of being an ancient civilisation with 5000 years of history. Students in middle school learn that China invented paper making around 100 BCE, created a bureaucratic examination selection system some 1400 years ago and sent the largest naval fleet to explore the world half a century before Christopher Columbus. They study teachings by philosopher Confucius from 2500 years ago and recite poetry written in 700 CE, in a language that has changed little. Some scholars estimate that China accounted for as much as 30% of the world economy around 1820 CE, before it suffered a long period of stagnation.[17]

The history of the 19th and 20th centuries, however, is much darker – plagued by domestic turmoil, colonial encroachment and foreign invasion that saw humiliating defeats in multiple wars and the secession of large amounts of territory. Although China was victorious in the Second World War and became a founding member of the United Nations, the country was beset by civil war that ended with the CPC establishing the People's Republic of China on the mainland in 1949. The country was not recognised by the United States and some other major western powers until the 1970s.

When China finally re-entered the international community in the late 1970s, it had been closed for nearly three decades. It was a poor country, with an economy that accounted for less than 2% of the world's GDP. It cautiously opened its doors to the west by setting up special economic zones in 1980 and sending its first batch of exchange students to the United States. The main objectives of its interaction with the outside world at the time were to learn about advanced foreign technology and import much-needed equipment and materials to help the country develop its economy while still preserving its socialist ideology.

Following much debate and many setbacks, China has gradually opened up further and integrated more fully with the rest of the world. Still, its foreign policy has for more than two decades adhered to Deng Xiaoping's mantra of – 'taoguangyanghui (韬光养晦)', or 'keeping a low profile' and avoiding being a leader. By the early 2000s, there were growing calls from the international community, including from the United States, for China to shoulder more international responsibility, including in the United Nations peacekeeping efforts.

As the size of its economy ballooned from USD 1 trillion in 2001 to more than USD 17 trillion in 2021, China's role on the international stage changed and, with it, the world's attitude towards it. With its rapid economic ascent, China suddenly found itself in a very different position – one of enormous economic influence, while still considering itself a poor country. The existing world economic order (which China had no part in shaping) did not have time to acclimatise or adjust to its rapid rise to prominence. China thus found itself in a position where it was still asking for accommodation from developed nations, but wielded an economic might that was unpalatable to many.

China's history plays an important role in how it engages internationally. Immensely proud of its culture and history, but humiliated by major powers over the past 200 years, the country is eager to project strength and become an equal of the big global players. This pride often prompts China's government and propaganda machine to show off the biggest and best to foreign visitors and the world and to under-report poor and backward elements.

State media also tend to emphasise (and often exaggerate) the government's role in China's economic achievement. Moreover, as a legacy of the planned economy, the government is traditionally not inclined to explain its policy plans or intentions to the market or the public, often leading to misinterpretation or misinformation. It does not help that most official speeches, even those made outside of China, frequently target the domestic audience, using language that is politically correct at home but hard to decipher abroad. Such unbalanced messaging and information sharing can make it difficult for other countries to grasp the policies and intent of the Chinese leadership.

Lacking experience, China also took time to understand that with greater power comes greater responsibility. China does not seem to be very aware of the impact of its domestic policies on the rest of the world and is unaccustomed to explaining its side of the story (more in Chapter 10). Meanwhile, the country's apparent ease with using its newly found economic power to punish or reward foreign companies or small countries, and its lack of coordination with global institutions (e.g., when investing in or lending to African countries) has often been met with suspicion and hostility.

China's rapid rise and its clumsiness in navigating the international stage may be among the main factors behind the significant negative shift in how the western world views China. A recent Pew survey of public opinion found that 75% of US respondents had negative opinions of China in 2021 – a historical high – while the majority of respondents in most developed countries had a negative view, compared with 30–40% just over a decade ago.[18] A recent Gallup poll in the United States also showed a sharp rise in unfavourable opinions of China over the past two years.[19]

Key elements in understanding China's economic dynamics

These are just some of the seemingly unfathomable contradictions and conundrums of China's economy. As we analyse China's economy in greater detail and try to decode some of these mysteries, we highlight a few key elements critical to better understanding its full dynamics: its population size, its starting point at the dawn of the 'reform and opening' period, the plan-to-market transitional nature of its economy, its political system, its governance structure, the rural–urban divide and social inequality, and the government's pragmatic and adaptive approach to economic policy.

Size matters

China has the world's largest population, totalling 1.4 billion people as of 2020. That is 18% of the global population and more than all of the advanced economies (38 OECD countries) combined. Bear in mind that this is after China implemented a strict population control policy for nearly 40 years – the country accounted for 22% of the world's population in the early 1980s. Moreover, this vast population lives in a country with relatively few natural resources (China's arable land per capita, for instance, is less than half the world average). Over millennia of Chinese history, grave policy mistakes combined with natural disasters have caused major famines, social upheaval and violent dynastic coups.

China's particular blend of size and a long history of disastrous social turmoil help explain why the government is obsessed with feeding its people and maintaining social stability. It helps to explain the gradualist approach the government has taken to reform and opening, its reluctance to rely heavily on imported resources, especially food (grain), and its insistence on maintaining control over economic affairs that are largely decided by markets in advanced market economies. It also illuminates some of China's unique policies, for example, its draconian 'one child' family-planning policy from the 1980s, lifted only recently, its strict controls on rural and urban land supply and the *hukou* household registration system that binds people to the land and to the social benefit system (see Chapter 6 for more on land policy and *hukou*).

China's girth also explains its enormous impact when it emerged onto the global stage in the 1970s. It clarifies the reasons behind the chasm between China's view of itself and the world's view of China. While China has gone to great lengths to emphasise its developing country status, highlighting its low-income level, consumption of resources and emissions per capita, the world sees the totality of the country's demand for resources and its pollution levels. When a 1.4-billion-strong economy industrialises at the record pace that China did, prompting hundreds of millions of people to migrate to cities in less than 20 years, it is no surprise that its commodity usage exceeds that of the world's most industrialised economies or, indeed, the largest economy.

The starting point

At the start of its reform period in the late 1970s, China was a centrally planned economy with little to no private sector and very little interaction with the rest of the world. It was a very poor and largely agricultural society, where most people were dependent on subsistence farming. This helps to explain its initial focus on stimulating agricultural production through various reforms while taking a gradual approach to introducing market forces and adopting a cautious attitude to SOE reforms. Over subsequent decades, China gradually shifted in the direction of a market economy, but did not undertake mass privatisation or make drastic changes to its institutions.

Considering where the Chinese economy started, its lack of markets and original economic institutions can help us understand the transitional nature of the economy and the incomplete nature of its reforms. This, in turn, can help us better assess both the progress made and challenges remaining in China's economy. At any point in the 1980s, 1990s or 2000s, China's economy was not as market oriented as the western economies or as many international economists and foreign investors had hoped. All the while, however, it was moving closer.

Today, China's economists and observers talk about the need for private companies to have a more level playing field with SOEs, for the market to play a decisive role in resource allocation (especially capital) and for the social welfare system to change to help achieve more sustainable and inclusive growth. In each of these key areas, the narratives and policy objectives have progressed significantly over the past four decades. From not having a private sector and debating whether to allow private companies to employ more than seven people in the 1980s, China privatised many SOEs and encouraged private-sector development in the 1990s. Now, the private sector plays a major role in the economy and the discussion is about fair access and competition.

On the resource front, prior to the reforms, the state allocated all resources according to plan. In the 1980s, it gradually introduced market pricing for goods and started to leave decision-making up to individuals and companies. In the 1990s, it established market mechanisms more broadly, including a capital market and, over the past two decades, it has further liberalised labour and the financial markets. Similarly, at the beginning of the reform period, people were not allowed to move home. Welfare was only afforded to the few who worked in urban SOEs. With the freedom to move around the country came massive rural–urban migration in the 1990s and 2000s. A nascent social welfare system followed in the late 1990s and has expanded significantly in the past decade. These are significant improvements.

Similarly, while China's current challenges are to move up the manufacturing value chain, master advanced technology and stave off decoupling pressures on the supply chain, it is important to remember that in the 1970s, China did not have the ability to produce much of anything, either to meet its own industrialisation needs or those of the international market. It was with the help of the right policies, foreign capital and the international market that China became the 'factory of the world' and the globe's largest exporter. It faced new challenges at every step: rapidly mobilising and accumulating capital, attracting labour-intensive industries at the outset with little protection for its own labour force or environment, and learning-by-doing with the help of industrial policy (but also learning when to abandon protection, with mixed results) to develop its domestic capabilities. While innovation is now considered one of China's biggest challenges, looking back at its starting point and seeing how production has become exponentially more sophisticated, how education has improved and how research and development (R&D) spending and patents have grown over the past couple of decades, it is also possible to see a path of success for the future.

Political system and governance structure

By classifying the country as being in the 'primary stage of socialism' in 1987,[20] the reformers in the CPC were able to incorporate private-sector development and market economics into China's socialist ideology and political system. The 14th CPC Congress in 1992 provided the ideological cover of the 'socialist market economy' for market-oriented reforms. However, the CPC has always insisted that the reforms and market liberalisation are meant to strengthen the socialist regime and that public ownership will remain a core part of the economic system.

This helps to explain why China was hesitant in tackling the SOE issues in the 1980s, never launched any mass privatisation programmes in the 1990s and, more recently, despite periods of significant difficulty with SOE performance, insisted on making 'big and strong' SOEs, which is the key objective of SOE reform. A flourishing private sector and the development of market mechanisms will always coexist with public ownership, especially in strategically important sectors.

China's governance structure is shaped by the political system, its size and its history. First, the CPC has absolute power over the political and governance system. Its leadership structure sits above the government administration. The party secretary of any government agency or organisation is senior to the administrative head (e.g., the party secretary of a province is senior to the governor).

Second, while China is still in the process of building and refining modern governance institutions in the economic sphere, including laws and administrative bodies to carry out policies and enforce laws and contracts, the CPC has a well-established and far-reaching network from top to bottom that can carry out policy orders. A key reform objective in the 1980s and 1990s was 'dangzheng fenkai' (党政分开) and 'zhengqi fenkai' (政企分开) – to separate the Party from the government and the government from enterprises. However, the former did not proceed very far and the CPC leadership has been strengthened in recent years. Thus, the CPC structure plays a crucial role in ensuring economic policy implementation, especially if formal administrative or legal channels are not well established.

Third, notwithstanding the strong central leadership of the CPC, China's local governments (provincial CPC secretaries and governors) hold a lot of economic sway and have always had some relative autonomy to carry out policies as they see fit for their regions. Given the size of the country and the different circumstances in each region, even emperors in the past had to contend with powerful local rulers, leaving them with some autonomy. In China's economic development and policy evolution, the interests and role of local governments cannot be underestimated.

Unbalanced regional development and gaping social inequality

It may not be apparent to people living in or visiting large coastal cities that are clean and devoid of the ghettos common to large emerging-market cities, but China's economic development is regionally unbalanced, with a deep rural–urban divide and serious inequality. While large cities on China's eastern and southern coast may be as developed and modern as any other major international city, regions in the middle of the country are far less wealthy, while many places in the west of the nation are still at in the early stages of modernisation and industrialisation. China's regional differences in economic development are perhaps greater than across the various countries of the EU, stemming from differences in natural endowment and geographical location (connection to the international market, for example), as well as the country's disparate policies on market liberalisation and fiscal decentralisation.

Moreover, China's rural–urban divide is sizeable, having widened in the first three decades of the reform period. Such a divide comes not only from the economic structure and the productivity gap between agriculture and non-farming activities, but also from institutions, including the *hukou* system, which deliberately created different tiers of access to education, healthcare, public services and economic opportunities for people born in different places.

For example, although rural residents now have rudimentary pension and healthcare coverage, they are a fraction of that enjoyed by urban residents. More than 200 million rural migrants who live in cities do not have the same access and benefits as their urban counterparts. This deep social divide and institutionalised inequality endanger social stability and sustainable growth, something of which the government is aware and has tried to remedy. This helps to explain in part its fiscal recentralisation moves and its striving for 'common prosperity', but narrowing the rural–urban gap and reducing social inequality will be no less challenging than in other parts of the world.

Pragmatic and adaptive policymaking

The state's role in China's economic evolution has been important in at least two regards: it has been an active, 'visible hand' in the economy and it has taken an adaptive approach to economic policy and development strategy. The first aspect we mentioned earlier – transitioning from a fully state-owned, centrally planned economy and retaining the socialist system, China's state has played a diminishing but still active role in the economy through state ownership, resource allocation, industrial policy and macroeconomic intervention. The second aspect requires us to review the history of China's economic development over the past four decades and observe how the government has shifted its growth model and policy focus over time as circumstances have changed. Understanding the government's pragmatism and adaptive policymaking will help us grasp why China has been able to overcome many significant challenges in the past and why predictions of the failure of China's strategies based on seemingly reasonable analysis of its flaws have not materialised to date. It can also help us understand how China's economy might evolve in the future.

China's 1980s reform was initially modelled on early reform experiments in Eastern Europe, such as those in Hungary, Poland and Yugoslavia, gradually reducing collective farming, allowing private ownership, liberalising SOEs and introducing market forces. China continued with this piecemeal approach even after the Eastern European countries adopted 'shock therapy' reforms following the fall of the Berlin Wall. From the mid to late 1980s, China also looked to East Asian 'miracle' economies such as Korea and Taiwan for inspiration,[21] mobilising high national savings rates to increase investment, promoting exports and foreign investment, and emphasising growth and macro stability.

Following Deng Xiaoping's tour of southern China in 1992, the pace of reform accelerated, which helped to establish a broad market economy. However, the incomplete nature of the reforms and long-built-up legacy issues led to SOE and debt restructuring in the late 1990s. In the process of restructuring, China's government began to realise the importance of building a scaffolding system to support the reforms, especially a social safety net, financial and other regulations, a sound and commercially oriented banking system and functioning capital markets. Entering the 21st century, China's policy mix and growth model continued to evolve, with the role of the government and the state enlarged in some areas, tax and administrative controls reduced in others, and the country becoming less export oriented.

Throughout this process, international opinion leaders and foreign investors viewed China's growth from myriad angles. While many were impressed by its rapid development and looked for explanations of its success, sceptics and critics pointed to the problems and vulnerabilities of its economy.

In the early 1990s, China was often compared with Eastern European countries and Russia, which were transitioning from socialist, centrally planned regimes to more market-oriented economic systems. Such comparisons often left China bathed in an unfavourable light. Mainstream economic thinking held that, for such a transition to be successful, a country must fundamentally change the ownership structure of its economy by breaking up the old system and establishing a new one. As China was taking a gradualist approach (Chapter 3) by allowing private ownership without dismantling SOEs, so the argument went, it would eventually be overtaken by Eastern Europe and Russia, which had undertaken mass privatisation to quickly bring about a private sector-dominated capitalist economic system. Although these economies were experiencing sharp declines in production and income levels, it was widely believed that the short-term pain of establishing the proper market mechanisms would ultimately pay off. Their growth and productivity would improve, while China's model was doomed to fail in the longer term. And while some Eastern European economies did see a marked improvement later on, China has seen sustained growth for three decades ever since.

From the mid-1990s, China was compared more with the East Asian 'miracle' economies in both the positive and negative sense. Sceptics underscored that China's growth performance, like that of East Asia, was mainly driven by capital accumulation rather than productivity gains and was not sustainable.[22] And, indeed, China's growth model seemed to run into problems in the late 1990s after a period of rapid debt-fuelled growth. Economic growth slowed sharply, most SOEs were loss-making, and millions of people were laid off in major urban centres. Many economists believed that data in the late 1990s overstated China's true growth rate[23] and understated its actual debt and unemployment issues. Some China bears also warned of the imminent collapse of China's economy.[24] Optimists such as Justin Yifu Lin, a prominent and highly influential economist in Beijing, in contrast, believed China could follow the growth trajectory of Japan and the East Asian 'dragons' and sustain high-single-digit growth for several more decades.[25]

Over the past 15 years or so, China has often been compared with other emerging economies, especially those of Latin America. The comparisons first focused on the dangers of debt accumulation and financial crisis after China used massive stimulus to grow out of the global financial crisis. More recently, they have honed in on the likelihood of a 'middle-income trap'.[26] Pritchett and Summers (2014) predicted that China's growth could soon follow 'regression to the mean' and slow substantially (to, say, 2%), as countries often do.[27] They argued that China's high level of state control, corruption and lack of the rule of law (relative to most advanced economies) meant that there was a significant chance of growth slowing suddenly and for a long period of time. Others have also pointed to China's institutional weakness from a western perspective and questioned the long-term sustainability of its growth. More recently, as the United States imposed restrictions on China's access to advanced technology and components, there has been growing scepticism as to whether the country can be innovative and move up the technology scale to sustain long-term growth.

These perspectives and criticisms of China's economy have often shone a light on the biggest challenges it faced at any given time. And yet, China has so far managed to continue to grow rapidly, despite the various challenges and deficiencies of its economic system. Interestingly, foreign direct investment in and profits from China have also continued to expand. So, why have most of the pessimistic predictions not materialised (yet)?

Here, the Chinese government's adaptive and pragmatic policies and approach to development have played a critical role in the past. They have helped the country to address the most pressing issues of the time, forging a dynamic development path and making any extrapolation unwise. For example, the role of the state has been more prominent in China than in most other economies, but has declined over the years, is now adjusting, and will undoubtedly continue to evolve over time and as societal demand changes. China did rely on capital accumulation as the biggest driver of growth, like the East Asian economies, but it also adopted market-oriented reforms, cut tariffs, introduced foreign competition and reformed domestic institutions to promote growth and macro stability. These reforms and policies not only made it possible for China to mobilise high savings and human capital resources to deliver consistent growth, but also resulted in strong productivity growth.

China still faces a debt overhang, but it has had successful episodes of debt restructuring in the past, avoiding a typical emerging market-type debt crisis. Faced with pressures on other countries to decouple their supply chains from China, as well as restricted access to advanced technology, China is increasing R&D spending and emphasising innovation and technological self-reliance. It has relaxed its population controls and has put policies in place to improve public services and create a social safety net to help address the challenges of its ageing population and social inequality.

Highlighting how the above elements have shaped China's economic evolution is not to say that conventional economic rules or lessons from other countries do not apply. They do and new challenges are immense. China's economy is simply multidimensional, with some of those dimensions unique. Policies and strategies have constantly evolved to deal with the challenges that emerge. As a result, extrapolation or simple comparisons with other economies may be flawed when it comes to analysing China's experience or predicting future outcomes or trends. It is crucial to bring together all of these elements, to put them in historical perspective and to remind ourselves of the ever-evolving nature of China's policies and economy.

Notes

1 Data from the World Bank's World Development Indicators Database.
2 Data from the World Bank's Poverty & Equity Data Portal.
3 Data from local statistics bureaus.
4 See People's Daily (2021b).
5 See China People's Daily (2021a) and RailServe (available from https://www.railserve.com/stats_records/railroad_route_miles.html).
6 See Lardy (2019), Rudd and Rosen (2020).
7 See National Bureau of Statistics (2019a).
8 See China General Administration of Customs (2022).
9 See National People's Congress of the People's Republic of China (2018).
10 See Nove (1969).
11 See McGregor (2012).
12 See Carney (2009) and Shih (2011).

13 This number is different to Bank for International Settlements (BIS) and International Monetary Fund (IMF) figures, probably as estimates of shadow credit differ. It does not include the debt of the financial sector.
14 See Reinhart and Rogoff (2009, 2013) and Schularick and Taylor (2012).
15 See IMF (2016). The BIS also warned in 2016 that China's extremely high credit-GDP gap might mean debt trouble in subsequent years (the credit gap measures household and corporate debt as a proportion of GDP compared with the long-term trend).
16 See Wolf (2018).
17 See Maddison (2007).
18 See Pew Research Center (2021).
19 See Gallup (2021).
20 See CPC (1987).
21 See World Bank (1993).
22 See Young (1995) and Krugman (1994).
23 See Rawski (2001).
24 See Chang (2001).
25 See Lin (2012).
26 See Eichengreen et al. (2012) and Im and Rosenblatt (2015).
27 See Pritchett and Summers (2014).

2 The evolving economic structure

The economy in 1978

Before we study how China's economic structure has evolved over the past few decades, it is worth looking at a snapshot from the start of its 'reform and opening' period. In 1978, when China emerged from its decade-long Cultural Revolution and decided to focus its energy on economic development, it was one of the poorest countries in the world. The country's per capita GDP was USD 156, ranking it 172nd globally, according to the World Bank.[1] It looked nothing like it does today.

Indeed, China's per capita income was lower than that of India (USD 205) and many sub-Saharan countries, less than a third of the levels of the Philippines and Ghana, and only one-tenth of that of Brazil (and 1.5% of the US level). Most of the population lived under the USD 1 a day poverty line, infrastructure was rudimentary and hundreds of millions of people did not have access to electricity or running water. Even so, thanks to its public healthcare and educational systems, China scored significantly better on human development indicators than countries at a similar stage of development at the time. For example, its life expectancy was 66 years in 1978 compared with 53 years for India and 60 years for the average middle-income country, according to the World Bank.[2] Its adult literacy rate was 65.5% in 1982 compared with India's 40.1%.[3]

China's economic structure in 1978 reflected the fact that it was still a largely agricultural society. It bore all the hallmarks of central planning and the exclusion of private commercial activity. Agriculture accounted for almost 30% of GDP in 1978 and industry accounted for 48%; the services sector was very much underdeveloped. In the two decades prior to that, China had focused on developing its industrial base, producing the metals, materials and machinery necessary to equip the country's military in times of war. Consequently, it had channelled resources to heavy industry and away from those required to meet the needs of households. Light manufacturing accounted for 43% of total industrial output in 1978 and the types of product were very limited. For example, there was no shampoo and only two or three types of bicycle.

DOI: 10.4324/9781003310938-3

GDP per capita (USD)

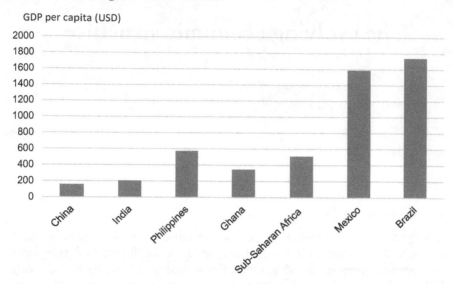

Figure 2.1 GDP per capita in international context, 1978.

Source: World Development Indicators, World Bank.

There were constant shortages in the economy – a phenomenon common in communist countries and astutely described by the Hungarian economist Jonas Kornai in his book, *Economics of Shortage*. Almost everything was rationed. Food rationing and coupon usage were widespread and highly specific, covering grain, meat, eggs, tofu products, edible oil and so on, as well as basic manufactured goods, such as fabrics for clothing. Bicycles and radios were considered luxury items and simply not available most of the time.

In line with the structure of the economy, more than 80% of China's population lived in rural areas in the late 1970s, while less than 18% lived in cities. As China's *hukou* system (also known as the household registration system) and severe mobility restrictions prevented people from moving from rural to urban areas or from region to region to make a living, there was limited rural–urban or intercity migration. Farmers were bound to the land through their villages and urban workers were allocated jobs by the government. And as grain and other food coupons were distributed by *hukou* and only to urban residents, rural people could not live in cities without a state-allocated job – not if they wanted to eat.

At the time, almost all economic activity was organised through the state planning system, while individuals had little economic freedom, decision-making power or incentive. There was no private sector to speak of and there were no markets for goods, services, labour or capital goods. Agricultural land was (and remains) collectively owned by villages (then called 'production units') and farmers were told what to produce, when to work and what portion of their produce to submit to the state. At the end of the year, each farmer's contribution was rewarded proportional to his/her labour input (measured by time and weighed by each person's physical strength score) from what was left over of the village's total output. Factories received allocated funding and produced according to bureaucratic plans, not demand. Workers lived in housing provided and owned by their employers and there was no material private property ownership.

There was no real financial infrastructure in 1978, no commercial banks, no securities, no financial markets. There was only one bank domestically, the People's Bank of China (PBC), which handled everything to do with money, but essentially functioned as the government's cashier (though there was also the Bank of China, which dealt with foreign trade-related banking services). All savings were deposited with the PBC, and all funds were allocated according to plans, so there was little need to calculate the cost of funds or to raise funds through different means.

China had few economic connections with the rest of the world. The Cold War was at its height in 1978 and China was not only closed to the western world because of its communist ideology, but also had patchy links with the Soviet bloc, as its relations with the Soviet Union had soured in the early 1960s. Faced with a hostile external environment in the 1960s and 1970s, China had adopted a policy of 'self-reliance' in a bid to build a complete set of industries on its own. In fact, in the early 1970s, China had moved or rebuilt sizeable industrial capacity in remote inland locations close to mountains (the so-called third front), away from the coast for national security reasons. China's trade accounted for less than 1% of total world trade in 1978 and its few exports were mainly primary products, such as food and coal. It imported machinery and materials that it could not produce. There was no foreign investment and there were no foreign businesses. Foreign exchange was rationed, and the exchange rate was overvalued to keep the cost of imports low (a practice similar to that of the Soviet Union and eastern Europe).

China also started with a very different population structure to today. Its population had grown rapidly in the two decades to 1980 and ballooned to about 1 billion, with almost half of it (46%) under the age of 20, according to the 1982 census. The dependency ratio – the number of children (aged 14 or under) and elderly (aged 65 or over) relative to the working-age population – was more than 80%. This high ratio meant that households were struggling to feed their young and the government was worried about creating jobs for its citizens. In just one decade, from 1970 to 1980, China's self-described '800 million people, 600 million farmers' had turned into '1 billion people, 800 million farmers'.

Moreover, China's resources per capita were low compared with other large countries such as the United States. While the United States has 0.48 hectare of arable land per person, China has just 0.09 hectares, less than half the world average. Always preoccupied with feeding its people and avoiding major disasters, by 1980, The Chinese government no longer considered the large size of its population an advantage as Mao Zedong had done in the 1950s, but a drag on resources and economic development. China's senior leaders thought that an improvement in living standards was going to be hard to achieve if population growth was not brought under control.

In all these respects, China's economic structure has changed significantly in the four decades since it launched major reforms and opened up. It has industrialised, urbanised, developed markets and a private sector, and become the world's largest manufacturer. Its population structure has aged rapidly, facilitated by strict population controls.

China's rapid industrialisation and commercialisation

China's economy has gone through a period of rapid industrialisation and commercialisation since 1978. In 2021, agriculture accounted for just 7% of GDP, down from almost 30% in 1978, while the service sector accounted for 53.3%, up from a mere 22% (Figure 2.2). The shift in sectoral weights did not follow a clear pattern during this period, however. In the 1980s, as the government focused on solving the issue of perpetual shortages, economic liberalisation began in the agricultural sector. This was followed by the emergence of individually owned businesses and private enterprises. Both the agricultural and services sectors grew far more rapidly than industry, and industry as a share of GDP declined from 48% in 1978 to 41% in 1990. Over the subsequent two decades, China industrialisation gathered pace, with agriculture shrinking as a share of GDP. Between 2010 and 2020, the 'rebalancing' of the economy led to faster growth in the services sector, while the share of industry declined again, weighed down by excess capacity in some sectors and slower export growth.

As China industrialised, its manufacturing capacity and capabilities expanded exponentially. This was reflected in the relative decline of simple manufacturing goods, such as processed raw materials and labour-intensive

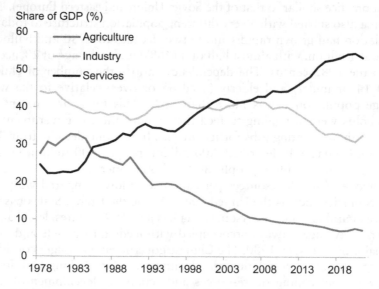

Figure 2.2 Structure of the economy, 1978–2021.

Source: NBS, author's calculations.

goods as a share of total manufacturing, and the rise in capital-intensive and higher-value-added goods. For example, in the late 1970s, China mainly produced simple light industrial goods, such as processed food, textiles and daily necessities, and basic heavy industrial materials, such as steel and coal. As it lacked manufacturing capabilities, it exported primary resources and raw materials, including food, coal, crude oil (until 1994) and cotton, and imported industrial materials and equipment. In 1980, primary products accounted for more than 50% of China's total exports, while over half of its manufacturing exports were textiles and clothing. Over the next two decades, as China's production capabilities improved, primary exports dropped sharply to about 5% of the total and its manufactured exports became ever more sophisticated.

The relative weights of consumer and investment goods (materials, metals and heavy machinery) shifted during that period as well, as sources of demand evolved and the government's policy focus changed. In the 1980s and most of the 1990s, to address China's widespread shortages and meet pent-up demand from the domestic population, the government focused on developing the light manufacturing sector, producing clothing, home appliances and daily goods. Heavy industry (investment goods) as a share of GDP declined from 57% in 1978 to just under 51% in 1998. From the late 1990s to the global financial crisis in 2008, a round of rapid domestic industrialisation, coinciding with a property boom, led to the sharp rise in heavy industry.

Notwithstanding the massive progress of the past four decades, China's industrial structure still has gaps and vulnerabilities. While the completeness and resilience of its industrial supply chain have been impressive and helped China to supply the world during the COVID-19 pandemic, its weaknesses have also become apparent in recent years as the US–China trade war has escalated. As officially acknowledged, China's strength in manufacturing remains mainly in relatively low-cost, labour-intensive areas, while it relies on imports for high-end machinery and equipment.[4] Even when it comes to its high-tech exports, such as computers and high-end consumer electronics, China's contribution centres largely on the assembly stage. Although China has increased its capabilities to produce intermediate components for the high-tech supply chain, it is largely absent from the production of the most advanced core components (advanced semiconductor chips, for instance) and it doesn't own the intellectual property of related technology. As we shall discuss in greater detail later, China's government has recognised these gaps and sees its heavy reliance on imports of advanced technology and components as vulnerable to potential supply disruptions.

Factors behind the transformation of China's economic structure

What lay behind China's economic 'take-off' and the shifts in its economic structure after 1978? It was a combination of factors. Agricultural reform in the late 1970s and early 1980s generated more food production, greater wealth and surplus labour. General economic liberalisation allowed private businesses to flourish, especially in services where there was only limited supply provided by typically unmotivated SOEs. The opening-up policy attracted foreign capital and imported advanced technology and knowhow to build and upgrade the industrial sector. SOE and urban reforms increased the efficiency of capital and resource allocation. Learning by doing and economies of scale stimulated innovation by firms. Over time, the external landscape and relative size of the domestic and external markets changed, especially after 2008. The rise of the urban middle class led to shifts in the demand structure, resource and environmental constraints became more apparent, and in response, domestic policy focus also evolved. All these things have come together to shape China's economic transformation.

Agricultural reform, especially de-collectivisation, proved a great stimulus for productivity gains, releasing surplus farm labour for non-farming activities on the one hand and producing more wealth for farmers to increase consumption on the other hand.[5] Township and village enterprises (TVEs), formed by surplus rural workers engaging in small-scale, local industrial and commercial activities (trading, transport and construction) under 'collective' village and township ownership, grew strongly in the 1980s. TVE development was important in the first stage of industrialisation and accounted for one-third of China's industrial production by the early to mid-1990s. Following the urban and SOE reforms of 1993, policy on TVEs changed. Despite their vibrancy and provision of millions of jobs, TVEs were considered to be inefficient in land and resource usage, insufficiently regulated and unfair competitors. Facing restrictions on land and credit access, TVEs were restructured in subsequent years, with many becoming private enterprises.[6]

Urban and enterprise reforms in the 1980s and 1990s introduced economic incentives and market factors to SOEs and local governments. While industries had previously seemed to perpetually lack funding for expansion, the reforms unleashed bank lending and SOE incentives to increase investment and production (Chapter 3) and, later, to increase competitiveness and profit to survive and expand. Also, once the CPC shifted its focus from politics to economics,[7] the government adopted policies to promote growth and industrialisation. For example, local governments provided industry with cheap or free land and basic infrastructure in industrial zones to attract investment. The fact that the government's main source of tax revenue was the corporate sector, not households, made local governments especially keen to attract industry, often at the expense of labour protections and environmental standards. There were also various subsidies for industry – foreign investors enjoyed preferential tax treatment until 2006, oil prices were subsidised until 2008, and large industrial-sector power users enjoyed lower electricity tariffs. SOEs did not have to pay dividends from 1994 to 2008, when China introduced its dividend policy, which meant they could retain earnings for reinvestment. These policy biases and subsidies contributed to the rapid growth of China's capital-intensive and energy-intensive heavy industry from the late 1990s until a decade ago, alongside a property boom triggered by housing reform.

Foreign investment was important in facilitating industrialisation and structural change. Starting with special economic zones in 1980, China expanded its preferential policies to attract foreign investment to many cities across the country. Money flowed in to soak up the surplus labour freed up by domestic reforms. The inflow of much-needed foreign equipment, capital and management knowhow first helped to expand China's industrial capacity, then helped increase its industrial sophistication.[8] As vividly portrayed in the example of a bra-hook factory in Peter Hassler's popular book, *Country Driving*,[9] 'learning by doing' was widespread – the experience and knowledge (and in this case, technology) gained in foreign invested companies led to the expansion of and improvement in domestic production and sophistication. Evidence suggests that indigenous innovation also took off, spurred by competition and economies of scale.[10] In this process, industrial policies promoting domestic content in joint ventures probably helped to boost China's own manufacturing capabilities, though they also led to over-investment and excess capacity in many cases, as we will discuss in Chapter 4.

Allowing private businesses to operate in service sectors in the late 1970s was instrumental in developing China's services industry. Services were largely neglected and, in some cases, strictly controlled prior to the reform. Economic liberalisation allowed individuals and TVEs to engage in commercial activities in services such as food markets, restaurants and shops, where there was limited SOE presence. This led to a boom in domestic commerce and trading and helped to increase the services sector's share of the economy to almost 30% in 1990. Later, as China moved steadily towards a market economy, the services necessary for a functioning market, such as financial services, business services and household services, emerged and grew. Into the 21st century, the emergence of the internet and e-commerce helped to further boost service industries, and real-estate and financial services developed rapidly. Demand from the burgeoning urban middle class also led to rapid growth in tourism, entertainment, education and healthcare, though the latter two have been mostly dominated by the public sector (except for after-school tutoring until 2021, as we will discuss later on).

Since the mid-2000s, the Chinese government has been concerned about imbalances in the economy and sought to redress them to reorient domestic demand from investment to consumption and to reduce the country's dependence on exports. China's investment and related heavy industry boom started in the late 1990s, when the government undertook large infrastructural stimulus to mitigate the shock of the Asian financial crisis and housing reform. The pro-investment policies, including energy subsidies and unchecked SOE investment from retained earnings, amplified the boom, as did middle-class demand for automobiles and homes. The explosive growth of energy-intensive heavy industry led to a sharp increase in pollution and commodity prices, however, exposing China's resource and environmental constraints. China started to 'rebalance' the economy soon after the global financial crisis, as weaker foreign demand led to a reorientation towards domestic demand. The reorientation from investment to consumption took longer to start, but it had become clear that the rising middle class was shifting demand towards services, wanting a better quality of life with a cleaner environment. In recent years, as excess capacity in some heavy industries, such as iron and steel, has emerged, the government has restricted their expansion. The share of heavy industry has stabilised or declined.

The rise of trade and shifts in trade pattern

China is currently the largest merchandise exporter globally, dubbed the 'factory of the world'. It has had the reputation of being an export-led economy for some time, especially following the country's entry into the World Trade Organization (WTO) in 2001. However, China has not always pursued an export-oriented development strategy and the economy's reliance on exports has declined since the global financial crisis.

Up until the late 1980s, China mainly deemed exports a means of earning foreign currency to buy necessary imports, not a key channel for creating employment or growth. Exports only accounted for around 6% of GDP in 1980, largely because the country did not produce much that could be sold internationally. In the first few years of the 1980s, China had not yet decided to open up more to the outside world or to become integrated into the world economy. The country's academics and policymakers worried that international trade could condemn the country to a fate of producing raw

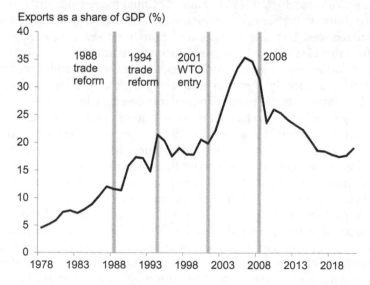

Figure 2.3 Exports as a share of GDP, 1978–2021.

Source: China Customs, NBS, author's calculations.

materials and basic goods for developed markets forever. That was one interpretation of the comparative advantage theory in international trade, popular among economists and governments in developing countries in the 1960s and 1970s. China's export ability was further hampered by its artificially overvalued exchange rate and the fact that a few state trading companies held a monopoly on international trade.

This changed when China adopted a more holistic market-opening strategy, launching its foreign trade reform in 1988 and its exchange-rate reform in the mid-1990s. It decided to enter into 'international circulation'[11] by importing components and raw materials and exporting assembled products to take advantage of its abundant cheap labour to generate more employment and growth. In the meantime, throughout the 1990s, as part of its efforts to join the WTO (and its predecessor, the General Agreement on Tariffs and Trade, or GATT), China reduced import tariffs significantly. These policies and the country's embrace of FDI helped to usher in a period of rapid export expansion. Entry into the WTO meant greater access to global markets as restrictions and export quotas were gradually removed, leading to another sharp increase in the country's export share. Strong US and global economic growth in the early to mid-2000s also contributed to the explosive expansion of China's processed exports.[12] By 2007, the country's exports had risen to 32% of GDP and its current-account surplus had ballooned to about 10% of GDP, with net exports contributing 2.5–3 percentage points a year to GDP growth in the three years up to then.

After the global financial crisis, as China's share of the global market continue to rise, exports as a share of GDP declined steadily. This was in part because global growth has slowed and in part because China had lost some of its export competitiveness as labour, land and other domestic costs rose. The latter was driven largely by changing domestic and external economic fundamentals, as well as deliberate policy adjustments. While rapid industrialisation and demographic shifts led to a sharp reduction in surplus labour and a rise in wages around the time of the global financial crisis, China's government also adopted a new labour law in 2008 and was paying more attention to social security contributions. It also phased out oil-price subsidies, increased land costs, stepped up the enforcement of environmental rules and began to require SOEs to pay dividends. Part of a package to rebalance the economy from investment to consumption, these measures also increased the real cost of exports, leading to the appreciation of China's real exchange rate (more in Chapter 11).

China's trade structure has also evolved enormously over the past four decades. In terms of product mix, the share of primary exports has declined steadily, while that of manufacturing goods has risen sharply. China's strategy to use its cheap labour to develop the processing trade prompted significant growth in light manufacturing exports, such as apparel, toys and footwear in the 1990s and electronics and electrical equipment thereafter. The country's WTO entry in 2001 accelerated its processing exports, which reached a peak of 55% of total exports in

2004, while primary exports have dropped to less than 5% over the past decade. As China's manufacturing capacity and sophistication increased, domestic firms started to take a big share of exports, and processing as a share of overall trade declined steadily to about one-third. Research also found that China's domestic value-added in the processing trade rose steadily.[13] The value added of its largest type of export, electronics, went from simple assembly to the production of more intermediate products, as skills and capabilities increased, according to the WTO.[14] China also became a large exporter of intermediate products and capital goods. Meanwhile, the share of textiles and clothing exports declined, dropping to 12% in recent years.

In tandem with the changes in China's export structure, the composition of imports also shifted. In the 1980s and early 1990s, the country's imports of light manufacturing goods waned as its domestic production increased. As it began to industrialise more rapidly from the mid-1990s, its imports of raw materials and commodities grew sharply, while its imports of metals shrank as domestic capacity expanded. Imports of machinery and equipment remained important, though the mix changed. Imports of transport equipment decreased as a share of total imports as domestic production grew with the help of foreign investment and joint ventures, while electrical machinery and electronics equipment increased. More recently, imports of consumer goods have increased, especially those from European countries. And as the Chinese have grown richer, outbound tourism has climbed faster

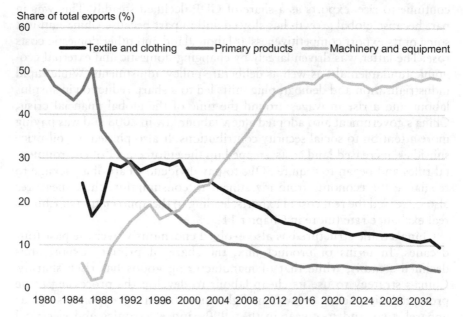

Figure 2.4 The changing export structure, 1980–2021.

Source: China Customs, UN Comtrade, author's estimates.

than inbound travel. Combined with the purchase of imported goods, this has led to a continued, significant increase in service imports – or it had, until the COVID-19 pandemic called a halt to international tourism. China has remained closed to international travel in 2022, while the rest of the world has reopened.

China's major trading partners have also evolved. In the 1980s and early 1990s, exports to Hong Kong accounted for 25–45% of China's total exports. With the development of the processing trade, however, exports to the United States and other developed markets have grown rapidly and the share of exports to Hong Kong has declined to just over 10%, including those eventually destined for other markets through the city.[15] On the import side, Japan accounted for 20% of China's total imports for much of the 1990s and was its largest source of imports until 2011, when it was surpassed by the EU and, later, South Korea. As China's integration with the global economy deepened and its supply chain lengthened, trade with the rest of Asia, especially South Korea, Taiwan and Association of Southeast Asian Nations (ASEAN) economies rose significantly, with China importing and, more recently, exporting processing components, machinery and equipment. China has also become the largest market for many commodity-producing countries, including Australia, Brazil, Chile, South Africa, Russia and Indonesia. Beyond commodities, as a production hub and with a large, fast-growing domestic market, China has also become the largest export destination for dozens of economies.

The transformation of the rural and urban landscape

As China industrialised, the rural and urban landscape transformed at an unprecedented pace and scale. As industrial, construction and transport activities burgeoned, what had once been farming areas became towns, towns morphed into cities and cities grew ever larger. Nowhere was the change more astounding than in Shenzhen, which burgeoned from a sleepy agricultural town of 600,000 people in 1979 to a mega city of 18 million people in 2020. Meanwhile, China's total urban population increased from less than 180 million to 902 million, with the urbanisation ratio surging from 18% to 64%.

This impressive urbanisation may underestimate the true degree of urban transformation, however. This is because Chinese cities are administratively defined, not based on shifts in the nature of economic activity or where people congregate. It is not uncommon to have densely populated, mostly non-farming areas still classified as rural rather than urban areas in the east and south of the country, where the rural–urban divide is increasingly blurred. Also, rural migrants who do not live in the same urban area for more than six months are not considered regular urban residents. China's true urbanisation ratio may be significantly higher, as the share of people employed in non-farm sectors was 76% as of 2020.

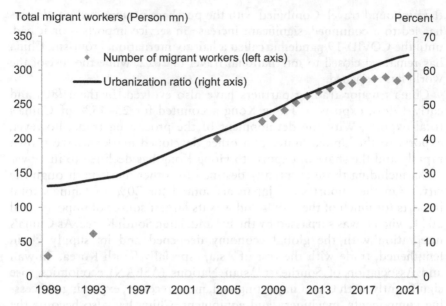

Figure 2.5 Rural–urban migration and urbanisation, 1989–2021.

Source: NBS, author estimates.

Like industrialisation, urbanisation got an initial boost from China's agricultural reform, which led to a productivity increase and release of surplus labour. As surplus farm labourers were put to work by local TVEs, the transfer of farm labour to non-farm labour – the prerequisite to and essence of urbanisation – began. The abundance of food being produced led to the eventual abolition of the *hukou*-related grain coupon system, making mass rural migration to urban areas possible.

Rural workers moved to coastal regions such as the Pearl River Delta and Yangtse River Delta to seek work opportunities, providing cheap labour for the newly arrived foreign-invested companies. By 1989, rural migrant labour had increased to 30 million from little to nothing in the late 1970s.[16] Rural–urban migration grew massively after the TVEs took a hit and the processing trade expanded in the 1990s, rising from 62 million in 1993 to almost 200 million in 2004. This included 120 million people who worked outside of their local areas, while the rest engaged in non-farm activities close to their villages.[17] As of 2021, 293 million people were considered rural migrant workers, with about 170 million people working outside their home region.[18] The central plains and the Sichuan basin were traditionally agriculturally rich areas and home to many people. Faster economic development in the eastern and southern coastal regions during the reform period drew mass migration from these labour-rich provinces and poor western part of the country.

In addition to rural industrialisation and rural–urban migration, China's rapid urbanisation has also been down to the significant expansion of investment in industry, infrastructure and property construction. Economic liberalisation in urban areas set off a lasting investment and construction boom, partly as city governments tried to catch up with rapidly increasing demand for infrastructure and housing, as well as industrial expansion. This was amplified by local governments' desire to accelerate urbanisation to help monetise land and promote economic growth (see more in Chapter 6).

The changing ownership structure

From nearly full public ownership in the late 1970s, the ownership structure of China's economy has grown more complex over the decades. This has been supported by the emergence and rapid growth of private companies, the rise and fall of TVEs, the presence of foreign firms, SOE restructuring and the development of the stock market. China's 2018 economic census put the share of employment in state-owned entities at about 15% of the total, and they may account for 30–40% of China's GDP.[19]

The first shake-up of the state ownership structure was the de-collectivisation of the agricultural sector in the 1980s. Although land officially remained collectively owned, farmers were given land-use rights at family level. Rural households became independent operators on their land and financially independent of village collectives. They gained greater freedom over what to produce and the prices at which they could sell their produce. More recently, they have been allowed to lease out their land or use it as collateral. Throughout the 1980s, the emergence of TVEs, permission to have individually owned private companies and incentives to attract foreign investment helped to reduce the dominance of the state-owned economy, especially in the industrial sector. By 1994, SOEs accounted for 37% of total industrial output, down from 78% in 1978, collectively owned enterprises (mostly TVEs) accounted for another 37%, and various forms of private enterprise accounted for 25%. The number of private entities had surged to 800 million from next to zero in 1978.[20]

From the mid-1990s, the acceleration of SOE reforms and related restructuring resulted in a significant reduction in SOEs' share of the economy. This was achieved by selling off or closing small SOEs and restructuring large ones (the so-called *zhuada fangxiao* or 'retaining the large, dispensing with the small' strategy), with the help of the stock market and private-sector participation. By 2004, the number of state-owned and state-controlled enterprises had fallen to 24,961 from 118,000 in 1995, while Gan (2008) estimated that close to two-thirds of China's SOEs were either privatised or subjected to some sort of non-state ownership between 1995 and 2005.[21] Official data also suggest that China laid off more than 20 million SOE workers between 1996 and 2003,[22] along with another estimated 10 million-plus workers from collectively owned enterprises. Meanwhile, private enterprises and foreign investments continued to grow.

From the early 2000s, China's export and housing boom led to a period of SOE revival. Demand and investment in the capital goods, mining and commodity sectors expanded rapidly, benefitting SOEs, as they were concentrated in these capital- and resource-intensive sectors. The revival of the SOE sector did not raise flags at the time, as the private sector also grew quickly due to the country's export and property booms. It became more pronounced following the global financial crisis, as the massive infrastructure stimulus programme was largely implemented by SOEs and local-government entities, while the private sector suffered more from the shock. The latter development brought about complaints of *guojinmintui* – the advance of the state and retreat of the private sector – although Nick Lardy, in his book *Markets over Mao* (2014), argues that this claim was exaggerated.

One reason it was hard to find statistical evidence of SOEs gaining share at the expense of the private sector may have been that the official classification of corporate ownership no longer accurately captured the underlying ownership picture. The National Bureau of Statistics (NBS) separates state-owned entities from share-holding and limited liability companies, although both of these categories contain companies that are majority owned or controlled by the state. Still, slow progress on SOE reform over the past decade, the government's plan to make SOEs 'bigger, and stronger' and the emphasis on strengthening CPC leadership in all enterprises have been key factors behind concerns that the 'state is striking back', to paraphrase Lardy.[23] Concerns grew to such an extent in 2018 that President Xi Jinping held talks with private entrepreneurs to reassure them that the CPC and the government would 'unwaveringly support' the private sector.[24]

One sector with a better ownership mix is the industrial sector. According to the 2018 economic census, five years ago, state-owned and state-controlled industrial companies accounted for 32% of total assets and 25% of total sales, but less than 12% of total employment.[25] Foreign-invested companies, and those with investment from Hong Kong, Macao and Taiwan, accounted for almost 20% of total industrial sales and 13% of total employment. In the services sector, SOEs and collectively owned enterprises accounted for 14% of total employment. Businesses in wholesale and retail, restaurants and catering, daily services and real estate are mostly private, while those in telecoms, banking and finance, and transport are mainly state owned.

Overall, data suggest that less than 15% of total employment in legal entities (almost 300 million) is by SOEs and collectively owned enterprises.[26] The figure for the whole economy is probably similar if one includes the almost 200 million farmers who work for themselves, the roughly 100 million self-employed people and the nearly 60 million public-sector employees, including those who work in education and healthcare.[27] In sum, the state-owned sectors (including majority state-controlled companies and the government sector) may account for 30–40% of GDP.[28] State-owned companies probably account for a higher share of total assets, as SOEs have enjoyed better access to credit and resources and their presence is skewed towards capital-intensive heavy industry.

Over the past four decades, the private sector has developed more rapidly in fields where there was no SOE dominance, or where there were specifically more liberal policies. For example, private businesses developed particularly fast in the Pearl River Delta in Guangdong province and in the

SOE share of total (%)

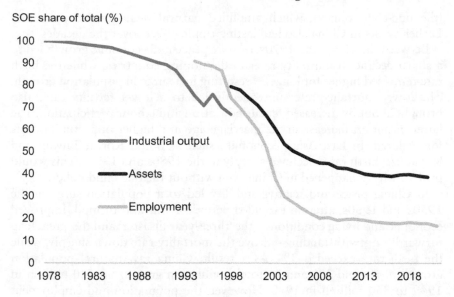

Figure 2.6 The falling share of SOEs in the industrial sector, 1978–2021.

Source: NBS, author's estimates.

Note: Data include both state-owned and collectively owned enterprises for output and assets and for employment up to 2002. Data for employment after 2002 are for state-owned and state holding companies. Total employmentdoes not include those individually employed.

Yangtse River Delta – especially in smaller cities outside the original large industrial centres of Guangzhou and Shanghai. Meanwhile, private-sector development has been relatively slow in the northeast region, China's old industrial hub, dominated by SOEs in resource-rich heavy industry. Also, private-sector development in state monopoly sectors, such as energy, telecommunications and finance, has been significantly slower than in manufacturing and consumer service areas.

China's ageing demographic structure

China's demographic structure has shifted dramatically over the past four decades; the country has aged faster than any other. At the time of the 1982 census, 46% of the population was under the age of 20. As of 1978, its youth dependency ratio – the number of people under the age of 15 relative to the number of people of working age (15–59) – was as high as 69%. In 2020, following a sharp 40-year decline in population growth, only 21% of the population was under the age of 20 and the youth dependency ratio had declined to 27%. The average age of the population had increased to 38.8 in 2020 from 27.1 in 1982,[29] and the working-age population shrank by 40 million in 2010–2020, having grown by more than 100 million each in the three preceding decades.

China's demographic transformation was down to two key factors: (1) the long period of global peace and economic development that drove major demographic shifts around the world and (2) its strict family planning rules (the one-child policy), which amplified natural demographic evolution. Earlier events in China also had lasting ripple effects over the decades.

Between the 1950s and 1970s, relative peace and economic growth led to a sharp decline in mortality rates in developing countries, while the birth rate remained higher for longer,[30] resulting in a surge in population growth. The lower mortality rate subsequently led to a lower fertility rate, also brought about by increased female education and labour participation. The latter meant an increase in the marriage age and higher opportunity costs for children. In East Asian economies such as South Korea, Taiwan and Singapore, birth rates declined sharply in the 1980s and 1990s. This would probably have happened in China even without the one-child policy.

In China, peace and relative stability led to a population surge in the 1950s and 1960s, after an extended period of war and turmoil. Improved economic and living conditions – the 'three-year disaster' and the 'great leap forward'[31] notwithstanding – drove the mortality rate down sharply, while the birth rate exceeded 3%. As a result, China saw natural population growth of around 2% and its total population grew from 540 million in 1949 to 830 million in 1970. However, the population and employment pressures had become serious by the early 1970s, prompting the government to launch a family planning policy in 1973 aimed at lowering the birth rate.[32] The modest policy turned into the draconian one-child policy in 1980 as China's population approached 1 billion. The birth rate dropped sharply from 3.3% in 1970. Apart from a mini baby boom around 1990, the downward trend has been largely maintained, with the birth rate dwindling to 1.2% as of 2010 and 0.9% in 2020.[33]

The decline in China's birth rate and dependency ratio was much more pronounced than in other countries and its subsequent population ageing also came sooner and more swiftly. As shown in Figure 2.7, China's youth dependency ratio dropped significantly from the late 1970s and the overall dependency ratio bottomed around 36.5% in 2010, clearly lower than that reached by Japan and South Korea, which had previously seen a similar trend. The plunge in the dependency ratio helped China to reap demographic dividends, as the productive working-age population grew faster than the total population it was supporting. It also helped to increase the savings rate and the educational levels of the labour force as parents focused on the education of their only child.[34] However, what goes around comes around; the more rapid decline in the birth rate and youth dependency ratio also meant a faster pace of ageing and a rise in old-age dependency compared with other economies. By 2020, the share of people aged 65 or older in China's population had reached 13.5%, up from 5% in 1982 (and the average retirement age was about 54. See more in Chapter 12). The United Nations Population Division (UNPD) predicts that this ratio could reach 17–18% by 2030 and 26% by 2050.[35] This is a faster pace of ageing than most developed countries have seen, and China is reaching these markers at a lower per capita income level.

The rapid ageing process has had and will continue to have a significant impact on the structure of the economy. The latest United Nations' World

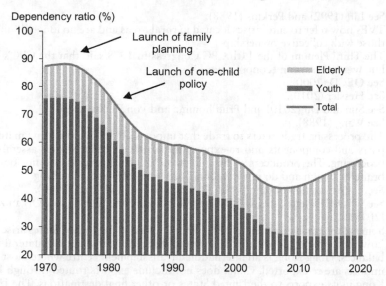

Figure 2.7 Youth and elderly dependency ratios.

Source: UNPD, author's calculations.

Population Prospect predicts that China's population will peak at 1.426 billion soon, though this did not seem to take into account the 2020 population census. Some Chinese scholars forecast that the population may have already peaked in 2022. This means that China's working age population may decline by another 40 million between 2020 and 2030. On the supply side, an ageing population means rising labour costs, which could lead to the relocation of labour-intensive manufacturing, as well as faster automation. On the demand side, the ageing population means greater demand for healthcare, old-age care and asset management businesses, for example. It will also put increasing pressure on the pension system and China's long-term fiscal sustainability.

Another important structural result of the one-child policy is gender imbalance. The policy prompted many traditionally minded people in rural areas, who favoured boys for working in the fields or continuing the family line, to selectively abort female foetuses or even commit infanticide. Consequently, China's male-female birth ratio rose steadily from 107 in 1982 (about the world average) to 117 in the mid-2000s, before receding to about 111 in 2020, according to the UNPD.[36] Some researchers contend that China's gender imbalance may have contributed to its high household savings rate and even its elevated urban housing prices.[37]

Notes

1　Data from the World Bank's World Development Indicators.
2　Ibid.
3　Data from the UNESCO Institute for Statistics and the World Bank's World Development Indicators.
4　See National Statistics Bureau (2018b).

 5 See Lin (1992) and Perkins (1988).
 6 TVEs now refer to enterprises located in rural areas and are no longer limited to those with collective ownership.
 7 The Third Plenum of the 11th CPC Congress in 1978 said that the CPC's basic line was to 'focus on economic work'.
 8 See OECD (2000).
 9 See Hessler (2010).
10 See Sun and Du (2010) and Prud'homme and von Zedtwitz (2018).
11 See Wang (1988).
12 The processing trade refers to trade that imports all or part of its raw materials, parts and components and re-exports the finished products after assembly or processing. The producers or assemblers of the final products do not own the brand or design and do not have influence over sales and marketing.
13 See, for example, Koopman et al. (2012), and Kee and Tang (2016).
14 See WTO, IDE-Jetro, OECD, UIBE and World Bank and World Trade Organization (2019).
15 Some of the trade disagreements between China and the United States arise from how they treat trade with Hong Kong in their measurement of bilateral trade balances. Hong Kong is an international transshipment centre where most of its imports are re-exported. China does not include exports routed through Hong Kong in its exports to the United States or other final destinations. The United States treats all imports from Hong Kong (including those possibly sourced elsewhere) as imports from China.
16 See China Labor Bulletin (2007).
17 See State Council Research Office (2006).
18 See National Bureau of Statistics (2022b).
19 Author's estimate.
20 See Jefferson (2016).
21 See Gan (2008).
22 Data from the China Labour Statistical Yearbook 2006 by Ministry of Human Resources and Social Security (2006).
23 See Lardy (2019).
24 See Xi (2018).
25 Author's estimates.
26 Data from National Bureau of Statistics (2018a).
27 See National Bureau of Statistics (2018a).
28 Author's estimate.
29 Data are from the Chinese census and China Statistical Yearbooks and estimates are from the United Nations Population Division (2019).
30 See Lam (2011) and Livi-Bacci (2001).
31 The 'Great Leap Forward' was an economic campaign spearheaded by the CPC between 1958 and 1960 (inclusive) to accelerate economic development. It set a target in 1958 of surpassing the UK economy within 15 years, starting by doubling steel production that year and accelerating the formation of agricultural communes. Grave policy mistakes at the time coincided with and aggravated three consecutive years of natural disasters, leading to severe famine.
32 See Attane (2002) and Wang (2012).
33 Data from the China Statistical Yearbook and the 7th population census.
34 See Modigliani and Cao (2004) and Choukhmane, Coeurdacier and Jin (2019).
35 See United Nations, Department of Social and Economic Affairs, Population Division (2022).
36 See United Nations, Department of Social and Economic Affairs, Population Division (2022).
37 See Wei and Zhang (2011).

3 The road to here

Key reforms since 1978

Since 1978, China has been transformed from an extremely poor, agricultural, centrally planned and closed economy into one with modern manufacturing and a vibrant private sector, deeply integrated into the world economy.

The single most important initial reform was, arguably, the adoption of the 'household contract responsibility system' – or rural land de-collectivisation – in the late 1970s. A plethora of reforms followed the Third Plenary Session of the 11th Central Committee of the CPC (the 11th Third Plenum) in December 1978. The first phase focused on 'liberating productivity' by reducing stifling economic restrictions, introducing price mechanisms and incentives, establishing special economic zones (SEZs) and allowing foreign investment. The initial reforms petered out in the late 1980s, but Deng Xiaoping's 1992 Southern Tour jump-started a second phase. Aiming to establish a market economy, policymakers attempted to tackle deep-rooted SOE operational issues, reform the state ownership structure, uphold private property rights and create the nuts and bolts of a functioning market system. The beginning of the third phase coincided roughly with the onset of the global financial crisis in 2008, with reforms and macro policies focused largely on addressing problems that had arisen from previous ones and on re-adjusting the role of government versus the market.

Phase one: reform and opening to liberate productivity

Most China economists and historians would probably cite the 11th Third Plenum as the birth of China's era of 'reform and opening'. It was at this meeting that the Chinese leadership decided to pivot away from 'class struggle' and focus instead on economic development, with a call to 'emancipate the mind'.[1] However, the arguably most important rural land reform came not from the top, but from the bottom. The 'household contract responsibility system' began in a small village called Xiao Gang in Anhui province (an area previously best known for food shortages), when the leaders of a production unit (village) secretly agreed to give 18 farmers land-use rights if they promised to produce the required amount of public grain.[2] The central government acknowledged the practice only after further pilots had

DOI: 10.4324/9781003310938-4

Grain production (million tons)

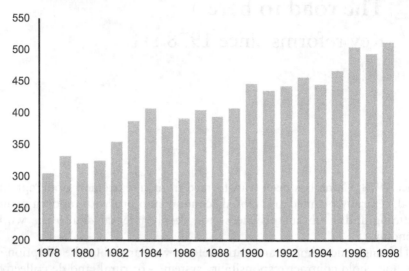

Figure 3.1 Grain production following the agricultural reform.

Source: NBS, Author estimates.

proved its success,[3] and soon it expanded across the country.[4] In 1982, the CPC explicitly affirmed household responsibility system as a form of production under the socialist collective farming system, thus providing full political cover for de-collectivisation.[5]

This rural land reform, as well as other agricultural reforms, such as increasing farm product prices, relaxing controls on what farmers could produce and reintroducing rural markets, was instrumental in boosting farmers' economic incentive and increasing agricultural productivity and output.[6] In addition to enlarging the food supply, reducing poverty and improving the living standards of hundreds of millions of farmers, the reforms also freed up millions of agricultural labourers to work in industry, commerce and construction. The surplus farm labour was first deployed in TVEs, then in cities as migrant workers.[7]

Other major reforms in the first phase (1978–1991) may have been less ground-breaking, but were also important when it came to addressing shortages and increasing productivity. These reforms, similar to those trialled in Eastern Europe from the late 1960s to the 1980s, were not about fundamentally changing state ownership or control of productive means, but decentralising economic decision-making and introducing market incentives.

Comprehensive urban reform

Witnessing the great success of rural reforms, China's government moved to liberalise decision-making in urban areas, including those of city governments and enterprises. It started a first pilot programme in 1981 in Shashi, a medium-sized city in Hubei province, expanding it to 58 cities by early 1985. In addition, the State Council granted 14 coastal cities the autonomy to step up market-opening measures. The key reforms in these pilot cities included (1) granting enterprises more power over production planning, procurement and sales, employee and salary management, and personnel decisions; (2) establishing a goods market and allowing all types of enterprise and producer to exchange goods freely, rather than according to the government's distribution plan and prices; and (3) giving city governments more freedom on construction and investment activities.[8] These moves were accompanied by other major reforms focused on creating economic incentives to release creativity and increase productivity in various areas. The main complementary reforms included price reform, enterprise profit-to-tax reform and local government fiscal reform.

Price reform

In 1978, the government set prices for 97% of all products in China (this ratio had declined to 3% by 2017). Price reform started in 1979, when the government raised the procurement prices of key agricultural products, including grain. The authorities undertook a more significant price reform in 1984, allowing enterprises to sell products at higher prices outside of the planned quota, establishing a dual-track price system.[9] In 1985, they further liberalised prices for key producer goods such as oil, metals and chemicals outside of the planned quota. Apart from a few key items, the system of centralised procurement and distribution for agricultural products ended in January 1985.[10]

The dual-track price system was meant to be an intermediate step, a compromise, to complete price liberalisation, but it led to rampant arbitrage and corruption, resulting in resentment and criticism from the public. China's top leadership decided to push for full price liberalisation in 1987–1988, calling it 'passing through the price gate' and deeming it critical to the success of overall reform. The prices of most manufacturing goods were freed up in 1987, while the prices of the most important food items (pork and grain) were liberalised in 1988.[11] A sharp rise in inflation and heavy public criticism led the government to reimpose some price controls in late 1988, however.

Enterprise profit-to-tax reform

Under the centrally planned system, enterprises – all of them SOEs – handed over their profits to the government and relied on the state for all operational and investment funding. Companies merely carried out government plans. They had neither the freedom to nor the responsibility of making profit or curtailing costs. In 1983, the government embarked on a pilot programme requiring SOEs to hand over corporate income tax rather than profit, something it refined in 1984. Under the profit-to-tax reform, SOEs could keep the remainder of their earnings after paying a 55% income tax levy and had the freedom to use the retained profit for worker compensation or future investment.[12] The reform also introduced a business tax for most SOEs in the service sector and levied value-added tax (VAT) and resource tax on SOEs in certain sectors.

Fiscal decentralisation

China had a highly centralised fiscal system before 1980. Although there were various revenue-sharing arrangements with local governments, the central government controlled most of the fiscal revenues and largely dictated spending plans.[13] Fiscal decentralisation started in 1980, when the central and local governments separated their fiscal accounts and divvied up revenue and spending responsibilities (dubbed 'eating from separate pots'). Local governments were bound by a lump-sum fiscal responsibility system, whereby they could keep a portion of revenues beyond the agreed 1979 base. The lump-sum fiscal responsibility system was refined and formalised in 1985 together with the SOE profit-to-tax reform, when central and local governments split SOE taxes from different sources.[14]

Fiscal decentralisation incentivised local governments to spend within their means, to actively support the economy to generate more fiscal resources[15] and, later, to create various new sources of revenue beyond the tax code. It not only motivated local governments to grow the local economy in the 1980s, but also generated problems. According to Lou (2014), one problem was that the central government still had many spending responsibilities, while local governments had more autonomy to retain revenues, eventually depleting central government revenue coffers.[16] Moreover, as the central government negotiated with local governments individually, it agreed numerous types of contract based on the power of and personalities in various local governments, resulting in a lack of transparency and equity (see more in Chapters 4–6).

Special economic zones

In the late 1970s, China's leaders were eager to learn from other countries in order to revive the economy and modernise the country. Comparing and contrasting economic performance between East and West Germany, South and North Korea and mainland China and Taiwan province of China, they recognised that the centrally planned and rigid economic system was not working all that well. They believed that institutions and policies could be reformed to achieve a far better economic outcome. Establishing SEZs was a way to experiment with western ways of economic management while keeping China's socialist economic structure and ideology intact.[17]

Four SEZs in Shenzhen, Zhuhai, Shantou (all in Guangdong province) and Xiamen (Fujian province) were established in 1980,[18] chosen for their proximity to Hong Kong, Macao and Taiwan, as well as their lack of strong industrial bases or SOEs. The latter meant that there would be few challenges to reforming the SOEs and a limited impact on the economy should the SEZ experiment fail. The SEZs created a market environment outside of the planned system and encouraged overseas Chinese and foreign firms to set up companies for export. The SEZ governments took care of land, utilities, transport and other infrastructure, while companies in the SEZ could operate independently and enjoy preferential tax rates and duty-free imports (as their outputs were destined for international markets).

Although the SEZs were initially developed with more domestic funding than foreign capital, their rapid economic growth was lauded by Deng Xiaoping and other senior leaders.[19] In 1984, the government permitted 14 other coastal cities to experiment with 'opening-up' policies. Over the years, the SEZs proved adept at attracting foreign investment, generating employment and export growth, and making a significant contribution to the country's economic growth.[20] Perhaps more importantly, the SEZs were used to pilot reform programmes and market mechanisms and to test the boundaries of reform in important areas such as the capital market and land supply.[21] Over time, many SEZ programmes and associated reforms were rolled out across the rest of the country.

International trade reform

Before the reform period, China's international trade was carried out by a few designated state-owned trading companies that followed government instructions, exporting excess goods and importing only necessary products.[22] By 1987, it was pretty much consensus among scholars and reform-minded policymakers that opening up China's economy even further was crucial to its development. The government decided on a new strategy to use China's comparative advantage of cheap labour to expand the processing trade and integrate the economy into international trade (what it called 'international circulation'). China launched significant trade reforms from 1988 onward, allowing state-owned trading companies to be commercially self-sufficient and to retain a portion of their export proceeds in foreign currency – a scarce resource. The government also granted export licences to some producers, introduced an import licensing system and removed or reduced taxes on export products.

China's trade reform coincided with the country's first round of negotiations with the General Agreement on Tariffs and Trade (GATT) with a view to 'returning' as a founder member. The negotiations made significant progress in the spring of 1989 and were expected to be completed by the end of the year. While unforeseen political events led to prolonged delays in its pursuit of GATT membership (and later membership of the WTO), China continued to open up its foreign trade. To this end, it reduced import tariffs significantly, from 43.7% on average in 1988 to 16.4% in 2001 (Figure 3.2).[23] These trade reforms, coupled with policies that increased domestic efficiency and attracted foreign investment, helped to boost China's trade

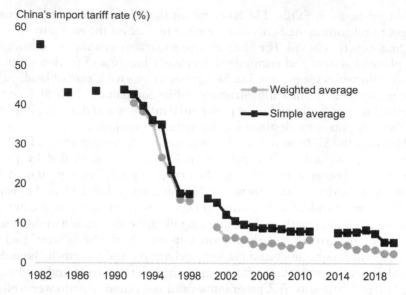

Figure 3.2 The substantial reduction of import tariffs before WTO accession.

Sources: Rumbaugh and Balcher (2004), WTO.

growth substantially in subsequent years. Its exports and imports grew by an average of 18% and 14% a year in US dollar terms, respectively, between 1987 and 1997. The blossoming of foreign trade brought related capital flows and exchange-rate reforms, which we shall discuss in more detail later.

The one-child policy

The strict family-planning policy introduced in 1980 was an important socioeconomic policy change that had a deep and far-reaching impact on the economy. As discussed in Chapter 2, China's population had approached 1 billion in 1980, even though family-planning measures introduced in the early 1970s had already slowed population growth. In 1980, the government adopted a more aggressive stance, explicitly encouraging a cap of one child per couple to keep the total population under 1.2 billion by 2020. Initially, the government gave subsidies and preferential treatment on schooling, jobs and housing to couples who opted to have just one off-spring. The one-child policy became mandatory in 1982,[24] however, though rural residents were allowed a second child if the first born was a girl, and ethnic minority groups were not subject to the policy.

From this point on, violators of the one-child policy were punished eco-nomically, socially and politically – public employees would lose their jobs in addition to being fined, while more draconian practices and punishments were often meted out in rural areas. China's population growth slowed sig-nificantly in the subsequent decades. Although the total population reached 1.27 billion in 2000, above the government's target, the birth rate dropped

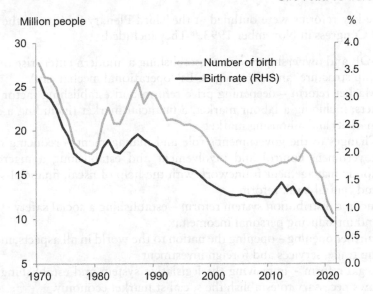

Figure 3.3 The decline in birth rate, 1970–2020.

Source: NBS, author's calculations.

sharply from 3.34 per 1000 in 1970 to 1.4 in 2000 and less than 1 in 2020. The dependency ratio declined dramatically, too, leading to a so-called demographic dividend (see more in Chapter 8). As mentioned in Chapter 2, this drastic change also brought about the more rapid ageing of China's population, posing challenges to long-term growth (see more in Chapter 12).

Phase two: establishing a socialist market economy

The first phase of China's reform petered out in the late 1980s, after price reforms led to high inflation and a public backlash, and as the international environment worsened. Deng Xiaoping's Southern Tour of 1992 kickstarted the second phase of reform, when he famously said that 'those who do not reform should step down'.[25] The 14th CPC Congress in 1992 decided to 'establish a socialist market economy',[26] formally incorporating the idea of a market economy into China's socialist ideology. This meant that reformers championing the role of the market no longer had to worry about being in the wrong political or ideological camp or being attacked as 'capitalists' (something Deng Xiaoping was accused of in the mid-1970s).

The new set of reforms was designed to establish a market mechanism as the economy's main operating system, rather than a mere supplement to planning, and to tackle deep-rooted SOE, ownership-structure and private property-rights issues. The sweeping market orientation and embrace of full trade liberalisation and FDI resembled the development strategies practiced by China's East Asian neighbours and echoed some of those advocated by the 'Washington Consensus'.[27]

The key reforms were outlined at the Third Plenary Session of the 14th Party Congress in November 1993.[28] They included:

- SOE and ownership reform – establishing a 'modern enterprise ownership structure' and changing SOEs' 'operational mechanism'
- Market reform – deepening price reform and establishing factor markets, including a labour market, a financial market (including a stock market) and a housing market
- Changes to the government's role and management – reducing direct government control and involvement and establishing a macroeconomic management framework with the help of fiscal, financial-sector and central bank reform
- Income distribution system reform – establishing a social safety system and introducing personal income tax
- Further opening – opening the nation to the world in all aspects, including trade, services and foreign investment
- Legal reform – improving the legislative system and establishing new laws necessary to establish the socialist market economy.

The first stage of the second reform phase largely took place between 1993 and 1996, when major reforms were rolled out on multiple fronts, focusing on market liberalisation of all types and fiscal reform. The second stage started around 1997 and mainly dealt with problems arising from previous and incomplete reforms, including SOE and bank restructuring and the construction of a social safety net.

Part 1: market liberalisation

The most notable reforms in the mid-1990s included SOE reform, price and exchange-rate liberalisation, financial-market and fiscal reform, and the full opening of the country to trade and foreign investment.

SOE reform

This focused on establishing a 'modern enterprise structure' for SOEs, so that they could become independent legal entities with clear ownership structures, rights and responsibilities that were separate from the government and which could function in accordance with a market system.[29] SOEs were given freedom in all aspects of their business operations, including production, sales, employment, compensation and investment.[30] They could establish shareholding structures, dispose of assets, dissolve operations or merge with or buy out other companies. Compared with the 1980s SOE reform, this was the wholesale liberalisation of SOE management and operations. However, while SOEs were given more freedom, they faced little market discipline. The 1992 Rules on Changing the SOE Operation Mechanism promised punishment for violations, but did not specify what rules SOE decision-makers were supposed to follow and mentioned little about budget constraints or cost control.[31]

Price reform

The government dialled back price controls considerably in 1992 and fully liberalised prices in the competitive sectors (those with little monopoly) in 1993.[32] In early 1994, it abandoned the dual-track pricing system for capital goods and stopped supplying grain at set prices[33] (although it still set procurement prices in some areas), long considered the most important consumer price in China. The liberation led to a 51% increase in grain prices in 1994, contributing – along with other price adjustments and the major investment boom – to 24% consumer price index (CPI) inflation that year. On the positive side, higher prices led to a persistent increase in grain and food supply in subsequent years. As the second phase of price reform coincided with overall market and SOE liberalisation, the initial sharp increase in prices stimulated investment and production and led to subsequent disinflation.

RMB exchange-rate reform

After some earlier adjustments of the exchange-rate system in the 1980s, the 1994 exchange-rate reform was a major step forward. China had been running a fixed exchange-rate regime (with multiple devaluations) for much of the 1980s, but a dual exchange-rate arrangement existed between 1988 and 1993. Under this system, the official exchange rate was fixed, but the

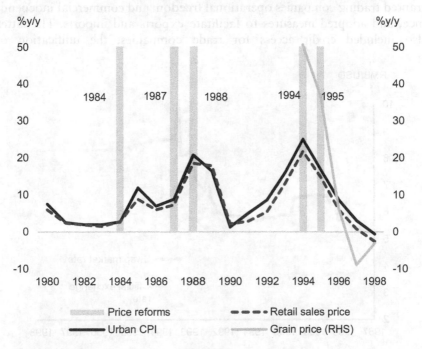

Figure 3.4 Price reforms and inflation in the 1980s and 1990s.

Source: NBS, Author estimates.

rate at swap centres – where those that needed foreign exchange outside of official plans could trade – was determined by market participants.[34] By the end of 1993, swap centres accounted for an estimated 80% of all current-account foreign-exchange transactions and the swap-market exchange rate had depreciated sharply to about RMB 10 per USD (Figure 3.5).[35] In early 1994, China devalued its official exchange rate from RMB 5.8 to the USD to RMB 8.7, unified it with the swap-market exchange rate under a managed float system and removed most trade-related exchange restrictions.[36] It also abolished the 'foreign-exchange certificate', which had rationed the use of foreign currency, helping to pave the way for the free use and exchange of foreign currency for all trade and services.

Observers have often cited the 1994 devaluation as a key reason for China's high inflation and even the subsequent Asian financial crisis. On the former, however, this view does not properly take into account the impact on CPI inflation of the major price reform in 1993–1994. As far as the latter is concerned, China's *de facto* devaluation of 1994 was far smaller than official numbers suggest, meaning any impact on trade was also far smaller.[37] As the swap-centre exchange rate was used in most transactions by 1993, the weighted average depreciation of the RMB in 1994 was only about 7%, not the 33% the official exchange rate would imply. Moreover, China's massive trade liberalisation in 1994 contributed to a subsequent explosion in trade. The trade reform abolished central export and import plans, granted trading companies operational freedom and commercial independence, and adopted measures to facilitate exports and imports. The latter also included credit access for trade companies, the unification of

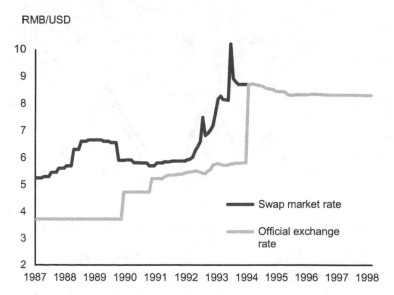

Figure 3.5 RMB exchange rate, 1980–2000.

Source: Fernald et al (1999), NBS, author's calculations.

trade-facilitating policies and rules across the country, nationwide opening to attract FDI and an export-tax rebate.

Financial market reform

A major financial-market reform in 1994 was the establishment of a commercial banking system. While China had set up three specialty banks and the country's first commercial bank (the Industrial and Commercial Bank of China) back in 1983, it was only in 1994 that these banks began to function like true commercial banks – commercially independent and allocating funds according to commercial factors and market demand rather than government credit plans. Meanwhile, a dozen or so joint stock banks were also established. The banking reform coincided with SOE liberalisation and easy fiscal and monetary policy, contributing to a period of rapid loan growth between 1993 and 1996. The 1993 Third Plenum also formally established the stock market as a proper channel for allocating capital[38] after the launch of the Shanghai Stock Exchange and Shenzhen Stock Exchange in 1990 and 1991, respectively.

In the 1990s, the stock market functioned mainly as a highly regulated capital-raising platform for relatively well-performing SOEs, which needed to meet a set of rules and get approval to be listed. No more than one-third of the shares could be purchased by the public (tradable shares), with the rest split between the government (either central or local) and other state-owned legal entities. This arrangement was to ensure the dominance of state ownership in listed companies, but created a host of long-lasting issues in the stock market until it was changed more than ten years later.

Another important reform was the institutionalisation of the People's Bank of China (PBC) as the central bank in 1995. To help carry out its mandate, the PBC started open-market operations using treasury bonds in 1996 after establishing an interbank foreign-exchange market in 1994. It also established a money market for banks and other financial institutions, whereby the latter could get funding and the PBC could influence liquidity in the financial system. Although the PBC introduced lending quotas and a directed lending system (formally abolished in 1998) to restrict bank lending and control inflation under Governor Zhu Rongji, market instruments were created and used since this period (see more details in Chapter 5).

Fiscal and tax reform

The fiscal reform of the 1980s not only incentivised local governments to focus on economic development and investment, but also led to a sharp decline in central government fiscal revenue and a segmented fiscal system with uneven taxation and spending responsibilities across the country.[39] The 1994 fiscal reform streamlined the fiscal system, recentralised taxation power and some tax revenues, introduced a VAT that was shared between the central and local governments, established a formal transfer payment and tax refund system, created a unified SOE corporate tax rate of 33% in place of lump-sum taxation and reformed budgetary management at local level.[40] The government could no longer use an overdraft from the central bank to monetise fiscal deficits. These reforms reversed the decline in fiscal revenue and the erosion of the central government's authority. The central government regained formal oversight of revenue and spending and obtained the means to adjust fiscal policy and help poorer regions. Importantly, a unified VAT system and the establishment of a central government tax collection system helped to ensure more even taxation across China's regions, facilitating the development of a national market.[41]

The 1994 fiscal reform faced immense resistance from local governments, however, and the central government was unable to bring all provinces under the same fiscal umbrella. The ensuing compromises with various provinces led to enduring problems, some of which have yet to be resolved. For example, rich provinces were able to keep more revenues, significantly limiting the central government's ability to address uneven development and regional differences. Resource taxes stayed mostly with local governments, contributing to the excessive and wasteful mining of natural resources to the detriment of efficiency and the environment. And while some revenues were recentralised, most spending responsibilities were left with lower levels of local government. This meant poorer regions had less to spend on education, while old industrial centres with a higher share of retired workers had to levy a higher tax on labour (more in

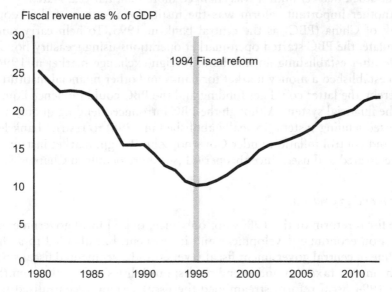

Figure 3.6 Fiscal revenue before and after the 1994 fiscal reform.

Source: NBS, Ministry of Finance, author's calculations.

Chapter 6). Also, most SOEs were exempted from paying dividends to state shareholders, contributing to excessive corporate savings and investment (more in Chapter 8).

Part 2: restructuring and building the social safety net

The second part of the second phase of reforms started in the late 1990s. It was devoted to deepening SOE and market liberalisation on the one hand and dealing with problems arising from earlier or incomplete reforms on the other hand. The most important elements included the restructuring of SOEs and the banking system, the expansion of housing-market reform and the development of a social safety net.

SOE restructuring

The wholesale SOE and market liberalisation process that began in 1993 not only led to rapid growth, but also created problems.[42] SOEs' new-found freedom, with little accountability or market discipline, led to over-investment, inventory building and poor profitability. Years of poor performance and losses were aggravated by the Asian financial crisis, with more than half of China's SOEs making losses in 1997. The government proposed a strategic restructuring of the SOEs in 1996, with the principle being to 'retain the large, release the small' companies. The CPC's 15th Congress endorsed the use of mergers and acquisitions (M&A), bankruptcy, sales (including management buyouts), leasing and labour shedding to help improve SOE performance.[43] By the end of 2001, three-quarters of SOEs had been restructured and at least two-thirds had been at least partially privatised.[44]

In this process, an estimated 20 million-plus people were laid off from SOEs and another 10 million-plus were made redundant from collectively owned enterprises.[45] The retrenched workers were called *Xiagang*, or layoffs, and excluded from the unemployment statistics. They were given lump-sum payouts that differed significantly from industry to industry, company to company and region to region, with many in the poor regions or the loss-making mining sectors getting almost nothing. While many were given some minimum subsistence funding by the government or saw an increased pension payout years later, the mass layoffs with limited severance constituted a quasi-default on the state sector's implicit pension and social safety responsibilities. The actual unemployment rate in urban areas was estimated at over 10% in the late 1990s.[46] This period saw a significant rise in social tensions and mass demonstrations,[47] prompting the government to focus more on maintaining relatively rapid growth and social stability.

In the process of SOE restructuring, banks had to accept suspension or delays in interest and principal payments, or forgive the debt. Where SOEs had failed, the government introduced the concept of 'policy bankruptcy', whereby the government helped provide minimum support for laid-off workers and asked banks to forgive debt, though this mechanism was not

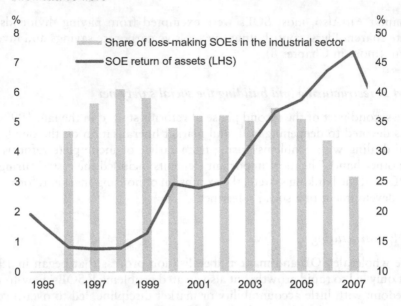

Figure 3.7 SOE performance before and after restructuring.
Source: NBS, author's estimates.

always smooth and depended on the fiscal resources of local governments. By stripping away redundant workers, reducing pension benefits and forgiving debt, the restructuring of the SOEs was instrumental in improving their performance in subsequent years.[48]

By the end of 2000, the profits of state-owned industrial firms had risen almost threefold from 1997 levels. Only one-third of the more than 6000 medium and large loss-making SOEs in 1997 remained in the red, though the total number of loss-makers remained above 30% for a few more years. However, anomalies and corruption in the restructuring process, partly due to the lack of independent third-party auditing and a market mechanism, led to a loss of state assets and a quasi-default on workers' benefits. These issues brewed resentment against SOE and market reforms in some quarters in later years, something that continues to inhibit reform.

Bank restructuring and financial reform

The credit boom of the mid-1990s led to problems that had to be cleared up over a subsequent ten-year period. Banks had the incentive to increase lending, as that upped their size and revenue, but had inadequate controls and risk management. In addition, lending was directed more at SOEs or companies with government ties than at more profitable firms.[49] When the economy slowed and SOEs got into trouble in the late 1990s, banks were basically insolvent, with an estimated non-performing loan (NPL) ratio of 50%.[50] The first stage of bank restructuring focused on writing off bad debts with the help of asset management companies (AMCs) and bank recapitalisation. The Ministry of Finance issued RMB 270 billion in special treasury bonds to recapitalise the big state-owned banks in 1998, while four AMCs took over more than RMB 1.4 trillion (or 14% of GDP) in bad assets in 1999.[51] China also abolished directed bank lending, enhanced banking supervision and started to implement a modern loan classification system, which assessed borrowers' payments, cashflows and collateral.

The second stage involved establishing a separate banking regulator, adopting macroprudential rules and listing the major banks. The China Banking Regulatory Commission (CBRC) was established in 2003, based on the PBC's regulatory and supervisory divisions, to strengthen bank supervision and reduce potential conflicts of interest between regulation and monetary policy – an issue heavily debated again in the mid-2010s. In December 2003, Central Huijin was established as a fully state-owned company and shareholder to help recapitalise the big state-owned banks and lead their restructuring and initial public offerings (IPOs). Huijin used USD 45 billion of the PBC's foreign-exchange reserves to recapitalise Bank of China and China Construction Bank at the end of 2003 and USD 15 billion to prop up Industrial and Commercial Bank of China in 2005.[52] The recapitalisation and subsequent shareholding reforms facilitated the successful listing of these banks on the Hong Kong Stock Exchange in 2005 and 2006. Huijin recapitalised the last of the big four banks, Bank of Agriculture, in 2008 and floated it in 2010.

Another important financial reform was interest-rate liberalisation, along with the development of a money market and a credit market. As in other countries, China liberalised money-market rates first, followed by bond yields and banking lending rates, with bank deposit rates coming last. The government removed the cap on interbank money-market rates in 1996, launching the China Interbank Offering Rate (CHIBOR). In 1997, interbank repo rates were liberalised. The PBC began to raise the lending-rate cap in 1998 and abolished the ceiling in 2004. It rolled out RMB interest-rate swap transactions in 2006 and the Shanghai Interbank Offered Rate (SHIBOR) started to operate in 2007. Over the next decade, bank lending and deposit rates were gradually liberalised until floors and ceilings were fully abolished in 2015, along with the introduction of a deposit insurance scheme. In practice, however, there has been soft guidance for banks, especially on deposit rates, to prevent too much deviation from the market 'average'.[53]

The period also saw a major stock-market reform in 2005, making non-tradable shares, or shares held by state-owned legal entities, tradable. This not only increased market depth and liquidity and removed a big overhang in the stock market, but also prompted significant market volatility and necessitated government rescue operations.[54]

Urban social safety-net reform

Before the reform period, government and SOE employees had lifetime employment, pension and social protection, but there was little in the way of a social safety net beyond that. As the economy liberalised, the private sector grew, and as SOE performance varied, the old pension and healthcare system, in which employers took care of everything, became increasingly inadequate. In 1991, the government decided to establish a national pension system and experimented with various programmes over the course of the decade. In 1997, it decided to establish a unified basic pension system for corporate employees, comprising a social pooling account and an individual account to fund a 'base' pension and individual annuity, respectively.[55] Around the same time, the government also set up a basic healthcare insurance system for urban corporate employees, with funding from corporate contributions and the state, along with an unemployment insurance scheme. It adjusted the parameters of the pension system in 2005 to make it more sustainable and expanded the arrangement to cover more self-employed people (see more in Chapters 8 and 10).

The government's fiscal situation in the late 1990s may help to explain two features of the initial social safety-net system: its decentralisation and its inadequate coverage of people who were about to retire or had not contributed enough to the new system. The former meant that both corporate contributions and average pension payments varied massively between cities and regions,[56] leaving corporate burdens uneven and inhibiting labour mobility between different areas. The latter meant that many laid-off workers or those near retirement saw a huge decline in their living standards once they stopped working. Nevertheless, the establishment of a basic pension and a social security system, including a minimum living assurance scheme, made it possible for the government to push through SOE restructuring and for companies to exit and fail with less devastating effects on staff.

Urban housing reform

Prior to China's reform, housing was provided by employers, who subsidised rents. There was a perpetual shortage of housing and urban living conditions were poor and cramped. After some experimentation, the State Council decided to deepen urban housing reform in 1994, calling for the commercialisation of housing and the establishment of a dual system of basic economic housing for low-income families and market-provided housing for others. Over the next few years, various pilot programmes were undertaken to reduce physical housing as a work benefit and increase cash compensation instead. Housing reform accelerated sharply in the late 1990s to help mitigate the shock of the Asian financial crisis. Physical housing distribution stopped in the second half of 1998 and was replaced with monetised housing distribution.[57] Here, a critical part of the reform was the privatisation of publicly owned housing and the sale of employer-owned dwellings to existing tenants in the late 1990s. This constituted a major wealth transfer from the state to households, while starting the process of land and property monetisation (to be discussed more in Chapter 8).

The reforms that took place from the mid-1990s to the mid-2000s were, in effect, a wholesale liberalisation that helped to establish a market economy in which market forces played an important and, in some cases, dominant role. During this process, government and public service functions often followed commercial principles (see Chapter 4 for more). With China's social safety net still nascent and the separation of public power and private market forces often hazy, this period also saw widespread rent-seeking and corruption (more in Chapters 6 and 10), a widening of income and social inequality and increased resistance to further reform.

The third phase of reform: deepening, rectification, rebalancing

The third phase of China's reform started in the mid-2000s with visibly less momentum than before. One reason was, perhaps, a reduced sense of urgency. China was growing rapidly, SOE and bank performance had improved significantly following restructuring, and the country had successfully joined the WTO. Another reason may have been the lack of consensus on various issues. After two-and-a-half decades of reform, much had been achieved, but there remained much to do. While everyone could agree on the problems – especially the build-up of imbalances, the rise in inequality and corruption – not everyone concurred on the causes and how they should be addressed. Some believed the problems existed because reforms had not been completed,[58] especially in the case of the SOEs, the separation of the state from the market, the continued presence of state monopolies and rigidities in the *hukou* and land systems. Others believed that marketisation had gone too far in many regards, that the market did not work in some areas and that the government should impose greater market oversight and discipline, as well as more equitable public services and social protection. Both groups were perhaps right to some extent.

Against this backdrop, the Chinese government tried to address some of the legacy issues while pushing forward with reform. A key aim was to readjust the role of the state versus the market, so that the market could play a greater role in some areas (allocating resources, for example) and the state could enhance its role in others (income distribution and regulation, for instance). Initial progress seemed limited outside of the social safety-net areas, so the comprehensive plans and principles of new reforms set out by the Third Plenum of the 18th CPC Congress in 2013 were welcomed.[59]

Developments since then have been uneven, however. There has been considerably more financial liberalisation and opening, but very slow progress on SOE and factor market reforms. Tax and fiscal reforms have progressed, but problems with intergovernmental relations and local government finances persist. And while the government has eased significantly the burden of administrative approvals and procedures, it has also tightened regulations in several areas. The social safety net has been expanded considerably, but public services and social protection remain highly unequal.

Financial liberalisation

Financial liberalisation over the past 15 years has proceeded on two main tracks: (1) liberalising financial services to facilitate more financial products and greater participation, and (2) opening up the market to foreign investors. The development of the interbank debt securities market has perhaps been the most impressive element of the former. Debt securities outstanding in the interbank market totalled RMB 134 trillion as of end 2021, or 86% of the total bond market, helped by the PBC's relaxed regulatory stance and interest-rate liberalisation. However, as shadow banking activities ballooned, the government was forced to tighten associated regulation in 2017 and 2018 (see more details in Chapter 9).[60]

When it came to market opening, meanwhile, China gradually expanded its Qualified Foreign Institutional Investor scheme[61] and launched the Stock Connect and Bond Connect schemes so that foreign investors could access China's stock and bond market, mainly through the Hong Kong Stock Exchange. China also relaxed controls on capital flows in the first half of the 2010s, helping to put the RMB in the International Monetary Fund's (IMF) Special Drawing Rights (SDRs) basket of currencies in 2015. However, it tightened certain controls again in 2016 amid significant outflows and depreciation pressure on the exchange rate. More recently, China has opened up more financial services to foreign companies in banking, insurance, securities and asset management.

Tax and local government fiscal reform

There have been three notable tax reforms in the past 15 years: (1) the abolition of the agricultural tax in 2006 – for the first time in Chinese history, farmers no longer had to pay tax on their agricultural produce (except for tobacco); (2) the introduction of a unified corporate income tax rate of 25% in 2008 – reducing tax for domestic companies and ending preferential tax treatment for foreign companies[62]; and (3) the switch from business tax to VAT for the services sector. Also significant in terms of incentives were an increase in the fuel consumption tax in 2008, an adjustment in the resource tax to a value-based system, and an environmental protection tax in 2018. The most prominent local government fiscal reform came in 2015, when China implemented a new budget law to officially allow local governments to borrow while restricting implicit debt financing through local government financing vehicles (LGFVs). China also realigned some spending responsibilities between local and central government, centralising further education and social and environmental spending – the former to partly compensate for the deterioration in rural finances after the abolition of the agricultural tax (Chapter 6). Budgetary management was also tightened, with bureaucracies and public institutions required to establish and follow a formal budgetary management process and disclose major spending to the public.

Provision of public services and social protection

From 2005, China significantly increased spending on basic public services and expanded the social safety net. It launched an urban resident healthcare insurance scheme in 2006 for people not covered by employee healthcare insurance and, since then, has greatly extended rural cooperative health insurance for serious illness coverage. As of 2021, about 90% of the population had basic health insurance, even though the coverage and payout ratio varied significantly between different population groups. A rural pension system was launched in 2009 and an urban resident pension system was launched in 2011 to supplement the urban employee pension system. Consequently, the number of people covered by a formal pension plan increased from 300 million-plus people in 2010 to more than 900 million in 2019. The government also stepped up its role in providing basic public services – including an increase in transfer payments to local governments for compulsory education in rural areas in 2010, helping to reduce the massive gap in basic education in rural areas.

Administrative reform and regulatory changes

Over the past decade, China has strengthened regulation in numerous areas to address issues of market failure and a lack of regulatory oversight. The main focuses have been on labour protection, work safety, food and drug safety and environmental protection.[63] More recently, the government has tightened rules on education, amended anti-trust laws, shored up rules on fintech and internet platforms, approved a new law on data security and passed another on personal data protection.[64] These new ordinances largely tried to rectify the previous absence of rules and regulations and bring China more in line with developed-country norms (more in Chapter 10).

While the sudden and concentrated way in which the recent new rules came about prompted investors to worry about an increase in overall government control, China's government was simultaneously trying to reduce control by streamlining state approval and administrative procedures. Since 2013, China has abolished or delegated many investment approvals to local governments and shortened the 'negative list' for foreign investment. In 2015, the State Council established a coordination group to streamline and reduce administrative and investment approvals, simplify business procedures and clean up fee collection. These reforms have cut red tape and lowered barriers to entry and operating costs for small private businesses, boosting new business registration (see more in Chapter 10).

SOE and factor market reforms

There has been no breakthrough in SOE reform in the past 15 years. While a shareholding structure has been introduced in most large SOEs, there has been limited progress on diversifying the ownership structure, despite attempts at mixed-ownership reform. While many SOEs operate on commercial principles and in a competitive environment, state monopolies persist in key sectors, and SOEs generally have better access to credit and a higher chance of government bailout if needed.[65] One notable area of progress on SOE governance has been the requirement to pay dividends to the state, although most have not gone to the general budget, but a separate SOE operating budget. In recent years, the government has emphasised strengthening CPC leadership in SOEs.

Factor market reform – letting the market play a decisive role in the allocation of labour, land, capital and resources – is a core part of the third phase of reform, as stipulated by the 2013 Third Plenum, but progress has been relatively slow. While *hukou* restrictions have been gradually reduced or abolished in small and medium-sized cities, they remain strong in larger ones. More importantly, unequal social benefits and access associated with the *hukou* system prevail. The government is proceeding cautiously on land reform, still testing the water with multiple pilot programmes in rural areas, while the urban land supply system remains largely unchanged (more in Chapter 6). There has also been some attempt at and limited progress on breaking down state monopolies and introducing private competition in key industries, including the financial industry, oil and gas, and power distribution.

Notes

1 See Communist Party of China Central Committee (1978).
2 See Lu and Wang (1981).
3 See Du (2005).
4 See CPC Central Committee (1980, 1982).
5 Ibid.
6 See Lardy (1983), Lin (1988, 1992), Perkins (1988) and Vendryes (2010).
7 See Ma (1991), Han (2008) and National Bureau of Statistics (1999b).
8 In 1984, the National Reform Commission published the Minutes of the Work Conference on Urban Economic System Reform Pilot Program. See Findlaw.cn Regulatory Library (1984). The conference focused on simplifying administration and decentralising power, 'enlivening' enterprises and empowering city governments.
9 From 1984, China gradually eased price management, allowing more prices to be adjusted by the market, and the 'dual track' system became a popular practice. In May 1984, the State Council passed 'temporary rules on further expanding SOE autonomy', allowing SOEs to sell capital goods exceeding the planned quota at a 20% premium. The rules were further relaxed in 1985.
10 In January 1985, the CPC Central Committee issued Ten Policies on Enlivening the Rural Economy, stipulating that the state would procure agricultural products from farmers at contract or market prices, ending the 30-year centralised purchase and dispatch system for agricultural products, with a few exceptions. See CPC Central Committee (1985).
11 In August 1987, the tenth meeting of the CPC Politburo decided to liberalise most prices with very few exceptions. Prices of key food items such as grain, pork and eggs were fully liberalised, while those of some capital goods, including coal, crude oil and electricity, rose significantly.

12 See Ministry of Finance (1984).
13 See Lou (2015).
14 From 1980 (see State Council, 1980), the central government and local governments separated their fiscal resources. This decentralised fiscal system was further refined in 1985 to establish the lump-sum fiscal responsibility contracts based on different tax categories. The central government took profit taxes from central government-owned SOEs and 70% of the tax revenues of resource companies, while local governments took profit taxes from local government-owned SOEs and the rest of the resource taxes. They shared revenues from VAT and business taxes.
15 See Lin and Liu (2000) and Bahl and Martinez-Vazquez (2006).
16 See Lou (2014).
17 Deng Xiaoping supported the proposal by Guangdong officials on establishing SEZs.
18 See NPC (1980).
19 See Wang (2013b).
20 See Ge (1999), Wang (2013a) and Zeng (2010).
21 See Yeung et al. (2009).
22 See Lardy (1992).
23 Data from the Chinese authorities, the United Nations Conference on Trade and Development (UNCTAD), the World Bank and WTO. See also Rumbaugh and Blancher (2004).
24 In March 1978, the National People's Congress passed the 53rd clause of the constitution on family planning. In 1980, the CPC Central Committee set the one-child policy as its basic stance on population policy. In 1982, the government distributed Instructions on further improving family planning work, making the one-child policy mandatory, emphasising the use of 'necessary rewards and restrictions' and 'disciplinary and administrative actions' to ensure full compliance.
25 See Zheng (2017).
26 See CPC Central Committee (1993).
27 The Washington Consensus is a term coined by economist John Williamson to summarise a set of policy reform recommendations for developing countries in crisis by Washington, DC based institutions such as the International Monetary Fund, the World Bank and the US Treasury. In its original sense, the term referred to policies that promoted the free market, macroeconomic stability, and trade and FDI opening. Specific policies included fiscal policy discipline, the liberalisation of trade and FDI, market-determined interest rates, the privatisation of SOEs, the legal security of property rights and the redirection of subsidies to spending more on basic education, healthcare and infrastructure. To the strong objection of Williamson, the term was later widely used to mean a broad and strong market-based approach and neoliberalism. See Williamson (1990, 2002, 2004).
28 See CPC Central Committee (1993).
29 See CPC Central Committee (1993).
30 See State Council (1992).
31 See State Council (1992).
32 See State Council Information Office (2001).
33 See State Council (1994a). The grain coupon, used for food rationing and distribution in urban areas, was also formally abolished.
34 China started to allow exporters to retain some of their foreign currency in 1979. In 1985, Shenzhen opened a swap centre for those with foreign currency to trade with those who had demand outside of official plans. In 1988, with the opening of another swap centre in Shanghai, China allowed the swap market exchange rate to be freely determined by market demand and supply. See Lardy (1992).

35 See Wang (2004).
36 See State Council (1993b) and PBC (1993).
37 See Fernald et al. (1999).
38 See CPC Central Committee (1993).
39 See Lou (2014).
40 See State Council (1993a).
41 See Lou (2015).
42 See Groves et al. (1994).
43 See CPC Central Committee (1997).
44 See China Labor Bulletin (2007) and Gan (2008).
45 See Jefferson (2016), Wang (2004) and Garnaut et al. (2006).
46 Author's estimate.
47 See Cai (2006) and Shen (2007).
48 See Hsieh and Song (2015) and Garnaut et al. (2006).
49 See Lardy (1998).
50 See Karacadag (2003).
51 In 1999, four AMCs were set up to take over the bad debt from the big four state-owned banks at face value: Huarong for the Industrial and Commercial Bank of China, Xinda for Bank of China, Orient for the China Construction Bank and Great Wall for Bank of Agriculture. The AMCs were initially funded by AMC bonds issued by the Ministry of Finance, held by the banks. By 'selling' RMB 1.4 trillion of bad debt at face value, the big four banks regained precious capital. The AMCs were meant to operate for ten years to deal with the bad debt, but later transitioned into 'real' asset management and financial services companies, engaging in investment, securities and asset management activities in addition to disposing of bad debt. At the early stages of debt disposal, the AMCs invited international firms to purchase debt packages. The recovery rate was relatively low given the lack of well-established debt disposal procedures and recourse for creditors. Later, the housing-market boom helped to push up SOE asset values and debt recovery rates.
52 China's use of foreign-exchange reserves to recapitalise the banks was an unusual operation. When the US$ 45 billion was transferred to BOC and CCB, the PBC's balance sheet showed a decline in foreign-currency assets and an increase in equity assets (shareholdings of banks). While not formally announced, BOC and CCB had to keep the US$ 45 billion in foreign currency on their books without selling it back to the PBC for three years. In 2007, the Ministry of Finance issued special treasury bonds to purchase Huijin's share from the PBC, replacing PBC's equity holding with treasury holdings (claims to government). Huijin also injected US$ 4 billion into China Re, US$ 20 billion into China Development Bank and RMB 24.4 billion into Everbright group in 2007.
53 From January 2020, banks were no longer allowed to price their loans off the benchmark lending rates, but use the Loan Prime Rate (LPR). The LPR is submitted by participating banks and the average is announced every month. Benchmark rates are no longer published regularly. This marked the final step in China's interest-rate liberalisation, according to the PBC. However, the LPR is priced off the rate of Medium Lending Facility, which is a policy rate set by the PBC. In addition, banks' deposit rates are closely monitored by the PBC to prevent 'excessive' rate competition 'disturbing market order'.
54 See China Securities Regulatory Commission (2005).
55 The 1997 pension plan stipulated that, on average, the corporate contribution to pensions should be about 20% of salary, of which 11% went into the 'individual account' and the rest into the 'social pooling' account. Employee pensions would comprise two parts: (1) a 'base' pension, equivalent to about 20% of the average salary of the region the previous year, paid from the 'social pooling' account, and (2) an individual annuity payment equivalent to 1/120th each

month, funded by outstanding money from the individual account. If a retiree lived longer than 10 years, the individual retirement payment would be funded by the social pooling account. In 2005, China amended some parameters. Contributions to individual accounts were reduced to 8% of average salary and payment was adjusted depending on life expectancy and length of retirement. The base pension payout was also adjusted to reflect the length of contribution and average individual salary.

56 For example, in the late 1990s, corporate pension contributions in Liaoning province, an old industrial base with many retired workers from SOEs, was as high as 30% of worker salaries, while that in Shenzhen, a migrant city with few retired workers staying to qualify for pension payment, was only 4%.

57 See State Council (1994b, 1998) and Ministry of Construction (1999).

58 See Zhou (2010).

59 See CPC Central Committee (2013).

60 The PBC and other regulators jointly issued Guidance on Regulating the Asset Management of Financial Institutions in April 2018.

61 The Qualified Foreign Institutional Investor programme was introduced by China in 2002 to provide foreign institutional investors with the right to invest in China's domestic stock market.

62 From January 2008, corporate income tax for domestic enterprises (SOEs) was reduced from 33% to 25%, while those for foreign companies were raised from 24% and 15% to 25%. Existing foreign companies were given a transition period. The end of preferential tax treatment was partly because domestic capital was no longer in short supply and partly because a large share of 'foreign' investment was domestic investment in disguise after companies set up shell companies in Hong Kong or elsewhere ('round-tripping'). The latter was to take advantage of lower tax rates (see Xiao, 2004).

63 For example, the Labor Law was amended in 2009 and 2018, the Production Safety Law was amended in 2009 and 2015, a new Food Safety Law and new Drug Safety Law were passed in 2015, and the Environmental Protection Law was amended in 2014.

64 The Education Law was amended in 2009 and 2015. In July 2021, the CPC Central Committee and State Council jointly issued 'Guidance on further reducing the homework burden and after-school tutoring burdens of students in the compulsory education stage', which sent the private education sector into a tailspin. The Data Security Law was passed in June 2021 and a Personal Information Protection Law was passed in August 2021.

65 See Cong et al. (2018) and Lardy (2019).

4   The state versus the market

How important is the state in China's economy today and how has its role evolved over the past four decades? The consensus is that the state plays a bigger role in China's economy than it does in the US or European economies. But is it a dominant role, as many people claim, or has China become a market economy as the government insists? Is the large role of the state the key to China's economic success, as some believe? Data on ownership structure suggest that most of China's economy is privately owned, but we need to analyse the role of the state from multiple angles, including how resources are allocated, the use of industrial policy, government intervention in the market and the state's role in the provision of public goods. We know from Chapter 3 (and will see later on) that China's economic success in the early decades of reform stemmed from the reduction of state ownership and government control. While government stimuli and proactive development strategy have helped China to respond to shocks and challenges, there are also many problems associated with the excessive presence of the state in some areas and its absence from others.

Ownership structure and resource allocation

The share of state ownership

As described in Chapter 2, China's economy started out in the late 1970s as almost fully state-owned with no private businesses. Poor economic performance drove the government to adopt market-oriented reforms and encourage the development of a private sector. The importance of the private sector in the economy grew steadily as state ownership shrank, even though China never had a mass privatisation programme like Eastern Europe or Russia.

The first big change in ownership structure was the de-collectivisation of farming in the early 1980s, which handed over agricultural production – nearly 30% of the economy at the time – to individual farmers. In the 1980s and 1990s, small-scale private companies and individually owned businesses were allowed to grow and TVEs to flourish. Most TVEs became

DOI: 10.4324/9781003310938-5

private companies later on. Another big shift happened in the late 1990s and early 2000s, when more than two-thirds of SOEs were restructured, with most small SOEs released from state control through sale, management buyout or other means. The listing of SOEs on the stock market helped the state to divest ownership and the private sector to boost its holdings, especially after a 2005 reform made it possible for the public-sector shareholders of SOEs to sell to private investors. The state-owned sectors now account for an estimated 30–40% of the overall economy (Figure 4.1).[1]

While this is high compared with most other developed economies and emerging markets, most of China's economy (60–70%) is in the hands of the private sector. More importantly, it is the rapid rise of the non-state sector and the reduction of state control of SOEs that has been behind the country's impressive economic performance since the 1980s, not the high level of state ownership. That said, the share of state ownership has changed little over the past 15 years or so, largely as a result of the SOE revival after the 1990s restructuring, a lack of major SOE reform since then and the government-driven stimulus that followed the global financial crisis. Although private businesses in many regions and sectors continued to flourish, especially where there was no SOE dominance, SOEs in resource-, financial- and infrastructure-related areas also grew rapidly. And while most in China acknowledge the SOEs' inefficiency, policymakers also view them as indispensable when it comes to economic security, the provision of jobs and social services.

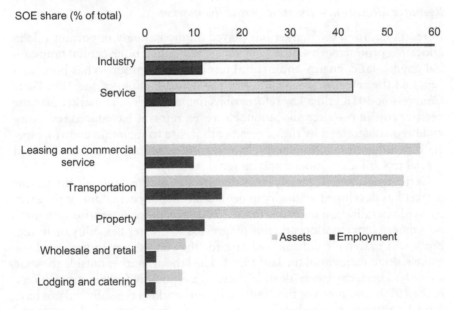

Figure 4.1 Ownership structure of selected sectors, 2018.

Source: NBS, author's estimates.

Invisible versus visible hands

An important dimension of the role of the state is how economic activities are organised – through the market or government plan, by 'visible hands' or 'invisible hands'. As detailed in Chapter 3, before the reform period, almost all economic activities were organised by the state through a centrally planned system. There was no market for goods or services, let alone labour or capital. Economic liberalisation reduced the role of planning and increased that of the market in the 1980s, starting with the market for farm goods. However, as late as 1987, the government still had a visible hand everywhere, with plans as detailed as the distributed quantity and price of specific types of wood and steel, for instance.[2]

The mid-1990s reforms helped to establish a market mechanism whereby economic incentives, price signals and competition became the driving force behind economic activity. The rise of private companies and the entrance of foreign firms amplified the importance of market forces – and even SOEs had to operate in the market. The rise of market forces, for example, is behind the millions of migrants from the Anhui and Sichuan provinces who now provide housekeeping and childcare services for families in big cities such as Beijing and Shanghai. Although the government still plays an active role in guiding China's development strategy and uses five-year plans to set medium-term objectives in key areas, especially large infrastructure investment, the plans today are nowhere near as all-encompassing, specific or binding as they were.

Resource allocation – the state versus the market

In recent decades, the market has played an increasingly important role in allocating productive resources in China, including labour, capital (and capital goods), land, energy and natural resources. But progress has been uneven, and the reforms are incomplete. The Third Plenum of the 18th Party Congress in 2013 said a key reform objective was to let the market play the decisive role in resource allocation. However, reforms have faced resistance and been constrained by the government's desire to maintain control, especially in industries such as energy, banking and telecommunications, deemed crucial to China's economic and national security.

Currently, labour is largely allocated by the market, though the labour market has developed gradually under a dual-track system. One of the earliest SOE liberalisation measures in the 1980s was more enterprise autonomy on worker compensation, and this progressed to greater flexibility on hiring. But it was extremely difficult and rare for the state sector to fire people or make redundancies until the late 1990s. The labour market outside the state sector had been extremely 'flexible', however, especially for migrant workers. In the 1990s and much of the 2000s, migrant workers typically did not have formal contracts or much labour protection, were often owed wages and could lose their jobs with no compensation and little warning.

In the past decade, the two segmented labour markets have converged somewhat. With the rise of large and vibrant private companies competing for talent, the urban employment market has become much less rigid. Meanwhile, demographic shifts and new labour laws have meant better labour protection and wages for migrant workers. The remaining issues with labour allocation hark back to the *hukou* system (and related social benefits, more in Chapter 6), which continues to hinder labour participation and mobility.

The market has played an increasing role in capital allocation, but the state has retained strong influence through its ownership of the banking system, lingering interest-rate controls and the involvement of local-government entities. The importance of the market in capital allocation grew when China set up commercial banks to extend loans rather than grants to enterprises, as interest rates gradually liberalised and the money market, stock market and credit market grew. Unlike the early years of reform, much of China's capital allocation is now driven by market forces. However, the banking system remains predominantly state owned, and the government interferes in banks' commercial decision-making, especially in times of economic shock or challenge (as in 2008–2009), pressuring banks to support growth.

The influence of local authorities over local banks (especially city commercial banks) is usually more pronounced. The state banks have incentives to lend to SOEs or large private companies thought to enjoy government support, enabling such debtors to borrow excessively due to easy access and expectations of a state bailout if needed. Aware of the problems, China has

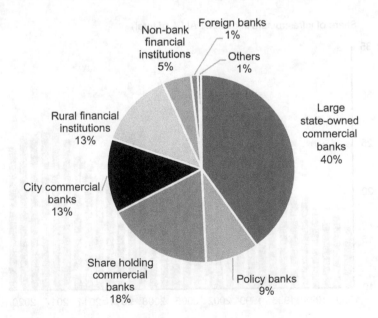

Figure 4.2 Ownership structure of the banking sector, 2020.

Source: CBIRC, author's estimates.

tried to expand 'direct financing' through the credit and stock markets since around 2010, as well as to develop small banks that better serve the private sector and SMEs. The heavy presence of state-owned entities in the financial markets and the lack of market discipline, coupled with distorted market signals, however, have led to more financing but not necessarily more efficient capital allocation (see Chapter 5 for more).

The capital goods market is also where the state still exerts significant influence. Although China has long abolished the dual track system, whereby SOEs enjoyed better access to cheaper energy, resources and investment goods, the government has retained control and even dominance of the 'commanding heights' industries considered strategically important to the economy and to national security, such as oil and gas, coal, power generation and distribution, rail and aviation transport, banking and telecommunications. Through SOEs and price controls, the state influences the allocation of these capital goods, though it no longer directly distributes them as it did under the planned economy and in the early years of reform.

The government also plays a critical role in resource allocation, thanks to its massive infrastructure investment. In the early days of reform, local governments provided land and infrastructure for free in industrial parks to attract investment and boost industrialisation. Large-scale infrastructure investment accelerated nationwide following the Asian financial crisis and, once again, after the global financial crisis. Over the past two decades or so, infrastructure investment has accounted for one-fifth to a quarter of total fixed-asset investment (FAI, Figure 4.3). Although not all infrastructure

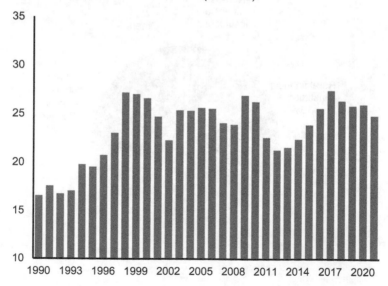

Figure 4.3 Infrastructure investment as a share of total fixed asset investment.

Source: NBS, Author estimates.

Note: Data before 2002 are for transport and utility sector investment.

investment is financed by the government, the state plays a dominant role in planning projects and mobilising resources. Corporate participation also tends to come mainly from SOEs. Infrastructure projects have typically not only been concentrated on transport, especially highways, bridges and railways, but also airports and ports. In the past decade, infrastructural investment has increasingly shifted to urban utilities, public transport (including subways), renewable energy, power transmission, and environmental and hydraulic projects.

The government still has a significant hand in land allocation, even though market forces have been introduced and land-use reform has been underway for more than 30 years. Urban land is state owned and new land supply can only be provided by local governments once procured from rural residents. Although most land is now supplied to the market by auction, not free government allocation (as it was until the 1990s), the fact that local governments are a monopoly supplier, owning LGFVs and some property developers on the demand side, demonstrates the persistent presence of the state's role in land distribution.

The role of industrial policy

The broad definition of industrial policy can refer to the 'developmental state' model, whereby the government actively intervenes in an economy to promote fast growth and guide structural transformation.[3] It is usually associated with the growth model of Japan and other East Asian economies. The narrower definition refers to the practice whereby a government selects certain industries, technologies or products and uses specific policy measures to accelerate their development more than others, often to gain competitiveness internationally.

While industrial policy has been widely used throughout history in many countries,[4] China has come under particular fire for its use of industrial policy over the past decade, though its critics do not always refer to the same concept. Many observers believe that China has increased its use of industrial policy in the past decade compared with the 1990s and that this was a critical factor behind its increase in international competitiveness. Such an impression may have largely stemmed from the changes in the overall reform backdrop.

China's industrial policy featured more prominently (in both the broad and the narrow definitions) in the early years of reform, with extensive government planning, SOE direct investment, directed lending and investment approvals. However, specific industrial plans did not stand out in the sea of government plans. Over the past 10–15 years, as government planning has waned, the focus on specific industries – and the use of more narrowly defined industrial policy – has become more apparent. The first period also coincided with powerful economic reform and liberalisation, which led to rapid developments that quickly rendered government plans obsolete. There was also a clear trend of declining state control in the first

20-plus years of reform. The recent period has seen no significant increase in the overall role of the market or decline in the role of the state, making industrial policy particularly notable.

The effect of China's industrial policy has been mixed. When the government was focusing on liberalising the economy through various reforms, introducing the market element and opening up to the world economy and foreign competition, the impact of industrial policy more broadly was overwhelmingly positive. Where government policies prioritised certain industries or products, be it during the more planned period or in the past 15 years through conventional industrial policy tools such as subsidies and preferential market access, the results have been less impressive and, in some cases, clear failures. While industrial policy has not been a particularly important factor in China's economic success, it has created distortions that have led to some legitimate complaints from trading partners.

Industrial policy in the 1980s and 1990s

China employed the broad definition of industrial policy long before its first official industrial policy document emerged in 1989. Indeed, as the state owned almost everything, production and investment were planned and funding came from state coffers, the government only had to increase investment in whichever industry or sector it wanted to prioritise. There was no need to incentivise indirectly or nudge enterprises into developing certain industries. For example, prior to 1978, China's development strategy was to catch up with the industrialised nations, so the government channelled investment into the capital goods sectors, including mining and metals (especially steel and oil) to facilitate industrialisation. After 1978, China shifted its industrial strategy towards the rapid development of light manufacturing to satisfy domestic demand, increase exports and create more jobs. The government adopted a broad set of policies to aid the achievement of that goal, liberalising the domestic economy, attracting foreign investment with subsidies and preferential taxes, and channelling more investment into light manufacturing while limiting funding for heavy industry.

China's first industrial policy document in 1989[5] stated the importance of 'identifying the key areas to be supported or restricted'. It said that the government would concentrate on developing 'foundational industries', including agriculture, energy, transport and raw materials, and control the development of ordinary processing. It also issued a catalogue listing industries and products/processes that were to be supported, severely restricted or terminated. As the economy was still a largely planned one, the decision was to be implemented by 'various departments and regions' to 'shrink FAI, adjust industrial structure, guide FDI flows [...] and arrange annual and five-year plans'. Banks were asked to come up with lending plans accordingly. In 1994, the government issued a National Industrial Policy Outline of the 1990s,[6] focusing on policies to foster competition and economies of scale and restricting the construction of 'below-standard' projects (which probably limited the development of TVEs thereafter). The same year also saw a new industrial policy for the automobile sector.

Actual development in the 1990s did not follow the government's industrial policy blueprint, as the sweeping economic reforms and market liberalisation overshadowed its plans. The flourishing of private firms and inflows of foreign investment led to the rapid development of the light manufacturing sector. China's export-oriented policies also sparked a surge in labour-intensive processing industries, including clothing, toys and shoes and, later, electronics assembly. Although the government achieved its plan of significantly increasing investment in mining and metals, energy and infrastructure during this time,[7] heavy industry as a share of total industry declined from 58% in 1990 to just below 51% in 1998. Moreover, the expansion led to excess capacity and SOEs faced severe retrenchment (Chapter 3). In other words, the economic success of the 1990s owed largely to market liberalisation rather than industrial policy.

Industrial policy since 2000

The release of Policies on Encouraging the Development of Software and Integrated Circuit Industries[8] in June 2000 marked the beginning of a new phase of China's industrial policy. The document was an example of the narrowly defined industrial policy, in which the government detailed specific measures, ranging from certification to investment to taxation and intellectual property, to encourage the development of two specific sectors. Strictly speaking, an integrated-circuit industrial policy had already been in place in the 1990s, but it was carried out mainly through direct government and SOE investment.[9]

High-tech industries, especially information technology and advanced manufacturing, became the main areas the government wanted to promote from 2000. In 2002, China issued a National Industrial Technology Policy, outlining technologies and processes to be promoted in almost all industries.[10] From 2004, multiple agencies jointly issued Guidelines on Key Priority Areas of High-Tech Industries every two years. The 2007 version established 130 focus areas, including information technology, biotech, aerospace, new materials and advanced manufacturing.[11]

More broadly, China also published industrial policy documents aimed at guiding general industrial upgrades and structural change. The 10th Five-Year Plan in 2001 emphasised the acceleration of industrial upgrades and digitalisation and the development of high-tech industries.[12] The 11th Five-Year Plan highlighted Indigenous innovation and the development of an advanced manufacturing sector.[13] It also aimed to accelerate services development and strengthen foundational industry and infrastructure development, and was accompanied by the State Council's Rules on Facilitating Industrial Structural Adjustment.[14]

In 2010, the State Council published a decision on building strategic new industries, setting industrial priority and the technological path for the 12th

Five-Year Plan.[15] After the global financial crisis, China rolled out 'indus-trial rejuvenation' plans for ten industries facing various difficulties, including the automobile, iron and steel, and shipbuilding sectors. The 13th and 14th Five-Year Plans continued to foster new, strategic industries, especially information technology, new energy, digital technology and related sectors, with industry-specific plans detailing policy measures to be used to promote certain technologies and products.[16]

Barry Naughton considers the National Medium- and Long-term Development Outline for Science and Technology (2006–2020) of 2006[17] to be the true start of China's industrial policy.[18] The claim may be exagger-ated, but the Development Outline gave comprehensive long-term guide-lines on industrial technology policy and key focus areas and called for implementation details from various government departments. It high-lighted policies, including fiscal policy, to encourage corporate innovation, government procurement policies to facilitate indigenous innovation and guidelines for technological standards.

By 2009, the country had rolled out 78 detailed implementation plans, while the provinces had issued more than 570 supporting policy docu-ments.[19] Specific policies included increased spending on science and tech-nology, tax deductions for R&D investment, tax deductions for high-tech firms, financing support for high-tech companies and government procure-ment of indigenous products. The Outline also established key projects on which the country could focus resources to help lead technology capabili-ties in some industries. Given its extensive use of industrial policy in the past, Naughton's impression that China has implemented industrial policy on a 'unprecedented scale' since 2010[20] may have more to do with the gen-eral slowdown in market reforms over the past decade.

China's more intense focus on developing advanced and high-tech indus-tries since the mid-2000s, triggered by major changes in the economy around that time, may have also attracted more scrutiny from developed economies. As mentioned in Chapter 2, it was around then that the govern-ment began to worry about economic imbalances – the rapid growth of heavy industry had led to environmental degradation, while the demo-graphic shift and a sharp rise in labour costs had made China's reliance on labour-intensive exports look unsustainable. Meanwhile, the explosive growth of information technology and the internet were transforming the globe. China's policymakers began to consider policies that would help the country move up the manufacturing value chain, maintain its competitive-ness and become more innovative, so that it was not left behind by the technological revolution happening around the world (more in Chapter 12).

The Made in China 2025 (MIC 2025) policy published in 2015 can be considered an updated version of the 2006 plan that reflected the desire to avoid being stuck with no advanced technology or cheap labour.[21] In line with China's long-term objective of becoming a modern, advanced economy by 2050, MIC 2025 was the first ten-year blueprint aimed at helping the country to advance up the global value chain, increase domestic capabilities in science and technology and catch up with advanced economies. It identified ten strategic sectors to be fostered, with actions focused on integrating digital technology into manufacturing (smart manufacturing), increasing indigenous innovation and domestic capabilities, and ensuring greener development[22] – clearly drawing on Germany's Industry 4.0 policy initiative.

The State Council also published its 13th Five-Year Plan on strategic new industries in 2016.[23] While the main MIC 2025 document listed 2020 and 2025 targets for R&D spending and patents, productivity, the digitalisation ratio and pollution reduction, the accompanying action plans for specific industries often listed targets and timelines for domestic production ratios. The latter implied restrictions on imports and foreign brands and attracted considerable concern and criticism from China's major trading partners.[24]

Chinese companies and local governments had often requested technology transfers from foreign joint-venture partners before, and China had set domestic content requirement for some time. However, it had not come as close to advanced-country levels in as many industries, or competed as directly with them, as when MIC 2025 was announced. Nor had the Chinese market ever mattered as much to the success of foreign companies. This was perhaps a key reason why MIC 2025 caused such an outcry in the United States and Europe. Moreover, China's emphasis on domestic innovation and production capabilities came at a time when it was not rolling out major market liberalisation measures (as it had in the 1990s).

Domestically, although the government formulated various plans to advance the agenda outlined in MIC 2025, actual implementation (other than using it to get project approval and investment funding in certain areas) and industrial development did not seem to be as driven by the plan as foreign commentators thought or feared. For example, the gap between China and the advanced economies in the semiconductor and similar high-tech sectors has not obviously narrowed since 2015. What's more, it is often difficult to identify new strategic industries amid rapid technological advancement and market development. In a 2021 report, the State Information Centre noted that the first list of new state strategic industries five years earlier contained only half the current new ones and did not include new energy vehicles and digital innovation.[25] In the face of strong criticism and sustained pressure from the United States and other key trading partners, China dialled back on MIC 2025, announcing policies to open the domestic market further, welcoming foreign investment and banning the forced transfer of technology. Meanwhile, China's quest for advanced technology and a move up the value chain continued in the 14th Five-Year Plan and other supplementary industrial plans.

The role and effectiveness of industrial policy

The role and effectiveness of China's industrial policy have been hotly debated. Critics can show numerous examples of the government's direct intervention failing to achieve intended objectives, creating distortions, leading to excess capacity or otherwise hurting the development of certain sectors.[26] Supporters can point to China's successful structural transformation and industrial upgrade.[27] It is hard to dispute the evidence that China's broadly defined industrial policy has had significant successes in helping the country to use its comparative advantages, gain and retain more advanced manufacturing skills and technologies, become internationally competitive and move up the value chain over time. Chapter 2 also showed how the government's pragmatic development strategy, including reforms and opening, has helped to transform China's economic structure.

However, proponents of China's industrial policy also acknowledge that industrial policy tends to work better when it tries to overcome informational, coordination and externality issues[28] and is combined with market liberalisation and greater competition. When the government has tried to pick winners in a certain industry, process or technology by substituting for the market and restricting competition, the results have been far less convincing.[29] A few examples help demonstrate these points.

Steel industry

From the beginning of the People's Republic, China was obsessed with producing enough steel, as it was considered the most important material for industrialisation, construction and building a modern military. In 1958, at the height of the 'Great Leap Forward', the government decided to double steel output and reach the United Kingdom's level of production within 15 years. The resulting massive investment in elementary iron and crude steel projects led to a surge in crude steel production in 1958–1960, but this diverted too many resources from other sectors and did not last. The economy shrank at a double-digit rate in 1961 and steel production halved, resulting in wasted capital and disastrous environmental impacts. In 1979, China invested a quarter of its annual FAI in establishing the Shanghai Baoshan Steel company, but the company required government support for years, as its high-end product was not competitive on the domestic market.[30]

From the mid-1990s to 2021, China's steel capacity expanded tenfold amid the central government's recurring efforts to restrict investment and capacity. The government repeatedly set policy and capacity-reduction targets seemingly without fully considering future economic developments and market demand or allowing for the full exit of failed companies. The government mandated a 10% annual cut in steel production from 1998 to 2000 after demand collapsed and steel production exceeded 100 million tonnes a year. However, small private steel mills did not adhere to the cuts and steel capacity continued to grow. Demand also rose sharply in the wake of the housing reform and property boom.

When China issued its first formal steel-sector policy in 2005, calling for consolidation, capacity had ballooned to about 400 million tonnes a year. In 2009, when crude steel capacity had exceeded 800 million tonnes and production was almost half of the world's total, China approved a plan to revitalise the steel industry and control steel production.[31] In 2015–2016, steel was again at the top of the state's excess capacity-reduction efforts, when crude steel capacity exceeded 1.1 billion tonnes.[32] And despite considerable success in reducing capacity in 2015–2016, both China's steel production and capacity have grown further since 2017.

Photovoltaic industry (solar panels)

No other industry, perhaps, can demonstrate the successes and challenges of China's industrial policy like the solar photovoltaic (PV) industry. China identified solar power and the PV industry among the new strategic industries it wanted to encourage in 2010 following the global financial crisis.[33] At the time, more than 300, or about half, of China's cities counted the PV sector as a strategic emerging industry.[34] In the first half of 2011, the capacity of large companies doubled, as did China's overall production and exports. China's output of PV products rose from 4 GW in 2009 to 21 GW in 2011, while its polysilicon output increased from 20,000 tonnes a year to 84,000 tonnes.[35]

As China's own plan to expand solar power capacity progressed slowly, the industry grew to depend heavily on exports. When the export market contracted following the eurozone debt crisis and, more importantly, after the EU launched anti-dumping lawsuits, production and exports collapsed and many Chinese companies went bankrupt. In 2012, 110 out of China's 260 PV companies closed. Since then, China has expanded its solar power generation significantly, which, together with the renewable energy drive worldwide, has helped put the PV industry back on a healthier path.

On the one hand, the government's PV policy, amplified manifold by local governments, led to an excessive build-up of capacity and disorderly competition, resulting in widespread closures and the waste of capital, as well as a global backlash against China. Subsidies from the Ministry of Finance in the early stages also led to fraud and encouraged low-level repetitive production and investment. On the other hand, the policy was instrumental in drastically increasing China's PV production, driving down prices and chasing out international competition with cheap products.[36] As the drop in PV costs helped lead to explosive growth in solar panel installation worldwide, China's solar panel industry benefited from its position of dominance.

The integrated circuit or semiconductor industry

The semiconductor industry is perhaps the one that China's government is most eager to develop, but 40 years of industrial policy have yet to prove successful in substantially aiding its development. Despite extensive and prolonged policy support to develop the semiconductor industry, China accounted for only 6–7% of global semiconductor production in 2020, but one-third of consumption. Moreover, China's firms are largely concentrated at the lower- to mid-end of the long semiconductor supply chain.[37] China's chip manufacturing ability is also widely considered to be a few generations, or about five years, behind the Taiwan Semiconductor Manufacturing Company (TSMC).

China had established a plan to develop the sector as early as 1981, focusing on importing new production lines and upgrading technology, with a deputy premier of the State Council leading the charge. In 1989, the Ministry of Machinery and Electronics proposed an integrated circuit development plan to build five key enterprises, and China launched two such major projects in 1990 and 1995. However, it took the government so long to decide and invest that the semiconductor industry had moved on to different technologies and paths by the time it had completed its investment.[38] By the late 1990s, China's integrated circuit industry had fallen further behind the United States and Japan, producing less than 1% of the global total.

Since 2000, China has continued to develop and intensify its semiconductor policy.[39] First, the government focused on developing a few major production centres. The 2008 special integrated circuit industry plan identified specific products, subsectors and processes on which to focus investment.[40] A 2011 plan specified tax, investment and financing, and R&D policies to further promote the semiconductor industry.[41] Another policy push came in 2014, when the government decided to establish national industrial funds with investment from the central government serving as a catalyst to lure private investment and open the sector to foreign investment.[42] The 2020 integrated circuit sector policy added the use of local government investment funds, as well as policies to attract talent, protect intellectual property, foster market application and support public listings.[43] The number of semiconductor-related companies in China increased by 58,000 from January to October 2020, some in the middle of nowhere, with no technology or plans, as new policies led to a gold rush of claims on subsidies and policy support from the government.[44]

The new policy push, especially the semiconductor sector funds, did help Chinese companies acquire foreign firms and make big investments, contributing to the country's progress on semiconductor assembly (packaging) and fabrication (manufacturing). However, in an industry that is extremely capital and knowledge intensive, where technology replacement occurs every year or few months, China's approach has not yielded a meaningful narrowing of the innovation or technological (and technical) gap.

Some suggest that the subsidies and financial support for big Chinese companies may have suppressed competition and dulled their sense of 'existential threat', thus proving counterproductive in spurring innovation.[45] Often, massive investments were made in companies with no core technology or product, leading to wasteful investment or even fraud.[46] There has been notable progress by the private sector in the integrated circuit industry, however. Huawei's HiSilicon, for example, grew after years of sustained large investment in R&D and by attracting talent from around the world.

The general role of government

From certain perspectives, China's government seems omnipresent – from controlling the banks and building highways to direct involvement in the local economy and its active pursuit of industrial policy. The past two years have seen the government increasing regulatory controls and emphasising common or shared prosperity.[47] These recent moves have led many in China and abroad to question whether a fundamental shift in the role of the state is on the way. Will China's government play a bigger part in every aspect of the economy? Does this mean China's transition towards a market economy has come to an end and could be reversed?

Reviewing the evolution of the role of the state more broadly over the past two-plus decades can help us better understand the factors behind the recent changes. While some recentralisation and regulatory reset may seem necessary, slow progress on reforming state monopolies reinforces the impression of ever-rising government controls, even though controls in some areas have been reduced. Moreover, the government playing 'saviour of last resort' in the economy also undermines the role of the market.

1990s government reform – reducing the fiscal burden and delegating power

In the early years of reform, the government continued to control almost all aspects of people's lives. This changed in the mid-1990s, when China introduced market forces and economic incentives to government management, absolving the state of many social and economic responsibilities. It was a time when fiscal revenue had dwindled to dangerously low levels and the government was facing serious challenges in covering its spending needs as inflation and private-sector wages soared.

The combination of wanting to reduce direct government control and a lack of fiscal resources prompted China to adopt the principle of 'zifuying-kui' ('自负盈亏'), or 'financial self-reliance', in almost every area, including government agencies. As a result, many ministries and government agencies set up 'institutions' (事业单位, or *shiyedanwei*) outside the government personnel and budget system to charge for services and engage in commercial activities to fund themselves.[48] For example, agencies that had data set up institutions that sold data or formed joint ventures to establish data platforms, while those with approval or certification functions set up institutions to run those as businesses. In addition, some former staff and relatives of civil servants set up intermediary companies to help businesses get government certification, licences and access to resources. In areas devoid of monetary benefit, there was a lack of government presence in the provision of public goods and services.[49]

Using commercial incentives to run public services and oversee government responsibilities led to widespread rent-seeking and the uneven implementation of rules and policies. Meanwhile, a government presence was lacking in areas such as market regulation, food and drug safety and environmental protection (see also Chapter 10). For years, for example, China's market supervision focused on granting qualifications or production approval to firms entering the market, but with no regular inspections afterwards. Local-level regulatory and supervisory agencies also typically reported to local governments, which had other priorities.

Such practices and a lack of proper supervision led to scandals and protests related to food and medicinal safety.[50] Pollution and emissions also worsened in the 2000s, even as local environmental agencies reported good compliance with official standards. The lack of proper regulation and supervision was also a major factor behind China's frequent deadly mining and industrial accidents of the early 2000s.[51] Indeed, research shows[52] that after coal-mine supervision was decentralised, collusion between local governments and mines led to a sharp increase in mining accidents and deaths. After the government moved the National Production Safety Inspection Bureau and the National Coal Mine Safety Inspection Bureau to the State Council, mining deaths declined sharply.

The mid-1990s reform to 'simplify administration and release power' (or 简政放权, 'jianzhengfangquan') also prompted the central government to delegate many responsibilities to lower levels of government. While local government may have had better information and the personnel to deliver public services, the vast difference in fiscal resources between poor and rich areas (provinces, counties, towns and villages) accentuated the inequality of public services provision across the country.[53] For example, poor regions in rural areas often did not have sufficient funding to pay for school building repairs or teachers' salaries after the fee-to-tax reform of the late 1990s reduced the revenues of lower-level governments. They, therefore, collected fees or sold expensive study materials to students to gain extra funding. Also, many public schools used the so-called school selection scheme and after-school tutoring to earn extra revenue.

Decentralised and localised public services, which are still largely based on the local *hukou* system, also led to inadequate service provision to the 'floating' population of migrant workers that lived and worked in cities, but lacked the rights of the local urban population, such as public security services, basic education and healthcare (more in Chapter 6).[54] The decentralised and compartmentalised government system also meant that the regulation and supervision of new industries and new forms of business could initially fall through the cracks. And while this may have given companies space for growth and expansion, it also led to sudden changes in the regulatory environment (see Chapter 10 for more).

Recentralisation and adjustment of the government's role

These deficiencies in government function are significant factors behind the recentralisation of certain government responsibilities, the consolidation of supervisory functions and the tightening of rules and regulations in the past decade. For example, the government introduced a basic rural pension scheme in 2009 and an urban one in 2011, and has increased central government spending on basic education since 2010 (Chapter 3). It has also enhanced the regulation and supervision of food, medicines and certain market behaviours since 2013[55] and tightened environmental rules since 2015.

The focus on common prosperity and regulatory tightening since 2021 can be seen as a further adjustment of the government's role. With China officially becoming 'a moderately prosperous society in all respects' in 2020[56] and moving closer to being an advanced economy, better social welfare and a more equitable society have become more important goals. The government made clear in its 14th Five-Year Plan (2021–2025) that the state was to play a leading role in basic public services provision, including basic education and healthcare, while the private sector could provide 'inclusive' services, or services not aimed at maximising profits, in these areas.[57] This will make the government, not the market, the main provider of public services, helping to ensure its public policy objectives.

On the regulatory front, as internet and related new industries have grown, previous regulatory loopholes and a lack of anti-trust rules have become more problematic. In addition, changes in the international environment have increased concerns about national security and data security when it comes to internet platforms and big data. In many cases,[58] China's recent regulatory tightening is to bring the country's regulations in line with the better practices of advanced economies. Nonetheless, the campaign-style regulatory tightening over a concentrated timespan, with little communication with the public or market, has fanned worries about the government's long-term intentions with respect to the private sector.

As part of these amendments to the government's role, since 2013, China has also been undertaking administrative reforms.[59] Over the past few years, the reforms have lowered barriers to business entry, shortened administrative timeframes and separated approval and registration processes. The government has significantly shortened the 'negative list' for market entry in recent years and pushed to lower the cost of funding for small businesses.[60] However, these reductions in government intervention have often been overshadowed by developments, such as tighter regulation, in the opposite direction. Also, while there has been some attempt to introduce competition to the state monopoly sectors, such as electricity and oil and gas, progress has been slow, while concerns about national security and related state controls have increased.

Government as the ultimate bearer of risks

There is a broad-based expectation in China that the government should not only be the lender of last resort, but also the 'saviour of last resort', bearing the ultimate risk and solving all kinds of issues in the economy and society. This may be a legacy from times past, when the government owned and controlled everything, but the public continues to expect the government to offer solutions – a sentiment often reinforced by government behaviour.

On the economic front, as the government is often directly involved and tries to maintain control through multiple channels, bad corporate behaviour (especially by SOEs) – be it monopolistic practices, the exploitation of employees or the pollution of the environment – tends to be attributed to the government. Moreover, the government has low-risk tolerance, so tends to apply soft budgetary constraints, even beyond the SOEs. For example, the default rate in China's corporate bond market is exceptionally low compared with other countries and with the corporate loan default rate.[61] It is also common for local governments to bail out local enterprises, including private companies closely linked to local government or considered important to the local economy.

The prevalence of implicit guarantees can lead to excessive risk taking in both SOEs and large private companies, forcing the government's hand on policymaking or eventual bailout. Such an ecosystem undermines market discipline, leads to distortions and the misallocation of resources, increasing financial and social risk. In the end, this increases the role of the government rather than that of the market in the economy.

Notes

1 Author's estimate.
2 See State Council (1987) and National Bureau of Statistics (1988).
3 See Johnson (1982).
4 See Rodrik (2004), European Commission (2010) and Block and Keller (2011).
5 See State Council (1989).
6 See State Council (1994c).
7 See NDRC (1991).
8 See State Council (2000).
9 Industrial policy on integrated circuits (semiconductors) in the 1990s was focused on direct government investment in certain areas. However, it usually took a long time for decisions to be made on a specific technological path and for SOEs to invest. In the end, investment in the integrated circuit industry was less than in other industries where the private sector took the lead and fell far below that of international peers. China's integrated circuit industry fell further behind the international frontier as a result.
10 See State Economic and Trade Commission et al (2002).
11 See State Council Office (2008).
12 See Government of the People's Republic of China (2001).
13 See Government of the People's Republic of China (2006).
14 See State Council (2005).
15 See State Council (2010).
16 See State Council (2016, 2021).
17 See State Council (2006).
18 See Naughton (2021).
19 See Zhang and Liu (2015).
20 See Naughton (2021).
21 See State Council (2015), Ministry of Industry and Information Technology (2015) and Shroff (2020).

22 The ten strategic sectors include new-generation information technology (including semiconductor chips, mobile communications technology, such as 5G and quantum computing, and software), high-end robotics and digital machine tools, aerospace equipment, oceanic equipment and shipbuilding, advanced rail transport equipment, new energy vehicles, power generation and distribution equipment, including smart grid, agricultural equipment, new materials, and biotech and medical equipment.

23 See State Council (2016).

24 See European Union Chamber of Commerce (2017) and the White House OTMP (2018).

25 See State Information Centre (2021).

26 See Jiang and Li (2010), Tian (2016) and Zhang (2016).

27 See Lin et al. (2018), Wang and Hua (2017) and Rodrik (2010).

28 See Lin and Monga (2010).

29 See Jiang and Li (2010).

30 See Yuan (2007).

31 See State Council (2009) and Ministry of Industry and Information Technology (2009).

32 See China United Steel Association and Greenpeace (2017).

33 See State Council (2010).

34 See Wang and Han (2015).

35 See China Photovoltaic Industry Association (2014).

36 See Meza (2014). According to the International Renewable Energy Agency, solar PV costs fell by 65–70% between 2009 and 2013 (see Yu and Wang, 2019).

37 The semiconductor industry mainly consists of integrated circuit design, chip manufacturing, packaging and testing, and equipment manufacture. According to the Semiconductor Industry Association (as quoted by Calhoun, 2021), integrated circuit design companies account for more than 50% of the total value added in global chip industry, while foundries – companies that manufacturing the chips – account for about 20%. At the top of the semiconductor industry are the United States (especially in integrated circuit design), Europe, Japan and South Korea, while Taiwan's TSMC dominates the most advanced chip-manufacturing business. China has a sizable market share of the (low-end) integrated circuit design segment, as well as lower-end manufacturing and packaging, but its share of advanced semiconductor design and manufacturing equipment is negligible.

38 See Zhang and Liu (2015).

39 The State Council issued policies supporting the integrated circuit industry in July 2000, outlining specific policy measures from certification to investment and taxation (see State Council, 2000). The Ministry of Science and Technology also approved the establishment of seven integrated circuit production centres. The 11th Five-Year Plan special integrated circuit industry plan was issued in early 2008 and identified specific products, subsectors and processes as special projects to be implemented (see MIIT, 2008).

40 See MIIT (2008).

41 See State Council (2011).

42 In June 2014, China released the National Plan on Advancing the IC industry (MIIT, 2014). The plan stated that China should narrow its gap in the semiconductor industry by 2020, with a compound annual revenue growth rate of 20% or more (which it achieved), and catch up with international levels in key areas of the supply chain by 2030. While emphasising the decisive role of the market and innovation, the document proposed the establishment of national industrial funds.

43 See State Council (2020).

44 See Zhong (2020) and China Economic Weekly (2020).
45 See Zhang and Liu (2015).
46 Tsinghua Unigroup is a recent example of failure in the chip industry. It got into the sector in 2013 when Unigroup bought Spreadtrum Communications, a US company, for USD 1.78 billion. It then acquired several other companies in subsequent years. With a short history, Unigroup expanded its presence in semiconductors by buying various assets, without its own core technology or investing in indigenous innovation. In 2017, Unigroup invested RMB 200 billion in Chengdu to build an international integrated circuit town and, a month later, another RMB 260 billion to build a semiconductor base in Nanjing. In December 2021, Unigroup filed for restructuring after failing to pay its debt, jeopardising the company's chip goals. Another company, Wuhan (弘芯), invested RMB 100 billion with no technology and no plan.
47 Common prosperity can be interpreted as 'getting prosperous together', in contrast to the 1980–1990s slogan of 'letting some people and some regions get rich first'. It means a more equal society and better public services and social welfare.
48 Government agencies reallocated staff to 'institutions' to cut costs and engage in commercial activities from the mid-1990s (see Sun, 2002 and Qu et al., 2009). Some government departments had monetary targets – for example, the police department was known to have fine-collection quotas.
49 See Qu et al. (2009).
50 In 2004, it was revealed that low-quality milk powder and infant formula had led to the malnutrition of hundreds of babies in Fuyang. The 2008 milk powder scandal involved the use of melamine to give the appearance of higher protein content, with hundreds of thousands of victims. There were also scandals about reused cooking oil, and invalid or outdated vaccines.
51 Fatalities in Chinese coal mines far exceeded those in other countries. In 2003, more than 6000 people died in coal-mine accidents and disasters, averaging four lives per million tonnes of coal, compared with 0.03 lives in the United States. See Zhong (2007).
52 See Nie and Jiang (2011).
53 See Dollar (2007).
54 For the migrant population, which often lives in the suburbs of big cities, public security is often provided by urban management teams rather than the formal public security bureau. Access to urban public schools is highly restricted, while there are few private schools. Until recently, health insurance did not cover expenses in urban areas or areas outside a *hukou* location.
55 China established a Food and Medicines Administration in 2013 to enhance the supervision of food and medicine safety. In 2018, the government set up the State Administration for Market Regulation to consolidate the regulation and inspection of food, medicines and various market structures and behaviours (including an anti-trust function), while establishing a new National Medical Products Administration to focus on the management of medical products.
56 President Xi Jinping made this declaration on 1 July 2021 at the centennial celebration of the CPC (Xi, 2021).
57 See State Council (2021).
58 Anti-trust matters in the internet space, for example, or individual information protection.
59 The Plan for State Council Organizational Reform and Functional Change in 2013 delegated some approvals to local government and abolished or consolidated the approvals and management of others in an effort to allow the market to play a more foundational role in resource allocation. In 2015, China established a coordination group in the State Council to facilitate government

functional change, focusing mainly on administrative approval, investment approval, professional qualification reform, fee collection clean-up, business procedural reform, etc.

60 See Li (2016, 2019).
61 According to Fitch Ratings (2022), China's domestic corporate bond default rate was 0.84% in 2021, while the China Banking and Insurance Regulatory Commission (CBIRC) (2022a) put the banking-sector non-performing loan ratio at 1.73%.

5 How does economic policy work in China?

To understand how China's economic policy works, we will review its key policymaking bodies, the broad policymaking process, its evolving policy objectives and policy implementation. We will dive deep into its monetary policy framework and outline its fiscal policy management process, which will also feature in Chapters 6 and 7.

Key policymaking bodies

China's most important economic policy decisions are made by the Politburo of the Central Committee of the Communist Party of China (CPC). The Politburo comprises 25 of the most senior members of the CPC, including the general secretary of the party, the chairman of the National People's Congress (NPC), the premier and vice premiers of the State Council (China's cabinet), and some local officials. The Politburo usually sets broad economic objectives and direction and weighs in on big issues when there are varying proposals or disagreements.[1] Once the Politburo decides, other agencies come up with policies accordingly. In recent years, the Politburo has also been holding quarterly meetings to discuss short-term economic policy. The fourth-quarter Politburo meeting precedes the annual Central Economic Work Conference (CEWC) in December, which sets economic targets and policy direction for the following year.

The most important long-term economic policies are typically decided at the plenary sessions of the CPC Central Committee, with a few hundred participants and broader representation of the Party. There have been three key plenary sessions for economic policy in the reform era. The 11th Third Plenum in 1978 launched China's reform and opening. The 14th CPC Congress in 1992 decided to establish a 'socialist market economy' and set the key reform direction and agenda for the following two decades. The 18th Third Plenum in 2013 laid out a comprehensive reform agenda for the new era. The CPC plenary sessions also approve proposals for China's Five-Year Plans.

The NPC is China's legislative body, where laws are made and amended and annual government budgets and economic plans are formally approved. Traditionally, the NPC is considered a 'rubber stamp' that approves all proposals and legislation submitted by the government, with little to no

DOI: 10.4324/9781003310938-6

dissent. In recent years, however, NPC scrutiny has increased. NPC committees and members send feedback, comments and critiques to the State Council, prompting the government to adjust, revise or amend proposals and plans. Budget laws, changes in the tax system and legislation governing the financial markets all need to be approved by the NPC. There are typically multiple readings of a draft law before approval. The NPC usually holds its annual meetings in March to approve the government budget and the premier's work report, among other things, while sub-committees and standing committees meet more regularly to carry out legislative work.

The State Council oversees detailed policymaking and day-to-day economic management. Almost all economic policies are proposed and issued by the State Council, which may issue ordinances or guidance itself or require various ministries or economic agencies to issue policy directives. Some policies may go to the Politburo for approval, especially if they require broader political support and local government buy-in. Some policies may require the formal approval of the NPC if changes or additions to legislation are required. The State Council helps to coordinate policies from multiple agencies. It has held weekly standing committee meetings in recent years, in addition to ad hoc meetings.

The National Development and Reform Commission (NDRC) has traditionally been the most powerful economic agency under the State Council. It has had many incarnations but, at its core, stems from the former planning commission. The NDRC and its predecessors previously set investment plans, approved projects, formed industrial policy and oversaw price setting. It used to be the agency that consolidated macroeconomic policy proposals from other ministries for the State Council, and its head traditionally ranked above the central bank governor and the minister of finance. However, in recent years, as the importance of investment plans and approvals has waned and prices have been liberalised, the NDRC's role has become less dominant.

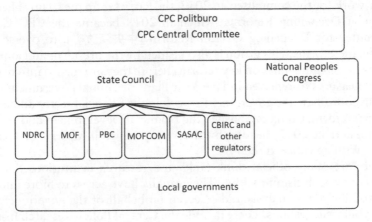

Figure 5.1 China's key economic policymaking bodies.

The Ministry of Finance formulates and implements the budget. It does not have tax-collection authority[2] and its role in fiscal policy decision-making is limited. It is responsible for drawing up detailed policy measures that are consistent with the big fiscal decisions made at a higher level and can decide the pace of fund distribution and degree of policy implementation. Due to China's decentralised fiscal system, the Ministry of Finance has less power than it appears, as local governments have strong financial autonomy and are often the most important entities when it comes to implementing central government policies (with discretion).

The PBC, China's central bank, traditionally ranked low in the hierarchy of ministries, has become more important to macro policymaking over the past two decades in tandem with the gradual modernisation of China's monetary policy and financial system. This has been helped by the prominence of ex-governor Zhou Xiaochuan, an eloquent speaker with many followers in academia and the market, and an uncanny ability to harness support from the market and the public for the PBC's agenda. The PBC is seen as being more professional, more reform oriented and more open to the outside than other economic agencies.

Other important economic decision-making agencies include the Ministry of Commerce, the State-owned Assets Supervision and Administration Commission, and regulators such as the China Banking and Insurance Regulatory Commission, the China Securities Regulatory Commission, the State Administration of Foreign Exchange and the State Administration for Market Regulation. Also, the Ministry of Industry and Information Technology and the Ministry of Human Resources and Social Security can issue policies that matter to the macroeconomy.

To help coordinate major economic policymaking and implementation, there are several high-level commissions. The Central Finance and Economics Committee of the CPC (中央财经委员会) is headed by the president and coordinates major economic policymaking. The Office of the Central Finance and Economics Committee (中财办) carries out detailed policy work for the committee. In 2013, the Party set up the Central Leading Group of Deepening Reforms, which in 2018 became the CPC Central Committee for Deepening Overall Reform (中央深改委), to oversee and coordinate reforms. This group is also headed by the president and approves proposals and guidelines on key reforms before they are turned into detailed policy measures or reflected in Five-Year Plans or annual government plans. To help coordinate the government's work in the financial sector and deepen financial reform, China established the Financial Development and Stability Commission in 2017, headed by the vice premier in charge of financial affairs, with an office in the PBC.

There are many official think-tanks and research institutions that help with economic decision-making. They usually have access to more information, conduct data analysis and research on behalf of the government and make policy suggestions. These include the Central Policy Research Institute of the CPC, the State Council's Counsellors' Office and Policy Research

Institute, the National Development Research Centre, the Chinese Academy of Social Science, the NDRC's macro research institute, the PBC's research bureau and the Ministry of Finance's Fiscal Science Research Institute.

How are economic policies made and implemented?

China's long-term economic policies typically go through a lengthy process. First, the authorities identify the trends and issues that need to be addressed, then official think tanks and other resources are mobilised to conduct research and formulate proposals – often drawing lessons from international experience or domestic pilot programmes. Next, policy proposals are discussed at senior government level or by various agencies. Then, formal policy proposals are submitted for approval by the State Council and/or the Politburo before policies are formally rolled out.

Towards the end of the process, the government may float some ideas to the public through research institutes or the media to gather feedback and test for support or resistance. If the government has already decided to push forward certain policies, it may campaign for support through economic or financial publications. There are exceptions: if the top leadership feels strongly that something ought to be done urgently to control macroeconomic risk or contain damage, rules and regulations can be issued quickly in the form of directives or opinions of the State Council office or CPC Central Office, or by relevant regulators and ministries. Meanwhile, a formal legislation process may be initiated to formalise government rules, though this process can be lengthy and the transitional rules may stay in place for years.

The long-term policies made by the CPC plenary sessions are usually directional and broad. Specificities are typically added to national five-year plans, supplemented by five-year plans at the provincial and industry level that contain more specific targets and supporting measures. Some longer-term targets are also broken down into annual targets, while short-term policies are formulated to help achieve them. These short-term targets can be and are often adjusted in line with developments and newly available data. For example, China did not set a 2022 energy-efficiency target in accordance with the 14th Five-Year Plan and long-term decarbonisation plan so as to avoid a repeat of 2021, when coal supply controls to meet the annual target contributed to power shortages and disrupted industrial production.

The medium- and long-term plans do not usually rank the importance of multiple objectives or specify how to balance competing ones. As a result, they are subject to interpretation by different government agencies. As each agency draws up and implements specific policies based on its core mandate, the compartmentalised policies that result may not be internally consistent and or serve the overarching objective. For example, strictly controlling local government debt or the property market in times of negative economic shock may make it harder to achieve stable growth, while pursuing the full opening of the capital account will make it challenging to ensure the stability of the RMB exchange rate. The overall policy leaning often depends on the economic circumstances of the moment, and any refinement needs to be gauged by the senior leadership, for example, in the quarterly Politburo meetings.

The fact that multiple layers of local government tend to implement economic policy complicates things. It is understandable that in a big country like China, local governments are given space and discretion to adapt broad-brush national policy to local circumstances. However, local government may not have the oversight or funding required to carry out policies consistent with the national plan. For example, if every local government tried to develop an automobile champion or solar panel producer, this could lead to repetitive investment, protectionist regional policies, excess capacity and a waste of capital (Chapter 4). Policies that require local government funding, such as an increase in public services or preferential tax treatment for certain sectors, are likely to see uneven implementation from region to region, as local fiscal circumstances vary. In addition, if every level of government delegated downwards, the lowest levels might not have the fiscal resources to carry out certain policy responsibilities.

Moreover, local government interests may often not be aligned with those of the central government, causing national policies to be undermined, resisted or circumvented.[3] For example, the central government tends to be more concerned about controlling risk and maintaining macroeconomic and social stability, while local governments are more focused on generating growth, investment and fiscal revenue. In the property sector, while the central government may want to prevent property prices and property leverage from rising rapidly, local governments may see a property boom as critical to driving local revenue and growth and view high property prices as a badge of success. Consequently, local governments may resist the central government's call to increase land supply to lower land prices. When it comes to market regulation, while the central government may want to enforce intellectual property protection and environmental rules, local governments may want to protect local firms because of the jobs and fiscal revenue they provide, or because local governments have stakes in them. In such cases, unless the central government has the means to enforce its policy, it may not happen. 'Policy directives do not get out of Zhongnan Hai' is a common refrain.[4]

The central government has more direct control over monetary policy, exchange-rate policy and fully funded fiscal policy initiatives. For policies that require local government compliance or implementation, China usually relies on the CPC network. If the Politburo or senior leadership holds local officials politically responsible for certain objectives, they are more likely to be achieved. In recent years, for instance, the central government has included local government debt and environmental measurements in local officials' assessment matrix, and major violations can scupper promotion. Most recently, a zero-tolerance policy on COVID-19 cases also prompted local officials to adopt extremely tight restrictions beyond national recommendations. While the CPC network can be very effective, overloading it can make it difficult for local officials to choose between competing objectives.

China is learning the importance of public communication in aiding policy implementation, but has not quite caught up. These days, the presence of vast, global markets (especially the fast-reacting capital market) and the prevalence of the internet and social media require policy information to be disseminated publicly, transparently and instantaneously to minimise any misunderstanding, distortion or unintended market volatility. However, the legacy of China's centrally planned economy means that the focus has been on conveying policies to various government agencies and subnational governments for implementation rather than to the public and the market.

In addition to official 'red headline' documents, the official media will carry speeches and comments on policy to rally support and encourage compliance. They serve to amplify the political importance and urgency of relevant policies rather than to present a subtle or balanced view. While China's economic system has evolved and the market, especially the capital market, has become increasingly important, government agencies often put limited effort into ensuring policy objectives and intentions are well understood by the public and the market. Such practices can lead (and have led) to misunderstandings and suboptimal policy implementation.

Evolving and multiple economic policy objectives

China observers may be familiar with the phrases 'development is the hard truth' or 'development is the solution to all problems' in official documents, which clearly put economic growth at the top of the agenda. In the past, the government has often set minimum growth targets and mobilised all possible policies to achieve its goals. This may give the impression that growth is and will remain the government's top priority to prevent mass unemployment and keep society stable (the implicit 'social contract'). The truth is a little more complicated than that, and the government's policy objectives have evolved as well.

It is true that the CPC and the government have emphasised economic development since 1978. However, maintaining stability – social, economic and political – has always been a top priority. Against this backdrop, China's key economic objectives have changed with time and circumstance. In the 1980s, the government's focus was on 'enlivening' the stagnant economy to deliver more food and goods to the population. Until the mid-1990s, rapid economic growth was seen as critical to galvanising public support for reforms and opening, but the government was not fixated on certain pre-set growth targets.

In the late 1990s, SOEs laid off millions of workers, while there was a high number of new entrants to the labour force. It seemed that the 8% growth rate the government had set was barely enough to prevent a considerable rise in unemployment and maintain social and economic stability. After the global financial crisis, the government gradually reduced its annual growth target, recognising that the correlation between new urban job creation and GDP growth was not constant, as the economic structure and labour intensity changed and labour supply had shifted. Since then, the government has also paid more attention to the long-term sustainability of growth and other economic objectives.

In recent years, the government's economic objectives have become increasingly multifaceted and complicated as it strives to maintain macroeconomic stability, including price, financial-system and exchange-rate stability, and safeguard economic security, including energy and food security as well as supply chain security. On the social front, the objective has gradually shifted from generating sufficient employment to also providing and expanding social welfare, ensuring work safety and protecting the environment.

On economic structure, the objectives include moving up the value chain, building complete supply-chain capabilities, advancing certain sectors and technologies, reducing imbalances in the economy and achieving carbon neutrality in the long run. Needless to say, some short-term priorities may run counter to medium- and long-term ones. For example, the government would like to rebalance the economy towards more consumption, reducing its reliance on investment in the long term. At the same time, it often makes growth the top short-term priority, stimulating investment to support it.

The objectives of various policy stakeholders also often differ. The central government emphasises macro and social stability, structural change and risk control in addition to GDP growth, while local governments make investment and growth their top economic objectives, as local officials have been promoted based on economic performance for most of the post-reform period.[5] National objectives and those of specific industries and related ministries may also differ. For example, on energy security, big oil companies want to develop or acquire overseas resources, even at the expense of China's diplomatic capital, while it may be in the nation's best interest to reduce energy dependence and move towards renewables. Within the State Council, the PBC is often reluctant to ease monetary policy to support growth due to its financial-stability and price-stability objectives, and often advocates more fiscal support. The Ministry of Finance usually wants to keep the deficit and debt in check and calls for more monetary easing.

In the end, while China's policies are typically guided by the Politburo or CPC plenums, the details are a consortium of policies reflecting different stakeholders' interests and interpretations. Many believe that China's one-party system and strong government control make it easy to coordinate policy, but it also faces the challenge of balancing different interest groups and stakeholders. While the top leadership, the Politburo (and its standing committee), is the top economic decision-making body, it simply does not have the time to decide on every economic policy detail or to coordinate all policy implementation.

How does China's monetary policy work?

As China's economy has grown, its monetary policy conduct has attracted more and more attention around the world. The PBC's moves are almost as closely followed as those of the US Federal Reserve. Despite periodic concerns about its high debt levels and property bubble, China has managed to maintain remarkable macroeconomic stability over the past two decades, especially compared with many other economies at a similar development level. So, how does China's monetary policy work? What is the policy framework?

Monetary policy framework and reaction function

China's monetary policy framework and the environment within which it operates have changed substantially over the past four decades. In the 1980s and 1990s, separate monetary policymaking did not really exist; monetary policy largely consisted of formulating and implementing lending quotas according to government plan. Commercial banks were just being established and were heavily influenced by the government, while the economy was going through a major transition. Significant volatility in both the money supply and economic growth coincided with major economic liberalisation.

Real monetary policymaking began in 1998, when China started to restructure its banking system, developed money and credit markets and introduced market interest rates. The PBC was able to use and test market-based instruments, observe the effect they had on monetary aggregates and study their relationships with economic growth and inflation. Administrative tools and directed lending became less important than before, growth volatility declined and price and exchange-rate stability improved. Since 2010, China has seen further financial liberalisation and the formation of its so-called dual-pillar monetary policy management.[6]

A few important features have remained. First, major monetary policy decisions are made by the government, not the PBC. Second, monetary policy has multiple objectives, some of which shift over time. Third, the policy framework is still in transition, with the PBC exploring the effectiveness of policy instruments and formulating its policy reaction functions to fit the economy, which is also in transition. Fourth, monetary policy management still relies heavily on quantitative and administrative tools, although the importance of interest rates has increased.

Unlike in most developed countries, where central banks have both legal and functional independence and are largely free to pursue consistent policy aims, the PBC mostly carries out decisions made by the State Council (and, at important junctures, the Politburo). The PBC's Monetary Policy Committee meets every quarter, but decisions are made outside these meetings. Key macroeconomic and monetary policy targets are formally decided at the State Council level, sometimes with the prior approval of the Politburo. Thus, other ministries can influence key monetary policy targets, while local governments and SOEs can also exert influence through the Party structure.[7] More recently, the PBC has gained some autonomy in the use of certain monetary policy instruments outside of policy rates and the exchange rate.[8]

Unlike the European Central Bank's single mandate of low inflation and the US Fed's dual mandate of maximum employment and stable prices, the PBC is subject to a broader set of policy objectives. Officially, the central bank law says the monetary policy objective is to 'maintain the stability of the currency, so as to facilitate economic growth',[9] but monetary policy has at least four objectives, according to former Governor Zhou Xiaochuan. They are 'low inflation, reasonable economic growth, relative full employment or a low unemployment rate, and a balanced external account'.[10] Moreover, monetary policy is often asked to help facilitate economic structural change by channelling finance to specific sectors. The 2003 amendment to the central bank law specifically put the PBC in charge of preventing and resolving financial risk and maintaining financial stability.

To help achieve these objectives, the PBC uses a 'dual-pillar' framework of monetary and macroprudential policy adjustment.[11] The first pillar uses conventional monetary policy tools; once the government establishes its growth and inflation targets, the PBC sets broad money (M2)[12] and credit aggregates (total social financing, or TSF)[13] accordingly as intermediate targets.[14] To achieve these intermediate targets, the PBC can alter base money supply[15] using tools such as open market operations (in treasury bonds or other securities) and required reserve ratios (RRRs) on commercial bank deposits and, and adjust interest rates to influence the cost of bank funding and lending.[16] The aggregate credit target itself can also be used to guide bank loan growth.

As for the second pillar, the PBC can use prudential rules to influence the amount and direction of bank lending, bond financing and shadow credit, along with administrative measures, such as sectoral credit policies, to restrict or encourage credit to certain sectors. The increased role of macroprudential rules is partly a result of the rise in shadow banking and the increased prominence of financial stability as a monetary policy objective. As shadow banking and mobile payments have developed, monetary aggregates such as M2 have become less representative of actual liquidity supply in the system, so the relationship between monetary aggregates and inflation has also diminished.

The PBC's monetary policy reaction function is hard to discern given the complexity of both policy objectives and instruments, especially in recent years, when the government has increased its focus on maintaining financial stability. If economic growth is reasonably strong, monetary policy tends to lean towards tightening to help contain the debt-to-GDP ratio. Prudential rules on high-risk sectors (such as property) are then tightened as well. When growth faces downward pressure, such as in 2020, or if policy tightening is viewed as overdone (as in late 2021), the government becomes more concerned about growth and employment, or large-scale corporate failures. Monetary policy is then eased to support growth. However, even during monetary easing, financial stability remains a key consideration, limiting the magnitude and message of any easing.[17] One needs to analyse high-frequency economic data and observe any change in policy tone in Politburo and State Council statements to assess the policy reaction. The monetary aggregate targets set at the beginning of the year can be exceeded or undershot with changes in the government's policy leaning.

To better understand monetary policy transmission in China, one must remember the importance of the state in the economy. The majority state ownership of most large banks means that the PBC can more easily use moral suasion (or 'window guidance') than other central banks to influence banks' lending. The state's active role in the economy also blurs the boundary between monetary and fiscal policy. An increase in government and LGFV spending can help ramp up credit demand in times of monetary expansion (as in 2009), while tightening local government debt management and project approvals can aid credit tightening. The significant role of the state in the conduct of monetary policy is down to the fact that China's economy has not yet completed its transition to a full market economy. It also helps to explain why the typical interest-rate transmission channel is less important in China.

Monetary policy communication is an important channel of policy transmission that the PBC is learning to use. In the 1990s and early 2000s, the PBC could call a few large commercial banks to learn about the liquidity situation and manage it accordingly. However, with the development of the credit market, especially the inter-industry bond market, on which hundreds of non-bank financial institutions (NBFI) and non-financial institutions trade all kinds of financial instruments, that was no longer adequate. This was a lesson learned from the June 2013 liquidity squeeze.

When the PBC injected funds into the market at the close of 20 June 2013 to supply extra liquidity, it did not disclose this information to the market to help quell fears of severe policy tightening, and the rates climbed further.[18] Subsequent explanation helped to calm things down, but since then, the PBC has become more proactive and transparent about its policy actions. Even so, the PBC often takes pains not to be seen as deviating from the Politburo's overall policy tone, downplaying its easing actions, which can confuse the market or even undermine its own policy moves. Conversely, when the PBC made a small exchange-rate adjustment on 11 August 2015, it referred to it as an 'important reform', causing the market to widely (and wrongly) believe that China meant to let the RMB depreciate significantly or even float freely, resulting in significant pressure on the currency.[19]

Details of monetary policy management

Quantity over price

Notwithstanding the significant increase in the use of interest rates over the past two decades, China's monetary policy still relies more on quantitative

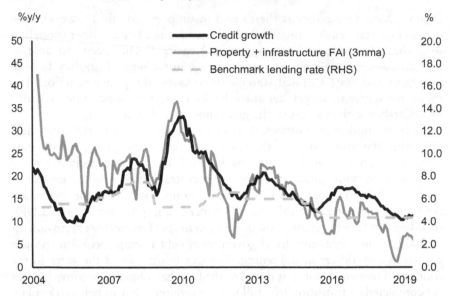

Figure 5.2 Construction and investment correlate well with credit, not with rates.

Source: NBS, PBC, author's estimates.

instruments and administrative tools. This is partly due to the transitional nature of the economy and its still developing financial market infrastructure. First, China still sets monetary aggregates as intermediate targets. Second, to achieve these targets, the PBC mainly adjusts base money supply using quantitative tools rather than short-term interest rates. Third, China uses prudential regulation and sectoral credit policy, as well as a generous helping of moral suasion, to influence the quantity and direction of credit. Meanwhile, transmission through interest rates is limited. Figure 5.2 shows the tight correlations of property and infrastructure investment with bank credit over the past 20 years, while the correlation with interest rates is weaker.

PBC's base money management

How does the PBC manage monetary aggregates? The PBC provides 'high-powered' base money to commercial banks, which in turn use these funds to create new loans and deposits via the money multiplier. The asset side of a central bank's balance sheet contains foreign assets, including foreign exchange (FX) and gold, and domestic assets, such as claims on domestic banks and the government (government bonds). Liabilities include reserve money – cash issuance and the reserves of commercial banks at the central bank – and the central bank's bond issuance, if any. To manage base money supply, the PBC can adjust the asset side by purchasing or selling foreign-assets or domestic assets from commercial banks. It can also tweak the liability side by changing the deposits commercial banks are required to hold with it (the RRR).

Until the end of 2002, the PBC mainly provided base money liquidity to commercial banks through on-lending and re-discount windows. From 2003 to 2012, it supplied base money passively by purchasing foreign exchange with renminbi from commercial banks (which got it from exporters) to prevent currency appreciation. Because FX inflows increased rapidly during that time, the PBC had to 'sterilise', or offset, part of its FX purchases to avoid excessive money supply. First, it sold central bank bills to commercial banks but, from 2006, it mainly relied on raising the RRR to 'freeze' commercial bank funds and lower the cost of sterilisation.[20] In subsequent years, it cut the RRR, as FX reserves declined or stagnated.

The PBC has also engaged in repurchase agreements (repos) of government bonds, commercial paper or reverse repurchase agreements (reverse repos) in its open-market operations with major financial institutions to adjust the base money supply. Here, it has most often used 7-day and 14-day reverse repos for regular liquidity management.[21] The PBC has also launched the Standing Lending Facility (SLF), Short-term Liquidity Operations (SLOs) and the Medium-term Lending Facility (MLF)[22] in recent years. The first two are short-term funding instruments, while the MLF is used to supply 3- to 12-month base money liquidity to qualified commercial banks and policy banks, collateralised by high-quality bonds. The PBC also uses the Pledged Supplementary Lending (PSL) facility, a collateralised on-lending facility for policy banks, of three or more years in duration, for special government projects such as lending for shanty-town renovations.[23]

An RRR cut transfers money from banks' required reserves to their excess reserve holdings without changing the size of the PBC's balance sheet, releasing liquidity permanently. Liquidity facilities such as the SLF or MLF,

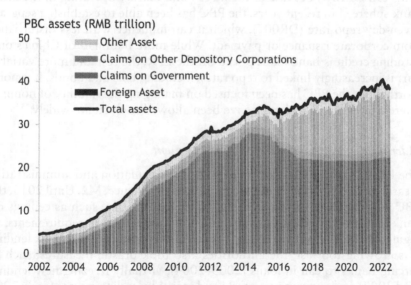

Figure 5.3 PBC balance sheet, 2002–2022.

Source: PBC, Author estimates.

in contrast, require banks to offer collateral (such as bonds) for the duration of the instrument's tenor (so is temporary), causing the PBC's balance sheet to rise (via 'claims on other depository corporations'). As can be seen in Figure 5.3, the PBC's balance sheet expanded sharply with the rise in foreign exchange holdings between 2003 and 2011, and has grown again recently with the expansion of domestic asset purchases.

Interest-rate management

For most of the past 30 years, the PBC has adjusted the benchmark deposit and lending rates to affect rates that commercial banks offer and charge. The PBC officially completed interest-rate liberalisation with the abolition of its deposit-rate ceiling in October 2015, but continued to publish benchmark rates until August 2019. Since then, the Loan Prime Rate (LPR) submitted by major commercial banks has been used to guide bank lending rates. The LPR is linked to the MLF rate.

In the past decade, the PBC has gradually increased the use of short-term money-market rates to gauge liquidity conditions and influence interest rates in the financial system. The most important short-term rate is the seven-day repo rate traded by depository financial institutions (backed by rate product collateral). The PBC can influence this rate by adjusting the quantity and price of its own short-term repos (it usually uses a seven-day repo).

In the process of establishing a short-term policy rate anchor, however, the PBC initially had some difficulties separating the interbank market (in which banks borrow from each other and the central bank is the lender of last resort) from the financial market at large (where NBFIs and non-financial firms can borrow) because of the large bond market operating in the interbank sphere.[24] In recent years, the PBC has been able to establish a separate seven-day repo rate (DR007), which it can influence with less disturbance from corporate issuance or payment. While more than half of China's outstanding credit is bank loans priced off the LPR, the rest and more variable part is increasingly linked to repo rates, including bills and bonds. It is noteworthy that the PBC has been focused on managing the stability of nominal interest rates, while real rates have been allowed to fluctuate widely.[25]

Macroprudential rules and credit management

The PBC and the government use prudential regulation and administrative measures to directly influence credit growth and, hence, M2. Until 2015, the PBC and the CBRC often used regulatory instruments, such as ceilings on bank loan-to-deposit ratios and capital or loan provision requirements, to regulate bank lending. In the first decade of this century, when bank lending was growing too fast, the authorities also took drastic measures, such as forcing banks to call in loans (2003–2004), virtually freezing new lending (end 2007) and imposing quarterly and monthly lending quotas (early 2008 and 2010).

In recent years, the PBC has established and fined-tuned its Macro Prudential Assessment (MPA) framework to influence banks' lending by regulating each individual bank's liquidity ratio and capital adequacy level and has rarely used such drastic measures of the past. At the same time, sectoral credit policies have been used more often. These include restricting credit to the property sector, LGFVs and high-polluting sectors, as well as increasing credit to SMEs, the rural sector and industries that the government wants to support. This has put more administrative tools in the PBC's monetary arsenal to respond to the increasingly complex and nuanced monetary policy objectives.

The authorities' reliance on administrative controls stems in part from the fact that the over-lending and over-investment issues of the past two decades have usually happened in a few sectors, such as property, mining and heavy industry, while other sectors have rarely experienced overheating. In recent years, the government has attempted to use 'targeted' easing and credit support to help resolve the credit access and cost issues of SMEs and certain private firms. This has been labelled 'drip-irrigation' and 'structural monetary policy'.

Perhaps the authorities believe that differentiated monetary instruments are better placed to deal with structural (sectoral) issues often caused by distortions. However, it is debatable whether monetary policy can achieve structural objectives, as money is fungible. Also, differentiated policies are discretionary, which may lead to rent seeking and credit rationing, which can undermine banks' commerciality. Moreover, credit risks may often be overlooked or underestimated, and credit may be channelled to unintended borrowers.[26]

Shadow banking and monetary policy

Over the past decade, the rise of shadow banking[27] has complicated China's monetary management, as it has become more difficult to use M2 or bank lending to judge financial conditions. Here, shadow banking refers mainly to financial intermediation done by NBFIs, such as trust companies, and to banks' wealth management products (WMPs) and other activities outside of the traditional deposit and loan realm.

In part to lessen the dominance of the banking system and to improve capital allocation, China gradually advanced financial liberalisation, easing controls on NBFI activities and shadow credit products while maintaining tight controls on large state-owned banks and bank lending.[28] This meant that whenever the authorities tightened bank credit, more credit would leak out through the shadow banking system, which was largely uncaptured by monetary and credit aggregates. Alarmed by rising shadow-banking risks, the authorities started to tighten regulations in late 2016, leading to a sharp slowdown in shadow credit.

The rise and fall of shadow credit growth meant that, for some time, overall credit to the economy was more volatile than the official monetary and credit aggregates suggested. For example, the PBC targeted TSF[29] credit growth of 13% in 2016, and official end-year TSF growth was 12.8%. However, if we take into account local government debt swaps and shadow credit through bank lending to NBFIs and other channels, the actual credit growth was an estimated 18%.[30]

Following the tightening of shadow credit, PBC data showed TSF growth slowing modestly from 12.8% in 2016 to 12% in 2017 and 9.8% in 2018, but actual broader credit growth halved between 2016 and 2018.[31] Underlying much of these large swings in shadow credit was the change in the non-deposit liabilities of banks and the financial system, which were not reflected in M2. The bigger overall liquidity swing may partly explain market perception of excessive credit tightening in 2018.

Questions and myths about China's monetary policy

What is the risk of China's exceptionally large M2?

One major worry about China's monetary policy over the past 15 years has been the very high level of broad money supply. M2 stood at RMB 238 trillion (or USD 37 trillion) at the end of 2021, equivalent to 208% of GDP and far exceeding the USD 19.1 trillion of US M2.[32] Excessive money supply is usually associated with high inflation, currency depreciation and, sometimes, asset bubbles. Yet, in China, inflation has been relatively moderate, the exchange rate has been stable and faced more appreciation than depreciation pressure for most of the past two decades. So, does China have excessive money supply, and what is the risk?

The rapid expansion of M2 in the late 1990s and first decade of this century was largely a result of financial deepening, not excessive money supply, as more and more areas of the economy and types of asset were monetised, especially land and property.[33] Moreover, the dominant role of banks in China's financial system, coupled with the underdeveloped capital markets, means that much of households' financial wealth is held in bank deposits, which are included in M2, rather than in bonds or equity holdings.[34] Bank deposits are used to finance credit expansion, generating more deposits. China also has high corporate and institutional deposits (RMB 97 trillion as of end 2021) due to its lack of a large corporate bond market, inadequate credit access for private companies and limited alternative destinations for excess corporate funds.

These factors help explain why the high level of M2 has not caused high inflation. Also, credit expansion in China has mainly been used to finance investment and expand the supply of goods, rather than boost consumption. Consequently, China's credit boom has often led to deflationary pressures (though usually preceded by commodity price inflation) over the past 20 years and, as domestic capacity has replaced imports, a sizable trade surplus that has supported the currency.[35]

However, money supply may have been excessive in some years and the consequences have yet to be fully understood. For more than a decade, the PBC set its M2 growth target a few (3–5)percentage points higher than its nominal GDP growth target, calculated by adding the real GDP growth target to the consumer price index (CPI) inflation target. In other words, if the government targeted 8% real GDP growth and 3% CPI inflation, the PBC often set an M2 growth target of 15–16%. This rule of thumb seemed to work well for some years, as faster M2 growth accommodated China's monetisation while inflation remained moderate. However, it was no longer suitable when monetisation slowed and the rise of shadow banking made M2 an inadequate gauge of liquidity. Moreover, China's overheating often led to producer price deflation (as more investment led to more supply), while its excess liquidity led to asset price inflation, especially property prices, both of which are not measured by the CPI. More recently, the PBC switched to setting M2 and TSF credit growth targets 'broadly in line' with nominal GDP growth.

Has China kept interest rates artificially low?

There is a wide perception internationally that China's interest rates have been held artificially low to ensure a low cost of capital for SOEs.[36] It is true that China has long had interest-rate controls. In the 1980s and the 1990s, interest-rate control was part of the old centrally planned system in which most prices were regulated. For most of the past 20-plus years, however, the authorities have kept a *floor* on bank lending rates, not a ceiling,[37] and banks could have raised actual lending rates if they wanted to.

Rather, China's low real lending rates are consistent with its high savings rate, similar to other East Asian economies.[38] Real interest rates, measured as the average of lending and deposit rates, were barely above zero in Japan and around 2.5% in the Asian tigers, including around their peak growth period – far below the real rate of economic growth (Figure 5.4). With average savings ratios of 35–40% of GDP during their high-growth periods, these Asian economies were not only able to sustain far higher investment ratios and, thus, far higher growth rates than their developed counterparts, but also with lower average returns on capital and lower interest rates. China's domestic savings rate has been even higher, at more than 35% of GDP since 1985 and at 45–50% since 2004. Weighted average real interest rates have fluctuated between 1% and 2%, meanwhile, very much in line with regional experience.

Will interest-rate liberalisation lead to better capital allocation?

In principle, interest-rate liberalisation should result in significantly higher deposit rates as well as an upward shift in the entire interest-rate structure.[39] It should also lead to more appropriate pricing of capital, higher returns to depositors, greater competition among commercial banks to

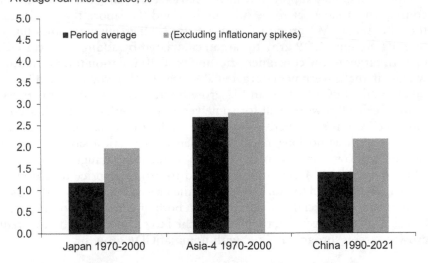

Average real interest rates, %

Figure 5.4 Average real interest rates in China, Japan and the Asian Tigers.

Source: Bank of Japan, Bank of Korea, CBC of Taiwan province of China, Hong Kong Monetary Authority, Singapore Monetary Authority, the PBC.

provide better products and cut costs, stronger incentives for banks to price risk appropriately and, therefore, better allocation of capital between large state-owned enterprises and smaller private firms.

However, the steady interest-rate liberalisation of the past two decades has not led to a notable increase in real interest rates. While bank deposit and lending rates were only officially fully liberalised in 2015, money-market rates, bill rates and bond yields had been set by the market long before then. Over time, these market interest rates became more important in financial institutions' funding and corporate finance. However, overall real lending rates did not see a trend increase along with the rate liberalisation. As noted, China's exceptionally high national savings rate likely helped to keep interest rates in check, as did its relatively closed capital account, though for much of the past decade, domestic rates have remained well above global rates.

It is also questionable whether rate liberalisation has led to better capital allocation. During the process of rate liberalisation, smaller banks and WMPs bid up the actual cost of bank funding, prompting banks to seek higher returns through shadow bank activities. However, China's shadow banking was mainly used for regulatory arbitrage, masking the risk and cost to banks while offering limited help to boost private-sector credit access.[40]

Moreover, both credit supply and demand remain distorted by the lack of market-clearing discipline at the corporate and financial institution level. Implicit guarantees are widespread, even for private companies and certain 'market' products, as evidenced by the government's bailout of WMPs and trust products. This means that although the cost of capital may be determined by the market, the behaviour of lenders and borrowers, especially

SOEs, may not be fully driven by market pricing. Without other structural reforms that fundamentally break the implicit guarantees, interest-rate liberalisation alone is unlikely to lead to better capital allocation.

Fiscal policy management

China's fiscal system has evolved tremendously over the past few decades. It was decentralised in the 1980s and has gradually been recentralised since the mid-1990s, along with major tax reforms and the formalisation of budgetary management. Current fiscal policy management has a few key features. First, China has a complicated fiscal structure: its general government budget is only one of four sets of budgetary plans, not including quasi-fiscal operations. The latter is where most of the policy action have been, but the government has tried to bring about more fiscal discipline and transparency since the Third Plenum of the 18th CPC in 2013. Second, like monetary policy and all important macro policies, decisions on fiscal policy are made at the State Council or Politburo level, and local governments are highly important in fiscal policy implementation. Third, in contrast to developed economies, China's overall fiscal resources tend to be spent more on investment and less on social welfare.

From quasi-fiscal to budgetary management

Among China's four sets of budgetary plans, the general government budget is the best known and is approved by the NPC every March. Spending is financed mainly by tax revenues and divided into central and local government portions. The government funds budget (政府性基金预算), meanwhile, is dominated by local governments and relies mainly on local land sales for spending related to land and construction. These two budgets form most of China's on-budget public spending. Since 2015, the government has issued local-government special bonds (地方专项债) to supplement the local funds budget and finance local construction projects. The government presents the local funds budget on an accrual basis and considers transfers from the budget stabilisation fund – carried-over unused revenue from previous years and special local-government bond financing – to be current revenue.

Figure 5.5 shows both the official budget and adjusted estimates of the 2022 fiscal balance to capture the actual fiscal stance. Here, we can see that while China's official budget deficit was set to narrow by 0.3 percentage points as reported in the general government budget, the combined fiscal deficit from both general and the funds budgets was set to widen by more than 3 percentage points in 2022.[41] Not presented here are: (1) the state capital operation budget, which is spending within the SOE sector, financed by a small portion of SOE dividends and transaction gains, which accounted for less than 0.5% of GDP in 2021; and (2) the social insurance budget, comprising social insurance funds operated mainly at local level, covering basic pension and healthcare insurance-related revenue and spending.

	2021 actual	2022 budget	2022 estimates
General government budget			
Revenue /1	20,254	23,343	21,014
% of GDP	*17.7*	*19.4*	*17.5*
of which local government revenue /2	*11,108*	*11,526*	*11,526*
Expenditure	24,632	26,713	26,713
% of GDP	*21.5%*	*22.2%*	*22.2%*
of which local government expenditure	*21,127*	*23,106*	*23,106*
General budget deficit (% of GDP)	**-3.1**	**-2.8**	
Underlying general budget deficit (% of GDP, 2021 is actual)	**-3.8**		**-4.7**
Government funds budget			
Revenue (2021 is actual) /3	9,802	13,899	9,864
o/w local government land revenue	*8,705*	*-*	*8,270*
Expenditure (2021 is actual)	11,366	13,899	
Total financing available for spending /3	13,127		14,299
of which local government spending	*11,046*	*13181*	*13,570*
Govt funds balance (% of GDP, 2021 is actual, 2022 is planned)	**-1.4**	**-**	**-3.7**
Total revenue including funds (% of GDP)	26.3	30.9	25.7
of which local government revenue /2	*17.9*	*17.4*	*17.4*
Total expenditure including funds (% of GDP)	31.5	33.7	34.1
of which local government expenditure	*28.1*	*30.1*	*30.5*
Combined general and funds budget deficit (% of GDP)	**-5.2**	**-2.8**	**-8.4**

Figure 5.5 The general government and funds budgets.

/1: The official budget includes surplus funds from the previous years as revenue, we treat them as financing.
/2: This does not include revenues that the central government transfers to local governments, which are substantial.
/3: The official budget counts proceeds from special local government bonds and one-off transfers as revenue, we treat them as financing.

Source: Ministry of Finance, NBS, author's estimates.

Most of China's fiscal expansion or contraction has taken place off budget in the post-reform period, but the government has tried to bring more actions on budget and into the open in recent years. The government has almost always tried to keep the general budget deficit under 3% of GDP, while public investment projects have been largely conducted and financed quasi-fiscally by LGFVs and other state entities, including using bank or policy bank credit.[42] For example, only about a quarter of China's famous RMB 4 trillion stimulus during the global financial crisis came from explicit government sources, while the rest was funded by credit to local and state entities.[43]

China's new budget law in 2014 helped to improve fiscal discipline and transparency. Local governments are prohibited from raising debt via LGFVs, but allowed to run a budget deficit and issue local special bonds to finance construction projects. The latter increased to 3.7% of GDP in 2020 from next to nothing in 2015. However, local governments circumvented the rules and continued to use LGFVs for financing, raising funding from policy banks and through public–private partnership (PPP) schemes for infrastructure and public projects.[44] As a result, quasi-fiscal channels became more obscured after 2015. Aware of this development, the government

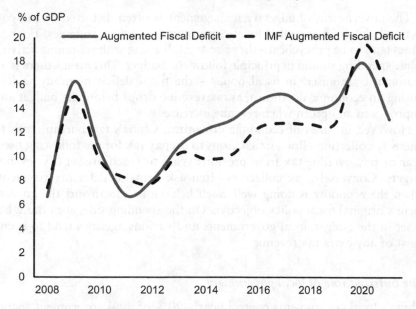

Figure 5.6 The augmented fiscal deficit, 2008–2021.

Source: NBS, Ministry of Finance, IMF, author's estimates.

clamped down on local government borrowing in 2017 and 2018, while the CPC network emphasised enforcement, making officials responsible for new local government debt over its lifetime.[45]

To capture the broad fiscal picture and understand the scale of 'true' fiscal policy stimulus or tightening, the IMF has been estimating an augmented fiscal deficit (AFD) for China, adding quasi-fiscal activities and channels of financing to the budget deficit. As shown in Figures 5.5 and 5.6, much of China's fiscal expansion and tightening was achieved through quasi-fiscal channels during the global financial crisis and in 2015–2016, but more has been done through the budget and local special bonds of late. AFD movements in the 2015–2016 period are likely to have been greater than estimated by the IMF,[46] as the Fund assumed compliance with the new budget law and did not consider the more hidden quasi-fiscal channels.

The government often uses multiple measures to adjust quasi-fiscal spending. When it wants to stimulate the economy, it can ease LGFV financing rules, lower the required share of local-government funding, pressure banks to increase lending to infrastructure and related projects, accelerate project approvals and/or ask SOEs to increase participation. Conversely, it can tighten LGFV financing, strictly enforce local government debt controls and slow or reduce project approvals on various regulatory grounds. As these measures are often administrative, non-transparent and hard to quantify, they make the true fiscal policy stance difficult to discern. Data on actual monthly infrastructure investment may be the best gauge, but they are no as proxies good beyond a couple of months.

The government's budgetary management is often distorted by tax-collection behaviour, as well as local-government spending strategies. Tax revenues tend to be procyclical – they rise and fall along with economic activity, while spending should in principle follow the budget. This means there is an 'automatic stabiliser' in fiscal policy – the fiscal deficit naturally widens during an economic downturn, as tax revenue drops below the budget and improves in an upturn when revenue increases.

However, in times of economic downturn, China's tax bureau tends to intensify collection efforts or ask firms to prepay tax for the following fiscal year or pay overdue tax from previous years to reach pre-set tax revenue targets. Conversely, tax collectors often ask firms to defer tax payments when the economy is doing well. Such behaviour can thwart the government's original fiscal policy objective. On the spending side, even though it is set in the budget, local governments and various agencies tend to spend most of any extra tax revenue.

The outsized role of local government

China's local governments control nearly 90% of total government spending (Figure 5.5), or even more if quasi-fiscal operations are included. One common misunderstanding about China's fiscal landscape is that local governments lack fiscal resources, as they do not have tax authority and too much revenue goes to the central government. In fact, local governments spend 85% of general budget resources, even though their revenue accounts for little over half. This is because about 60% of central government revenue is transferred to local governments, a significant portion of it in the form of tax rebates (see Chapter 3). In addition, local governments account for more than 90% of the government funds budget, of which over 90% is financed by local land sales and spent on land-related and infrastructural projects. Quasi-fiscal spending is also overwhelmingly controlled by local governments through LGFVs and other entities, with just a few controlled by central SOEs.

The outsized role of local spending helps to explain the importance of local government in fiscal policy implementation. This largely came about after the 1980s fiscal decentralisation and has not changed fundamentally ever since, despite the central government's efforts to recentralise some fiscal resources and spending responsibilities. Moreover, on the one hand, the central government has been reluctant to run a larger explicit budget deficit, while on the other hand, it has demanded that local governments deliver growth. This combination has contributed to the rise of land-related financing (see more in Chapter 6) and quasi-fiscal spending at local level.

Of course, China's governance structure is also one that gives local governments a lot of power. For example, the CPC heads of key provinces and cities are Politburo members, but no ministers are – including the minister of finance. The central government's lack of fiscal resources and the relative political power of local governments also help to explain why China sometimes has to lean on the CPC network to rein in local-government borrowing or boost local-government spending.

A prudent and pro-investment fiscal stance

There seems to be an innate tendency at the Ministry of Finance to run prudent fiscal policy. This may be partly because the ministry is tasked with controlling the fiscal deficit, even though the policy stance is decided at the top. It may also stem in part from the legacy fiscal principle of *liangruwei-chu* (量入为出), or 'spending according to revenue', which prevailed prior to and during the early reform period.

This kind of thinking is reflected in how the government defines easy fiscal policy. The fiscal policy stance is deemed 'proactive', or supportive of the economy, whenever the government runs a deficit, even when the deficit is declining and the fiscal impulse is negative. Regular China watchers may note that the country's official budget deficit almost never exceeds 3%, the limit EU countries are required to follow by the Maastricht Treaty. Another reason for controlling the explicit budget deficit while allowing quasi-fiscal spending is perhaps the government's lack of confidence that fiscal funds will be spent as well as borrowings from banks. Fiscal funding may be considered 'free' money, while the latter needs to be repaid. And bank loan officers may scrutinise projects or borrowers more closely, or at least have more resources to do so than budget officers.

Compared with developed countries, more of China's fiscal revenue comes from the corporate sector and less of it is spent on social protection and public services (Figure 5.7). In the general budget, personal income tax accounted for only 8% of China's total tax revenue, or 1.2% of GDP, in 2021. More than 60% came from VAT (collected at firm level) and corporate tax on profit, meaning that revenue is much more skewed towards the corporate sector than in OECD countries. In overall budgetary spending, only 8.9% of GDP was spent on 'people's well-being' in 2021, including healthcare, education, culture and recreation, social protection and social housing.[47] This share would rise to 16.7% if local social security spending were included. That still pales in comparison to 27.5% for OECD countries and 33% for the EU. China, in contrast, spends more on investment, including infrastructure funded by special bonds and land sales, especially if quasi-fiscal spending is also included.

The pro-investment and pro-business nature of the budget is also reflected in the way the government uses fiscal stimulus. China has usually relied more on spending increases, especially infrastructure spending, to stimulate the economy, though it has cut corporate taxes significantly in the past few years.[48] This is perhaps because the fiscal multiplier of infrastructure investment is greater than that of tax cuts during an economic downturn.[49] Moreover, tax cuts usually take longer to formulate and are usually permanent,[50] while an investment spending increase can be cut back more easily.

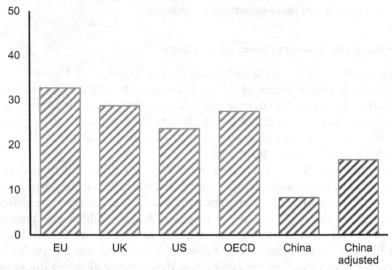

Fiscal social spending (% of GDP)

Figure 5.7 Share of social spending in the budget, China versus OECD countries.

Source: OECD, Statistical Office of the European Communities, China NBS. NBS, Ministry of Finance, IMF, author's estimates.

Note: Social spending covers spending on housing and community amenities, health, recreation, culture and religion, education and social protection.

Data for China is 2021 and for all other countries, 2019.

China has been extremely reluctant to use fiscal support for the household sector or consumption. While the low level of personal income tax may leave limited scope for tax cuts, China did not provide much income support or subsidies to households during the 2020–2022 COVID-19 pandemic either, unlike other major economies. Instead, the government emphasised that cutting corporate taxes would indirectly boost employment and consumption.

Notes

1 For example, in the 1990s, when there were debates as to whether socialism could accommodate a market economy.
2 Taxes are collected by the General Tax Bureau, which focuses on revenue generation.
3 See Qu et al. (2009) and Fewsmith and Xiang (2014).
4 Zhong Nan Hai is where the offices of China's senior leadership, including the State Council, are located in Beijing.
5 See Zhou (2007, 2008).
6 See also Huang et al. (2020).
7 For example, the reporting system and central government-led outreach means local governments or large SOEs can pressurise for monetary or credit easing through the State Council or CPC channels.
8 See PBC (2020).

9 See NPC (1995).

10 See Caixin (2012).

11 See Li (2018). The 2020 amendment to PBC law formally added macroprudential policy to the PBC's mandate.

12 Broad money is a measure of the amount of money, or money supply circulating in the economy. In China, broad money is defined as M2, which includes RMB cash in circulation (M0), demand deposits and the time deposits of households, companies, institutions and non-bank financial institutions. It does not include money-market funds or wealth management products, though some of these can be easily converted into money.

13 Total social financing is total financial-system credit provided to the corporate, household and government sectors. It currently includes bank lending, corporate bonds, local and central government bonds, and banks' off-balance sheet lending, such as trust loans and entrust loans, as well as undiscounted bills.

14 An intermediate target is an economic variable that the central bank can control with a reasonable time lag and with a relative degree of precision. It has a relatively stable or at least predictable relationship with the final target of monetary policy.

15 Base money, or the monetary base, also known as high-powered money, is the amount of money created by the central bank. It includes cash in circulation and commercial banks' reserves held at the central bank.

16 See Huang et al. (2020) and Sun (2011).

17 For example, monetary easing was more modest in 2020 than in 2009 and compared with other countries.

18 See Wu (2013).

19 See PBC (2015a).

20 The RRR was raised from 7.5% in 2006 to 17.5% in 2008 and, again, to 20% in 2011.

21 See Wang (2020).

22 The SLF is a one-day to one-month tenured facility for all banks, with high-quality bonds and credit assets as collateral, created in early 2013. The SLO is a repo agreement provided to qualified primary dealers in open market operations to supplement the OMO, normally for fewer than seven days.

23 See Wang (2014a).

24 See Wang (2014b).

25 For example, from 2011 to 2012, real lending rates surged as the economy slowed, producer prices fell and financial liberalisation pushed up market rates. The trend finally turned in mid-2016, when China's PPI moved back into positive terrain.

26 For example, credit support for SMEs may have ended up in LGFVs with few staff (technically also small firms) or channelled into property investment, as the latter are backed by collateral.

27 In line with the definition of the Financial Stability Board of the Bank for International Settlement (BIS), 'shadow banking' refers to all financial intermediation outside the traditional banking system and bank non-loan products.

28 For example, banks' RRR was more than 20% in 2011, while they also faced a strict loan-to-deposit ratio requirement and capital adequacy requirement.

29 At the time, TSF included banking-system loans, all corporate bonds, trust loans, entrust loans, newly issued local government bonds and undiscounted bills. It did not include local government debt swaps or shadow credit, such as non-loan trust assets or some NBFI credit to the economy.

30 Author's estimate.

31 See Wang et al. (2016a), Zhang and Wang (2017a).

32 Data from the PBC and the US Federal Reserve.

33 See Yu (2002).

34 Deposits accounted for an estimated 50%-plus of China's household financial wealth in 2020, down from 66% in 2010 and almost 80% around 2000. In the United States, that share was only 15%, according to the Federal Reserve.
35 See Anderson (2007).
36 See Lardy (2008).
37 Recently, however, they have pressurised banks to keep rates low for SMEs.
38 See Anderson (2007).
39 See He et al. (2015).
40 See Sun (2019).
41 Author's estimates.
42 Except for some key national projects and central SOE investment (such as railways), most of China's infrastructure projects are carried out at the local level, for which government budgetary funding accounts for only 15–20% usually.
43 See Wang (2009). Ministry of Finance and PBC data.
44 Caixin reported in 2015 the issuance of RMB 800 billion in special construction bonds by policy banks, but the report was latter taken down and no official announcement was ever made. Another RMB 1 trillion was reportedly issued in the first half of 2016. The proceeds were reportedly used as seed capital for public projects at the local level, as the 20–25% down-payment required for borrowing from banks for such projects. Meanwhile, the assets of China Development Bank reportedly rose RMB 900 billion in H1 2016, or 27% y/y, helped by additional funding from special construction funds and the PBC's PSL facility.
45 See Ministry of Finance (2018).
46 In the author's view.
47 Author's estimates based on the Ministry of Finance's 2021 budget.
48 The government cut corporate taxes and fees by RMB 2.36 trillion in 2019.
49 Vagliasindi and Gorgulu (2021).
50 China did roll out temporary tax cuts and tax waivers in 2020 and 2021 to help firms cope with the COVID pandemic.

6 Urbanisation and the urban–rural divide

The great urbanisation

China entered the late 1970s as a predominantly agricultural economy. Since then, economic liberalisation and rapid industrialisation have transformed the rural–urban landscape. As of 2020, 902 million people lived in cities – about 64% of the total population and 720 million more than in 1978. The number of Chinese cities also grew from 77 in 1978 to 672 in 2018, while the number of townships reached 20,000. The urbanisation ratio was more than 64% if measured by the share of people active in the economy outside of farming, but only 45% based on the number of people with an urban *hukou*. There are nearly 100 cities in China with a population of more than 1 million. Together, four Tier 1 cities – Beijing, Shanghai, Shenzhen and Guangzhou – are home to more than 80 million people. Among the Tier 2 cities, mostly provincial capitals, a few have a population of around 10 million, such as Tianjin, Chongqing, Chengdu, Wuhan and Nanjing.

What has led to this rapid urbanisation? Economic reforms since the 1980s first generated significant agricultural productivity gains and released surplus labour for industrialisation and rural–urban migration, followed by a lasting investment and construction boom in urban areas, partly to meet the rising housing and infrastructure demand. Unlike the rest of the world, however, China's urbanisation has not been that 'natural'. Mobility restrictions, the *hukou* system and a two-track urban–rural land system have inhibited urbanisation in numerous ways, while the construction of industrial zones, the drive to expand urban areas and administrative reclassification[1] have accelerated it.

Before the reform period, China's urbanisation was slow – while industry as a share of GDP increased from 17.6% in 1952 to about 50% in 1978,[2] the urban share of the population rose only from 11.2% to 18%.[3] This was in part down to China's pursuit of an industrialisation path focusing on capital-intensive heavy industry, which provided limited employment opportunities and left little funding for urban infrastructure and housing development. Moreover, from 1958, strict mobility restrictions based on the *hukou* system and land allocation prohibited movement

DOI: 10.4324/9781003310938-7

from rural to urban areas. In addition, low agricultural productivity and food shortages limited the food supply available to sustain a bigger urban population. The progress of urbanisation, therefore, stagnated in the 1960s and 1970s.

Urbanisation accelerated after 1978. The urban population swelled as the government gradually eased population mobility restrictions and embarked on agricultural reform and economic liberalisation. First, more than 10 million urban youth who had been sent to the countryside during the 'cultural revolution' returned to cities between 1978 and 1980.[4] Second, the government allowed immediate family members (spouses and children) of certain urban technical workers to move from their rural *hukou* to an urban or township *hukou* in 1980, granting them grain and food quotas – a must if you wanted to live in a city at that time.[5] Third, and perhaps most importantly, the agricultural reforms (see Chapter 3) not only greatly increased productivity and released surplus labour into non-farming activities, including rural industry, but also re-opened rural markets for an increasingly rich array of agricultural produce. This led to a rise in the population of small towns, as well as an increase in the non-farming population around towns and small cities.

Between the mid-1980s and late-1990s, urban reforms, the relaxation of *hukou* policy in small cities and administrative reclassification were key factors behind rising urbanisation, with the ratio reaching 35% in 2000. As China's reform focus shifted to urban areas from 1984, urban governments were given more freedom and incentives to carry out construction and invest in infrastructure and housing. The *hukou* policy for small cities and towns was also gradually relaxed.[6] The rise and rapid growth of TVEs, which turned millions of farm labourers into industrial and commercial-sector workers, also contributed significantly to urbanisation during this period.

To keep up with the expansion of the non-farming population in rural areas and to spur related construction, there were major administrative reclassifications during this period. The number of prefectural cities increased by 50 between 1983 and 1985 alone and more than doubled to 410 between 1986 and 1996,[7] with many counties upgraded to cities. China also converted thousands of former communes and village clusters into administrative towns as the non-farming population in those areas increased.

From 2001, rural–urban migration and the expansion of urban areas were the main drivers of urbanisation. China's urbanisation policy formally switched to developing both large and small/medium-sized cities,[8] ending previous restrictions inhibiting the expansion of large cities. Rural–urban migration was encouraged, which, combined with the slowdown in TVE development and the boom in the processing trade in coastal regions, led to a rapid increase in migration to the coast and larger cities. The population in cities and towns of all sizes ballooned. During this period, rural–urban migration, rather than administrative reclassification, contributed more to urbanisation, especially in large cities. According to the World Bank,[9] rural–urban migrants accounted for 43% of the 100-million increase in the urban population in 2000–2010, while the expansion of existing urban areas was responsible for another 40%-plus. Meanwhile, the number of cities changed very little.[10]

In 2014, China's urbanisation strategy was adjusted to promote '人的城镇化', or people urbanisation.[11] The new strategy recognised existing problems, including the low urbanisation ratio, the lack of urban public services for the 230 million migrants counted as urban residents, the wasteful use of land resources[12] and the constraints on integrated urban–rural development. It therefore promoted 'people-urbanisation', emphasising the granting of *hukou* to migrants who had long lived in cities and the provision of public services to those residents without urban *hukou*.[13] The plan also aimed to develop city clusters, mainly in the east, to help spur regional development and to increase connectivity among cities, partly because small cities and towns were having trouble creating enough jobs to sustain urbanisation.

Since then, and especially during the 13th Five-Year Plan (2016–2020) period, *hukou* policies for medium-sized and large cities (up to 3 million people) have been eased, helping to achieve the government's target of increasing the urban *hukou* population by 100 million by 2020.[14] Meanwhile, extra-large cities (with a population of 5–10 million) and mega-cities (with a population of more than 10 million) have continued to attract migration, which the government has tried to address by developing surrounding satellite cities and transport links.

Official statistics may underestimate the degree of true urbanisation in China. Measured by the economic essence of urbanisation – the agricultural population moving away from farming to non-farming activities and living in a manner similar to urban residents – China's urbanisation ratio could be significantly higher. According to official statistics, 76% of China's employment was either in industry, construction or services as of 2020, with only 24% still in agriculture. One key reason the official urbanisation rate remains low is because cities and towns in China are designated administratively, rather than naturally based on a change in population or the nature of economic activities. It is not uncommon to have densely populated, mostly non-farming areas still classified as rural areas, especially in the east and south of China, where the urban–rural divide is often blurred.

Perhaps more importantly, China's *hukou* system treats migrants in cities differently to the existing urban population. Workers who originate from rural areas (and, hence, have a rural *hukou*) but have worked and lived in the cities for many years are still considered '农民工', or peasant workers (and sometimes the '流动人口', or floating population, if they have not obtained an urban *hukou*). They are also excluded from urban statistics if they have not lived in a fixed urban location for more than six months.

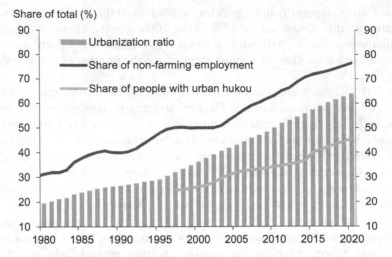

Figure 6.1 China's rapid urbanisation – different classifications.

Source: NBS, Author estimates.

Hukou urbanization data: 2015–2020 are from govt; others are calculated.

NBS, author's calculations.

China's rapid and massive urbanisation over the past 40-plus years may have been triggered by economic liberalisation and industrialisation, but it has also facilitated the country's economic transformation. As people moved from farming to more productive jobs in industry and services, urbanisation helped boost productivity and lift hundreds of millions of people out of poverty. The agglomeration effect of urbanisation is evidenced in the increasingly important roles cities play in generating economic growth and innovation.

It is remarkable that China's urbanisation process has been largely devoid of large-scale ghettos formed spontaneously by migrants in urban centres, high unemployment rates and paralysing traffic jams often seen in other emerging-market economies.[15] This may be in part down to the fact that China has been able to maintain rapid economic growth over the past 40 years while investing heavily in urban infrastructure. In addition, China's *hukou* and other policies have helped to control migration to large cities, while rural land-use rights have served as a safety net for migrant workers who become unemployed (or at least they did in the first 30 years of the process).[16]

However, the hukou system and related policies are also at the root of China's incomplete urbanisation and persistently deep urban–rural divide. Moreover, the country's dual land system, which treats rural and urban land differently, has amplified urban spatial expansion, supercharged urbanisation and contributed to the widening of the urban–rural wealth gap.

China's steep and persistent urban–rural disparity

China's large urban–rural income disparity has existed for a long time and worsened since the late 1980s. At the beginning of the reform period, China was known as a relatively egalitarian society. Estimates suggested that its Gini coefficient, which measures income inequality and has a value between 0 and 1 (the lower the more egalitarian), was below 0.2 in cities and 0.21– 0.24 in rural areas around that time. These figures were below that of most developing countries (e.g., it was 0.57 for Brazil in 1981).[17] However, even then, China's urban–rural income ratio was about 2.5, significantly higher than in other low-income Asian economies (1.5) and higher than in middle-income countries, according to the World Bank.[18] This was partly attributable to the government's development strategy, which kept agricultural product prices low to subsidise industrialisation. In addition, urban residents received most consumer goods and services in kind as an implicit subsidy, something that was not available to the rural population.[19]

The agricultural reforms of the early 1980s led to faster rural income growth and a significant narrowing of the urban–rural income gap, but that chasm started to widen again from 1986.[20] Although the urban–rural income ratio declined from 3.33 in 2009 to 2.56 in 2020, China continues to have one of the biggest urban–rural income gaps globally (Figure 6.2). Moreover, taking into account the various implicit subsidies that urban residents enjoy, such as food and housing subsidies, healthcare and pension benefits associated with formal urban employment and in-kind income, the disparity is actually far larger than official statistics suggest.[21]

The widening of the urban–rural divide over most of the reform period can be explained in part by the naturally more rapid productivity gains of the urban industrial and services sectors relative to the agricultural sector. In addition, research has found that pro-urban policies and pro-heavy-industry development strategies contributed to the widening of the gap in the 1990s and 2000s.[22] These included keeping agricultural prices low while

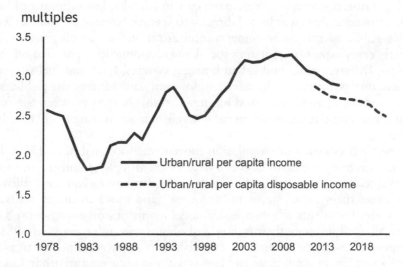

Figure 6.2 The urban–rural income gap, 1978–2021.

Source: NBS, Author estimates.

providing subsidies to the urban population, as well as a relative reduction in rural fiscal resources. The capital-intensive growth meant less absorption of rural surplus labour in the job market.

What has been most striking, however, is perhaps the dual systematic and institutional setup that has codified the urban–rural divide and sometimes amplified the disparity – the *hukou* system, the dual land system and the separate fiscal and administrative structures that go with them. This institutionalised divide persists even after rural people have 'urbanised', increasing the disparity between different groups of people in urban areas. Indeed, the modest improvement in urban–rural inequality over the past decade has been the result of greater fiscal spending and social welfare coverage in rural areas, the gradual reform of the *hukou* system and a modest move away from heavy industry.

The evolution of the *hukou* system and its role in the urban–rural divide

Origin and evolution

China's *hukou*, or household registration, system has existed for more than 2000 years in one form or another. The feudal *hukou* system was used for recording population statistics, collecting taxes and assigning military duties.[23] Soon after 1949, when the People's Republic of China was established, land reform redistributed plots to farmers across the country and a new *hukou* system was established. The system did not become a tool for restricting population movement until 1958, when the *hukou* registration rule formally established a two-track social and economic structure.[24]

The *hukou* rule required people to get government approval and documentation to obtain a *hukou* and move location. It set strict rules on registering births, residential moves, marriages and deaths. The rationing of food and daily necessities was linked directly to specific *hukou* locations, as were strict public security, government administration and employment rules. Nearly every aspect of a person's social and economic life depended on their *hukou*. Different rural and urban housing systems, food and fuel supplies, educational systems, healthcare, employment and retirement, public services and social welfare formed an impenetrable barrier between the rural and urban population, stopping rural dwellers from moving freely to urban areas.[25]

The strict controls on population movements loosened after 1980. The easing was marginal up to 2000, however. First, in 1980, family members of certain technical workers and officials with an urban *hukou* were allowed to change their 'rural' status to 'non-rural' and move to urban areas. In 1984, rural residents who worked in local townships on a long-term basis were allowed to move their *hukou* and obtain a grain ration.[26] In 1985, a temporary residence system was established to allow rural people to work legally and live in small cities and towns without obtaining an urban *hukou*. In 1992, the Ministry of Public Security rolled out a so-called local effective urban *hukou* (blue book), allowing long-term migrants in special economic zones and small cities to obtain transitional status.

More formal *hukou* reform started in 1997, with pilot programmes in small cities where migrants with stable employment and residence and/or those who had lived in the city for a certain period of time and bought a dwelling there could obtain an urban *hukou*. A pilot programme of *hukou* reform in large cities started in 2001 in Shijiazhuang, the provincial capital of Hebei Province, outside Beijing. As various experimental reforms took place across the country, the State Council had to stop local governments from forcing rural–urban *hukou* conversion to expropriate collective land.

The government issued a new national urbanisation plan in 2014, abolishing all restrictions on obtaining *hukou* in towns and small cities, 'orderly' liberalising *hukou* rules in medium-sized cities (with a population of 500,000 to 1 million) and 'reasonably' easing those of cities with a population of 1–3 million people.[27] In 2016, the central government asked cities with more than 3 million people to relax *hukou* rules in suburban districts and expand the resident card system to cover all of the non-*hukou* urban population. The latter was to facilitate better administrative and other public services to non-*hukou* residents. *Hukou* has since been fully liberalised in cities with fewer than 3 million people. However, migrants still need to meet certain conditions to qualify for an urban *hukou* in large cities including contributions to social security and proof of long-term residence.[28]

Over the past four decades, economic reforms and liberalisation have reduced the restrictions the *hukou* system has imposed on the rural population. The most important changes, perhaps, were the agricultural reform and market liberalisation of the 1980s. They not only increased food supply, which made the government less worried about farmers leaving farming and rural areas, but also made it possible for migrant workers to buy food from the market outside of the planned system and the government food rationing tied to the *hukou*. As such, moving outside of one's *hukou* jurisdiction became possible. Later, the emergence of a labour market, housing and rental market and private services, including private schools, also facilitated rural–urban migration.

Hukou-related restrictions and inequalities

Although the *hukou* policy no longer prohibits movement from rural to urban areas, many *hukou*-related restrictions and inequalities persist, especially between rural and urban residents. Indeed, property policy tightening in many large cities over the past decade has increased the importance of *hukou* once again, amplifying the large gap in benefits that exists between different *hukous*. The main restrictions/inequalities are as follows:

- *Social welfare and public services*. Although food and daily supplies no longer depend on *hukou* status, pension and healthcare benefits still differ significantly between the different tiers of cities, especially between rural and urban areas. Benefits for rural residents tend to be a fraction of those for urban residents and differ greatly from city to city. Also, non-local *hukou* workers cannot participate in local urban resident pension and healthcare insurance plans; participation in employment-related pension and healthcare schemes cannot easily be transferred.[29]

- *Education.* School admission is based on *hukou* and housing location. Rural and non-local *hukou* students need to pay extra to be admitted to schools and are not allowed to take college entrance exams in locations other than their *hukou.* However, migrant students also need to have a student registration and record of studying in their original *hukou* location to take the college entrance exam. This combination of policies effectively excludes migrant children from studying in local high schools. Meanwhile, migrant private schools are subject to heavy restrictions by urban governments, which have tightened in the past few years.

- *Employment.* Many urban jobs require a local *hukou*, especially in large cities. Employers usually offer less labour protection and fewer benefits to migrant workers and do not contribute to work injury and unemployment insurance schemes on their behalf. Migrant workers also usually do not have access to free local employment services and vocational training.[30] The government has since called for greater labour protection and services for migrant workers, though it is hard to verify implementation at the local level.

- *Housing.* As part of measures to rein in housing prices, local governments have explicitly restricted the purchase of urban housing by non-*hukou* residents in large cities since 2008.[31] Such policies have made top-tier city *hukou* even more valuable than before. In addition, while the government has undertaken massive shanty-town renovation projects and built social housing or cheap rentals for the urban poor, rural migrants have little to no access to cheap rental accommodation or housing subsidies.

- *Other services.* The non-*hukou* population can fall through the cracks in the public administration of areas such as serious infectious disease prevention, social relief, disaster relief and disability services. Some migrants in large cities can even face deportation. The rebuilding of old towns or other initiatives can lead to the closure of migrant business establishments or the tearing down of rental properties, often with little warning and no compensation.[32]

Fundamentally, the *hukou* system has systematised unequal access to social welfare and public services, and contributed to the uneven distribution of public resources.

Impact

China's *hukou* system and related restrictions helped the government manage the size of cities, prevented the formation of large-scale ghettos, stopped mega-cities from growing even bigger and distributed services efficiently. One could argue that, in the early stages of reform, the lack of benefits for rural migrants helped to create a separate and extremely 'flexible' labour market outside of the SOE-dominated urban one, facilitating private-sector development, attracting FDI and, indirectly, fostering urbanisation. However, as the economy continued to develop, the *hukou* system entrenched and amplified social inequality in terms of access to public services, educational and employment opportunities and housing.

With more than 200 million 'floating' urban dwellers who cannot avail in full of urban public services and benefits (unlike formal urban residents), *hukou* policies have led to incomplete urbanisation, inhibiting the consumption of this large group. Moreover, as recognised in the government's new urbanisation plan, this dual structure in urban areas has created many social challenges, chief among them the phenomenon of 'left-behind' children and increased vulnerability for the elderly.[33] The *hukou* system and the lack of fully portable social benefits also impedes urban residents from moving to seek opportunities elsewhere (e.g., from the old industrial centres of the northeast to the coastal regions).

Rozelle and Hell (2020) suggest that the current urban–rural divide and its associated barriers are having a significant negative impact on the education of China's next generation of workers.[34] With the *hukou* system and related restrictions hindering family migration, hundreds of millions of rural migrants are seeking jobs away from home, leaving children and family behind. According to a 2013 study commissioned by the All-China Women's Federation, in 2010, China had 61 million children under the age of 18 with at least one parent away from home for more than three months in the year.[35] Among them, close to 30 million were of compulsory education age (grades one to nine) and some 8 million were not enrolled in schools, though the number of left-behind children has since declined substantially.[36]

Rozelle and Hell's study showed that the left-behind children were growing up 'without basic resources they need', undernourished and developmentally delayed.[37] This means that the urban–rural divide manifests itself already in early childhood. The fact that more than half of China's children have grown up in rural areas and not been given a better education has already had damaging consequences on the labour force. Data from the 2010 population census showed that only 30% of China's labour force had a high-school education, the lowest level among similar economies.[38] And while 44% of China's urban labour force had a high-school education, the ratio was only 11% for the rural labour force.

China's government has adjusted policy to try to reduce the urban–rural divide since then, by making education from grades one to nine free, for example, and trying to recentralise some spending responsibility for basic education to ensure funding in poor areas.[39] It has also significantly increased direct and indirect fiscal spending to reduce rural poverty, among other things, by improving rural roads, electricity, water supply and telecommunications coverage.[40] The 13th Five-Year Plan (2016–2020) targeted and achieved a goal of reducing the size of the population living in poverty by 50 million, effectively eradicating extreme poverty. On education, official data show a significant improvement over the past decade. While only half of people aged 30–39 have a high-school education or above, that ratio was two-thirds for 20- to 29-year-olds in 2020.[41]

However, while increased government spending has led to a significant improvement in enrolment, better school buildings and better teachers in rural areas, the *hukou* system still makes the rural education system profoundly different to the urban one. Even those children who move with their parents to cities have to go to separate 'migrant children's' schools. These are generally of lower quality, and children often have their education interrupted, which can have a sustained negative impact into adulthood.[42]

Moreover, as a joint NDRC and United Nations Population Fund (UNPF) report pointed out, China's incomplete urbanisation, with working migrants living in cities and their children and elderly left in rural areas, means hundreds of millions of people have had their lives disrupted, creating deep social and cultural issues.[43] This urban–rural divide has led to a rise in social contradictions and unrest, including mass social protest, migrant labour disputes over unpaid wages, inadequate compensation and the irregular termination of contracts, as labour and social protection laws usually do not apply to migrant workers.[44]

The dual land system and its impact on urbanisation

The dual land system and modest policy adjustments

China's land policy has played a major role in the speed and shape of urbanisation, as well as the persistent urban–rural divide. In the initial stages of reform, de-collectivisation, which allowed rural families to use collectively owned agricultural land under a contracted responsibility system, was critical in generating sufficient food and the surplus labour necessary for urbanisation. In the latter stages, the urban–rural dualism of the land system, whereby rural land could not be considered part of the urban construction market unless it was first expropriated by the local urban government, helped to both expedite urbanisation and exacerbate the urban–rural split.[45]

In China, rural land[46] is owned collectively by villages, while urban land is owned by the state. Rules on rural agricultural land have been increasingly solidified since the 1980s to protect the land-use rights of farmers.[47] However, rules and policies on rural land for non-agricultural construction changed in the late 1990s and early 2000s, giving urban governments the exclusive right to alter the purpose of land use and the right to most of the value gains.[48] In the 1980s, farmers were encouraged to use rural land to establish TVEs and conduct industrial and commercial activity. Land used by TVEs expanded 3.6-fold between 1978 and 1985.[49] This policy changed in the 1990s, when the government stipulated that collectively owned land must be first brought under state ownership before it could be converted for other purposes.

The 1998 version of China's Land Management Law specified that the right of use of collectively owned land could not be transferred or leased for non-agricultural purposes.[50] Land expropriation by local urban governments became the main channel through which rural land was converted to non-agricultural use for development in the second half of the 1990s and early 2000s. This period saw local governments use cheap land to build industrial parks to facilitate industrial development and attract foreign investment.[51] This was also a period in which urban land area expanded almost twice as fast as the urban population.

The central government became increasingly aware of the problems associated with land expropriation and the rapid expansion of urban development in the late 1990s and 2000s. The burgeoning of urban construction land led to an increasingly unsustainable reduction in agricultural arable land and the wasteful, inefficient use of urban land.[52] Free land allocation by local administrations also led to corruption, the loss of state assets and social conflict.[53] Indeed, the increase in land expropriation led to widespread grievances and even mass demonstrations by farmers who lost land and were not (or poorly) compensated.[54]

To alleviate these problems and social tensions, China's government amended its urban land acquisition and transfer policy, reducing free land allocation and increasing distribution through paid concessions. From 2001 to 2010, urban land supplied through tender and auction jumped from 7.3% to 88.3%.[55] Meanwhile, the government also adjusted the land expropriation system – with the 16th CPC Congress proposing to reduce the scope of land expropriation and to increase compensation for farmers from 2005. The State Council in 2004 demanded that local governments notify and compensate farmers appropriately when commandeering their land and to gradually shift to land acquisition.[56] The CPC plenary session in 2008 undertook more land policy reform, such as allowing collective construction land to be used for commercial purposes on approval and to enter the market, greatly increasing compensation for land use.[57]

However, although compensation for land increased gradually from the mid-2000s, land expropriation reform progressed slowly despite various pilot programmes. In the meantime, land sales revenue surged as tenders and auctions became the dominant channel through which local governments supplied urban construction land to the market, spurring them to monetise land for the local coffers.[58] Official statistics suggest that land sales increased from RMB 100 billion in 2001 to RMB 1 trillion in 2007 and RMB 8.4 trillion in 2020,[59] accounting for more than 50% of all government revenue in some localities. In addition, the central government encouraged local governments to set up LGFVs and borrow against their land reserves after the global financial crisis, leading to a sharp increase in land-collateralised local-government financing.

As the property market became a key channel for the monetisation of land, local-government finances and their urbanisation-driven growth have been increasingly linked to property development over the past two decades (see more in Chapter 7). Consequently, local governments often use their monopoly power over urban land supply to maximise land revenue. For example, when property sales and prices corrected in 2014 following the previous rapid build-up, local governments significantly reduced land supply for residential real-estate construction in the following years[60] to support property prices and maximise land revenue. At the same time, local governments have the incentive to expand city areas, turning suburban counties into urban districts, using their legal powers to convert rural land into urban land and resisting pressure to allow rural land to enter the urban construction market through other channels.[61]

Impact on urbanisation and the urban–rural divide

The dual land system has helped local governments to drive faster urbanisation in recent decades, first by supplying cheap land to support industrialisation, and then by monetising land through the property market to fund urban construction and investment. The former happened largely before the central government increased the paid use of land for urban construction in 2005; local governments expanded industrial parks and development zones using cheap land to attract industrial and commercial investment and achieve urbanisation.[62]

Since 2005, the focus has been on monetising land (after acquiring it from farmers) through the urban property market on the one hand, and using land reserves as collateral to leverage financing for urban infrastructure and other construction on the other hand.[63] In both stages, local governments benefitted from land valuation gains. Farmers and rural collectives who were the original owners of the land enjoyed little of the valuation gains, even after compensation was increased. Urbanisation has become a key source of local government revenue, and both the objective and means of achieving it.[64]

Thus, the dualism in rural and urban land, like the *hukou* system, has been key to the dual social and economic structure in Chinese society.[65] Not only are rural and urban people born into different circumstances, but also the *hukou* system ensures that their access to education, healthcare and job opportunities are different, while the dual land system also means that rural and urban property accrue vastly different benefits to their owners. While urban homeowners, who do not legally own the land on which their property sits, can enjoy the valuation gains of their homes, farmers, who have legal ownership of the land, cannot realise value from their land property rights, at least not in full, when their land is appropriated for urbanisation.[66]

Meanwhile, local governments' monopolistic control of the urban land supply perpetuates a sense of shortage, pushing up urban property prices. Prohibitively high urban property prices, in turn, add another barrier to the integration of rural migrants. The inequality of land rights has also contributed significantly to the valuation and growth gaps in urban and rural housing, amplifying the wealth gap between rural and urban households. A 2019 survey by the *China Economic Daily* suggested that the wealth of an average urban resident was 3.34 times that of an average rural resident, with housing accounting for 71% and 52% of urban and rural wealth, respectively.[67]

The dual land system has given local governments strong incentives to broaden the valuation gap between rural and urban land and made them focus more on the property aspects of urbanisation than on the provision of jobs or urban public services. The financial incentives associated with land have also led to over-construction and a bias towards tearing down old cities rather than preserving traditional architecture or the natural environment.

Continued urbanisation – where to from here?

China's urbanisation process since 1978 can be roughly divided into three key phases. The first involved the economy shifting rapidly towards non-farm activities as rural people left farming after agricultural reform and market liberalisation, with urban areas seeing a construction and investment boom. The administrative adjustment was a significant factor behind the increase in the number of cities. The second phase began in the mid-1990s and saw a surge in rural–urban migration and the expansion of urban land area, the latter motivated by the use of land to finance industrialisation and urbanisation. Changes in urban land acquisition and supply policies and the housing reform and property boom were instrumental here.

While China's first phase of urbanisation was largely the result of industrialisation, in the second phase, many government officials viewed urbanisation as the driver of economic growth and industrialisation. The dual land policy and local authorities' fiscal reliance on land and property gave local governments added incentives to expand urban construction. The urban construction boom did create more jobs and fuel demand for construction materials and equipment, leading to more industrial investment.[68] However, urbanisation requires sustainable underlying economic activity to prevent over-construction and excess capacity – as the lessons of 2014–2016 showed (Chapter 7).

The third phase started after China rolled out its new urbanisation plan in 2014, with an emphasis on 'people-centred urbanisation'.[69] The shift in focus came after the government had become increasingly concerned about environmental, energy and financial constraints, as well as the sustainability of its earlier urbanisation path, not to mention the persistent urban–rural divide and related social issues.[70] This phase has focused more on integrating migrants into urban areas, broadening public services and social welfare coverage and making urbanisation more sustainable in terms of land usage, financing, environmental impact and job creation.

There has been progress on increasing land supply for social housing construction in the past few years, though rural construction land is still not
entering the urban land market to any great extent. Property and construction
have remained a significant part of urbanisation, but their importance seems
to be waning, judging by the slowdown in property prices and overall investment since 2015. The 14th Five-Year Plan (2021–2025) announced plans to
further increase public services coverage for migrants in cities and rural areas
and to expand the provision of public housing rentals.[71]

At the current juncture, the dual land system and local governments'
land-property financing system continue to entrench the urban–rural divide,
however. While most experts agree on the dangers and causes of the existing
problems with China's urbanisation, addressing them is not so simple. For
example, the central government cannot simply mandate local governments
to grant long-term rural migrants the same rights to urban public services
and social welfare, as this would require significant fiscal resources that
local governments do not have. It would also require the transfer of resources
from localities where people have emigrated from to areas they have moved
to, but the former tend to be already fiscally challenged, poor regions.

Moreover, even if funding were not constrained, building sufficient pub-
lic-service facilities (schools and hospitals) without compromising quality is
difficult and takes time. This would likely lead to the original urban *hukou*
population feeling that their rights and (relative) privileges were being compromised, resulting in resistance to policy change. Indeed, after the State
Council asked local governments to allow migrant children to take college
entrance exams in cities where their parents lived, Beijing and Shanghai
residents with local *hukou* protested strongly that such policies 'violated'
their rights and benefits, as more competition from migrant children would
lower the chances of their children getting accepted into better universities.[72] Amidst strong social resistance, most local governments have continued to put up high barriers. In 2014, only 0.5% of eligible high-school
students who took the college entrance exams did so outside of their *hukou*
jurisdiction.[73]

There are also strong reasons why some stakeholders may resist land
policy reform. Local governments could potentially lose trillions of renminbi in land revenue if rural land could be supplied directly to the urban
market. This would hamper local governments' ability to support economic
growth when called upon. In addition, local governments are politically
powerful as a group and cannot easily be ordered around by the central
government, especially when their economic interests are at stake. Also,
rural land entering the urban market may lead to a sudden increase in land
supply, while the resulting decline in urban land prices could prompt a drop
in existing home prices. Given the importance of property to the economy
and as a share of household wealth,[74] the government may want to avoid
such an outcome. Lastly, some experts also worry about farmers losing land
as their social protection of last resort before sufficient and universal social
protection has been built.[75]

Therefore, policy changes to address the deep-rooted urban–rural divide and incomplete urbanisation are likely to be gradual, especially reforms of the *hukou* and land system. In the meantime, progress along the following lines is being made and can be expected to continue. First, the central government is providing some financial incentives for cities to absorb more migrants into the urban *hukou* population. Second, the central government is allocating more resources to basic public services and social welfare (e.g., expanding healthcare coverage and the payment ratio), gradually reducing the entitlement gaps associated with different *hukou*. Third, the government is fostering the development of rural areas and small towns,[76] reducing the pressure on migrants to move to overcrowded large cities where the treatment of rural and urban people is most different. Fourth, the state is gradually reforming urban land supply policy so that an increasing share of rural land value gains can be accrued to rural people, while local governments have less incentive to expropriate land and focus on property development and more incentive to provide services to the urban population.

Hukou and land system reforms along the above lines, coupled with adjustments to public finance and the expansion of public services and social welfare to reduce the urban–rural divide, could lead to better education of the next generation of workers, boost domestic consumption, address brewing social issues and reduce the risk of social and economic instability from the systematic discrimination against a large portion of the population.

Notes

1 See Zhang and Li (2021).
2 See National Bureau of Statistics (1999a).
3 See Xu (1988).
4 See Xu (2006).
5 He and Yu (2003).
6 Before 1984, the policy slogan was 'leaving land but not hometown', which encouraged local industrialisation.
7 See Zhu (2000) and Zhang and Li (2021).
8 See Wang (2010a).
9 See World Bank and Development Research Center (2014).
10 See Zhang and Li (2021).
11 See State Council (2014).
12 Between 2000 and 2011, completed urban areas expanded by 76.4%, far exceeding the growth rate of the urban population of 50.5% during the same period, according to the New Urbanization Plan 2014–2020.
13 The National New Urbanization Plan 2014–2020 set a target of granting at least 100 million people urban *hukou* and asked local governments to allocate resources for public services, such as basic healthcare based on the number of regular urban residents rather than *hukou* residents.
14 See National Bureau of Statistics (2021a).
15 See World Bank and Development Research Center (2014).
16 See Chen (2014).
17 See World Bank (1983).

18 See World Bank (1983).
19 See Zhao (1992) and Cai and Yang (2000).
20 See Zhao and Li (1997).
21 See Li and Luo (2007).
22 See Lu and Chen (2004), Chen and Lin (2013).
23 See Wang and Wang (2008).
24 See Zhu (2003).
25 See Wu (2002).
26 See Wang and Wang (2008).
27 See State Council (2014).
28 See Zhang (2012a) and Zhang and Li (2012).
29 See NDRC and UNPF (2014).
30 Ibid.
31 Restrictions including a ban on purchasing one's first home until after a certain number of years of social security contributions and a ban on buying a second home.
32 See Caixin (2014) and Reuters (2016).
33 See State Council (2014).
34 See Rozelle and Hell (2020).
35 See All-China Women's Federation (2013).
36 According to the Ministry of Civil Affairs, a more narrowly defined left-behind children (under the age of 16 living with no one with guardianship capacity) numbered 9 million in 2016.
37 See Rozelle and Hell (2020).
38 China's share of labour force with high-school education is less than Thailand, Mexico and Turkey (according to Li et al. (2017).
39 China had a highly decentralised fiscal system after the 1980s reform, where basic public services including compulsory education spending were delegated to the lowest level of government, at village and township level. Following the fee-to-tax reform in the late 1990s, lower levels of government had even fewer resources to meet these obligations. The central government gradually increased funding to local governments for compulsory education in 2010, improving basic education conditions in poor rural areas. However, vast gaps remain.
40 See Zhu and He (2018).
41 See China Statistics Yearbook, various issues.
42 See Lu et al. (2022).
43 See NDRC and UNPF (2014).
44 See Huang (2013) and World Bank and Development Research Center (2014).
45 See Liu (2005b, 2018a) and Ding and Lichtenberg (2011).
46 Rural land consists of rural agricultural land, rural collective construction land and rural family homesteads. The property and use rights associated with and rules governing each type of land are different. Agricultural land and construction land are collectively owned, but rural families have strong property rights on their homesteads.
47 See Kung and Liu (1997), Liu et al. (1998), and World Bank and Development Research Center (2014).
48 See Zhou (2004), and Liu (2018a).
49 See Liu (2018a).
50 See Liu (2018) and NPC (1998).
51 See Tan et al. (2005), Liu (2005b), Cartier (2001), and Ding and Lichtenberg (2008).
52 See Tan et al. (2005).
53 See Cai (2003) and Ho (2005).
54 See Yu (2009), Page (2011) and Deng et al. (2020).
55 See Liu (2018a).

56 See State Council (2004).
57 See CPC Central Committee (2008).
58 See Whiting (2010) and Zheng et al. (2014).
59 Data from the China Statistics Yearbook. See also Li et al. (2013).
60 Land supply was only two-thirds of 2013 levels in 2015–2016, according to official statistics.
61 See Liu (2018a).
62 See Tao et al. (2007, 2010) and Liu (2005b).
63 See Zheng et al. (2014) and Wong (2013).
64 See Liu (2018a).
65 See Andreas and Zhan (2015).
66 See Liu (2018a) and Ye and Wu (2014).
67 See China Economic Daily (2019).
68 Investment as a share of GDP rose significantly between late 1990s and 2010, while the share of heavy industry also expanded. See Chapter 2 for more.
69 See State Council (2014).
70 See Tang and Côté (2021), Gallagher (2013) and Lu et al. (2014).
71 See State Council (2021).
72 See 21st Century Business Herald (2012) and Wang (2010a).
73 See China Education Daily (2014).
74 The property sector contributes about a quarter of China's GDP, while property accounts for more than 60% of household wealth. See Chapter 7 for more.
75 See Chen (2014), Cai (2016) and Cheng and Chen (2006).
76 The government is pushing for 'rural rejuvenation', for example, investing more in rural infrastructure and human capital.

7 The property market and local-government finance

Property is arguably the most important sector in China's economy. Over the past two decades, the property boom has put hundreds of millions of people in modern housing and changed the country's landscape. It has also helped to power China's economic growth, monetise land and finance local governments, and has led to a global commodity boom. From the very start, the government has grappled with multiple objectives in the property market, wanting to see the housing market flourish and housing become affordable for most people. The debate about a property bubble persisted, often leading to policy shifts that have amplified if not triggered property cycles. The 2021–2022 property cycle is still unfolding. After foreign investors voiced concern about China's 'Lehman moment' in late 2021 and as the property market weakened further since the second quarter of 2022, the government has eased policy to try to stabilise the sector and the economy, and to minimise the macro and financial risks of a sharp downturn.

China's property market: types of property and housing stock

Before we discuss China's property-sector development and its intricate links with the rest of the economy, as well as the fiscal and financial system, we need to understand some basics. When talking about the property market, we are referring exclusively to China's urban housing market. Before the reform era, dwellings for urban residents were generally provided by state-owned employers at subsidised rents, based on rank, years of work and family need. Decades of under-construction and population growth resulted in extremely cramped living conditions; the per capita urban living space was about 7 square metres in 1980. China increased housing construction significantly in the 1980s and 1990s, boosting per capita living space to 14 square metres in 1990 and 18.7 square metres in 1998. But it was only after the housing reform of the 1990s that China saw an urban housing-market boom.

The urban housing reform formally started in 1994, but expanded nationwide in 1998 (see Chapter 3). Housing was gradually commercialised and became available outside of the employment context. A housing provident fund was soon launched. Employer-owned housing units were sold at

DOI: 10.4324/9781003310938-8

cost to existing tenants in the second half of 1990s, constituting a significant transfer of assets and wealth from the state to the household sector. Millions of households promptly owned private housing, which could then be traded or upgraded, kick-starting the urban housing market.

Commodity housing, economic housing and various types of social housing

'Commodity housing' came into being in the late 1990s. It refers specifically to residential housing built by property developers for sale on the market, as opposed to properties built by employers and allocated as a work benefit. The latter was supposed to have ended in the late 1990s, but never really did, as government agencies and universities alike realised that they could not increase salaries sufficiently for their employees to afford commodity housing. They could, however, access cheap land to build them homes. Nevertheless, commodity housing construction grew rapidly after the housing reform. Its share of total new urban residential housing grew from about 30% in the late 1990s to 72% in 2006 and has remained in the 70–80% range ever since. The cumulative completion of urban commodity residential property between 1995 and 2021 totalled 13.5 billion square metres, or about 127 million units, while non-commodity housing added another 90–100 million units.

Thanks to the post-reform property construction boom, per capita urban residential space rose from 18.7 square metres in 1998 to almost 40 square metres in 2019, even though the urban population more than doubled to over 800 million during that time.[1]

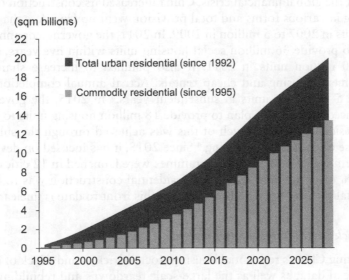

Figure 7.1 Cumulative urban residential housing completion, 1995–2021.
Source: NBS, author's estimates.

Since the start of China's housing reform, the government has tried to create a two-track housing system, whereby social housing is provided to low- and middle-income households and the remainder of housing is provided by the market. At first, the government tried to provide social housing within the commodity housing market through 'economic housing' – relatively small residential units built on land provided by the government at a lower cost.

The rules on economic housing were published in 1994 and amended in 2007,[2] though the guidelines for qualification were often unclear. Households had to apply to buy economic housing and local governments would decide whether they qualified. Complaints about the large size of economic housing allocated to relatively well-off households led to the rise of 'double restriction housing' after 2007 – economic housing with a ceiling on both price and size (90 square metres). Such price-restricted housing could not be resold on the market for eight years after purchase to discourage property flipping. Demand for both types of economic housing far outstripped supply and distributional problems were widespread.

Since 2008, the government's social housing scheme has focused more on supply outside the commodity housing market and has included shantytown renovation, cheap private-sector rentals and public long-term rentals. Shantytown renovation refers to the rebuilding or replacement of housing that is in poor condition, typically old housing built by SOEs in old city centres or mining areas. Cheap rentals and public rentals involve the construction of smaller units on land provided by the government for lease to low-income households; the former are typically privately owned, while the latter state owned.

After the global financial crisis, China increased its construction of social housing in various forms and total provision went up from less than 2 million units in 2007 to 5 million in 2009. In 2011, the government announced plans to provide 36 million social housing units within five years, starting with 10 million units in 2011. It also planned to increase shantytown replacement housing and cheap rentals. Actual annual completions were around 5–6 million units in subsequent years.[3] In 2015, the government announced a three-year plan to provide 18 million housing units to shantytown residents, though much of this was achieved through the subsidised purchase of commodity housing.[4] Since 2018, it has focused on developing long-term rental units. Pilot programmes were launched in 12 cities, where 30–50% of urban land supply for residential construction was to be used for rental properties. Actual progress on this front to date is unclear.

The stock of urban residential housing

Estimating China's residential housing stock is tricky amid a lack of consistent official data, as well as the large-scale teardowns and rebuilding of old city centres. The 2010 census reported that 79% of urban households lived in homes they own, while that share for rural households was significantly higher. It further reported that residential space totalled 17.9 billion square metres in urban areas, compared with 20.6 billion square metres in rural areas, amounting to about 1 unit per household on average for both urban and rural households, though a significant share of the homes were of poor quality and without a kitchen or toilet.[5] Between 2010 and 2020, another 9.6 billion square meters of urban residential housing (or about 100 million units) was built,[6] though some old housing has been torn down and replaced.

The 2020 census showed that urban residential space stood at 29.5 billion square meters while rural housing amounted to 22.3 billion.[7] Judging from the fact that a sizable share of urban housing was reportedly 'self-built', a significant portion of originally rural housing has likely been reclassified as urban following urban expansion. The share of urban households who lived in their own homes stayed at 79%,[8] though urban home ownership may be higher, as some homeowners may live in rental units. A 2019 PBC survey suggested that 96% of urban households owned residential properties and that urban residential units amounted to 1.5 per household.[9]

Put another way, assuming that housing built after the mid-1990s is of modern design and better quality, China has built a total of 220–230 million housing units since 1995, of which more than 60% is commodity housing. This does not include some of the 20 billion square metres of rural homes built since then that have been reclassified as urban housing after rural areas became cities or towns.

Estimates of the value of China's housing stock vary a great deal. Two parameters affect it most: the share of old urban housing that has been demolished each year and the valuation of properties. The former depends on the speed of old town teardowns and shantytown renovation, while the latter needs to take into account the vast differences in valuation from city to city and the different quality of housing. Taking these into consideration, China's urban housing stock is estimated to have been worth about RMB 165 trillion in 2020, or over 160% of GDP and more than half of total household assets.[10] This is consistent with the 2019 PBC household survey, which reported property as accounting for 59% of household assets.[11] This may seem high compared with the United States (where housing is about 30% of household wealth), but this may be due in part to China's shallower financial market, different tax regime and idiosyncratic policy elements.

Outside of residential real estate, commercial property (including office buildings and retail space) also features in China's property story. In 2017 (the last time the government published such data), commercial property under construction was equivalent to about 80% of residential space under construction, while completion was one-third higher. However, unlike the residential market, most commercial properties were not 'commodity' properties, which means they were not built by developers for sale on the market. Historically, commodity property has only accounted for 15–20% of total commercial property, though this share has increased recently to 25%. Most commercial properties have been built by owner-occupiers – companies (including many SOEs), and local governments. Traditionally, the commercial property cycle has tended to track the residential property market, but changes in local-government debt management and tighter controls on SOE spending are likely to have had an impact in recent years.

The key drivers of China's housing demand

China has completed more than 200 million residential housing units since the mid-1990s. Urban residential sales rose from about 100 million square metres in 1998 to almost 1.6 billion in 2021. What has driven such strong housing demand?

The most important drivers of the residential property boom have been upgrades from extremely poor starting living conditions and rapid urbanisation. Upgrade demand was particularly significant in the first 10–15 years after housing reform. In 1998, per capita urban housing living space was only 18.7 square metres, and this did not include the millions of migrant workers who lived in temporary sheds on construction sites or in cramped factory dorms.

Moreover, mass constructions prior to the mid-1990s were of relatively poor quality and most were not up to modern specifications, so had to be gradually replaced.[12] As recently as 2010, about 18 million urban households lived in housing built before 1980 and another 39.4 million lived in dwellings built in the 1980s. What's more, as household income has grown rapidly in the past two-plus decades, demand for bigger and better housing has also surged. In addition, the government's shantytown renovation programmes and local governments' drive to renovate old city centres has created extra or brought forward upgrade demand, especially from the lower-income population.

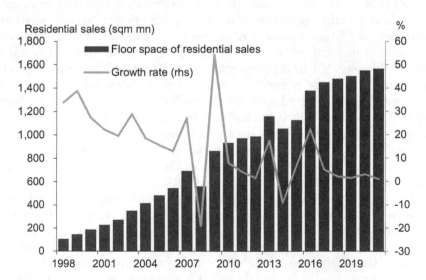

Figure 7.2 Urban commodity residential sales, 1998–2021.

Source: NBS, author's calculations.

Urbanisation has been a major driver of housing demand in two respects: rapid urban population growth and urbanisation as a goal and means of boosting economic growth (see Chapter 6 for more on the latter). The urban population has more than doubled in the past 20 years, creating a substantial increase in housing demand. Also, as local governments have incentives to monetise land through the property market, they have boosted urbanisation to generate and amplify property demand, including tearing down old city centres to rebuild.

Calculations of incremental housing demand should not just be derived from changes in the official urban population, however. A significant share of urban population growth has involved the administrative reclassification of towns and suburbs, and there were existing properties in those places that were not all torn down and replaced with new ones. In fact, the 2020 census showed that about 21% of urban residents live in 'self-built' homes which were likely rural homes originally. Another big bump-up in urban population growth has come from rural migrants, but they have been largely unable to participate in the urban housing market, as they either cannot afford to purchase urban housing or their non-local *hukou* status disqualifies them from social housing. That said, an estimated 20% of migrant workers have purchased urban homes in the past few years compared with 1% a decade ago,[13] though mostly in lower-tier cities closer to their hometowns, not in the larger cities where many of them work and live.

The decline in urban household size is also an important contributor to urban housing demand. While natural population growth (outside of urbanisation) has slowed considerably in China in recent years, the change in household structure may have played a significant role in housing demand. The 2020 census showed that the average household size declined from 3.44 in 2000 to 2.62 in 2020, while the urban household size declined from 3.13 to 2.57. The number of single-person households in urban areas grew from 13.8 million in 2000 to 34.2 million in 2010 and about 81 million in 2020.[14] Thus, the shrinking size of households has probably increased urban housing demand significantly over the past decade.

Demand for property as an asset – often known as investment demand or speculative demand – has played an increasingly important role in housing demand over the past ten years as well. There have been various incentives for households to invest in property: the lack of property holding tax, light taxes on rental income, low deposit interest rates and an underdeveloped capital market for alternative investment vehicles, to name but a few. Two ways to estimate the overall size of investment property are to look at vacancy rates and multiple home ownership.

The 2017 household finance survey by the Southwest University of Finance and Economics found that 22% of urban households had more than one property, while the vacancy rate was about 21.4%.[15] A 2019 survey by the PBC found that 41.5% of urban households had at least two residential properties[16] and that property accounted for 59% of household wealth among the 30,000 households surveyed. Various housing purchase intention

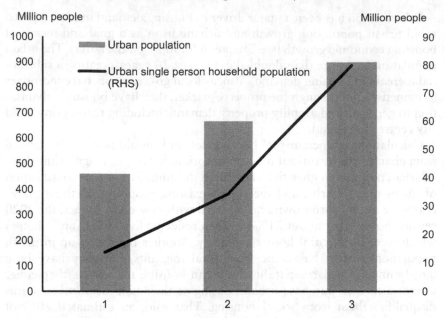

Figure 7.3 The rise in urban population and single-person households.

Source: NBS, author's estimates.

surveys conducted by the UBS Evidence Lab typically found that 30–33% of home buyers said they were buying homes for investment purposes.[17] The share of investment demand is likely to fluctuate over time and with changes in house-price expectations, monetary policy and property policies.

Property as an engine of growth and industrialisation

The Chinese government has viewed the property sector as a pillar industry and engine of growth for more than 20 years, though it has recently tried to reduce the country's reliance on the sector. Previously, when housing was in very short supply in the 1980s, the government just wanted to provide more residential homes to the urban population as fast as possible. After the introduction of commodity housing, government policy focused on providing affordable dwellings to the mid- and low-income urban population. It was after the Asian financial crisis that China started to see the property sector as a key driver of economic growth and, arguably, it has been the most important driver of growth for much of this period (Figure 7.4). Property's contribution to GDP growth was especially large between 2000 and 2010 and has dropped in the past ten years.

Between 2001 and 2021, real-estate sector fixed-asset investment accounted for almost a quarter of China's total fixed investment. The total value-added of the construction and property sectors rose from less than 10% of GDP to about 14.5% during that period. To capture a fuller picture

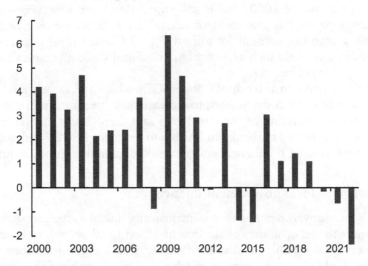

Growth contribution (ppt)

Figure 7.4 The property sector's contribution to GDP growth.

Source: NBS, author's estimates.

of property's importance to China's economy, it is useful to look at the whole supply chain using an input–output table. One way to estimate this is to treat property as the final output and sum up the shares of product value in each sector contributing to it as an input. Estimates using this method, based on China's latest available input–output tables (2018),[18] suggest that property and related construction (excluding non-property-related construction, such as factory plant) account for about 25% of GDP, roughly half of it through the sector's long supply chain.[19] However, even this does not fully capture how property development has helped to propel and finance China's urbanisation and related infrastructure investment, as described in Chapter 6.

The input–output analysis helps reveal the importance of property in leading the build-up of industrial capacity and a global commodity super-cycle in the 2000s. Real-estate fixed-asset investment grew by an average of 26% a year in nominal terms between 2000 and 2013 (though growth has slowed to less than 7% a year since then), and residential floor space under construction expanded tenfold to 4.9 billion square metres, leading to a sharp increase in demand for construction materials and machinery. This strong demand lifted China's fixed investment in non-metal products (including cement) by 33% a year and that in metal products and machinery by 37% a year in the decade to 2013. China's crude steel capacity rose from less than 200 million tonnes in 2000 to about 1 billion tonnes in 2013, almost half of the world's total. Cement production also surged to 2.4 billion tonnes in 2013, accounting for 59% of the world's total.

China's property and heavy industry boom led to a sharp increase in commodity imports, especially minerals and metals, including iron ore, copper and coal. Strong demand from China helped to drive up global commodity prices in the 2000s and is still supporting them now (Figure 7.5). This development has also changed China's trade structure. For example, imports of iron ore account for almost 7% of China's total imports, and commodity exporters such as Australia, Brazil and Chile all count China as their largest export market.

The property boom also helped China's SOEs, which are concentrated in the mining and heavy industry sectors, to increase their revenues and profits following the restructuring of the late 1990s and early 2000s. Moreover, the property boom helped the banks and AMCs to restructure SOEs' bad assets, as the land collateral of those assets saw tremendous valuation gains (Chapter 9).

Property and local-government finance

China's local-government finance is intrinsically linked to the property market thanks to the evolution of the decentralised fiscal system and the dual urban–rural land policy, as discussed earlier. Local governments are often directly involved in the property market and have multiple incentives to boost both construction activity and property prices.

As we saw in Chapter 5, land revenue and various property-related taxes account for one-third of total local-government revenue on average, and more than half for many local governments. This is a result of the evolving decentralised fiscal system and incomplete fiscal reform.

The 1980s fiscal decentralisation gave local governments fiscal autonomy and incentives to maximise revenues. After the 1990s' fiscal reform

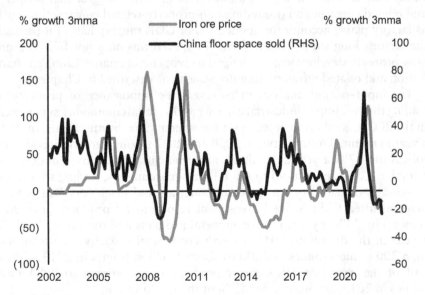

Figure 7.5 China's property sales and the global iron-ore price.

Source: NBS, World Bank, author's calculations.

introduced tax-sharing with the central government, local governments collected various fees for their 'out-of-budget' spending, which became difficult after the fees were formalised into taxes or abolished in the early 2000s.[20] Meanwhile, the SOE restructuring of the late 1990s transferred many social responsibilities, including healthcare, pensions and social services to local governments. In addition, local governments were pressured into supporting growth and employment. With no mandate to raise taxes or issue debt (until 2015 in the case of the latter), local governments increasingly relied on land sales revenue, made possible by a change in land supply policy and the property boom.

China's dual rural and urban land system, the adoption of tenders and auctions as a key form of urban land supply, and the housing boom combined to create a 'land finance' era in which local governments monetised land to fund fiscal spending.[21] Recall from Chapter 6 that rural land can only enter the urban land market for property construction after being acquired by urban governments. Although land compensation to farmers has increased significantly over time, there are still enormous valuation gains after rural land is converted for urban use and auctioned off to developers. Such valuation gains are largely taken by local governments and can be used for urban infrastructure and other investment projects outside the general budget.

In addition, local governments and LGFVs can use land reserves as collateral to borrow from banks and finance investment projects. Land revenues can fund construction investment directly, while cheap land can be used to cross-subsidise the industrial sector by indirectly facilitating industrial investment. Both contribute to local investment, tax revenues and GDP, important performance indicators for officials keen on promotion. These incentives have led local governments, as the monopoly suppliers of urban land, to push up land prices and construction activity and, at times, ration land supply.[22]

LGFVs are an integral part of the 'land finance' scheme. Local governments had begun to operate investment companies in the late 1980s, but LGFVs developed more rapidly after the housing reform of the late 1990s and really took off after the global financial crisis, encouraged by the central government. As local governments could not officially borrow until 2015, they set up LGFVs, injecting them with state-owned assets or land and using them to borrow from banks or to issue bonds to finance various infrastructure, property or other projects, often pledging future fiscal or land revenue as debt payment.

LGFVs can be directly involved in operating local land reserves, procuring and selling land, have land as an asset and collateral for financing, or even own property or construction companies directly. LGFVs' involvement in the urban land and property market gives local governments additional incentives and means to manage land revenue and the property market. Higher land and property prices mean LGFVs can raise more financing and profit more from their land assets. When the property market declines, local governments can use LGFVs and linked property companies to fix land auction prices to stabilise collateral value and, indirectly, property prices.[23]

Attempts to separate LGFVs from local-government finances have not fully succeeded. China formally banned local governments from using LGFVs to borrow on their behalf in 2014. However, such practices continued in roundabout ways, as mentioned earlier. To overcome this problem, rules on local government debt and LGFV financing have been more strictly implemented, and local governments have been allowed to issue more special bonds to finance infrastructure projects in the past few years.

There have also been discussions on creating new sources of revenue for local governments, but the planned property tax is still on the drawing board after a decade and personal income-tax reform remains controversial. In any case, without significant changes in the way local governments are relied on to support growth, or amendments to the country's land supply policy, the property market and local government finances will remain enmeshed. Indeed, tighter local debt management may make property activities even more important to local economies, as local governments have a reduced ability to borrow.

China's policy-driven property cycles

Property policy objectives and instruments

China has had many property cycles over the past 20 years, and they have often been triggered by policy changes as the government used property policy to stimulate growth or cool overheating. In recent years, the government seems to have been constantly caught between wanting the property sector to support growth while trying to control property prices and the property bubble. Although it has tried to focus on social housing and let the market meet normal upgrade housing demand for the past 10–15 years, the government has never really given up trying to control the pace of construction or price changes in the housing market.

There are two types of property policy instrument in China – nationwide policies controlled by the central government and differentiated policies managed by local governments. The most important nationwide policy is on credit to the property sector. The government can tighten or ease credit by adjusting mortgage down payment ratios and interest rates, modifying banks' property loan quotas and changing bond-market and bank-loan access rules for property developers. The central government can also use land supply and social housing policy tools, though the implementation of these is undertaken by local governments. Local governments' policy instruments include purchase restrictions, price restrictions, window guidance on local banks' mortgage provision, adjustments of the quantity, price and payment of land auctions, and the provision of credit to connected developers.

Despite much discussion over the past ten-plus years, a property holding tax has not yet been rolled out, except for two insignificant pilot programmes in Shanghai and Chongqing. Proponents argue that a property tax could discourage property speculation by adding a carrying cost and help supplement local fiscal revenue. Opponents question the basis for levying a property tax when the land on which the property is built is owned by the state and worry that such a tax would tank the property market. Most importantly, there seems to be strong resistance from the urban population to such a tax, as more than 80% of people own their homes. In 2022, the government announced a delay to the planned expansion of property-tax pilot programmes.

Different central and local-government policy objectives often complicate the property cycle. Local governments are usually happy to amplify central government's policy to speed up housing construction and support growth, but reluctant to cool the property market when the central authorities are concerned about overheating or overly rapid price gains. Local governments' reluctance sometimes triggers more heavy-handed tightening measures from the central government, causing a sharp downturn in property activity. Likewise, local governments are not eager to provide social housing to low-income people, as this requires them to provide land for free (at the cost of acquisition). They are also less concerned about property bubbles or macro-financial risks, which are the concern of central government.

Notable property cycles

While policy-induced property cycles started soon after housing reform of the late 1990s, three particular cycles merit a more detailed look.

One is the overheating of the property market in the mid-2000s, which was quelled by rounds of policy tightening, culminating in a sharp downturn in 2007–2008. The cycle started in 2003, when the State Council formally declared the property sector a pillar of the economy, leading to a set of policies supporting property-market development.[24] As property investment grew by more than 30% a year in 2003 and 2004, worries of overheating led to policy tightening.[25] After moderating briefly in 2005 and 2006, property investment growth climbed once again to more than 30% in 2007.

More serious policy tightening followed: higher down payments on second mortgages (40–50% rather than 20%), restricted lending to developers for land purchases, a requirement for developers to put a bigger portion of their own capital into property construction and limitations on land hoarding. The PBC also raised interest rates five times in 2007. More policy tightening ensued in 2008 as the Ministry of Construction expanded restrictions on housing size and required developers to start construction within three years of land purchase or face fines or forfeiture. The CBRC capped loans to developers at 70% of collateral and two years in duration. These measures and overall credit tightening brought about a sharp slowdown in the property market in autumn 2008, just as the global financial crisis hit. Property sales contracted by 19% in 2008, after growing 26% in 2007, and property investment growth slowed by 10 percentage points.

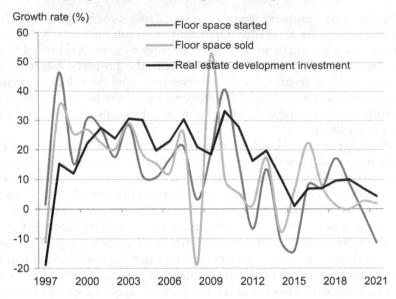

Figure 7.6 China's property cycles, 1997–2021.

Source: NBS, Author estimates.

The global financial crisis led to a 180-degree turn in China's property policies. The government cut mortgage down payment requirements and interest rates (with mortgage rates cut significantly more), lowered the property transaction tax, eased lending to developers, poured credit into the whole economy and encouraged local governments and platform companies to engage in property and urban construction. In 2009, the State Council set a minimum increase in new lending (of RMB 5 trillion) for banks,[26] which they exceeded. Thanks to the strong policy and credit stimulus, property construction and prices rose sharply. By 2010, property policy had tightened again.

The second notable property cycle was the sharp correction in 2014–2015 after the over-construction of 2012–2013, followed by a de-stocking campaign in 2016–2017. China's property market was on a recovery cycle in 2012 thanks to more stable property policies, easier monetary and credit policies, and better affordability. Residential housing sales grew 18% that year. While policies focused on controlling prices in large cities using purchase restrictions, the governments of lower-tier cities rushed to construct more industrial parks, new city centres and residential properties under the banner of accelerated urbanisation as the new growth driver. Residential construction per capita rose to 1.5 square metres in 2013 and investment grew 20%.

The ensuing downturn in 2014–2015 resulted from both high inventories in most cities and policy tightening, including a clampdown on local-government debt and property trusts, and tighter credit access for homebuyers.[27] In the wake of the deep downturn (housing starts at end 2015 were 27% lower than in 2013), the government eased property policy and embarked on a multi-year de-stocking campaign. Down payment requirements for mortgages were reduced, purchase restrictions were abolished or eased and, most importantly, local governments used shantytown renovation funds to subsidise home-buyer property purchases from the market.[28] Property sales started to rebound in 2015 and rose by more than 22% in 2016.

The 2013–2016 property cycle demonstrated that in China, it was more important to monitor property sales and construction volumes than prices for signs of a downturn. While nationwide affordability and leverage ratios did not get much worse before the downturn, residential floor space under construction reached 5.7 billion square metres at end 2013, six times the completion rate and five times sales that year. Unsold inventories climbed sharply in lower-tier cities.

This cycle also showed that the impact of a property downturn was largely felt through the supply chain rather than through household balance sheets. At the time, China's relatively low level of household debt and the limited leverage of home purchases[29] meant that households were not forced to sell their properties or default on mortgages. Meanwhile, the drop in property construction led to a decline in demand for steel, cement, coal and aluminium, leading to excess capacity of 20–30% in these industries and a sharp fall in industrial revenue. Together, debt problems in the property and related industrial sectors posed significant risk to the financial system, even though China avoided a banking crisis (see Chapter 9 for more).

The ongoing 2021–2022 property cycle has been caused by a combination of fundamental factors and policy tightening. With population growth in the

Figure 7.7 Urban residential floor space under construction.

Source: NBS, Author estimates.

key homebuying cohort (aged 25–44) and rural–urban migration slowing, urban housing ownership already high, and household leverage rising to 100% of disposable income, the fundamentals supporting China's underlying property demand have weakened. Demand has been adjusting back to the long-term trend after being pushed up by the government's shantytown subsidy scheme in 2015–2018 and the post-COVID-19 property boom. As property prices and activities grew strongly and China's economy recovered from the pandemic in late 2020 and early 2021, the government rekindled its desire to rein in property prices and contain property leverage by tightening developer financing (the 'three red lines')[30] and mortgage lending. After mid-2021, debt troubles at the largest developer effectively shut down financing channels for almost all developers and weakened market sentiment.

The double-digit decline in property sales and starts triggered gradual policy easing from late 2021 onward as the government refocused on containing the property downturn and the associated negative impact on the economy and financial system. However, the emergence of new COVID-19 cases and enhanced mobility restrictions hit the property market hard in the second quarter of 2022. With sales contracting almost 40% year on year in volume terms, cash flows for many developers began to dry up, leading to more project suspensions and debt defaults. While local governments and banks were asked to work on ensuring the delivery of pre-sold homes and more than 100 cities eased or removed home purchase restrictions, these measures have had little apparent effect as of November 2022. The effectiveness of policy easing was seriously limited by persistent COVID-related restrictions in most of 2022, as well as weakening overall economy and confidence. As a result, the

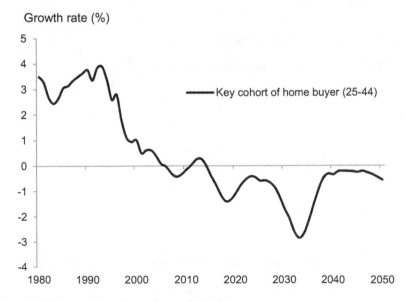

Figure 7.8 The number of people aged 25–44 years.

Source: UNPD, Author estimates.

ongoing property cycle has been the deepest yet, and due to the changes in long-term fundamental demand, it may also have the weakest recovery.

Over the past 20 years, government policies have often been behind property-market ups and downs. Multiple, incompatible objectives and frequent changes have made it difficult for the market to form long-term expectations.[31] Because of the importance of the property sector, the government has often abandoned or reversed policy tightening mid-way, amplifying moral hazard in the sector by underpinning the belief that the government will always save it (or large developers, or home buyers, or never let home prices fall). In recent years, a broad consensus has formed on China's need for multiple types of housing supply, including rentals, the importance of policy continuity and long-term solutions (e.g., a property holding tax), as well as the need for the economy to gradually reduce its reliance on property as a growth driver. Actual implementation of this vision remains challenging.

The property-bubble debate: measurements and unique Chinese features

In the recent property-market downturn, debate about China's housing bubble surfaced once again, as it frequently has for around a decade. From many perspectives, China's housing market shows clear 'bubble' signs, yet it has defied many predictions of its demise. Housing prices and construction have continued to rise, though they have slowed considerably in many lower-tier cities in recent years.

This section will show that measured by affordability ratio, rental yields, the importance of property construction and the vacancy rate, China's housing market resembles housing bubbles elsewhere. However, China's relatively low mortgage leverage and government control, including of land supply, make it difficult to time the end of the bubble. At the same time, the distorted incentives that have perpetuated the property boom cannot last and, together with China's slowing population growth and urbanisation rate, make it likely that the property bubble will eventually burst.

Usually, an extended period of rapid home-price rises or a high price-income ratio could signal a housing bubble. Official statistics in China show that the average price of new urban residential housing in 2020 had increased more than fivefold since 2000 (corresponding to an annual growth rate of 8.5%) and was eight times the average urban household disposable income (prices were as much as 20 times income in a few large cities such as Beijing).[32] However, during the same period, household disposable income had grown 10.2% a year, meaning the price-income ratio had declined (or affordability had increased), even though it remained higher than in developed markets.[33]

But there are problems with both the price and the income data. Official housing prices are not adjusted for location or quality – newly built homes are increasingly further away from city centres, though their quality is also better. Price restrictions and mandated social housing supply may have skewed average home prices to the downside. Data from national real-estate brokers show far more rapid price increases in large cities than the official

Average price of a 100 sq m property over average annual urban household
income (%)

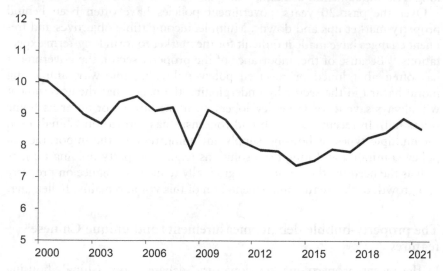

Figure 7.9 The housing affordability ratio, 2000–2021.

Source: NBS, Author estimates.

data. In contrast, the official data also underestimate household income, especially the incomes of the higher-income population.[34]

The experience of other countries suggests that a credit boom almost always accompanies or predicates a property bubble. China's property-market boom has also been helped by credit expansion. Mortgage lending grew 21.3% a year between 2004 and 2021, far outpacing overall bank lending (about 15.6% a year), though mortgages have only existed for 20 years. Overall household debt rose from about 17% of GDP in 2004 to 62% in 2021. Household debt relative to disposable income also surpassed 100% in 2021 (see Chapter 9 for more).

However, high down payment requirements – 20–30% for the first mortgage and 40–60% for the second as of 2021 – have limited leverage in home purchases. The estimated loan-to-value (LTV) ratio of new mortgages, proxied by new mortgage finance relative to the value of new commodity residential sales, has generally been below 60%.[35] And even in those years when down payment financing was not restricted, the estimated new LTV ratio was still 80%, in sharp contrast to the near 100% seen in the United States just before the subprime crisis.

Another sign of a property market bubble is a period of sharp and sustained rise in construction activity. In the United States, real-estate and construction as a share of GDP rose to 16.4% in 2007, while in Spain, it rose to 19.2% in 2008, before their housing bubbles collapsed.[36] Just before the Asian financial crisis, the economies that later saw their property market bubbles burst, such as Korea and Hong Kong, all experienced a surge in

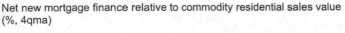

Net new mortgage finance relative to commodity residential sales value (%, 4qma)

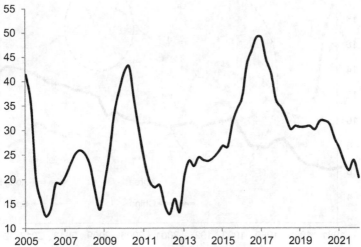

Figure 7.10 Estimates of the LTV ratio of new mortgages.

Source: NBS, PBC, Author estimates.

construction activity. China's real-estate and construction share of GDP remained relatively stable until 2008, but has risen continuously over the past decade, reaching 14.5% in 2021.

In terms of physical construction, China was building about 1 square metre of housing per capita on average in the first decade after the housing reform. That climbed to 1.5 square metres in 2013, on a par with the speed of Japan's construction in the late 1980s and close to that of Spain before the global financial crisis, but not quite as high as that of the United States in 2007 or Korea before the Asian financial crisis.[37] This number has since come down to about 1 square metre per capita, but that is probably under-estimated due to the under-reporting of completions.

Housing stock and the vacancy rate are also typical indicators of a housing bubble. Data from the seventh population census suggest that China's urban housing stock was just above 300 million units in 2020, slightly above the number of urban households, at 295 million (excluding those with 'collective' *hukou* and live in dormitories).[38] However, the 2019 PBC survey suggested that each urban household had 1.5 residential units, on average. One potential reason is that some 'rural' housing in the suburbs may have been counted in the survey. As mentioned, some surveys and estimates put China's housing vacancy rate at 15–20%.

These measurements may not convincingly define China's property sector as being in a bubble state for most of the time it has been called such. However, there are clear distortions in the market that have made China's property market fizz. First, high household savings with limited financial investment opportunities[39] means property is seen as a good alternative

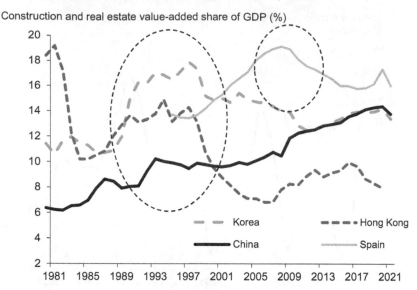

Figure 7.11 Construction as a share of GDP: China versus selected economies.

Source: Bank of Korea; Hong Kong Census and Statistics Department; China NBS; Spanish National Statistical Institute; author's estimates.

asset. The allocation of household wealth to property assets could cause self-fulfilling price increases without too much household leverage. Second, the lack of a property tax or capital gains tax, and low taxes on property income are incentives to hold property. Together with low bank deposit rates, these make people tolerant of low rental yields or keep homes vacant, the latter reducing the supply of rental properties.

Third, local governments, as monopoly suppliers of urban construction land, have incentives to push up land prices. Meanwhile, suburban housing built on rural land cannot be sold to urban residents and city governments do not provide 'urban' infrastructure and public services accordingly. Fourth, until a few years ago, SOEs paid little dividends, so could use retained earnings to invest in property and land.[40] Collateral-focused lending practices also facilitated the injection of corporate loans into the property sector. These features and distortions have likely pushed up China's property construction and prices beyond the normal fundamentals of housing market supply and demand.

The impact of a property bust: transmission channels and possible remedies

In autumn 2021, many China observers and investors were once again worried about the potential calamity of a sharp fall in China's property market. These concerns intensified in 2022. Given the importance of the property sector to China's economy, local-government finance, household wealth and the banking system, those worries were warranted.

Analyses of property downturns elsewhere usually focus on the correction in property prices and the transmission of the consequences through household and banking-sector balance sheets. This is because property bubbles are usually driven by a housing credit bubble, and burst bubbles are usually the outcome of a financially driven collapse.[41] In such cases, the fall in housing prices reduces household wealth and significantly increases mortgage defaults, the latter partly due to housing values falling below the level of mortgage debt.

In China, real estate accounts for 60–70% of household wealth, according to various estimates. However, home purchases have not been backed by excessively high leverage, as down payment requirements have been high. Estimates of the LTV ratio for outstanding mortgages averaged about 30% in 2019, according to a UBS survey.[42] Meanwhile, house prices have grown fivefold in the past 20 years on average. As such, Chinese households may have more staying power when it comes to their properties, and the risk of large defaults on mortgage loans and large foreclosures is small. Banks have persistently reported low mortgage default rates through the various property cycles. While the decline in property prices is likely to hurt household wealth, which could affect household consumption, the high down payment should limit 'fire sale' of homes and price decline, and home equity loans are not common in China, both of which should limit the impact.

Other transmission channels are potentially more important when it comes to how China's property market affects the rest of the economy, including the long property supply chain, local-government finances and total banking-sector exposure.

As mentioned earlier, property construction volumes matter more than prices in China, as the sector's long supply chain is the most important transmission channel when it comes to impact on the economy. Estimates suggest that a 10 percentage-point drop in the growth of construction volumes would result in a 2.5 percentage-point drop in real GDP growth, half of that indirectly through other sectors in the supply chain. Weaker construction, for example, would mean less demand for steel, cement and construction machinery, leading to less investment in those sectors, and so on. Other closely linked sectors include furnishings, automobiles and financial and transport services. In light of this, a significant negative impact on the economy could come solely from a fall in sales and construction volumes, without necessarily a large price correction. This is perhaps why China's government has always watched property construction volumes and related heavy industry activity closely, easing property policy or embarking on infrastructure support to stabilise the economy when property construction saw a sharp fall.

Another important transmission channel is local-government finances. Land sales revenue has consistently financed about 30% of local-government spending and 'net' land sales (subtracting land-related expenses) has contributed 15–20% of China's infrastructure investment.[43] A property downturn not only reduces land revenue, but also lowers the collateral value of land and property, limiting local governments' ability to carry out infrastructural investment. That said, local governments can reduce land supply and use their influence over LGFVs to keep land prices from falling too much during a downturn. This would help stabilise expectations and the collateral value of local land and property, limiting the second-round impact of falling land prices and a credit crunch. Even so, given the importance of land to local finances, a property downturn could lead to a sharp deterioration in local-government debt sustainability, especially the ability of LGFVs to service debt.

A serious property downturn could cause significant damage to banks' balance sheets and threaten financial-system stability. At end 2021, just under 30% of total bank loans were to the property sector, including about 21% in mortgages and 6% to developers.[44] Also, banks may hold half of the bonds issued by developers and construction companies, as well as substantial shadow credit to the property sector via non-standard assets on or off-balance sheet. This means that direct bank exposure to the property sector could be equivalent to 40% of total loans. Banks also have indirect exposure through lending to the non-property sectors that are collateralised by land and property, including loans to LGFVs. Moreover, the balance sheets of some industrial companies, especially in metals and mining, would worsen significantly in a property downturn, making it difficult to service debt. All in all, the total exposure of the banking system to the property sector is substantial.

Typically, a deterioration in bank balance sheets can lead to a credit crunch, as banks rein in their loan books to preserve capital and as the loss of confidence in the banking system drains liquidity from the system. The credit and liquidity crunch would exacerbate the fall in asset prices, which would lead to additional decline in credit and economic activities – a downward spiral. This is how financial crises often play out. In the case of China, there are a few safety valves built into the system to prevent such a course of events.

First, as discussed earlier, local governments, with the help of LGFVs, SOE developers and state-owned banks, can work to prevent land prices (and indirectly, property prices) from declining sharply. This would help stabilise the collateral value of bank loans and prevent large-scale loan call-backs. Second, liquidity is unlikely to dry up, as banks do not rely heavily on the market for funding and the PBC has consistently proved ready, willing and able to provide liquidity. Third, as previous episodes of bank clean-ups have shown, regulators would allow the banks to gradually recognise and dispose of bad assets to limit any credit crunch. And lastly, with banks predominantly state owned, the government can help organise orderly debt restructuring while pressuring banks to continue lending to support the economy.

With China's property-market fundamentals having changed, a few factors could trigger a sharp correction followed by sustained weakness in the property sector. Urbanisation-related housing demand is diminishing because of the already high levels of home ownership, the mass upgrade of old housing and slowing rural–urban migration. Housing demand will also be weakened as the population peaks and the working-age population continues to decline, though the rise of single-person households will act as a demand buffer, to a certain extent.

Against this backdrop, if households reduce additional asset allocation to property because of stagnant or falling prices or better returns on alternative investments, or if a nationwide property tax is introduced, housing sales could drop significantly. Such a downturn could also be triggered by land reform that increased the effective urban land and property supply, so that prices fell substantially, or, like the ongoing downturn, triggered by the government tightening property credit and local-government finances and aggravated by an exogenous shock. The decline in property sales would then lead to a drop in construction volumes. With the changes in demand and supply fundamentals, it would become more difficult for the government to reverse the downturn and sustain long-term trend growth in the sector.

As noted, China has a few ways to limit the damage of a severe property-sector downturn and prevent it from triggering a financial crisis. However, this does not mean a sharp property dip would not cause serious damage to the economy, be it in the form of depressed economic activity, the inefficient use of resources as banks carry bad assets longer term, constraints on the PBC's ability to conduct monetary policy, or a knock to market confidence in the RMB exchange rate.

Notes

1 See China Statistics Yearbook, China Urban and Rural Construction Yearbook, various issues. Also, cumulative rural residential completion between 1995 and 2021 exceeded 21 billion square meters, some of which may have been made into 'urban' housing, as formerly rural areas were reclassified as urban areas.
2 See Ministry of Construction (1994, 2007).
3 See NPC (2011) and National Audit Office (2013).
4 See Zhang and Wang (2017b).
5 See National Bureau of Statistics (2011) and Liu et al. (2013).
6 China Statistical Yearbook, various issues (http://www.stats.gov.cn/tjsj/ndsj/).
7 See National Bureau of Statistics (2022c).
8 See National Bureau of Statistics (2022c).
9 See PBC (2020).
10 Author's estimate.
11 See PBC (2020).
12 The 2010 population census reported that 15.6% of urban housing units did not have in-house toilets, for example.
13 See Li (2020).
14 Data from the NBS census (http://www.stats.gov.cn/tjsj/pcsj/) and author's estimate.
15 See Gan (2018). The survey defines property with no one living in it at the time of polling as vacant. This includes housing that is used during weekends or when owners come back from their workplace outside of town.
16 See PBC (2020).
17 See, for example, Lam et al. (2020).
18 See National Bureau of Statistics (2021b).
19 See Wang (2011b) and Wang et al. (2022). Some estimates that use a different methodology put the share higher. See Rogoff and Yang (2021).

20 See Lou (2014).
21 See Ye and Wu (2014) and Zheng et al. (2014).
22 Not all governments do this, as some local governments in lower-tier cities increase land supply to keep costs from rising too much, so their tax revenue from industrial companies and businesses can grow.
23 Such practices happened during the 2014–2015 property downturn, as well as in early 2022, when the media reported that only SOEs bid for land at auctions during the deep property downturn.
24 See State Council (2003).
25 Policy tightening started in 2004, with stricter rules on land acquisition by developers. In 2005, preferential interest rates on mortgages were abolished and the requisite down payment was raised from 20% to 30% in some areas. The government also called for more land supply for economic housing and fewer old-town teardowns in March 2005 and tried to regulate property prices in May 2005. In 2006, the State Council reined in property trusts, required 70% of new housing to be less than 90 square meters, levied business tax and personal income tax on second-hand property sales and banned speculation by foreigners.
26 See Wen (2009).
27 The rise of wealth management products as an alternative investment channel, the increase in overseas investment opportunities, and anti-corruption policies and uncertainties related to property tax may have also contributed to property-market weakening in 2014.
28 The shanty-town monetary subsidy scheme contributed to an estimated 18–20% of total residential sales between 2015 and 2018.
29 The down payment requirement for a first mortgage was 20%, while 40% was required for a second mortgage in 2013, even after the reduction.
30 The 'three red lines', introduced in August 2020, refer to the requirements that property developers' (1) liability asset ratio excluding pre-sales receipts not be higher than 70%, (2) net liability ratio not be more than 100% of assets, and (3) cash to short-term liabilities be no less than 1. Developers that do not meet any of the three red lines are not allowed to increase interest-bearing debt, while those that meet all three can increase it by 15%. See 21st Century Business Herald (2020).
31 See Qin (2019).
32 China Statistical Yearbook, various issues (http://www.stats.gov.cn/tjsj/ndsj/).
33 Housing price/disposable income ratios in developed markets usually range between 4 and 6.
34 See Wang (2010b).
35 Author's estimate based on PBC credit data and NBS property sales data.
36 Author's estimates based on data from the US Bureau of Economic Analysis and Spanish National Statistical Institute.
37 Calculated as residential completion per person per year. For China, it is urban residential completion per urban population.
38 See National Bureau of Statistics (2022c).
39 Even in 2021, more than 40% of households' financial wealth was in the form of bank deposits with regulated deposit rates.
40 The government attempted to address this issue by forcing non-property sector SOEs to exit the property business in 2012–2013.
41 See, for example, Duca et al. (2010).
42 See Yan et al. (2020).
43 About half of land sales revenue is used to cover the cost of land acquisition and preparation, the latter including the tearing down of old construction and the installation of basic infrastructure and road connections.
44 See PBC data (2022) (http://www.pbc.gov.cn/goutongjiaoliu/113456/113469/4464086/2022013010434016509.pdf).

8 The slow move towards a consumer economy

As far back as the 19th century, the vast potential of China's consumer market had foreign companies salivating. An enterprising Englishman was famously quoted in the 1850s as saying that if he 'could add an inch of material to every Chinaman's shirt-tail, the mills of Lancashire could be kept busy for a generation'.[1] A 2005 book, *One Billion Customers*, explored the emergence of a new era of Chinese consumers.[2] In recent years before the COVID-19 pandemic, the Chinese have flocked to European and Asian cities buying luxury Swiss watches, Italian bags and French couture. It seems that Chinese consumers have finally landed on the global stage – and were missed when the COVID-19 pandemic hit international travel and purchases.

At the same time, however, China's domestic consumption seems to be lacking; excess capacity has emerged, with the country producing more than it consumes. Some prominent economists have laid part of the blame for the US subprime crisis on the Chinese consuming too little and saving too much, enabling Americans to borrow excessively.[3] China's government has been trying to rebalance the economy towards consumption over the past 15 years, while the 14th Five-Year Plan saw a new iteration of such policies in the name of 'internal circulation', placing greater emphasis on expanding domestic demand and improving supply structure and efficiency.[4]

What is China's true consumption picture? Why do the Chinese consume so little? Why is the savings rate so high? And what could drive a shift and rebalancing?

The true state of Chinese consumption

Strong growth and continued upgrades

Total consumption comprises household consumption and public consumption. The latter encompasses consumption by the government and public institutions, including public spending on healthcare and education.[5] In 2019, before the COVID-19 pandemic struck, Chinese consumption totalled USD 8 trillion, having grown by 8.6% a year in the decade before and 10% a year between 1991 and 2010 in real volume terms (the nominal

DOI: 10.4324/9781003310938-9

increases were more striking at 12% and 15% a year, respectively).
Consumption reached USD 9.3 trillion in 2021. While China's total consumption in 2019 was less than half that of the United States, it had
increased from USD 3 trillion in 2010 (and USD 770 billion in 2000).
China's USD 5 trillion increase just outpaced that of the United States (USD
4.9 trillion). In other words, China had become the world's largest growth
market for consumer goods. According to official statistics, a total of
26 million cars were sold in China in 2021, compared with 15 million in
the United States, while estimates put smartphone sales at 343 million and
147 million units, respectively.

The rapid growth in China's consumption has been driven by even faster
growth in the economy and household income. Between 1990 and 2010,
China's GDP growth averaged 10.5% in real terms and 15.5% in nominal
USD terms. As a result, China became a USD 6.1 trillion economy in 2010,
up from USD 1.2 trillion in 2000. By 2021, the size of the economy had
reached USD 17 trillion, and China's per capita GDP had risen to USD
10,550 from about USD 350 in the early 1990s and USD 4,500 in 2010.

As Chinese consumers' income has grown, their spending patterns have
changed dramatically. While consumer spending in every category has burgeoned in recent decades, the consumption of certain discretionary and luxury items has grown far faster, as more and more people have become
sufficiently well off to afford such items. One example is automobiles.
Research suggests that car ownership starts to soar when per capita GDP
reaches USD 5,000.[6] While China's per capita GDP did not reach USD 5,000
until 2011, the number of people earning more than USD 5,000 had grown

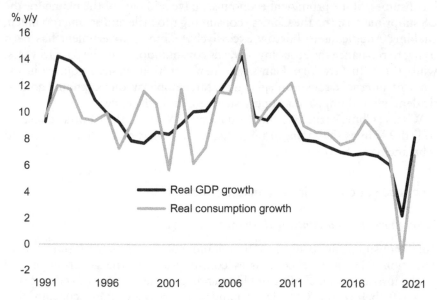

Figure 8.1 Real consumption and GDP growth, 1991–2021.

Source: NBS, author's calculations.

exponentially. As a result, China's car sales rose sharply from less than 2 million in 2000 to over 14 million in 2011 and 26 million in 2021.

The picture is similar for luxury items. While the average Chinese person cannot afford most of these things, the number of those who can has grown rapidly. Foreign consumer goods companies initially focused on selling products to people living in the four Tier 1 cities, with a combined population of more than 80 million and an average disposable income of more than USD 10,000 in 2021. Increasingly, they are now targeting Tier 2 cities, where income levels and consumption patterns may be a few years behind those in Tier 1, but there is still a combined population of about 200 million.

Consumption upgrades have been evident over the past 30 years in every income group and major consumption category, with spending on durables (especially transport and communications) and services significantly outpacing the rest of the consumption basket (Figure 8.2). For example, household consumption spending on food dropped from roughly 45% in 2000 to 38% in 2010 and 30% in 2020. Within food, spending on staples, such as grain, declined, while that on meats, dairy and fruits increased as a share of total spending, along with expenditure on dining out (until the COVID-19 pandemic).

In terms of durable goods, urban households saw the penetration of home appliances, such as colour televisions and refrigerators, rise to near saturation in the 1990s, followed by rural households 10–15 years later. Over the past decade and a half, ownership of air conditioners, computers, mobile phones and cars has increased, with urban households again leading rural residents by at least a decade. In addition to spending more on

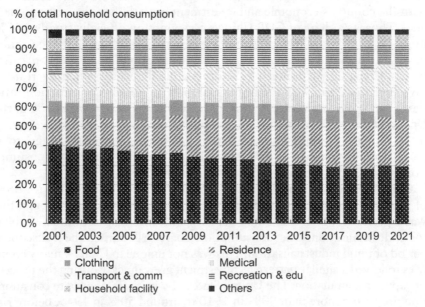

Figure 8.2 The shifting consumption pattern, 2001–2021.

Source: NBS, Author estimates.

housing services, healthcare services and leisure, more people are also trav-
elling abroad. Outbound tourism increased from USD 13 billion in 2000 to
USD 55 billion in 2010 and USD 277 billion in 2018, before the pandemic
caused travel to collapse.

E-commerce and mobile payments had already been advancing rapidly in
China, but COVID-19 significantly accelerated the pace of growth. China's
large number of mobile internet users, the high penetration of mobile payment systems,[7] its high population density[8] and cheap labour for delivery all
helped to foster stronger online sales growth than elsewhere. Online sales
grew from less than 4% of retail sales in 2010 to 21% in 2019.[9]

COVID-19 triggered a surge in e-commerce and online services usage,
including online entertainment. According to the National Statistics Bureau,
online sales accounted for almost a quarter of all goods sales in 2020. Many
people found themselves downloading online shopping apps for the first
time during pandemic lockdowns and continuing to use them after mobility
restrictions were lifted.[10] COVID-related disruptions to the labour supply in
the early days of the pandemic were also a catalyst for the increased use of
smart household appliances and heavier reliance on the internet and digital
systems.[11] The rise in the number of single-person households due to population ageing and the greater social and economic independence of women
also contributed to the trend.

Weak relative to the rest of the economy

While Chinese consumption has grown rapidly, it has been weak compared
with the country's economic and investment growth over the past two decades. Thus, as a share of GDP, China's consumption officially stood at 55%
in 2019, with household consumption less than 40% of GDP (the ratios
have since dropped as the pandemic hit consumption significantly). In other
words, China only consumed 55% of its annual output, saving the rest for
investment or a rainy day. That puts China's household consumption ratio
(less than 40%) among the lowest in the world, compared with 68% in the
United States, 60% in India, 49% in South Korea and an OECD average of
60%. China's consumption share was even more meagre a decade ago; total
consumption fell as low as 49% of GDP in 2010, with household consumption at just 34%, after a steep decline from the late 1990s.[12]

Consumption had not always been so weak. In fact, it accounted for 66%
of GDP in 1980 and household consumption about 52%, even though this
was a period in which China had kept wages low to help accumulate capital
for industrialisation. The consumption share fell during the subsequent
period of rapid industrialisation. This was not unique to China – many countries followed a similar pattern as investment grew quickly during the process
of capital accumulation. The United States saw its share of private consumption drop from more than 90% in 1910 to around 50% in 1945, before rising steadily in the subsequent decades.[13] Japan between the 1950s and 1980s
and South Korea between 1960 and the end of the 1980s also saw a steady

decline in their consumption shares.[14] India's consumption-to-GDP ratio has been falling since 1990. What is unique is that China's private consumption as a share of GDP decreased to a level not seen in any other country.

That China's household consumption rate was as low as just one-third of GDP (and remained not much above that for many years) seems incredible – and, indeed, there are reasons to believe consumption has been underestimated. One reason is that the NBS uses flawed household surveys to estimate household consumption. It has acknowledged these data issues, including the under-reporting of income and expenditure, especially among higher-income households.[15] The 'grey' economy (including unreported consulting services, some domestic help and rent-seeking transactions), is perhaps not well captured in the official statistics either,[16] though this has likely led to the underestimation of both GDP and consumption (see more discussion on data issues in the Appendix).

More importantly, housing services, especially those related to owner-occupied housing, are likely to be seriously underestimated. China's households have spent a growing amount on buying homes over the past 20 years, and housing ownership in China is more than 80% (see Chapter 7). Buying a home is not consumer spending, but investment; but a home provides services for the residents. Official statistics put housing services provided by owner-occupied housing at just 3–4% of GDP (although close to 80% of urban residents and more rural residents live in homes they own), less than half the level in most developed economies. Overall housing

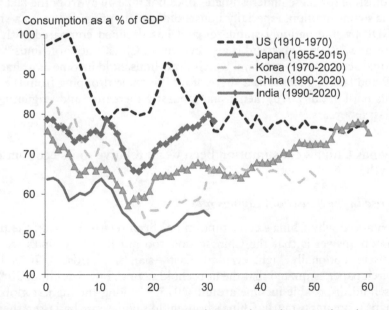

Figure 8.3 The fall in the consumption ratio during industrialisation, selected countries.

Source: US Bureau of Economic Analysis; Japan Economic and Social Research Institute; Bank of Korea; Ministry of Statistics and Programme Implementation of India; China NBS; author's estimates.

services, which also include rents and utilities, account for roughly 7% of GDP,[17] far lower than in other countries (roughly 13% in the United States and the euro area, for example).

The underestimation comes from the NBS's use of the cost of the original construction to estimate own housing services rather than imputed rents, largely because the rental market has been relatively small and prevalent mostly in bigger cities.[18] Many people also rent from the government or pay subsidised rents to SOEs (a legacy from pre-housing reform days), or, more recently, have cheap public rentals. Using alternative estimates of housing services, China's household consumption as a share of GDP would be about 5 percentage points higher than the official data suggest,[19] albeit still relatively low from a global perspective.

Consumption may have also been underestimated somewhat in recent years because certain small e-commerce retailers may not have been fully captured in retail sales data. Official retail sales data collect information directly from medium and large wholesale and retail establishments, while sales by smaller vendors are estimated using sample surveys. This means that while sales made on large internet retail outlets are included, those by small retailers, including the many individual players on Taobao (the customer-to-customer platform of Alibaba), may only be partially captured. Amid rapid online sales growth, a non-negligible share of internet sales may not be included. The rise of services relative to goods in overall consumption and in online sales may also not be fully reflected.

Adjusting for these underestimates does not take away from the fact that China's consumption, especially household consumption, is low as a share of GDP by international standards and has declined compared with the 1980s and 1990s. This trend is also evident in China's flow-of-funds[20] and national accounts income data, which show household income as a share of GDP and labour income as a share of total income dropping from the late 1990s until about 2010, then rising modestly thereafter and stagnating in the last few years.[21]

Why has China's consumption been weak relative to its economic growth?

The rise in the household savings rate

When asked why China's consumption has been relatively weak, the most common answer is that the Chinese save too much. And China's savings rate is exceptionally high, even by East Asian standards. A 2018 IMF research paper estimated that the household savings rate was about 30% of household disposable income around 2015,[22] among the highest globally. Perhaps more importantly, China's household savings rate had risen sharply over the previous 35 years, from 5% in the 1970s – the Chinese did not always save so much. This steady increase in the household savings rate is a key cause of the relative weakness in consumption.

So, what is behind the sharp rise in the household savings rate? Modigliani and Cao (2004) attribute the rise to faster economic growth and changing demographics, the latter leading to an increase in the ratio of employment to total population and undermining the traditional role of family in providing old-age support.[23] As discussed in Chapters 1 and 2, China's population control policies from the mid-1970s drove down the dependency ratio – the ratio of the young and old relative to the working population – in the 1980s and 1990s. With fewer children, families needed to spend less on food and education and could save more. At the same time, people needed to save more to prepare for old age; family transfers had been the main source of old-age income prior to this, especially in rural areas. Zhang et al. (2018) found that demographic shifts accounted for about half the increase in China's household savings, making it the most important factor.

The breakdown of the social safety net in the early stages of China's economic transition to a market economy also led to a rise in precautionary saving. With the de-collectivisation of agriculture in the early 1980s, basic rural healthcare under the Cooperative Medical Scheme, which had covered most of the rural population, also collapsed. In urban areas, SOE reform in the late 1990s did away with the lifetime employment and pension 'iron rice bowl' (see Chapter 3). More than 30 million workers from SOEs and collectively owned enterprises were laid off, with little pension or social safety net, while those still employed could no longer expect the same job or pension security as before, and had to pay more out of the pocket for healthcare.[24]

The latter helps to explain the notable increase in the household savings rate from about 20% in the mid-1990s to 25% a few years later. However, social safety-net issues cannot really explain the further increase in the household savings rate from the mid-2000s, as the government had started to establish and enhance social security from that point, with both pension and health insurance covering most urban and rural residents.

The worsening of income inequality in the 1990s and 2000s also probably contributed to the rise in the household savings rate during that time. According to the World Bank, China's Gini coefficient, which measures income inequality, rose from 0.32 in 1990 to 0.44 in 2010 (and has since moderated somewhat), while China's official estimate of the Gini coefficient peaked at around 0.49 in 2008–2009.[25] Piketty et al. (2017) also showed that while the top 10%'s share of income rose from 27% to 41% between 1978 and 2015 in China, the bottom 50%'s share declined from 27% to 15%. Higher-income people have a higher propensity to save, while the poor tend to consume a bigger share of their income – as data from the Chinese Household Income Project shows, with the top earners saving about 50% of their income.[26]

In addition, the inadequate development of a consumer credit market until recently may have contributed to the high savings rate. There are also hypotheses that China's low interest rates and high housing prices may have added to the rise in the household savings rate, though empirical evidence has been mixed.[27]

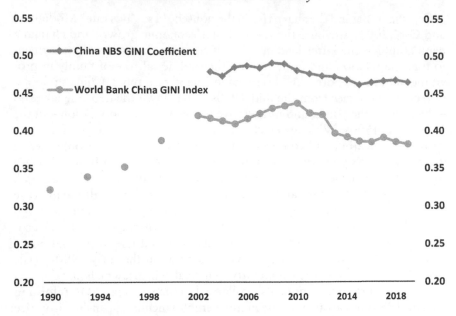

Figure 8.4 China's Gini coefficient, 1990–2019.

Source: World Bank, NBS, Author estimates.

The relative decline of household income and the rise of corporate savings

The high and rising household savings rate was not the only reason why the consumption share dropped from the late 1990s to 2010. Standard economic theory suggests that income is the most important determinant of consumption. It is, therefore, not surprising that during this period, household income as a share of national income also declined sharply. According to the NBS's national accounts income data, household disposable income fell from nearly 70% of GDP in 1998 to just below 60% in 2008. The decline was driven by a 10 percentage-point drop in the share of labour income – the most important component of household income – during that period.[28] The household income share has gradually increased since 2010, though it is still about 5 percentage points lower now than it was in the late 1990s.

Why did the share of labour income decline significantly between the late 1990s and 2008? The SOE reform of the late 1990s led to a large drop in urban employment and social benefits, but the one-off adjustment does not explain the decade-long income decline. The more likely reason is the capital-intensive growth model the government was pursuing at the time – with increased capital input leading to higher capital income relative to labour. Research finds that growth from the mid-1990s was predominantly driven by capital accumulation in the industrial sector while the shift in labour to higher-productivity sectors slowed sharply.[29]

Industry-heavy, capital-intensive growth during that period was not only helped by the property boom, but also amplified by various government policies and institutional factors. Local governments favoured industry and investment over services and consumption, partly because local officials advanced through the ranks on the former, and because tax revenues came mainly from industrial production.[30] Banks favoured lending for investment in industry and infrastructure, particularly to large enterprises and SOEs.[31] Meanwhile, services-sector development suffered from tight restrictions and regulation.[32] In addition, the movement of labour and, hence, urban employment growth were inhibited by *hukou*-related restrictions and discrimination, as well as non-portable labour and social benefits across the country (see Chapter 6).[33]

The factors underlying the drop in China's labour income share during the 2000s also help explain the increase in the corporate savings rate. China's corporate savings rate was roughly on a par with the household savings rate in the early 2000s, bringing the national savings rate to as high as 50% at the time.[34] The rise of the more profitable private sector and the increased profitability of SOEs following the late 1990s restructuring (Chapter 3) helped to boost corporate savings in the early 2000s. Moreover, the absence of dividend payments for SOEs and the national growth strategy favouring industry and investment lifted both corporate investment and savings at the same time.

As capital input rose with investment, total returns on capital also increased and were retained for investment in industrial capacity. These mutually reinforcing developments helped China to rapidly build up capital stock and expand industrial capacity, driving a period of fast economic growth (averaging 10.2% a year between 1998 and 2008). The capacity expansion also helped China to increase its non-processing exports and reduce its net imports of metals and machinery. Corporate investment is a form of saving from a macroeconomic perspective – it is output that is not consumed in the current period. Moreover, high total corporate earnings helped to lower the net borrowing of the corporate sector; leverage actually declined during this high-investment period. Between 1998 and 2008, the corporate savings rate increased by about 10 percentage points, reaching 23% of GDP,[35] while China's overall national savings rate reached 50% of GDP in 2008.

The corporate savings rate only started to decline after the global financial crisis, partly as China tried to move away from the investment-driven growth model. The government reduced energy subsidies, required SOEs to pay dividends, tightened environmental rules, increased the minimum wage and fostered services development.

Why and how should China boost consumption?

Why should China worry about the relative weakness of consumption if it has been growing rapidly, especially as history shows that the consumption share usually declines during rapid capital accumulation and then recovers?

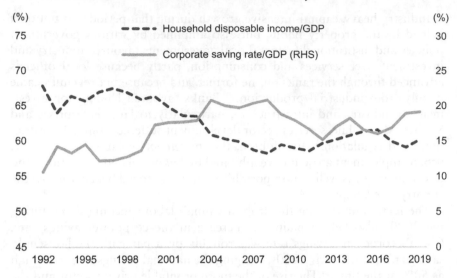

Figure 8.5 The household income share and the corporate saving rate, 1992–2019.

Source: NBS, author's estimates.

Well, because an exceptionally low share of consumption over a prolonged period can endanger economic sustainability, create structural imbalances and threaten social stability.

Investment growing faster than consumption and GDP could cause production capacity to expand faster than domestic absorption, requiring greater foreign absorption through exports. Indeed, rapid expansion in China's current-account surplus in the 2000s coincided with a climb in the national savings rate (Figure 8.6). This is to be expected: basic macroeconomic theory suggests that a country's domestic savings-investment balance is the flip side of its external balance. However, the persistent expansion of exports and the current-account surplus had become increasingly challenging after the global financial crisis and as China's share of global exports reached a high level (15%). The backlash against globalisation and protectionism against Chinese exports has been growing ever since in some major markets.

Moreover, too much investment results in excess capacity when output is not absorbed by consumption or exports, making investment wasteful. Even infrastructure investment, which improves the efficiency and productivity of the productive capital stock, could be wasted. This means that some investments would not lead to an increase in the productive capital stock, even though they contributed to GDP growth at the time, meaning future growth would require ever more investment. This is not sustainable. Excess capacity and wasteful investment also mean no return on those investments, leading to the accumulation of bad assets.

What's more, a low consumption share also means that the household sector is not sharing the fruits of growth as much as it should, while low

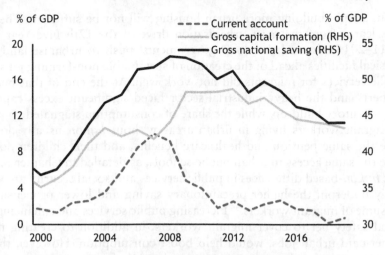

Figure 8.6 Savings, investment and the current-account surplus.
Source: NBS, author's estimates.

household income relative to capital income exacerbates income distribution problems. Both could worsen social stability.

No magic turning point for consumption

For some time, there was a belief that when a country reached the midpoint of the middle-income phase, with per capita income of USD 4000–5000, consumption would take off, as people would become 'consumers'. However, international experience shows that there is no clear income level that prompts consumption to rise as a share of GDP. China's own experience also refutes this notion. What does change after income reaches a certain level is, perhaps, the types of products and services that households consume.

Another common belief is that, as an average Chinese urban resident spends 2.9 times as much as an average rural resident, speeding up urbanisation could boost consumption growth. Many have proposed upping the pace of urbanisation by accelerating the construction of urban centres, reforming the *hukou* system so migrant workers can become official urban residents, and moving suburban farmers into urban-type living arrangements.

An average urban resident earns 2.5 times as much as an average rural resident and has three times the disposable income (Chapter 6). The urban–rural income difference explains more than 90% of the spending gap, even though urban residents tend to have a higher savings rate. If a rural resident can earn more income, be it through farming or non-farming work, their consumption will increase too. Urbanisation can help boost consumption growth to the extent that it creates more long-term non-farming jobs that pay more.

But simply building more urban housing will not be sufficient. The lessons learnt from the mass urbanisation drive of the 12th Five-Year Plan (2011–2015) showed that local governments' push to urbanise land and physical facilities ahead of the creation of sustainable non-farming jobs and public services for migrants did not work well. At the end of that period, property and the heavy industrial sector faced significant excess capacity and inventory build-up, while the share of consumption stagnated.

Migrant workers living in urban areas without *hukou* usually do not have the same pension and healthcare benefits, and their children do not have the same access to urban public schools, as detailed in Chapter 6. The vast *hukou*-based differences in public services and social security are what really underpin the higher precautionary saving and lower propensity to consume of migrant workers.[36] Increasing public services and enhancing the social safety net to cover migrant workers, in addition to creating more higher-paid urban jobs, would help boost consumption. However, this is not as simple as changing migrant workers' *hukou* status, as it would require more spending from national and local government, which, in turn, would require public spending reform.

Policy plans to promote consumption

China has recognised that it has an unbalanced economy and announced various policy plans to boost consumption over the past decade. To an extent, this transition has already started, albeit at a very gradual pace. The official (underestimated) consumption share of GDP rose from 49% in 2011 to 56% in 2019. It declined to 52% in 2021, however, and weakened further in 2022 as the COVID-19 pandemic and related restrictions hit consumption hard and the government opted to support businesses through tax cuts in the hope of limiting job losses, rather than subsidising consumers directly.

Given the aforementioned factors underlying the country's relatively weak consumption, policies supporting sustainable consumption growth should include those that boost household income, especially labour income; lower the household savings rate, especially precautionary savings; reduce income inequality; and reduce the corporate savings rate. In sum, China needs policies that facilitate a change in the growth model and enhance the government's role in public services and social welfare.

Increasing household income

Since the 18th Party Congress in 2012, the government has promoted the theme of 'common prosperity', and both the 13th and 14th Five-Year Plans called for policies to support household income growth, especially labour-income growth. To this end, the government encouraged the development of labour-intensive service industries and small- and micro-sized enterprises. Policy measures included tax reductions for small companies, easier credit access, and a reduction in red tape related to starting a business or making an investment.[37] Business registrations increased and the World Bank's ease of doing business index improved.[38] Nevertheless, other restrictions and practices may be denting the effectiveness of some of the policies.[39]

Other policy initiatives to increase labour income were to enable faster wage growth and increase labour protection. The minimum wage was increased by an average 13% a year in the 2011–2015 period, after which the adjustment was suspended or left at local governments' discretion. In 2019, in the midst of the downturn, government efforts to compel private companies to boost compliance with social-security contributions were met with resistance, leading to a watering down of the policy and cuts in the official corporate contribution rate.[40] Stipulations in China's labour law about worker compensation and benefits, as well as working hours, have not been well enforced, although there now seems to be a greater intent to implement some of these rules, at least among internet-based companies, where non-compliance with rules has been more visible.

The government has also wanted to support growth in other income for households, especially from property. However, attempts to boost the wealth management market have had mixed success, as many earlier wealth management products gave false guarantees while investing in high-risk trust products, endangering financial stability.[41] Returns on wealth management products have come down since new asset-management rules were put in place in 2018, while negative economic shocks since then have also kept interest rates on households' savings deposits low. Attempts to reform rural land policy to give a higher share of land valuation gains to farmers have progressed slowly as well.

Lowering the household savings rate

China's household savings rate should theoretically moderate along with the ageing population, as the rising old-age dependency ratio reduces the employed population as a share of the total. East Asian economies such as Japan and Korea experienced a notable decline in the household savings rate as their populations aged and economic development reached a certain level.[42] However, the rise in the dependency ratio alone may only prompt a very slow drop in the savings rate, as evidenced in China over the past decade.

An inadequate public pension system may accentuate the desire to save more for the future.[43] Therefore, it is still important to reduce the household savings rate by enhancing social security and reforming public finances and services to help reduce inequality, as well as to increase support for the poor. China's stronger emphasis on 'common prosperity' since 2021 suggests that the government plans to redouble its efforts along these lines while regulating monopoly income.

China has made notable progress on improving the social welfare system since the late 2000s. Since the government introduced a rudimentary rural pension plan in 2009 and a basic urban resident pension plan in 2011, overall pension coverage has increased significantly, covering 1.03 billion people as of the end of 2021. The next step in the government's plan is to coordinate the rural and urban pension plans and make them more portable between regions. Basic health insurance coverage has also increased to 1.36 billion people and benefit levels are to be increased during the 14th Five-Year Plan. Spending on public services increased from 7.4% of GDP in 2010 to 9.8% in 2020, and there is an ongoing initiative to increase the role of the state in providing basic education, healthcare and social housing.

On social housing, the government has helped to provide more than 60 million units of shantytown replacement housing over the past decade through renovation, construction and subsidies, and it plans to build more public rentals going forward. China has also made inroads into *hukou* reform, with about 100 million people obtaining urban *hukou* between 2016 and 2020. *Hukou* rules are also being relaxed in cities with fewer than 3 million people. However, as we discussed in Chapter 6, despite progress, millions of migrants are still facing fundamentally unequal treatment in cities where they live and work, and do not have full access to public services and social protection. In addition, the government needs to significantly increase public services in rural areas to help reduce the urban–rural gap.

Improving income distribution

Various recent government documents have mentioned improving income redistribution to help reduce inequality,[44] inevitably leading to questions about potential tax increases and other forms of redistribution. As China's personal income tax system has a narrow tax base with a limited re-distributional function, it is reasonable to expect some gradual changes. As discussed in earlier chapters, China's tax system relies heavily on taxes collected from businesses, while personal income tax accounted for just 8% of total tax revenue and 1% of GDP in 2021.

Although China has made several amendments in recent years, personal income tax remains largely a salary or labour income tax. The marginal income-tax rate is relatively high, at 45%, but certain in-kind compensation elements are not taxed. In addition, capital gains, dividends, property income and other personal income are either not taxed or taxed at far lower rates.[45] As a result, less than 10% of the population pays income tax, according to estimates,[46] while most of the wealthy are not subject to income tax at all. Over time, more incomes are likely to become taxable, while more family expenditures will be deductible. Efforts to reduce the tax evasion of high-profile, high-income earners are likely to increase too. Nevertheless, expanding personal income-tax coverage is likely to face strong public resistance and be implemented very gradually.

Lowering the corporate savings rate

As the high corporate savings rate and policies that amplified the invest-ment-led growth model were key reasons for China's high national savings rate and relatively low household income share, they had to be changed to boost consumption. To this end, over the past decade, China has reduced energy subsidies to heavy industry, tightened environmental rules and enforcement, increased SOE dividend payments and transferred some SOE stakes to the national pension fund.

However, it is still common for the government to reduce electricity costs or provide subsidies in times of economic downturn.[47] Most SOE dividends are still paid to a central SOE operating budget rather than redistributed to the household sector or used by the government to increase public spending on social security. Moreover, tax and public-finance reforms to steer local governments' focus away from investment and land sales and more towards providing public services have progressed very slowly.

Do Chinese households have too much debt?

In developing countries, an underdeveloped credit market often constrains household consumption, as households are unable to smooth savings and consumption over the lifecycle.[48] Naturally, developing a consumer credit market was deemed a positive step in supporting consumption.[49] However, over the past decade, China's household debt has surged and there have been reports suggesting that many young people in large cities are already carrying large debt burdens. Have Chinese households already accumulated so much debt that it could constrain their future ability to consume?

China's household debt rose from 27% of GDP at end 2010 to 62% as of end 2021, largely due to a sharp increase in mortgage borrowing (and rising property prices). That debt ratio does not look excessive by global standards, compared with 57% in Japan, 58% in the euro area, 79% in the United States and 94% in South Korea. However, as a share of disposable income, China's household debt is already quite high.

If we assume that all household debt is borrowed by urban residents and use income data from the household survey, China's debt-to-disposable income ratio was about 120% at end 2021. If we assume half of rural resi-dents also have access to consumer loans, this ratio drops to about 106%, while debt-to-total household disposable income is over 95%.[50] While China's household debt-to-disposable income ratio is lower than that of the United Kingdom (134% in 2021) and Korea (188% at end 2020), it is similar to that of Japan (108%) and the euro area (108%) and higher than that of the United States (93%).

The results of multiple UBS Evidence Lab China online lending surveys since 2017[51] show that the availability and high penetration of online lend-ing have been an important reason for the rapid increase in consumer credit since 2015, although many of the borrowers also had sizable savings. The

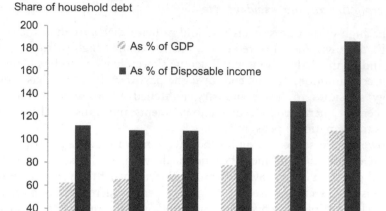

Share of household debt

Figure 8.7 International comparison of household leverage, 2020.

Source: NBS; Bank of Japan; Office of National Statistics; Eurostat; Federal Reserve Board; author's estimates.

Note: Data for China are for 2021.

median debt payment-to-income ratio across surveyed respondents averaged in the mid-teens in the 2018–2020 surveys,[52] comparable to that of the United States. Although borrowers' outstanding debt mainly consisted of mortgages and was not that high, their monthly payment ratio was high relative to monthly income, and mostly owed to online creditors.

Furthermore, low-income borrowers and those who use multiple platforms to borrow cash loans were most at risk of being unable to service debt should there be a sudden income shock. This was perhaps one reason why the government started to tighten regulations on internet consumer lending supervision in late 2017. Although mortgages remain the biggest part of outstanding household debt in China, the surveys found that, on average, around a quarter of mortgage borrowers' monthly income was used to service it. The average loan-to-value ratio of existing mortgages is estimated at about 30%.[53]

Can consumption be China's growth engine?

Economists and China observers generally agree that Chinese investment will inevitably slow in the coming years. There had been hope that with the right kind of policies, implemented effectively, China could move to a more consumption-oriented economy, where consumption drove up economic growth in place of investment. Unfortunately, this is not particularly realistic.

When it comes to long-term growth drivers, economists look at production factors – capital, labour, other resources and, of course, the way these production factors are put together – what is called total factor productivity (TFP). Productive capacity is accumulated by investing in physical and human capital, in technology, in institutions that can help improve the efficiency with which capital and labour (and other factors) are put together. In other words, investment in physical capital or areas that help to improve productivity, technological breakthroughs and institutional changes that can improve overall productivity are the long-term drivers of growth, not consumption. Indeed, countries that have seen a rise in consumption as a share of GDP have tended to experience slower investment and GDP growth during the same period.

Of course, as mentioned, too much investment can be wasteful and growth cannot be sustained. Therefore, striking a balance between investment and consumption is important, as consumption helps to ensure that output is absorbed, investment realises its value and there is no systematic excess capacity. Put another way, increasing consumption can help ensure more sustainable growth in China, but not necessarily a faster growth rate, which must come from the more efficient allocation of resources through structural reform and innovation. As China's long-term trend growth slows, and as most China watchers predict, consumption growth will also slow, even as it rises as a share of GDP.

Although rebalancing China's economy towards consumption is unlikely to drive faster growth, it will still have important implications for the rest of the world. Over the coming decade, China is likely to be the largest contributor to global consumption growth. With consumption outpacing investment, China's import demand for commodities will slow or decline, which could, depending on developments on the supply side, lead to a reversal of the worsening of its terms of trade (and those of many other non-commodity exporters). The slower growth in China's production capacity relative to domestic absorption could lead to slower exports, or import substitution, which could result in a smaller trade surplus. And as the current-account surplus declines and households diversify some of their assets overseas, China may see its foreign-exchange reserves stop growing or even decline.

Notes

1 See The Economist (2011).
2 See McGregor (2005).
3 See Bernanke (2005) and Bernanke et al. (2011).
4 See the Government of the PRC (2021).
5 See National Bureau of Statistics (2019b).
6 See Wu et al. (2014).
7 According to China Internet Network Information Centre (2021), China had 1.01 billion internet users, 1 billion of which were mobile internet users as of June 2021. Mobile payment system users reached 872 million in June 2021. The digital payment share rose from 72.5% at end 2018 to 86.4% at end 2020.

8 China's official population density is only 153 per square kilometre, significantly lower than South Korea's 511 and United Kingdom's 278. However, about 70% of China's population lives in areas where the population density is more than 700 people per square kilometre. See Liu et al. (2010).

9 See Ministry of Commerce (2019).

10 See Wang et al. (2020).

11 COVID-19 led to a sharp increase in the adoption of a combined online-offline hybrid model. Digital grocery penetration (online sales) received an outsized boost as the consumption of staples and daily necessities shifted online.

12 See China Statistics Yearbook, 1999–2010. http://www.stats.gov.cn/tjsj/ndsj/.

13 According to data from the US bureau of economic analysis.

14 Data from the CEIC.

15 See Shi (2010).

16 See Wang (2010b).

17 Based on official national accounts data for 2011. Detailed data on different consumption categories have not been released since, but no apparent change in statistical methods has been observed or announced.

18 See National Bureau of Statistics (2022a).

19 See Wang et al. (2012) and Cai (2014).

20 The flow-of-funds accounts show the sources and uses of financial resources for households, enterprises, the government and rest of the world, through which we can discern the production and distribution of income by these sectors.

21 Data from China Statistical Yearbook, 1999–2021. http://www.stats.gov.cn/tjsj/ndsj/

22 See Zhang et al. (2018).

23 Wei and Zhang (2011) suggest that the male-female imbalance, a by-product of China's one-child policy, also contributes to household saving behaviour.

24 See He et al. (2018).

25 Data from World Economic Indicators, the World Bank and the National Bureau of Statistics.

26 See China Household Income Project (http://www.ciidbnu.org/chip/index.asp?lang=CN) and Yang et al. (2011).

27 See Chamon and Prasad (2010) and Zhang et al. (2018).

28 See China Statistical Yearbook, various editions. Income breakdown by labour and capital is only available at the provincial level, so the national-level labour income data are a summation of provincial data. There was a structural break in the data in 2008, so the author adjusted data before and after that year to make them consistent.

29 See Kuijs and Wang (2006).

30 The government promoted industrialisation by keeping the prices of energy, electricity, utilities and land low and by not strictly enforcing environmental regulations at local level (see Chapters 6 and 10).

31 PBC research (Liu, 2005a) described how banks' lending policy made it extremely difficult for small and medium-sized enterprises, especially those in the services industry, which do not have much real estate or plant/machinery to serve as collateral.

32 See World Bank (2003).

33 See Whalley and Zhang (2004).

34 See Kuijs (2005).

35 Estimates from China's flow-of-funds data.

36 See Chen (2018).

37 China cut tax for SMEs multiple times between 2016 and 2020, followed by additional tax waivers and cuts in 2021–2022 in response to the COVID-19 pandemic. The PBC used on-lending facilities and targeted RRR cuts to encourage banks to increase lending to SMEs, while the CBIRC set a floor on bank lending

to SMEs at low interest rates. The administrative reforms since 2013 also abolished hundreds of approvals and procedures (Chapter 10).

38 World Bank Indicators (2020).
39 For example, bank lending typical relies on collateral, which does not bode well for small services businesses; private companies may face implicit entry barriers or discrimination in certain sectors; and, in 2021, the government tightened regulations on private businesses in education, healthcare and cultural areas.
40 See State Tax Administration (2019a).
41 See Wang et al. (2017c).
42 Japan's household savings rate peaked in 1974 at about 25% and fell to about 10% in the subsequent two decades. It has been almost zero in recent years. Korea's household savings peaked in the early 1990s at about 27% and fell sharply after the Asian financial crisis, before recovering somewhat.
43 See Wang and Mason (2004).
44 See the 14th Five-Year Plan, for example (see Government of the PRC, 2021).
45 Rural income is also not subject to personal income tax, as there were separate agricultural taxes that every farmer had to pay, though the major agricultural tax was abolished in 2006.
46 Author's estimate based on official press release. http://www.npc.gov.cn/npc/c13335/201809/cb86a8a6ae4b498993c211eb9acb0c3b.shtml.
47 For example, China lowered electricity tariffs by 10% in 2020 to help the corporate sector to cut operational costs.
48 See Morduch (1995).
49 See China Banking Regulatory Commission (2016) and Zhou (2016).
50 Excluding 'operating loans', which are mostly business loans to individually owned businesses from household debt, the debt-to-disposable income ratio would drop by about 25 percentage points.
51 The UBS Evidence Lab has conducted China online lending surveys each year since 2017, with each survey receiving more than 1500 online responses from dozens of cities across the country. See Yan et al. (2021) and Wang et al. (2021).
52 See Wang et al. (2021).
53 The loan-to-value ratio of new mortgages, as proxied by the ratio of flow of mortgage loans to the sales value of property each year, is estimated have come down from about 60% in mid-2016 to below 30% in 2021.

9 How serious is the debt problem?

How much debt does China have and where is it?

In the past decade, economists and investors have become increasingly concerned about China's rising debt levels and the potential for a debt crisis. China's government embarked on a deleveraging campaign in 2017 and has maintained debt control as one of its top policy priorities. So, how much debt does China have?

A country's total debt typically refers to the combined debt of the non-financial sector, namely, the government, household and corporate sectors, and does not include the debt of the financial sector. Estimates of China's total debt level vary, often due to different estimates of shadow credit. The Bank for International Settlements (BIS) estimated China's total credit to the non-financial sector at 290% of GDP in 2020 (up from 263% in 2019), while the IMF put it at 278%.[1] China's National Institution for Finance and Development (NIFD), a think tank of the Chinese Academy of Social Science, estimated that total debt rose from 247% of GDP in 2019 to 270% at end 2020.[2]

By any estimate, China has one of the highest debt-to-GDP ratios in the world. Using the BIS figure to facilitate international comparison, China's debt ratio of 290% of GDP at end 2020 exceeds other emerging-market economies at a similar level of development, such as Brazil (189%), Chile (202%), Mexico (87%) and Malaysia (212%). China's debt ratio is also higher than that of many developed economies (including South Korea (258%)), and on par with that of the United States (296%).

China's total non-financial-sector debt declined from an estimated 296% of GDP in 2020 to 287% in 2021.[3] This estimate includes bank loans, corporate and government bonds, external debt, shadow credit included and not included in official TSF, and cumulative debt written off by banks in recent years. Of that, government debt accounted for roughly 84% of GDP, household debt about 62% and corporate debt about 140%.

Here, government debt includes both explicit central and local-government bonds, most bonds issued by local-government platforms (LGFVs), quasi-fiscal financing through corporate balance sheets, the debt of the national railway corporation and the legacy bad debt of the banking system

DOI: 10.4324/9781003310938-10

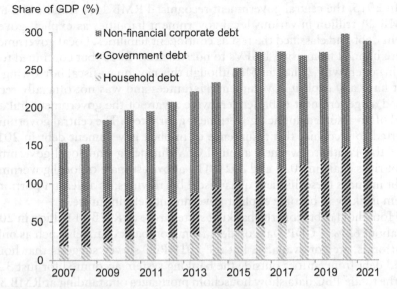

Share of GDP (%)

Figure 9.1 Estimated total debt by sector, 2007–2021.

Source: PBC, Ministry of Finance, author's estimates.

that was taken over by China's AMCs (see Chapter 3). Household debt includes banking-sector debt to households, but not most of the recent debt taken out through internet finance channels, such as cash loans or instalment loans provided by e-commerce companies. Corporate-sector debt includes credit from bank and non-bank financial institutions (NBFIs), but not all intra-corporate credit and not the quasi-fiscal debt issued by corporate entities that is counted in government debt.

China's corporate debt is also among the highest in the world and dominated by the debt of SOEs. As a share of GDP, the BIS estimates that China's corporate debt was 161% at end 2020 (though this includes some *de facto* local government debt included in our estimate of total government debt). This is significantly higher than the 114% of the eurozone, 85% of the United States, 116% of Japan and 110% of South Korea. While there is no official breakdown of SOE and non-SOE debt, estimates put SOE-related debt at about 60% or two-thirds of the total, equivalent to 100–110% of GDP, based on data on SOE liabilities and bank lending to enterprises by ownership.[4]

China's total government debt reached an estimated RMB 96 trillion in 2021, up from about RMB 15 trillion in 2008.[5] This includes about RMB 23 trillion in central government bonds, RMB 30 trillion in local-government bonds and RMB 6 trillion in railway corporation bonds (which is not officially included in government debt). The rest is made up of contingent or quasi-fiscal liabilities that have not been recognised by the government. Recall that China's local governments were officially not allowed to borrow before 2015, but did so through investment companies or LGFVs.

In 2015, the central government recognised RMB 15.4 trillion of a total RMB 24 trillion in various local-government liabilities as explicit government debt and classified the rest as contingent liabilities. Local governments were banned from using LGFVs to borrow from 2015, but continued to do so in covert ways (Chapter 5). Although this new quasi-fiscal borrowing did not have any explicit government guarantees and was not officially recognised as government debt, lenders were aware of the government linkages and often assumed implicit government guarantees. The central government started to recognise this resurgence of implicit government debt in 2018,[6] and the Politburo warned about LGFV financing and local-government debt risks again in 2020 and 2021. The above estimate of local government debt includes these 'hidden' quasi-fiscal borrowings, as at least a portion of them is likely to become explicit government debt in future.

Household debt from the banking system rose to RMB 71 trillion in 2021, or about 62% of GDP. Data on debt from non-bank channels, such as online platforms, are not available, but the 2019 PBC survey suggests that household debt from entities outside the banking system accounted for just 3.2% of the total.[7] PBC data show household mortgages outstanding at RMB 38.3 trillion at end 2021, though some household 'operational' loans and other consumer credit may also be linked to property. The second-largest category of household debt is household operational lending, which largely comprises loans to individually owned small businesses and farmers. Car loans, credit-card debt and other consumer credit make up the rest. Household borrowing from banks that was 'facilitated' by internet platforms should already be included in the statistics, as banks would record this funding as consumer loans, though internet lending outside of the banking system is not.

Why has China's debt risen so much?

From a position of very little debt 40 years ago, China has become one of the most indebted countries globally. Debt accumulation has been particularly rapid since the global financial crisis, with the debt-to-GDP ratio almost doubling during that period. How come?

China's investment-driven growth model over much of the past few decades has been a major reason for the debt accumulation. After China shifted SOE funding from government allocation to bank lending in the 1980s, the credit-fuelled, investment-driven growth model quickly took shape. The slow establishment of proper prudential rules in the financial sector and rampant soft budgetary constraints in the SOE sector helped to fuel credit growth in the 1980s and the mid-1990s (Chapter 3). This fast debt growth powered fixed-asset investment growth of 22% a year between 1984 and 1996. By the end of the 1990s, corporate loans stood close to 100% of GDP, based on estimates from PBC data. China was able to stabilise and reduce its debt-to-GDP ratio between 2003 and 2008 after lengthy SOE and bank restructuring, but then the global financial crisis unleashed another period of debt-driven investment growth. Corporate debt rose from

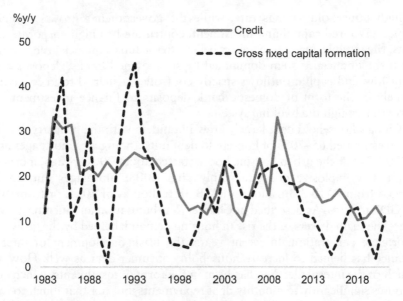

Figure 9.2 Credit and investment growth, 1983–2021.

Source: NBS, PBC, author's estimates.

Note: Credit growth is proxied by loan growth prior to 2002 and total social financing thereafter.

87% of GDP in 2008 to 160% in 2016, while fixed-asset investment rose by 12% a year.[8]

China's investment-driven growth model has also been fuelled by the increase in government debt, especially since the global financial crisis. Estimated overall local-government debt rose from just over 21% in 2007 to 40% in 2015 and 57% in 2021.[9] Local governments had a long history of using provincial or city-level state-owned investment companies to borrow and invest. Such borrowing was not officially considered government debt, but lenders often treated it as such. Meanwhile, as related investments were funded by credit rather than the budget, they received less scrutiny from the government.

After the global financial crisis, China encouraged local governments to establish LGFVs to borrow and support growth. LGFVs carried out government-mandated projects and engaged in property and infrastructure investments. Although the central government started to restrict bank lending to LGFVs in 2010, shadow bank credit, such as trusts and LGFV bonds, rose sharply in its place. After commercial LGFVs were barred from taking on debt on governments' behalf in 2015, new and more hidden local-government liabilities increased through public-private-partnership schemes, credit from policy banks and LGFV bonds.

China's high savings rate and financial repression helped to sustain this debt-financed growth pattern. As explained in Chapter 8, the sharp decline in the dependency ratio from 1980 to 2010, the lack of a widespread social safety net and skewed income distribution led to the increase and sustained a high household savings rate, while the government's growth policies, which favoured capital and investment, contributed to high corporate savings. Meanwhile, many researchers believe that China's financial repression – with the financial system dominated by state-owned banks, deposits rates kept low and capital outflows strictly controlled – helped to keep savings largely in the form of domestic bank deposits to finance investment and growth through the banking system.[10]

China's household debt largely grew in tandem with the property market, as an estimated 65–70% of household debt outstanding was mortgages as of 2020.[11] While the urban housing boom started about 20 years ago, mortgage loans saw explosive growth, mainly after 2008; mortgages outstanding surged from RMB 3.3 trillion to RMB 38 trillion as of 2021, or from 10% of GDP to 37%. As described in Chapter 7, urbanisation and income growth were the main drivers of the rise in housing demand, helped by the growth in mortgage penetration. In recent years, the brisk development of internet finance has helped to increase household consumer debt as well. However, much of the internet lending has been in the form of instalments, which contributes significantly to monthly debt repayments, but not that much to total debt outstanding. Since 2019, tighter regulation of peer-to-peer (P2P) and internet lending has led to a slowdown in internet consumer credit growth.

The rise and containment of shadow credit

The development of shadow credit over the past decade, especially that involving mainstream financial institutions, has played a significant role in China's debt accumulation. According to the BIS, the shadow banking system 'can be broadly defined as the system of credit intermediation that involves entities and activities outside the regular banking system'.[12] This includes credit activities by NBFIs, as well as the off-balance-sheet activities of banks, including corporate bonds and bills. In other words, it is a very broad set of financial intermediation activities that are very different to what people usually understand as 'informal', or underground lending.

China initially allowed – and at times encouraged – shadow credit growth to help create alternative channels of financing for private companies, especially SMEs. While this may have happened to some extent, shadow credit over the past decade has mainly allowed debt to companies and local governments to continue growing in the face of general credit tightening, or attempts by the government to control credit to excess-capacity sectors, the property sector and local governments (Chapter 5).

Before these broadly defined shadow banking activities took off, China's most famous informal lending market was in Wenzhou, a municipality in the coastal province of Zhejiang, known for its tens of thousands of small and medium-sized private companies, which rely heavily on an active informal lending market, as well as speculative investment in property markets everywhere and the latest, most fashionable assets. A 2011 PBC survey showed that almost 90% of households and 60% of firms in Wenzhou participated in the informal private lending market, and that the size of this informal lending was 20% of formal bank lending, or about RMB 110 billion as of June 2011.[13] Many thought it could be significantly larger.[14] Nationwide, the size of informal lending around 2011 was estimated to be about RMB 3–4 trillion, or about 5–7% of total bank lending.[15] The informal lending markets in Wenzhou and elsewhere saw rapid growth around 2010–2011, when the government tightened formal bank lending. Informal market interest rates also shot up at the time to 20–40%, with most of the funding channelled into the property sector or other short-term lending.[16]

It was around 2010–2011 when broad shadow banking started to take off. As banks faced credit-quota constraints and rising reserve requirements, while demand for credit remained very strong, off-balance-sheet lending by banks and credit intermediation by NBFIs (including trust companies), rose sharply. Banks off-balance-sheet credit was estimated to be roughly RMB 12 trillion in mid-2011, compared with RMB 56 trillion in total banking-sector loans.

Between 2011 and 2016, although the government tightened rules on some shadow credit products, banks' off-balance-sheet intermediation ballooned. Various channels were created or used to facilitate banks' shadow credit activity, including wealth management products, trusts, and products of security firms and asset management companies. As a result, shadow credit swelled from about RMB 14 trillion in 2010 to RMB 58 trillion in 2016,[17] including corporate bonds, banks' off-balance-sheet assets (such as commercial bills, trust and entrust loans),[18] and securities companies' asset management businesses,[19] some of which were not covered by official TSF. Shadow credit accounted for about one-third of China's total credit at end 2016, up from just 10% in 2006, and stood at around 80–90% of GDP.[20] The expansion of shadow credit helped finance the continued debt expansion of the corporate and local-government sectors, even as the government tried to tighten bank credit.

Regulators initially took a relaxed and somewhat encouraging attitude towards shadow banking. While the government was tightening bank rules and bank lending to reduce financial risk, it still wanted to sustain rapid growth and was happy to rely on financial 'innovation' and shadow banking to achieve it.[21] Also, the consensus among financial-sector policymakers was (though to a lesser extent now) that China's financial system was dominated by the state-owned banks and bank lending and that such 'indirect' financing for companies was neither inclusive (as banks tended to favour large companies over SMEs) nor efficient (as banks also favoured SOEs over more profitable private firms). More importantly, this system also meant that all risks stayed with the state-owned banks, which would have to be bailed out by the government when trouble brewed, as happened in the late 1990s and 2000s.

Therefore, more direct financing would not only deliver better capital allocation (with more funding channels and easier access for SMEs and the private sector),[22] but also reduce the government burden – as the state would not have to bail out investors in the capital markets.[23] Thus, shadow

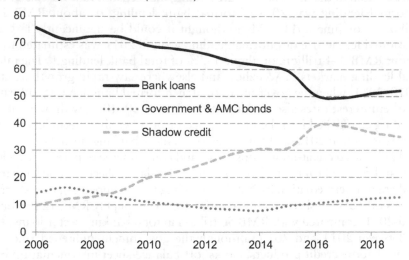

Share of adjusted total credit (% of total)

Figure 9.3 The rise of shadow banking, 2006–2019.

Source: PBC, Ministry of Finance, Asset Management Association of China, author's estimates.

banking was initially considered a useful channel for private-sector and SME financing.[24] Regulators readily allowed NBFIs or non-financial institutions to conduct financial intermediation while keeping a tight rein on private banking licences and strictly regulating bank lending.[25]

The frequent use of prudential regulation for monetary policy may have also contributed to the development of shadow banking to circumvent regulations. For example, the PBC raised banks' RRR significantly in the few years preceding 2011 (up to 20%) as a cost-saving way of sterilising the significant rise in foreign exchange. This helped the central bank avoid passively easing monetary policy too much, while keeping the RMB exchange rate stable. But the high reserve requirement was equivalent to a tax on banks and created more incentives for them to divert deposits to wealth management products. In addition, regulators used the loan-to-deposit ratio to restrict bank lending.[26] This, plus strict capital requirements, led banks to develop non-loan assets, including off-balance-sheet assets.

Competition for influence among regulators and the fact that China's financial supervision was institutionally focused rather than functionally based may have made regulatory circumvention easier.[27] Regulators often encouraged the development of financial institutions under their authority to gain influence. For example, the securities regulator, the China Securities Regulatory Commission (CSRC), wanted to see securities companies and various asset managers, including private equity funds, grow in number and boost their assets under management, while the banking regulator, the CBRC, wanted to see banks and trusts grow their assets. When the two types of institution collaborated (banks used NBFI balance sheets and the latter used banks' access to depositors and corporate clients) to circumvent regulations, the joint businesses were not effectively regulated. Such collaboration was also helped by the PBC's success in creating a credit market under its influence – the interbank bond market,[28] where banks, NBFIs and non-financial corporates could trade bonds, bills, commercial paper and other credit products.[29] This market facilitated financial businesses among institutions where the underlying risks were masked, as the risks and the liquidity treatment of interbank assets were substantially different to bank loans.

As shadow banking-related risks increased and more credit events emerged, China started to tighten the rules governing certain segments of the market, including leverage in the bond market in 2016 and off-balance-sheet wealth management products in early 2017.[30] More serious regulatory tightening occurred in the spring of 2017, when the then CBRC issued multiple documents demanding stricter supervision and the implementation of existing regulations in the banking sector, especially when it came to inter-institutional business and wealth management products.[31] The tighter rules required banks to include all their inter-institutional businesses in the liquidity risk monitoring system, have a unified bond investment monitoring system for direct, indirect and off-balance-sheet investments, apply the so-called penetration principle to more accurately measure risks masked by multiple layers of inter-financial-institutional business, make adequate provisions, and reduce dependence on interbank financing.

The tightening of regulation and supervision culminated in a new set of rules for all types of asset management products in 2018, after the 2017 Central Financial Work Conference set the direction for tighter regulations and deleveraging. The new asset management rules overhauled the segmented

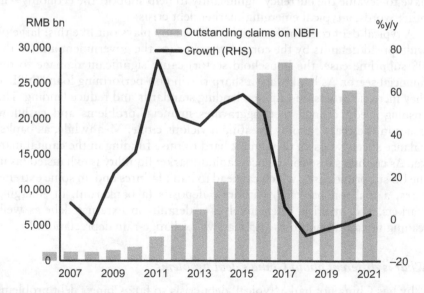

Figure 9.4 The rise and fall of bank lending to non-bank financial institutions.

Source: PBC, author's calculations.

and lax regulations governing different types of asset management business, formally banned the practice of using multiple layers and channels to cover illiquid non-standard debt intermediation, and established a holistic approach to reducing regulatory arbitrage.[32] Tighter rules led to the stagnation and gradual decline of inter-institutional lending, a gradual unwinding of illiquid, non-standard debt products, and the consolidation of wealth-management product balances. They also helped with corporate-sector deleveraging.[33]

Why has China not had a 'traditional' debt crisis? And why no 'Minsky moment' as yet?

Concerns over and predictions about China's looming debt crisis have been around for the past 20 years. In the late 1990s, as the Asian financial crisis unfolded, China faced a mountain of debt, a large share of SOEs were loss making, and the banking sector was practically insolvent (Chapter 3). Some predicted an inevitable collapse of China's economy.[34] During the global financial crisis, as China's exports plummeted and the government rolled out massive stimulus to support the economy, the sharp rise in local-government debt also rang alarm bells.[35]

Worries about China's debt issuance rose to new heights in 2015–2016, as debt rose sharply to finance excess-capacity industries after the property downturn.[36] That was also the time when China lost US\$ 1 trillion in foreign-exchange reserves, as capital outflows increased and foreign debt unwound after China tried to open its capital account and let the RMB exchange rate be more flexible. Many predicted that China was about to face its 'Minsky moment',[37] while some investors worried that China would have to devalue the currency significantly to help support the economy – in other words, a typical emerging-market debt crisis.

A typical debt crisis or financial crisis usually plays out like this: large or widespread defaults by the corporate sector (or the government and, in the US subprime case, the household sector) cause significant damage to the financial sector. As banks face a sharp rise in non-performing loans (NPLs), they increase provisions, tighten lending standards and reduce lending. The ensuing credit crunch then aggravates financial problems and cashflow issues in the real economy, creating a vicious circle. Meanwhile, as banks' balance sheets worsen, they find it hard to raise funding in the capital market. As creditors lose confidence, capital-market liquidity is exhausted (as in the US subprime case), which can lead to bank failures and, in some extreme cases, a rush on banks to withdraw deposits (a bank run). In emerging markets, a debt crisis often involves a default on external debt as well, leading to capital outflows and massive exchange-rate depreciation.[38]

What is different about China's debt problem?

Why has China not had a 'typical' debt crisis so far? China's debt problems have a lot of similarities with other highly indebted countries: a rapid rise over a relatively short period of time (in the few years after the global financial crisis), a sharp increase in the debt-servicing burden, new debt being used to finance the servicing of existing debt or zombie companies with little to no cash flows,[39] and a rise in defaults and bad debt. There are also key differences, however. As mentioned, a key reason for the large increase in China's debt has been the investment-driven growth model. In other words, most of the debt has been used for investment, not consumption, which should, presumably, generate some assets and returns, even if a portion of the investment is wasted or yields a poor return. In the case of government or quasi-fiscal debt to finance infrastructure investment, most should generate decent long-term returns that the government can expropriate over time, even though short-term returns may be poor. In the case of SOE debt, SOE assets could be used to help pay down some of the debt. As of end 2020, China's non-financial-sector SOEs had combined assets of RMB 269 trillion and combined liabilities of RMB 172 trillion, with state equity of RMB 72 trillion.[40]

However, debt crises are often liquidity crises of the financial system, which can arise from the duration and currency mismatch of assets and liabilities and/or a loss of confidence in the financial system, regardless of long-term returns on assets. Having features that can help limit the risk of a liquidity crisis is where China may truly differ from many others: (1) its debt is mainly in the form of bank loans and banks are predominantly state owned; (2) China has an exceptionally high national savings rate (still around 45% of GDP), and capital controls help keep domestic savings largely at home; and (3) SOEs and the government sector account for more than 60% of total non-financial-sector debt.

How do these features help? A high savings rate and a largely closed capital account mean that almost 95% of China's debt is financed domestically. The small share of external debt makes China less vulnerable to potential sharp swings in foreign investor sentiment and capital flows. As most debt is financed by deposits or quasi-deposits in state-owned banks, the banking sector as a whole does not really rely much on wholesale funding and is not that vulnerable to domestic capital-market sentiment and liquidity changes.[41] State ownership of the banks and the government's guarantees on deposits (explicit since 2015) and track record also make banks less vulnerable to bank runs. State ownership also means the government can prevent banks from withdrawing credit or otherwise causing a credit crunch. Meanwhile, the government can also inject capital or liquidity to support the operation of the banking system. The fact that most of the debt is owed by the state sector also means that the government can exercise strong influence on debtors to coordinate more orderly debt restructuring, as opposed to market-enforced deleveraging, which can often overshoot.

These factors can help explain why China has not experienced a typical liquidity-driven debt crisis with a rapid, one-time disruption, and why the current property downturn will unlikely lead to a financial crisis. The state can prevent the plug being pulled on the credit cycle and enable a continued rise in leverage. However, this does not mean that China is immune to serious debt issues. Indeed, China has experienced severe debt problems twice in the past two-and-a-half decades: once in the late 1990s, which took almost a decade to mop up, and again in the wake of the global financial crisis, which is still being dealt with.

China's experience of debt restructuring

Late 1990s debt and SOE restructuring

China's late-1990s debt restructuring ensued after rapid credit expansion – which paired investment-hungry SOEs and local entities with not fully commercialised banks[42] – ran out of steam, while the build-up of excess capacity and the Asian financial crisis drove down economic growth. More than half of SOEs were loss making even before the Asian financial crisis, and banks were basically insolvent, with an estimated 50% NPL ratio.[43] As detailed in Chapter 3, debt restructuring at the time mainly involved the establishment of four AMCs to take over major banks' NPLs at face value in 1999, and the recapitalisation of the four big state banks in 1998 and again in 2003, 2005 and 2008, prior to their initial public offerings.

In addition, the government enhanced regulation and supervision while practicing regulatory forbearance. The former included setting up a separate bank regulatory body, the CBRC, gradually implementing a new loan classification system, and aligning with Basel capital requirements to help improve bank soundness and risk management. Meanwhile, regulatory forbearance allowed banks to continue lending to the economy and avoid a sharp credit crunch. The government also pushed for the gradual disposal of bad debt and the restructuring of SOEs. Each bank set up its own debt disposal department, while SOE restructuring involved policy bankruptcies, management buyouts, SOE debt write-offs and the *de facto* default of SOE social-welfare and implicit lifetime retirement benefits (Chapter 3).

The housing market reform of the late 1990s and China's entry into the WTO in 2001 both helped with its debt restructuring. The former led to a lasting property boom, which not only drove demand for construction materials and related fixed investment, pushing up commodity prices that were vital to large SOEs, but also helped to turn SOE legacy bad assets (such as old factory land in prime urban locations) into valuable ones. The latter led to an export boom that boosted employment and income growth, and more profitable economic growth. China did not follow other Asian economies in letting its currency depreciate sharply during this period. Rather, it tightly managed the capital account to limit capital outflows and kept the exchange rate fixed. While this may have contributed to a more painful real adjustment in the economy initially (higher unemployment and deflation), over time it may have proved a less painful option – as countries that saw large depreciation during the Asian financial crisis also saw a loss of confidence exacerbate market and macroeconomic volatilities.

The unconventional debt restructuring of 2015–2016

The debt restructuring that started in 2015–2016 involved some unconventional practices and, to some extent, is still ongoing. In 2015, China's total debt had reached 251% of GDP, 100 percentage points higher than in 2008. Moreover, a sharp property downturn has cooled growth and exposed serious excess capacity issues. Producer price inflation (PPI) had been in decline for more than four years, mirroring a decline in corporate revenues and profits. A growing share of new credit was being used to keep loss-making companies afloat or to service their debt.

China's government adopted a set of measures that helped to reduce debt risk, some of them unconventional and controversial and some that arguably might have sowed the seeds of future problems. The measures included stimulating growth with more fiscal and quasi-fiscal spending on infrastructure investment; easing property policies (including providing subsidies for home purchases); cutting capacity and controlling production; controlling new credit flows to excess-capacity sectors; tightening rules on shadow credit; and conducting a large-scale debt-swap programme. By September 2016, China's growth had stabilised, PPI had turned positive for the first time in 54 months, industrial revenue and profit had rebounded sharply, and NPL formation had slowed.

The conventional wisdom for dealing with a debt crisis, one that has been often prescribed by the likes of the IMF, is fiscal consolidation – cut fiscal spending and lower the deficit. However, China expanded fiscal spending and eased monetary policy, similar to what the United States did after the global financial crisis, albeit more modestly and mostly through quasi-fiscal means. Quasi-fiscal spending boosted infrastructure investment, helping to underpin demand for products from the excess-capacity sectors. In addition, the government eased buying restrictions, encouraged mortgage lending[44] and subsidised the purchase of unsold housing inventory in lieu of shantytown construction to reverse the property downturn. The property rebound, in turn, helped to support heavy industrial sectors such as construction materials, automobiles and appliances.[45]

China also adopted an unconventional approach to corporate deleveraging. Typically, corporate debt restructuring in a market economy involves the closure or bankruptcy of loss-making companies, with market clearing imposed by creditors or the equity market. Such a process is not only clear cut and transparent, but can also be disorderly and have a significant negative effect on employment and banks' balance sheets. Rather than go down this path, China's government took a planned economy approach of forcing production cuts and capacity reduction in several industries.

This method was used most notably in the coal sector, where the prevalence of SOEs helped ensure compliance. The central government imposed a production cap of 276 days' average annual production (rather than more than 330 days a year previously) between May 2016 and October 2016, enforced by production quotas, highway transport controls and fines. This led to a double-digit decline in coal production for most of 2016, pushing up coal prices sharply.[46] The government also imposed quotas for capacity cuts in key sectors, aided by the fact that some were already suspended because of deep losses. As part of this process, the government often opted to use mergers and acquisition and let the merged company cut capacity and jobs slowly, rather than close some companies. For example, rather than allow the loss-making Wuhan steel to go bankrupt, the government let the profitable SOE Baoshan Steel merge with it. The new Baowu group cut some capacity in Wuhan steel and laid off workers there, but continued to carry the original debt and kept most of the jobs.

China's approach to corporate deleveraging may have rewarded inefficient companies (as all companies had to cut production and capacity) and been biased against smaller companies (which are usually privately owned), which were let fail more easily. However, it did manage to limit job losses and the associated social impact, and stave off a bigger rise in NPLs (debt taken over by a new company would still be a going concern rather than the debt of a bankrupt one) in the short term. It also helped to push up producer prices and, in turn, industrial profits.

The rebound in mining-product and raw-material prices directly contributed to an estimated half of the PPI turnaround in 2016 and a greater share of the increase in industrial profits.[47] The turnaround in producer prices from protracted deflation helped to change market expectations and business behaviour; companies no longer wanted to delay their spending. Rising prices and profitability were also great news when it came to reducing the debt burden. As producer prices increased, real interest rates on and the debt-service burden of the corporate sector declined sharply. And as companies become more profitable, they no longer needed to borrow as much to stay afloat, so they could service their debt again, lowering the formation of new NPLs.

The most important way of dealing with China's public-sector debt was perhaps the debt swap. Local governments were allowed to issue provincial-level government bonds with an average maturity of 5–7 years to replace previous LGFV debt, which largely comprised bank loans or corporate bonds with an average maturity of three years or less. From 2015 to 2018, some RMB 12.5 trillion of debt was swapped, according to the Ministry of Finance. The swap helped to significantly reduce the debt-service burden of local governments, though the debt stock was not reduced. Indeed, local-government debt rose further, even as the corporate sector deleveraged, as it had resorted to more hidden channels of implicit borrowing.

The 2015–2016 debt restructuring is still ongoing, to some extent. After stabilising in 2017 and declining in 2018, China's debt-to-GDP ratio rose again in 2019 and jumped sharply in 2020, as the government eased policy to deal with the impact of the US–China trade war and the COVID-19 pandemic.

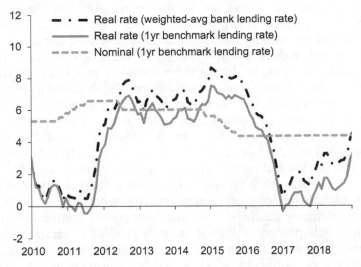

Real rate (% per annum, CPI & PPI avg deflated)

Figure 9.5 The end of deflation helped to lower real interest rates in 2016.

Source: NBS, PBC, author's estimates.

Deleveraging resumed in early 2021 following a strong rebound in growth, though the effort was once again suspended amid a sharp property downturn and a new wave of COVID-19. To a certain degree, the shantytown subsidies and quasi-fiscal easing that had been useful in dealing with debt problems a few years previously may have had delayed negative consequences.

One long-term and ongoing change introduced in 2016 was tighter financial regulation, especially of shadow banking. It has been gradually implemented over the past few years and expanded to cover internet finance, including P2P platforms in 2018, cash loans in 2019 and other aspects of internet finance in 2020–2021.

What are China's debt risks and what to watch?

Despite repeated warnings of a debt crisis, China's experience to date has shown that there is no one debt level at which a debt crisis will occur. While research has shown that rapid debt build-ups or debt above certain levels are highly correlated with debt crises, they do not always cause one.[48] In fact, debt crises can happen at different debt levels. For example, Mexico ran into trouble in 1992 when its debt-to-GDP ratio was 62%, significantly lower than China's current level. South Korea, meanwhile, experienced its debt crisis in 1997 when its debt-to-GDP ratio was 166%.[49] Conversely, Japan's debt level has been rising ever higher since the early 1990s without triggering any obvious financial-sector distress.

Not having had a typical debt crisis does not mean China will never have one, however, nor does it mean that the country has no major debt problems.

First, evidence suggests that a significant portion of the massive increase in Chinese debt since 2008 has gone to non-productive or inefficient sectors, making its debt-financed growth unsustainable. While most of China's debt has been used for investments that should have generated assets and returns, debt in the non-productive sectors has risen far faster than that in the productive sectors. For example, debt in the real-estate sector has risen eightfold since the global financial crisis, far outstripping the threefold increase in the industrial sector. Real-estate assets have also risen sevenfold, but this has mainly been driven by valuation gains rather than reasonable rental yields.

The estimated return on assets in the industrial sector also declined between 2008 and 2010 and between 2012 and 2016. The continued rise in debt going into the real-estate and excess-capacity sectors, as well as the less efficient SOEs between 2008 and 2016, meant that the debt-financed asset build-up did not generate sufficient returns to justify or service the debt.[50] It also meant that while the debt-financed investment contributed to GDP growth as it happened, it did not generate productive capital to support continued growth without additional debt. Consequently, growth would necessitate ever more debt, which would be unsustainable. The situation improved between 2016 and 2018 as corporate earnings improved and leverage was controlled. However, it has deteriorated again since then and could continue to worsen unless the improvement in corporate profitability proves lasting and growth can be less debt driven in the long term.

Second, the development of the shadow credit and financial markets has complicated the lability structure of the financial system. Although it has been curtailed by recent deleveraging efforts and tighter regulation, shadow

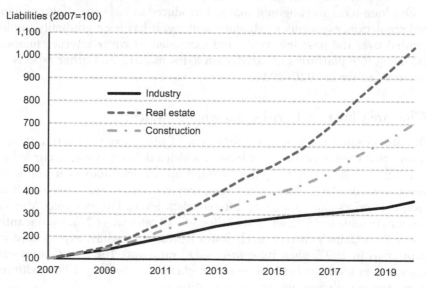

Figure 9.6 The rise of liabilities in industry and real-estate, 2007–2020.

Source: NBS, author's estimates.

credit has still become an important source of debt accumulation over the past decade. With the rise of wealth management products and asset management businesses, some of which are not necessarily provided by properly regulated financial institutions (e.g., wealth management products issued by property developers such as Evergrande), traditionally stable banking intermediation – bank deposits financing bank loans – has been eroded. This means that some banks and almost all NBFIs rely on the market for financing, so liquidity could dry up for them. While the central bank will probably always want to prevent funding problems from spilling over to the whole system, it may not be able to quickly identify where they are. Remember that most financial crises are liquidity crises.

Third, the continued rise in debt can be problematic even if it never leads to a typical debt crisis. If debt consistently rises faster than output over a prolonged period and a growing share is allocated to non-productive sectors, this means that there is a misallocation of resources and some waste. Even though China's unique features may facilitate a much longer and more stable credit cycle than in other economies, this could still depress corporate profitability and investment, leading to lower long-term productivity gains and stagnant economic growth. This is because, without market discipline to clear the low returns or failures of investment, inefficient and wasteful investments will crowd out more productive and profitable ones. The wasted resources will eventually end up as non-performing debt, the cost of which will have to be borne by the financial sector and, ultimately, savers.

Fourth, the debt overhang is likely to constrain China's capital-account opening and monetary policy conduct going forward. China's closed capital account helped to keep its high domestic savings at home to finance the rising debt. This means that further relaxation of controls on capital outflows could jeopardise domestic liquidity and, therefore, financial stability in times of market pressure. This became clear in 2015–2016, when the earlier *de facto* easing of capital outflows combined with a deterioration in the domestic economy and confidence led to a loss of almost US$1 trillion in foreign-exchange reserves. China promptly tightened controls on capital outflows and has not attempted any meaningful liberalisation since. Its high levels of debt and concerns over the soundness of the domestic financial system may prevent China from completely opening the capital account and making the RMB fully convertible anytime soon. This is likely to constrain the growth of the RMB as a major international reserve currency.[51] Similarly, the high level of debt is likely to make (and has already made) the PBC reluctant to ease monetary policy significantly, for fear of even more debt and, eventually, bigger problems.[52] At the same time, China's high debt-service burden also means the central bank may be constrained in raising interest rates significantly in future or fully liberalising interest rates.

At a sector level, while most attention has been paid to China's local-government and corporate debt, the recent sharp increase in household debt is also a concern. While household debt was only about 62% of GDP in 2021, it was more than 100% of household disposable income (Chapter 8), having more than doubled since 2010. The 2019 PBC survey reported urban households' average debt service-to-household income ratio at 18.4%, almost double that of the United States.[53] A 2020 UBS consumer credit research report found that following an industry clean-up, the use of both online cash loans and instalment loans had contracted, contributing to a decline in the household debt-service burden.[54]

To monitor the evolution of China's debt and related risks, the most important indicators are still the level and speed of change in the overall debt-to-GDP ratio. The credit-gap measure developed by the BIS[55] could be another useful indicator. The size of shadow credit relative to traditional bank lending is important to watch, too, as a rise in shadow banking would reduce the stability of financial-system liquidity and the government's control over it. The structure of banking-sector funding can be measured by the loan-to-deposit ratio, with proper adjustments for non-loan assets and quasi-deposits on banks' balance sheets. As discussed, any major relaxation of capital outflow controls could erode the domestic liquidity buffer, even if net capital outflows do not occur right away.

As has been the case over the past few years and in earlier episodes of debt restructuring, China's debt cycle can be a drawn-out process. The government's desire to balance growth and defuse debt problems, its control over banks and state-sector debtors, and the PBC's liquidity provision are likely to help China avoid any sharp credit slowdown. Debt restructuring will be gradual, with regulatory forbearance and liquidity support ensuring continued bank lending growth. To fundamentally address the debt issue, China needs to deepen its structural reforms and change its debt-fuelled growth model, also by applying market discipline over time to reduce moral hazard for borrowers and by levelling the playing field for more resources to be allocated to the more efficient private sector and less debt-dependent sectors.

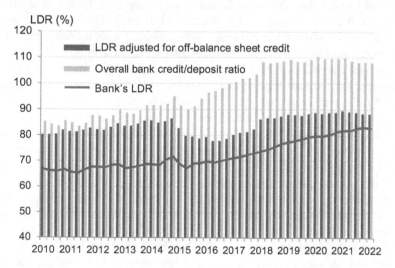

Figure 9.7 Banking-sector loan-to-deposit ratio, 2010–2022.

Source: PBC, author's estimates.

Notes

1 See BIS (2022) and IMF (2022).
2 See NIFD's macro leverage ratio database.
3 Author's estimates.
4 Aggregate SOE liabilities were equivalent to 76% of total non-financial debt at end 2020, though these include intra-corporate debt, such as accounts payable, and overstates total SOE-related debt from the financial sector. At end 2016, 'state-controlled' and 'collectively controlled' enterprises together accounted for 61% of total loans. The PBC put the SOE share of banks' corporate lending at 53% as of end 2018 (see PBC, 2019).
5 Author's estimate.
6 See Ministry of Finance (2017, 2018).
7 See PBC (2020).
8 NBS and PBC data releases.
9 Author's estimate.
10 See Lardy (2008).
11 Official data suggest mortgages accounted for just under 60% of total household debt, but some household operational loans and other consumer credits were probably also for real estate.
12 See Shiina (2012).
13 See Zhang et al. (2013).
14 See China Economic Weekly (2014).
15 Wang (2011c).
16 Ibid.
17 This estimate includes shadow credit listed under TSF, namely, undiscounted bills, trust loans and entrust loans, as well as corporate bonds and shadow credit 'missing' from the official credit numbers. The 'missing' part is estimated by subtracting secondary market investments (such as bonds, equities and money-market funds) from assets outstanding in trusts and securities asset management subsidiaries to get the proxy for non-standard assets not captured by TSF. See Wang et al. (2016a).
18 So-called entrust loans or designated loans are corporate-to-corporate loans arranged by banks. In other words, the bank puts money on deposit at one company to lend to another company under an 'entrust' scheme, with the bank making a fee and the credit risk taken on by the deposit-bearing company.
19 Securities firms raise funds from investors, sometimes in cooperation with banks, and invest in the products of their asset-management subsidiaries, which use the funds to invest in non-standard assets such as trust asset or loan-like equity products. See CBIRC (2018).
20 See Wang and Zhong (2016).
21 See IMF (2017).
22 See PBC (2012).
23 This turned out not to be the case, as the government acted to bail out the stock market in 2015 and to repeatedly bail out wealth management products.
24 For example, the PBC consistently reported the rise of shadow credit assets as an achievement of increased direct financing or improved support for SMEs (see PBC, 2015b). In meetings with market analysts, including the author, regulators often dismissed concerns about regulatory arbitrage, excessive risk taking by local governments and property developers, and hidden risks that still resided within the banking system.
25 Between 2014 and 2019, regulators approved the establishment of only 19 private banks, including those backed by internet companies.
26 Until 2016, banks in general could not lend more than 75% of deposits and this ratio was significantly lower for large banks such as ICBC.

27 See IMF (2017).
28 The interbank bond market has become the dominant bond and corporate bill market since its launch in the late 1990s, with 90–95% of all bonds traded on it, while exchange-traded bonds have become relatively small.
29 Strictly speaking, this is an inter-institutional market under the National Interbank Funding Centre, not just a market between banks or even financial institutions. In 2005, the PBC issued its 'Measures for short-term bill management', opening the doors for companies to issue short-term bills (with a duration of less than a year) on the interbank bond market (see PBC, 2005).
30 See PBC (2017).
31 For example, Documents No. 6 and No. 46. See CBRC (2017).
32 See CBIRC (2018).
33 See Wang et al. (2017a, 2017b).
34 For example, Chang (2001).
35 See Shih (2010).
36 See IMF (2016). BIS (2016) also warned that China's extremely high credit-to-GDP gap might mean debt trouble in the following few years.
37 'Minsky Moment' is a term coined by Paul McCully of Pimco, referring to Hyman Minsky's theory, to 'describe a situation when debt levels reach breaking-point and asset prices across the board start plunging', according to the Economist (2016). For warnings about China's debt problem, see Pesek (2015) and Cassidy (2015). The Fed was believed to have delayed and reduced its rate hike in 2016 because of concerns on about China's debt risk.
38 For example, Mexico in 1982 and 1994; the Asian financial crisis in 1997–1998; Argentina in 2001 and Turkey in 2001.
39 An IMF research paper by Maliszewski et al. (2016) found that in 2015, 15.5% of corporate loans were 'potentially at risk', as those borrowers had less cash-flow to cover interest payments.
40 See National People's Congress of the People's Republic of China (2021b).
41 The rise of shadow financing between 2010 and 2016 complicated banks' financing structure and significantly raised liquidity risks in the financial system. This has been partly addressed since regulations and supervision have been tightened.
42 The direct lending quota was only formally abolished in 1998 when a proper five-tier loan classification system was first established, before being fully adopted only in 2004.
43 Karacadag (2003).
44 As their balance sheets looked healthy, households were encouraged to lever up to help companies deleverage. See Zhou (2016).
45 Auto sales have also been helped by tax cuts and the rapid expansion of auto credit.
46 See National Bureau of Statistics (2017).
47 See Wang et al. (2016b).
48 See Reinhart and Rogoff (2013), Schularick and Taylor (2012) and Dell'Ariccia et al. (2012).
49 BIS data.
50 See Lardy (2019) and Wang and Zhong (2016).
51 See IMF (2012, 2017).
52 For example, China's monetary policy easing in 2020 in response to the COVID-19 pandemic was more modest than in other major economies.
53 See PBC (2020) and FRED (2022).
54 See Yan et al. (2020).
55 See BIS (2016).

10 The environment, public health and the government management challenge

Two major events of 2020 are set to have a broad and lasting impact on China and the rest of the world. At the beginning of the year, coronavirus disease 2019 (COVID-19) swept through Wuhan, the capital of Hubei province, and soon spread to the rest of the world. Towards the end of 2020, President Xi Jinping announced that China would aim to achieve net zero carbon emissions by 2060. China's handling of COVID-19 – its first missteps in Wuhan, its ability to control the spread of the virus in subsequent months across the rest of the country, and its uncompromising policy two years later to clamp down on the Omicron variant – demonstrated both the strengths and weaknesses of its public health and governance system. In announcing its net zero plan, meanwhile, China joined the world's major developed economies in moving to cap the global temperature increase in the coming decades. It was a culmination of China's recent efforts to recognise and address its environmental and ecological issues.

How does China manage major public issues such as public health crises, environmental protection and climate change? How have its governance system and guiding principles evolved over time? What are some of the challenges it will face in future?

Over the past four decades, China's public management system has seen significant changes in priorities, administrative systems and institutional arrangements. The role of the public and the media, including social media, has also evolved. In the 1980s and 1990s, the government focused primarily on providing food and jobs for the vast, poor population. This meant that public policy was designed to create an environment of rapid economic growth, far more than providing public goods or managing the environment, safety standards or labour protection.

The balance started to shift when the most urgent issue was no longer sustaining the population. Over time, matters such as controlling pollution, public health, social protection and climate change became more politically salient. The rise of the middle class helped to shape these changes, as it led to shifts in public demand for things such as public health, clean air and the safety of food and medicines. Public opinion in this regard has found voice in various forms (including protest), which can be more easily expressed and amplified by the internet and social media.[1] Moreover, the rise of the

DOI: 10.4324/9781003310938-11

internet and social media has led to greater public scrutiny and the disclosure of government information, in turn helping to increase government accountability.

The way the government manages these issues has also changed. In the 1980s and 1990s, it moved away from controlling all aspects of people's lives, bestowing more freedom on individuals and companies and targeting a reduction in the fiscal burden and an increase in government efficiency (often measured in commercial terms). Over the past two decades and especially in recent years, the government has begun to build regulatory frameworks and a public service system rather than just focus on speed or the commerciality of public administration.

It has also started to delegate authority to appropriate agencies and provide public services and basic support for low-income earners. In addition, a more formal institutional governance structure has begun to take shape, gradually moving away from relying on administrative measures driven by competing short-term economic interests. This means that the role of rules, regulations and legislation has increased, helping to formalise government policy and public management. There has also been a concerted effort since 2013 to streamline government departments and institutions and reduce administrative approvals and procedures to reduce systematic rent-seeking practices.

The evolution of China's public management over the past few decades is testament to its pragmatic, self-correcting mechanism of governance. Once government priorities shift or public pressures intensify, rules and regulations and institutions can change, sometimes swiftly, after long periods of seeming immobility. Three key drivers have helped to bring about change in public management: (1) the priorities of the Chinese government have shifted from fulfilling the basic needs of the population to addressing the consequences of rapid growth; (2) demand from an increasingly affluent society for a better quality of life and greater security has helped drive the government's policy agenda, underpinned by the internet and social media; and (3) the government has acquired more technocratic capability, sophistication and fiscal resources to deal with increasingly complex issues.

There are still limitations to China's public management system, however. Before formal rules are established – or in parallel – there is generally some tolerance of informal mechanisms and practices outside the existing system. This is consistent with an administrative culture that prefers to retain discretionary executive power. The fear of erosion of the Party's leadership has also led to an increased emphasis on strengthening the CPC leadership in the past few years. Using the CPC network to sway public policy may not only help to overcome resistance to policy implementation, but can also run the risk of undermining the government's other institutional frameworks. In addition, there is a need for more channels to engage the public in discussions on key policies to facilitate a better understanding of public demand and smoother policy implementation.

China's public health crisis management since SARS

Lessons from SARS

The first case of an unknown pneumonia-like severe acute respiratory syndrome (SARS) was recorded in Guangdong province in November 2002. From February to April 2003, SARS spread rapidly to multiple cities and several countries, most severely affecting Hong Kong and Beijing. China was unprepared for such a sudden public health crisis; there was no emergency response system, and officials in Guangdong and Beijing first tried to play down and cover up the outbreak for fear of causing public panic and disrupting normal activities.[2] The lack of proper information about SARS aggravated the spread within hospitals, while rumours proliferated through the internet and society. After the seriousness of the outbreak in Beijing was revealed to foreign media by a retired military doctor,[3] China's central government took quick action to control it. On 20 April, the mayor of Beijing and minister of health were replaced, the government started to report daily new cases and, on 23 April, the State Council established a SARS-control command headquarters to coordinate nationwide efforts.[4] A new hospital was built in a week on the outskirts of Beijing to treat SARS patients and, on 9 May, the State Council rolled out a new regulation on handling public health emergencies.

SARS happened at a time when China's old 'prevention first' public health system[5] had declined while the new system was still being formed. In the three decades prior to 1980, with limited medical resources, China had a public health system that focused on preventing and controlling epidemics and the communicable diseases that had plagued the country (and most other poor countries), such as malaria.[6] Between the mid-1980s and 2003, China's healthcare reform tried to reduce the government's fiscal burden by expanding healthcare and medical treatment with the help of the market, but still preserving the state ownership of hospitals.

Hospitals were constrained in raising the price of most healthcare services, but were allowed and even encouraged to use a portion of revenues from medicines and various medical services to supplement public funding and increase staff compensation.[7] Between 1992 and 2003, public spending on healthcare consistently grew by less than GDP[8] and declined as a share of total healthcare spending (Figure 10.1). The fiscal resources allocated to disease prevention and control institutions were relatively scaled back and these institutions had to charge for their services to finance themselves.[9] As a result, most public health institutions were under-funded, their capacity for epidemic control was severely compromised and the epidemic control network was badly damaged, with the situation worst in rural areas.

According to Xue and Liu (2013), the SARS outbreak not only exposed serious flaws in the public health system at the time, but also revealed the long absence of an emergency response system in China's public administration. The segmented administrative system meant that power and resources

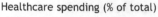

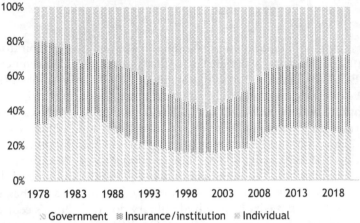

Figure 10.1 Healthcare spending, public versus private.

Source: NBS, author's calculations.

were scattered across different parts of government with different and divided interests, so there was a lack of information sharing and coordination. Xue and Liu believed that the sudden outbreak, combined with an under-developed public health and epidemic prevention system, a fragile social management mechanism and a flawed public information dissemination system led to a public emergency that threatened economic and social stability and undermined trust in the government.

After SARS, China established a nationwide public health reporting system. This early warning system, or the Network Direct Report System,[10] with its hub in the Chinese Center for Disease Control and Prevention (CDC), was designed to discover the early onset of epidemics and trigger a nationwide emergency response. The system covers five levels of government administration, from the central government all the way to townships and villages. It requires every hospital to report within hours to the local CDC and the central CDC through the network, bypassing layers of administration. It is online and real time, and covers all local CDC centres, 95% of county-level hospitals and above, and 70% of village clinics.[11] By 2006, this direct reporting system has helped to accelerate the speed of infectious disease reporting, according to the CDC.

China also launched a new round of healthcare reforms after SARS to significantly improve the public healthcare system. Hospital and medical facilities expanded greatly after 2003, including basic healthcare facilities in small cities and rural areas. The number of doctors and hospital beds per thousand people increased from 1.48 and 2.34 in 2003 to 2.9 and 5.1, respectively, in 2020.[12] In 2003, China also launched a new rural cooperative health-insurance system that provided major illness insurance for rural residents, with modest initial funding, of which two-thirds came from the

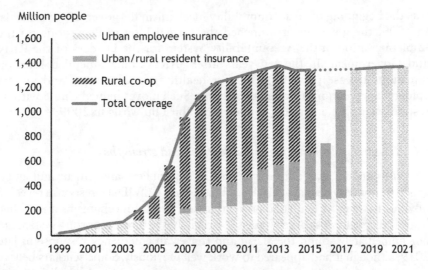

Figure 10.2 The expansion of health-insurance coverage.

Source: National Healthcare Security Administration, author's estimates.

Note: 2016/17 data for urban/rural resident insurance did not include rural co-op, but include it from 2018.

government. By 2010, the new rural cooperative healthcare insurance scheme had covered 80% of rural areas and the government's contribution had quadrupled. A basic healthcare insurance scheme was introduced in 2007 for urban residents as well. When the rural and urban resident health-care insurance schemes merged in 2017, 95% of the population had some sort of medical coverage, with an increased government contribution.

SARS also led to the establishment of a formal public emergency response system. The State Council issued the National General Emergency Response Preparatory Plan in May 2003, providing a general framework for the emergency response system, covering natural disasters, major catastrophes, public health events and social-security events. In 2006, the government required all urban districts and rural villages, as well as all companies and institutions, to set up emergency response plans. On the legal front, the Emergency Response Law of the People's Republic of China was implemented in 2007. Institutionally, the State Council established an emergency management office to help consolidate information and coordinate responses from different departments. From a procedural perspective, the government published Regulations of the People's Republic of China on the Disclosure of Government Information in 2007, specifying formal requirements on the scope, process and monitoring of government information disclosure. Many ministries launched press/news spokesperson systems and official weibo (microblog) and internet information platforms.

SARS triggered a legislative response and government administration reforms too. The dismissal of the mayor of Beijing in 2003, for example, was the beginning of an accountability mechanism for government officials. In 2009, the government launched the formal Interim Provisions on the Implementation of the Accountability System for the Leaders of the Party and Government. In the ten years after SARS, China amended laws on infectious disease prevention, border health and quarantine, and animal epidemic prevention, among other things. Such moves helped China with its response later on, including to the H1N1 'bird flu' virus in 2009.[13]

COVID-19 pandemic exposes weaknesses and strengths

Notwithstanding major improvements in the public management and emergency response system since SARS, China's early COVID-19 response revealed obvious flaws in its epidemic prevention and control mechanisms and public health emergency response systems.[14] Crucially, the direct reporting system did not immediately sound the alarm and trigger an emergency response in late 2019, although it had appeared to work well previously. Some scholars believe that the management structure of the reporting system may have disincentivised local hospitals from reporting COVID-19 to the CDC sooner. According to Hua et al. (2020), as local managers of the direct reporting system fall under the purview of local health administrations rather than the CDC, hence face potential local political pressures and administrative punishment, they may be reluctant to report every potential epidemic case if the disease is unknown and the reporting could inconvenience local officials.[15] What actually went wrong in late 2019 and early 2020 is hard to know, but the tension between incentives and responsibilities in many local agencies may indeed be an issue.

Despite the early COVID-19 response issues, the improvements in the public health and nationwide emergency response systems did help China control the pandemic in subsequent months. In contrast to what happened with SARS, China's National Health Commission issued a public notice on 20 January 2020, triggering a nationwide response mechanism. Subsequently, local governments activated the first-level public health emergency response system, enabling coordinated measures, such as mobilising medical and material resources, closing schools, cancelling mass gatherings and, for most provinces, adopting the enclosed management of communities and districts.

The State Council set up a Joint Prevention and Control Mechanism to coordinate efforts from 32 government agencies. The organised and coordinated emergency response helped to reduce the spread and contain the outbreak. In addition, the expansion of hospital facilities and health-insurance coverage since the SARS outbreak helped to provide large-scale testing and treatment of COVID-19. The government's decision to provide COVID-19 treatment free of charge and build makeshift special medical facilities for thousands of Wuhan residents also helped to contain the outbreak and limit the number of deaths, even as forced quarantine imposed significant social costs on affected families.

The involvement of Chinese society, with the help of social media, was important in exposing the COVID-19 outbreak to the public in the early days and in the response thereafter. When local health officials did not immediately report the onset of the COVID-19 outbreak, a few medical staff in Wuhan passed on information and sounded the alarm through social-media channels.[16] Later, WeChat and other social-media channels contributed to the dissemination of COVID-19-related information and prevention tips, acted as platforms for volunteers across the country and helped to source medicine and equipment from and for Chinese communities around the world. This probably helped to plug the gap caused by the initial delay in the official response. The rapid proliferation of social media turned every citizen into a potential news reporter, exposing problems where they appeared, giving voice to public opinion and playing a role in shaping the official response and public policy.

A key characteristic of the Chinese public emergency response was the mobilisation of resources and aid from other provinces and regions. This is an informal response system, often used by the government, which drew on political and CPC channels to source funding, materials and volunteers through state-owned companies, medical facilities, public institutions and the military. During the 76-day total lockdown of Wuhan, according to the State Council, 42,600 medical staff from across the country went to work there. Other medical resources, including medical and personal protection equipment, were also gathered across the country and sent to Wuhan.

China's COVID-19 control relied heavily on severe lockdowns implemented first in Wuhan, then in other places, supplemented by the confinement of communities and districts and strictly enforced mandatory quarantines, with no exceptions and no family considerations taken into account. These measures, combined with extensive contact tracing and mandatory mass testing, were effective in containing the outbreak in 2020 before vaccines were available. While other countries also adopted lockdowns and quarantines, popular resistance tended to be greater and enforcement was far less strict. In China, these strict measures were implemented by the country's extensive local-government and community management structures, with the help of public propaganda campaigns and surveillance equipment. In addition, the zero-COVID policy was conveyed to all levels of government as the No.1 priority. Local officials who were seen as failing to achieve this goal were severely punished, sometimes losing their jobs. This incentive system prompted local governments to enforce restrictions that went far beyond CDC requirements, often adopting extreme local measures – including doubling the national required quarantine period, refusing entry and accommodation to travellers from areas with any COVID cases, and suspending non-COVID medical treatments.

For two years, this approach of mass testing, contact tracing and lockdowns was effective in minimising the number of COVID-19 cases and deaths, but it may have led to complacency. China was seriously tested once again in dealing with the more transmissible Omicron variant in 2022, with multiple cities implementing lockdowns, some repeatedly, but with less success in fully eradicating new cases.

The lockdowns and other draconian measures taken by local governments in April-May 2022, such as roadblocks, highway closures and travel and public transport bans, had a sharp negative impact on the economy as well as on people's lives. While the rest of the world adjusted its pandemic policies and returned to normality, China maintained its 'zero COVID' approach unwaveringly until early December 2022. The sudden easing of nearly all restrictions in late 2022 may have been partly due to growing public disquiet and complaints as well as unsustainable tolls on the economy and local governments' finances, though the government's apparent lack of planning for the exit from the 'zero COVID' policy is puzzling. The extended campaign-style crisis mode of public management and its abrupt unwind reveal challenges in dealing with complex social and economic issues without a well-established real-time feedback loop and public policy adjustment mechanism.

In general, local governments' incentive structure is critical to governance and public management in China. Local administrations are the ones that carry out public management actions and respond to public emergencies, as they are close to the source of information and have the institutional structures and personnel to do so. However, they have multiple roles and objectives that may compete or conflict at times. Their role in developing or facilitating the development of the local economy has been the dominant goal since the 1980s and 1990s[17] and can sometimes be at odds with their roles of regulating the market, protecting investors and consumers, and providing social services. Such conflicts of interest may be a major reason why proper supervision and the enforcement of regulation is still lacking in some areas of government administration, such as safety in the workplace, food and medicines safety, and environmental rules and regulations.[18] Many readers will recall the vaccination scandal of 2018[19] and a number of major work accidents.[20] Environmental issues, however, may be where the number of cases has been most concentrated.

Environmental protection and decarbonisation: changing policies

The rapid economic evolution of the 1980s and 1990s, coupled with the de facto 'develop first, fix it later' attitude at local level under China's 'developmental state'[21] led to severe environmental degradation at the end of the last century. The dire picture was detailed in a World Bank special report in 2001.[22] While China had taken measures to address some of the consequences through afforestation and technological upgrades to reduce industrial emissions and wastewater, new environmental problems soon became overwhelming. Land degradation was widespread, for instance, while water quality deteriorated, especially in the North of China. In 2001, water in 67% of all cities failed to meet China's Class 2 criteria, while 40% had one or more pollutants in a concentration of more than Class 3.[23]

While China's government started to pay more attention to environmental issues in the late 1990s and passed multiple environmental laws,[24] the situation deteriorated further during the 10th Five-Year Programme period (2001–2005). Environment-related targets were not met, largely due to the rapid development of energy- and pollution-intensive heavy industry. Total energy consumption increased 70% between 2000 and 2005, with coal accounting for three-quarters of that. This led to a significant rise in China's SO_2 emissions during that period.[25] In fact, SO_2 emissions were 42% higher than targeted at end 2005, causing acid rain in many areas. According to official statistics, 53% of the 341 cities monitored in 2003 (58% of the urban population) reported annual average PM_{10}[26] levels twice the US annual average.[27] Only 1% of China's urban population at the time lived in a city where air quality would be considered acceptable by the major developed countries. During the same period, some 54% of China's main rivers contained water deemed unsafe for human consumption.[28]

The severe degradation of China's environment and ecological system came at a significant health cost and inflicted considerable economic damage. The World Bank estimated the cost of air and water pollution in China at between 3.5% and 8% of GDP in 2003.[29] The National Statistics Bureau and State Environmental Protection Administration (SEPA) put the pollution damage at about 3% of GDP in 2004.[30] The public was also becoming more aware of and disgruntled about the serious environmental problems and the damage to their health. Complaints received by environmental agencies rose by 30% to 600,000 cases a year in 2003 and 2004, while the number of environment-related mass protests jumped.[31] A 2002 report also found that urban residents in China placed great value on health and were willing to pay as much as those in advanced economies to reduce the environmental damage.[32]

The rising cost of and public focus on environmental issues led to a rethink of China's development strategy. President Hu Jintao's 'scientific outlook on development' was in part a response to China's uneven and unbalanced economic model. The 17th CPC Congress in 2007 also proposed building an 'ecological civilisation' as part of China's goal to be a moderately prosperous society in all regards by 2020.[33] The 11th Five-Year Plan (2006–2010) put environmental protection at the top of the agenda, set reductions in the total discharge of major pollutants as mandatory targets, and pursued a 20% decline in the energy emissions intensity per unit of GDP. Premier Wen Jiaobao's work report at the 2007 NPC cited 'environment', 'pollution' and 'environmental protection' 48 times.[34] Some actions were swiftly taken: for example, from June 2008, all retail establishments were banned from providing free plastic bags.

The government's attempts to overhaul the country's economic structure were rudely disrupted by the global financial crisis and the massive stimulus that ensued to counter its effects. The stimulus-fuelled property and construction activity further boosted energy and pollution-intensive heavy industry. Air pollution continued to worsen during and after the 11th Five-Year Plan period. Moreover, while China revised and passed more environmental legislation and regulations with stricter requirements, enforcement was poor.

One factor may have been a lack of implementation guidelines for the numerous and complex laws and rules. As of 2011, there were around 236 environmental protection laws issued by the NPC, 690 sets of environmental regulations from the State Council and 8600 local-government rules and regulations related to environmental protection.[35] Another factor behind the poor enforcement may have been that the central government authorities that set the rules did not have much control over how they were implemented at local level, as local governments tended to focus more on economic growth and tax revenue.[36] Wang and Wheeler (2000) noted that China's pollution levies depended on polluters reporting the emissions and that levies could be negotiated or even eliminated at the discretion of local regulators.[37] Moreover, regulators tended to lack good data and sufficient punitive measures for violations and complaints needed to be supported by evidence gathered by the complainants.

Two major developments helped to move the dial on environmental protection. One was the large-scale air pollution that occurred in Northern China, including Beijing, in 2011, which triggered public outcry. The second was the production and capacity cuts in heavily polluting industries in 2015–2016.

That the air quality in Beijing was poor and worsening after the 2008 Olympics was clear to anyone who lived there. One could often smell the sulphur in the brown coal-induced haze that enveloped the city; the only relief came from strong, cold winds that blew the pollution away for a couple of days now and then. In 2008, the US Embassy began to monitor and inform US citizens of the air quality in Beijing through a Twitter account, @beijingair. Gradually, more people became aware of the US Embassy index, which often differed from the official measures. At the time, the latter focused on PM_{10} – course particulate matter – not $PM_{2.5}$, the finer

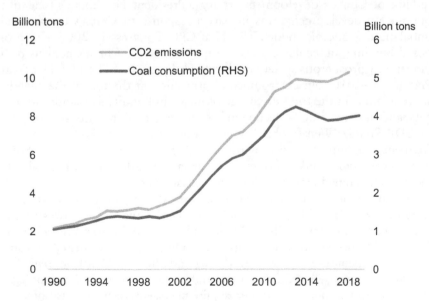

Figure 10.3 Coal consumption and CO_2 emissions, 1990–2019.
Source: NBS, World Bank.

particles that were 2.5 microns or less in diameter and more easily inhaled into lungs and bronchioles.

When the US Embassy's $PM_{2.5}$ reading surged to about 550 micrograms per cubic metre on 19 November 2010, about 20 times higher than World Health Organization (WHO) guidelines, the Embassy declared they city's air quality 'crazy bad'.[38] Although Beijing's official air quality index also deemed the air 'heavily polluted' that day, the US Embassy reading grabbed widespread attention. Government agencies initially tried to stop the Embassy from releasing such data, but the increase in public awareness and criticism, combined with the continued deterioration in air quality the following year, prompted a different response. In January 2012, the Beijing government started to monitor and release $PM_{2.5}$ data and, by end 2013, 113 cities in China were monitoring it, in line with the new Environment Air Quality Standards in March that year.[39]

The step-up in official monitoring revealed the severity of China's air contamination, especially in Northern China around Beijing. According to the Ministry of Environmental Protection, while more than 90% of cities met the old air quality standard in 2012, only 41% met the new standard, even though it was still considerably less stringent than that recommended by the WHO. The beginning and end of 2013 also saw multiple incidents of smog engulfing large parts of China, which attracted significant public attention. In one such event in January 2013, smog covered 17 provinces, almost a quarter of China's land area, affecting about 600 million people.[40] The severity of air pollution also spurred a rise in pressure on the government from the urban middle class for a change in policy.[41]

The State Council issued an air pollution control plan in September 2013.[42] The five-year action plan set specific targets for reducing inhalable particles. It required the gradual retirement of polluting facilities and the retrofitting of power plants to reduce pollution, a phased transition to cleaner energy and the establishment of a 'goal responsibility' system on pollution control for local governments. To this end, the central government signed an accountability document with each local government, whereby local officials would be evaluated each year on their performance against pollution control targets. Local governments also rolled out their own action plans.

Overall budgetary spending on environmental protection and energy conservation in 2017 was almost double that of 2012. By 2017, according to the Ministry of Ecology and Environment, PM_{10} national emissions had declined by 23% from 2013 levels, while $PM_{2.5}$ emissions had declined by almost 40% in the Beijing-Tianjin-Hebei region.[43] One of the key contributing factors was a massive conversion from coal to gas heating systems,[44] which was aggressively pushed by local governments around Beijing, especially in 2016–2017. While instrumental in improving air quality, the switch in the midst of an energy price surge and natural gas shortage, however, led to some rural residents being left without proper heating, for which the government came under fire.

Production and capacity cuts in the energy-intensive sectors in 2015–2017 were also important to the success of the action plan. The 2014–2015 property downturn exposed excess capacity in a number of sectors[45] and the government took action to reduce it in the steel, coal, cement, flat glass, aluminium and shipbuilding industries. In the steel sector, China reduced capacity by 65 million tonnes in 2016 and another 50 million tonnes in 2017. In addition, more than 100 million tonnes of substandard steel capacity, so-called ground-mould steel, were eliminated.[46] In the coal sector, in 2016, the government retired 800 million tonnes of capacity and implemented strict production controls. While both steel and coal capacity subsequently increased again as the economy grew, capacity reductions – especially at the lower, more polluting end – contributed significantly to the improvement in air pollution.

The tightening of environmental rules and better enforcement since 2015 are also likely to have been critical in reducing China's pollution. According to the Ministry of Ecology and Environment, China passed or amended many new laws and regulations related to environmental protection between 2016 and 2020. These included a new environmental protection law, water, soil and solid-waste pollution prevention and control laws, and more than 500 new environmental standards.[47] Importantly, the government reformed the compensation system for ecological and environmental damage, and the Supreme Court issued stipulations on rulings involving environmental damage cases, including in civil law.

After President Xi made environmental clean-up a top three priority of his administration, the government established an environmental target responsibility system, holding local officials accountable for missed environmental targets or serious violations. To improve compliance, four rounds of environmental inspections were conducted in 2016–2017. These were undertaken jointly by environmental agencies and the CPC Central Committee, which greatly increased their authority, as the Party system has the power to decide on officials' future. Also, the inspections targeted local CPC and government officials who tolerated pollution, making them more impactful, given the typically collusive nature of the violations. The inspections dealt with 135,000 cases and held more than 17,000 officials accountable during the two-year period.[48]

The new scheme to enhance compliance was not without controversy. The stricter application of environmental rules helped to weed out many high-polluting factories in the 2016–2018 period, most of which were small and private companies, which tended to be less compliant, but more profitable, than large and state-owned companies. Critics of the policy believed that this led to an erosion of private ownership and the further strengthening of SOEs, especially as the latter saw profit surge after industry capacity was reduced and prices rose sharply.

The evolution of China's environmental policy and its enforcement shows that people's key priorities shift with economic development. The Party leadership and the government have responded to the change in public demand and proved adaptable. During this process, public information and involvement have been crucial in pushing through changes in policy and the law. Once the government has decided on a certain direction, new policies and implementation can be swift – especially when the top CPC leadership has expressed a clear opinion. The local-government goal responsibility system and Central Committee inspections are important here. The Party structure and political mechanism help reinforce the policy changes.

China's policy on climate change is another example of the government's adaptive approach. When the Kyoto Protocol[49] came into effect in 2005, many in China saw climate change as a distant threat and resisted committing to emissions targets, which some considered unfair and a hinderance to economic development.[50] Policies focused mainly on the clean-up of local pollution, such as SO_2 and $PM_{2.5}$ emissions, though these goals were consistent with carbon emissions targets. However, as China quickly overtook the United States as the largest carbon dioxide emitter and, as the negative impact of frequent climate-related extreme weather conditions increased, the government's position started to shift.

US–China cooperation in this area under the Obama administration may have also helped China to see the strategic importance of combatting climate change.[51] China formulated a national strategy on climate change in 2013 and, at the 2015 Paris conference, President Xi Jinping committed China to reaching peak carbon emissions by 2030. In 2020, at the UN General Assembly, President Xi announced China's commitment to achieving net zero carbon emissions by 2060. The government published a framework white paper in October 2021, outlining key areas where China would take action to achieve its climate and decarbonisation goals. It called for significant change in China's economic, transport and energy structures, the mobilisation of fiscal, monetary and regulatory policy instruments, and investment in green technology and renewable energy.[52]

Because of senior leadership's strong commitment to decarbonisation, China's political system was quickly mobilised to formulate and implement policies to achieve this goal. Every local administration and government agency was required to come up with specific action plans, with some announcing preliminary proposals to cut production in certain high-energy areas as soon as 2021. In July 2021, China launched a nationwide online carbon trading market. The government has actively promoted green financing,[53] making China's green financing one of the largest such markets in the world. China's outstanding green loans totalled RMB 12 trillion (or US$ 1.8 trillion), while its outstanding green bonds were worth RMB 800 billion.[54]

The initial push towards decarbonisation came up against a severe energy and power shortage in autumn 2021, however, which required some policy adjustment. As the government drafted plans and launched campaigns to lower energy and carbon intensity, economic growth turned out to be very energy intensive. While consumer services were still muted by COVID-related restrictions and cautious sentiment, goods production rose sharply to meet both domestic construction and export demand. Energy demand was further boosted by the government's electricity tariff cuts between 2019 and 2021. The resulting sharp rise in energy consumption made it extremely difficult to achieve the annual energy-efficiency target.

In addition, coal and power shortages appeared as environmental and work-safety concerns limited coal supply growth to 3.7% in the first nine months of 2021, while thermal coal consumption – mainly for power generation – grew 12%.[55] Meanwhile, renewable power generation fell short of target due to weather factors. The resulting coal and power shortage led to widespread power cuts and production outages, trigging upward revisions of electricity tariffs and an easing of coal production controls. It also sparked debates about the speed and manner in which China's decarbonisation transition should take place. This may have led to China's less ambitious commitment to cutting absolute coal consumption at the COP26 climate conference November 2021.[56] China also did not set a specific energy-efficiency target for 2022.

Rules and regulations: easing vs. tightening

Over the past decade, China's government has taken meaningful steps to reform its administration, institute major organisational reform and systematically cut administrative red tape and approval procedures. In 2018, it established the Ministry of Emergency Management and the National Healthcare Security Administration to coordinate and oversee the systematic management of public emergencies and healthcare insurance. It also re-established the Ministry of Justice and the National Intellectual Property Administration and streamlined the management of natural resources and environmental protection, market supervision and regulation, national assets, government audit and local and central government tax collection.[57]

Between 2013 and 2017, the State Council abolished hundreds of administrative approvals and related certification and intermediary services.[58] China also launched the 'Fang Guan Fu', or 'release, management and service' reform, in 2015 to simplify administration and delegate authority, improve management, and enhance government services. These reforms have led to a sharp reduction in the number of days required to start a business (to around 5 from 20),[59] an increase in the registration of private firms (to 60 million between 2016 and 2020)[60] and greater transparency in administrative information and services (including public security and business registration).

However, despite the improvement and formalisation of government management, China still faces significant challenges when it comes to public administration. While the central government has been pushing for deregulation, the overall impact outside of the ease of business registration is difficult to gauge. Local interests may be hard to overcome, while the few tightly controlled rules may be the critical ones. In addition, policy changes are sometimes ad hoc and hard to predict. This was especially notable in 2021, not just in the way that some local governments took extreme measures to

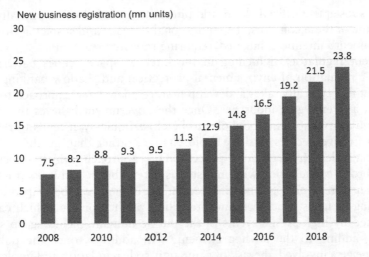

Figure 10.4 Annual new business registrations, 2008–2019.

Source: State Administration for Market regulation, author's estimates.

implement the zero-COVID policy, but also in the regulatory storm that swept through many sectors. In the first eight months of 2021, China saw dozens of rules and regulations announced in the areas of internet finance, internet platforms, data privacy and data security, education and gaming, leading to a sharp correction in the share prices of related stocks. In the education sector, the Offices of the CPC Central Committee and the State Council jointly issued their "Opinions on Further Reducing Student Homework and After-school Tutoring Burdens during the Mandatory Education Period", or 'double reduction' policy.[61] It significantly restricted after-school tutoring, with some measures to be implemented immediately.

In retrospect, the principles of education reform had already been laid out in 2017 by the CPC and State Council and, again, in a speech by President Xi in 2018.[62] The increased marketisation of education, with many public schools maximising matriculation and profit and the after-school tutoring sector crowding out regular compulsory education, had pushed up the cost and inequality of education.[63] People deemed educational costs to be one of the 'three big mountains' they had to climb (the other two being housing and healthcare costs). Even so, the market was still surprised by the sweeping and comprehensive tightening of rules on 24 July.

This may be partly down to the fact that while China's government issues important long-term policy plans and its senior leadership makes important speeches quite often, the speed and scale with which these are turned into enforced rules and regulations varies a great deal. The concentrated timeline of the regulatory amendments in 2021 prompted investors and China observers to wonder about the motivation and timing of the changes. People questioned whether China intended to increase government controls in every sector and was moving away from its long-standing market orientation.

While subsequent official clarification in some areas helped to partially dispel some of these concerns, the reputational damage and suspicion over the government's intentions lingered, requiring repeated reassurance.[64]

Recent regulatory tightening in the internet space echoes patterns in China's regulation of environmental protection and shadow banking. The government typically takes a 'develop first, regulate later' approach to new sectors and emerging industries. Once the government believes that there are regulatory gaps and loopholes to be closed quickly, it tends to rely on administrative decrees to drive rapid change, rather than go through the potentially lengthy legislative process. This approach, which sometimes lacks broad consultation with industry, is often abrupt and lacks transparency. The timing and specifics of rules and regulations can be shaped by the lobbying of firms concerned and prevailing public opinion, which can be triggered by high-profile events in the public domain, including on social media, adding to the ad hoc element.[65] In addition, once the political machine gets involved, the risk of campaign-style regulation and implementation emerges – with every agency participating and state media amping up the message. Lastly, in the absence of official, public explanations, clarifications or rebuttals, the various interpretations of quasi-official channels can make policy and regulatory changes seem unclear and fuel misunderstanding. This and misguided implementation can lead to a public backlash.

The State Council officially passed a Temporary Regulation on the Procedure of Major Executive Decisions in 2019. It stipulated that major executive decisions needed to involve public participation, expert consultation, a risk assessment, a review of legality and collective discussion.[66] Implementation of the regulation seems to have been patchy, however. Government agencies usually conduct research and consultations in principle with experts in the background before important decisions are made. But the extent of such research and consultations may vary depending on the issue or agency involved, as there are no specific requirements. Thus, some government decisions may still come as a surprise to the public. In addition, there is often a lack of consultation and study on operational feasibility and the potential impact of implementation.

Challenges in moving towards a modern public management system

Reform of China's public management first involved the decentralisation of power to local governments and to the market, then the selective recentralisation of some government authority and public responsibilities. There has been a gradual formalisation of governance, including increased reliance on legal procedures and formal institutions. Nevertheless, a clear feature of China's governance system and public management has been the discretion and flexibility of local government and government agencies when it comes to policy implementation.[67]

The central government has informally tolerated and even encouraged such local-government discretion and flexibility. The system lets local administrations incorporate regional and circumstantial differences into policy implementation, creating flexibility and scope for the development of new industries, new business models and new forms of government management. However, such discretion and the government's informal tolerance thereof has also led to uneven or weak compliance in the area of environmental protection, the patchy provision of public services and unfair competition.[68]

Moreover, discretion can translate into ambiguity, uncertainty and instability of public policy. Discretion can be given and expanded when something is seen mainly as a positive force to be encouraged, but also taken away with little warning when it is seen as a threat to be restricted. The latter can be triggered by a major public event, a corruption scandal or the emergency of a significant negative effect, often prompting the central government to use a strong hand to bring about swift change. This path, rather than a more upfront and clear legislative process, can create room for policy flexibility to deal with an uncertain future. But it can also lead to campaign-style execution that causes collateral damage, a lack of transparency and unsustainability.

The discretionary approach to public management may also increase doubt and spawn a backlash from the public, the business community and foreign investors. Even if the government is responding to long-entrenched issues of complaint, its reactionary and offhand approach can fuel the perception that it is trying to control too many things against the public's wishes. Such examples include curtailing the marketisation of education, regulating internet data collection and usage, and investor/consumer protection. Another factor that may lead to such misunderstandings is the lack of a formal mechanism for the government to acknowledge mistakes and assume responsibility, even when it does recognise policy errors and adjust them quietly afterwards.

In the past few years, there has been a tendency to rely more on the CPC leadership and network to drive public policy change, including on poverty reduction, environmental protection and education. While this may be effective in cutting through red tape and resistance, it can also boost the importance of politics to the detriment of public management institutions in the long term. China needs to think of how to establish a modern public management system that can systematically deal with the challenges of an increasingly complex world and balance administrative efficiency with transparency and fairness.

It needs to balance multiple objectives, reflect different interests in society, maintain effective control and supervision while not choking off innovation and the vitality of society and the economy, and provide efficient and equitable government services. It will also have to contend with a more informed and demanding public that is increasingly adept at using the internet and social media.[69] The government is likely to need a more institutionalised and transparent approach and will have to establish more formal channels for public participation and effective communication. The latter is especially important for those who may lose out in any policy or rule change and may quell fears of encroachment on the public interest. It should also help bring about more harmonised public policymaking and implementation.

Notes

1 See Qin et al. (2017) and Luo and Harrison (2019).
2 Xue and Liu (2013).
3 Time Magazine's article 'Beijing's SARS Attack' on 8 April quoted a retired doctor from a military hospital reporting significantly higher SARS cases and deaths than had been officially announced. See Time Magazine (2003).
4 See State Council information Office (2003) and China News (2003).
5 See Dai (2003) and Li (2014).
6 See Dai (2003) and Wu (2009).
7 See Li et al. (2008).
8 See Du and Zhu (2016).
9 See Wang et al. (2019).
10 The full name is the epidemic information reporting management and public health emergency reporting system.
11 See China CDC (2011).
12 See China Statistical Yearbook, various issues.
13 See Huaxi Metro Daily (2020).
14 See Xi (2020).
15 For example, in the case of Wuhan, the time of Chinese New Year celebrations and the local People's Congress meeting may have been a consideration.
16 See Xinhua News Agency (2020).
17 See Oi (1992).
18 See Wang (2014) and Zheng and Wu (1994).
19 See Di and Li (2018).
20 The Tianjin port storage explosion in August 2015 and the Jiangsu Xiangshui chemical plant explosion in March 2019, for example.
21 See White (1988, 1991).
22 See World Bank (2001).
23 See State Environmental Protection Administration (2001). China classifies water into five categories. Class II refers to lightly polluted water that can be used for drinking after treatment. Class III refers to more polluted water that needs serious water treatment. Class IV and V waters are not suitable for direct human contact.
24 They include a water pollution prevention law and solid waste pollution law in 1996 and 1999–2000; an ocean pollution prevention law in 1999; a new air pollution prevention law in 2000; and an environmental impact evaluation law and clean production facilitation law in 2002.
25 See World Bank (2007).
26 PM_{10} refers to particulate matter that is inhalable and has a diameter of less than 10 micrometres.
27 See China Environmental Yearbooks 2004 and 2005.
28 See World Bank (2001, 2007) and SEPA (2001).
29 See World Bank (2007).
30 See Ministry of Ecology and Environment and National Bureau of Statistics (2006).
31 See Ma (2007).
32 See ECON Centre for Economic Analysis (2002).
33 See CPC Central Committee (2007). The 'Scientific Outlook on Development' was added to the CPC charter.

34 Wen (2007).
35 See Luo and Cao (2011).
36 See ECON Centre for Economic Analysis (2002).
37 See Wang and Wheeler (2000).
38 See The Guardian (2010).
39 Ministry of Ecology and Environment (2014).
40 See China People's Daily (2013).
41 A 2015 documentary about air pollution, 'Under the Dome', was watched 200 million times within 48 hours of its release online, before it was taken off air.
42 See State Council (2013b).
43 See Ministry of Ecology and Environment (2018).
44 In the outskirts of Beijing and surrounding provinces, direct coal burning was the main form of winter heating. This apparently accounted for more than 20% of the fine particulate matter in the area, as the direct burning coal could generate as much as 10 times the pollution of centralised coal-fired power plants per unit of coal consumed. See Wei et al. (2016).
45 According to the State Information Center, the capacity utilisation rate was only 67% for crude steel and 65% in the coal sector in 2015. See Zou (2016).
46 See China United Steel and Greenpeace (2017).
47 See Ministry of Ecology and Environment (2020).
48 See China Economic Weekly (2017).
49 The Kyoto Protocol commits industrialised countries and economies in transition to limit and reduce greenhouse gas (GHG) emissions in accordance with agreed individual targets. It was adopted in 1997 and entered into force in 2005. China signed the Kyoto Protocol in 1998.
50 See Ding et al. (2010).
51 China and the US issued a joint announcement on climate change in 2014 after US President Barack Obama's visit to China, committing to work together. This was widely seen as having helped to make Paris 2015 a success. See The White House (2014).
52 See State Council Information Office (2021).
53 The PBC announced various green finance facilities in 2021, including RMB 200 billion of green on-lending facilities.
54 See PBC (2022).
55 According to the China Coal Transportation and Distribution Association.
56 See US State Department (2021).
57 See State Council (2018).
58 For example, government certification of professions, government-appointed intermediary services and central government-mandated local-government approvals.
59 See NPC (2015).
60 See Li (2020).
61 See CPC Central Office and State Council (2021).
62 See CPC Central Office and State Council Office (2017).
63 See Yang (2021).
64 Vice Premier Liu He's speech in mid-March 2022 at a Financial Development and Stability Commission meeting helped to reassure the market. See Xinhua News Agency (2022).
65 See Zhang (2022).
66 See State Council (2019).
67 See Zhou (2011) and Zang and Zhang (2019).
68 See O'Brien and Li (1999) and Zang and Zhang (2019).
69 See Zheng (2014).

11 China and the world

China's economic reintegration into the world after 1978 has helped shape both its own economy and the global economic landscape. Over the subsequent four plus decades, China has gone from being virtually closed to gradually and steadily building relationships and integrating with the rest of the world. These connections span trade and investment, financial markets, technology, supply chains and education. Initially, for China, 'the West', which was still very much in the throes of the Cold War, not only posed threats to the country's ideology, but also presented opportunities. These included access to more advanced equipment and technology, funding, new ideas and alternative models for development. For the western world, China's opening and reform was an opportunity to access a new market, as well as to make the country more like the west – embracing a market economy and liberal values. As time went by and connections grew deeper, how China viewed the world and how the world viewed China evolved.

The steady integration of trade and investment

China has integrated with the rest of the world economy in all respects. The greatest progress has been on trade and foreign direct investment (FDI), but over time, linkages through financial markets, supply chains and tourism have increased as well. Technological relationships have received immense attention of late and are facing increasing hurdles to move forward.

Trade was perhaps the first and most notable channel through which China established connections with the rest of the world. It was also the most visible way for the rest of the world to become exposed to China. Its share of global exports rose from less than 1% in 1980 to 3.8% in 2000.[1] After China joined the WTO in 2001 and was freed of many restrictions and the uncertainty of the annual US review of its Most Favoured Nation status, its trade took off and global brands sourced ever more products there to take advantage of its cheap labour. Before the US–China trade war in 2018, estimates suggested that Walmart, the largest US retailer, imported a quarter of its merchandise from China, while China's exports accounted for about 15% of the global total, the largest share of any nation. From

DOI: 10.4324/9781003310938-12

toys, shoes and daily goods to smartphones, air conditioners and household appliances, China exported everything to developed and developing markets on every continent. During the peak of the COVID pandemic in 2020–2021, when the global supply chains experienced production disruptions and transport backlogs, China gained market share, thanks to its comprehensive industrial base and resilient domestic supply chains.

As China's exports gained market share globally, from 2009, the country also became the world's second-largest importer. China's imports rose from USD 18 billion in 1980 to USD 1.8 trillion in 2020, second only to the United States, accounting for about 10% of global merchandise imports. It has also become the largest trading partner for dozens of countries and is by far the most important market for many commodities, including iron ore, coal and copper. China has further become the world's largest crude oil importer, buying in 10.85 million barrels a day in 2020.[2] Outside of raw materials, China has also become one of the largest markets for industrial machinery and components, such as semiconductors and machine tools, agricultural products, such as soybeans and meat, and luxury consumer goods.

China's integration into global trade has also been mirrored in its ncreasing role in the global supply chains, or global value chains (GVCs), since the mid-1990s. Research has found a continued increase in the Chinese domestic content of other countries' exports as China has exported more intermediate goods.[3] As the 2019 *Global Value Chain Development Report* puts it,[4] 'China is no longer just a 'factory' exporting huge amounts of final goods to the world', but thanks to its rapid industrial upgrades, is integrated through GVC trade networks with large-scale exports and imports

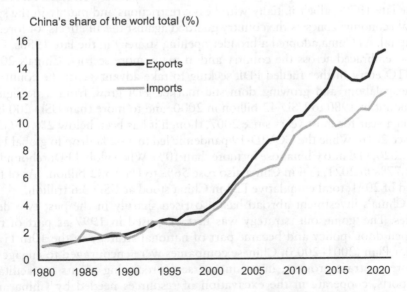

China's share of the world total (%)

Figure 11.1 The rising shares of China's exports and imports in global trade.

Source: IMF, author's calculations.

of intermediate goods and services. Through its interconnectedness with other Asian economies, China has played a central role in forming 'Factory Asia'. The Asian economies, as a bloc, have seen linkages with both Europe and North America increase through the GVCs, especially in the information and communication technology sectors.

China's trade in services has also grown significantly. Some of it, such as insurance and shipping, has expanded along with merchandise trade and investment activities, but the fastest-growing sector has been tourism. In the 1980s and 1990s, China posted a tourism surplus, as the rest of the world was curious about the ancient country, while China's population was too poor and restricted to explore the world. Over the past two decades, China's outbound tourism has risen sharply. In 2019, before COVID-19 severely disrupted global travel, China's outbound tourism spending reached USD 255 billion, with 155 million visits abroad, while inbound visits reached 145 million.[5] Peppered among the macro numbers are anecdotes about Chinese companies buying Club Med, French wineries and US golf courses, and building resorts in Thailand to accommodate the rising number of Chinese tourists.

Another more recent sign of integration can be found in education. In 2019, more than 700,000 Chinese students went to study abroad, almost 100,000 of them to the United States, followed by the United Kingdom, Australia, Japan and Canada. Meanwhile, about 400,000 foreign students were studying in China as of 2019. From 1978 to 2019, a cumulative 6.56 million Chinese people studied abroad, of which 1.65 million remained there (more than 350,000 in the United States), while more than 4 million returned home.[6]

As part of China's opening to the outside world, it has welcomed FDI since the late 1970s, albeit initially with heavy restrictions and mainly in the special economic zones as the country guarded against the 'ill effects' of foreign capital. As China adopted a broader opening strategy in the late 1980s, FDI was embraced across the country and in many more sectors. China's 2001 WTO entry further fuelled FDI, seeking to take advantage of the country's cheap labour and growing domestic market. FDI grew from a negligible amount in 1980 to USD 42 billion in 2000, and to more than USD 200 billion a year for most years since 2007, though it has been below 2% of GDP since 2016. While the COVID-19 pandemic led to a 42% drop in global FDI in 2020, FDI into China rose by more than 10%. When global FDI rebounded by 77% in 2021, FDI in China also rose 56% to USD 332 billion.[7] As of the end of 2021, total cumulative FDI in China stood at USD 3.6 trillion.

China's investment abroad has also risen sharply in the past two decades. The 'going out' strategy was first proposed in 1997 as part of the 'open door' policy and became part of national strategy in the 10th Five-Year Plan (2001–2005). Chinese companies were encouraged to engage in more contract projects, invest in overseas processing plants to facilitate exports, cooperate in the excavation of resources needed by China and develop multinational operations. In the early to mid-2000s, as China's domestic property boom led to a sharp increase in commodity demand and prices, Chinese companies, especially state-owned mining and resource companies, went abroad in search of energy and resources with the support of state-owned banks.[8] This was when China's investment in Africa started to rise sharply, attracting much attention and criticism.[9]

In the late 2000s, export-oriented companies, especially those focusing on labour-intensive products, began to shift some production to cheaper places in Asia and Africa. Nike had already been making more shoes in Vietnam than in China since 2010. China's share of US and European clothing imports has dropped from 42% in 2011 to about 30% in recent years. Since 2013, the private sector's move to diversify investments outside of China and the government's Belt and Road Initiative (BRI) have led to increased outward direct investment (ODI) in other areas, including property and infrastructure, while investment in resources, brand names and technology, as well as manufacturing to avert trade restrictions, has continued. China's cumulative ODI reached USD 2.6 trillion at end 2021.

Unlike the trade and direct investment channels, China has been more cautious when it comes to other capital flows. One of the key lessons it learned from the Asian financial crisis was that a country should not rush and open itself up fully to potentially volatile cross-border capital flows before the domestic financial system and the monetary policy framework are robust enough to deal with them.[10] The global financial crisis and the European debt crisis may have also reinforced that lesson, though some in China argued that it was an opportunity for greater RMB internationalisation. Nevertheless, the further opening up of financial services and markets was

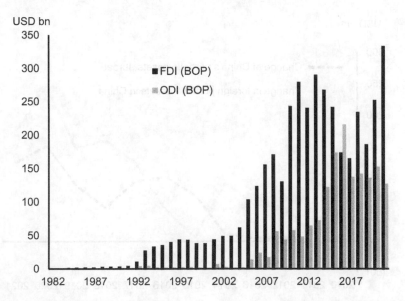

Figure 11.2 Inbound and outbound foreign direct investment, 1982–2021.

Source: SAFE, author's calculations.

a WTO commitment, something successive US administrations have demanded in bilateral economic negotiations, and an objective that China's government also actively sought to achieve.

Financial opening is aligned with the PBC's push for RMB internationalisation, which necessitates freer capital flows and more foreign participation in China's financial markets. Partly motivated by joining the IMF's SDR pool of currencies, China has increased its capital-account and financial-market opening since 2009.[11] Both financial inflows and outflows have risen to an average USD 200–300 billion a year over the past five years, significantly higher than a decade ago, and sometimes with sharp swings. Carry trades by Chinese companies and banks have played a sizable role in the past decade, as onshore-offshore liquidity conditions have often diverged, aided by the RMB's relative stability against the US dollar, though they have been reined in since 2016. In addition, the PBC has generally encouraged cross-border RMB flows to facilitate RMB internationalisation.

Significant progress has been made on opening up financial services in the since 2018 (Chapter 3), including in most areas the US administration had sought. China has also further relaxed controls on portfolio inflows. Financial-market opening did not just signal China's continued embrace of opening up to the outside world, but the government also saw the benefit of bringing international institutional investors and best practices onshore and facilitating domestic capital-market reforms. As global investors had relatively light exposure to Chinese assets and as the country offered decent bond yields relative to other major economies, there had been a steady and sizable inflow into China's bond market before 2022, mainly into sovereign debt.

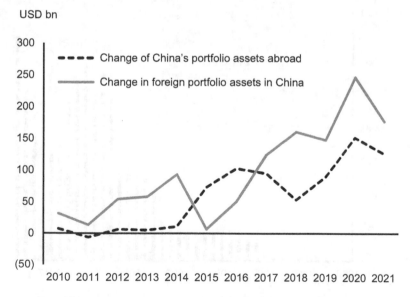

Figure 11.3 Portfolio investment flows, 2010–2021.

Source: SAFE, author's calculations.

At the end of 2021, foreign equity and bond holdings each exceeded USD 600 billion, accounting for 4.3% and 3.5% of China's markets, respectively, not including foreign holdings of Chinese companies listed in Hong Kong. Also, a total of 253 Chinese companies were listed in the United States as of March 2022, though their total market cap had halved from May 2021.[12] Further financial-market opening is seen as a way of increasing foreign investment in China, to cushion the country from pressure by some foreign politicians to decouple it from the world economy. In most of 2022, aggressive rate hikes by the US Fed and increased uncertainty over China have led to some capital outflows.

Changing views

How the world sees China: from exporter and market to competitor and disrupter

As China's connection with the world deepened, the world's view of China gradually changed. In the first couple of decades, China was seen as an exporter of cheap, low-end products. One Chinese official famously said that China needed to export 800 million shirts to buy a Boeing or Airbus plane.[13] In the 2000s, China was increasingly seen as a major source of demand and another engine of global growth for many emerging-market economies. This came particularly to the fore soon after the global financial crisis, when China's economy powered ahead with massive imports of commodities, industrial equipment and luxury goods, while developed economies suffered a serious recession. Between 2001 and 2010, China's imports rose from USD 0.2 trillion to USD 1.2 trillion and became the largest market for many economies. With car sales increasing from 2 million units to 18[14] and construction surging, China's crude steel production almost quadrupled and iron ore imports increased ninefold to 619 million tonnes over the decade.

That was also the decade that saw China gain its reputation as a heavy polluter. While China's environment deteriorated throughout the 1990s,[15] it was not until the mid-2000s that the world began to pay more attention to its pollution levels. Along with its rapid heavy-industry growth, China's coal consumption rose from about 1 billion tonnes in 2000 to 3 billion tonnes in 2010. As a result, according to the World Bank, China's CO_2 emissions grew from 3 billion tonnes in 2000 to 8.15 tonnes in 2010, surpassing the United States in 2005.[16]

Around the time of the global financial crisis, China also came to be seen as a disrupter and serious competitor to some industries in the developed world. Previously, it had been known to compete mainly with other emerging economies on cheap, labour-intensive products. By 2010, however, China's electronics processing trade had taken a sizeable leap, while exports of steel and machinery had also increased, putting Chinese firms in direct competition with companies in the developed world. The solar panel industry is a good example. China's production quadrupled between 2009 and

2011 thanks to government support and subsidies (Chapter 4), prompting it to export its excess to Europe and the United States, driving down prices and squeezing many other producers out of the market.

There was a sea change in the western world's view of China. One reason may have been that China's gain in terms of global market share had become more visible, while the United States and Europe were slow to recover from the recession that followed the global financial crisis. It was common for politicians and opinion leaders to focus on how globalisation and imports from China were contributing to the loss of manufacturing jobs in developed markets, including the United States,[17] while downplaying other key factors, such as technological change[18] and the absence of structural adjustments to boost education and infrastructure. Meanwhile, more holistic research showing how trade with China had helped US companies to become more competitive and had boosted overall US manufacturing employment[19] did not receive nearly as much airtime.

China's high-profile acquisitions of western firms at large premiums, backed by the government with easy financing (e.g., ChemChina's purchase of Syngenta in 2015), may have also triggered suspicion and wariness among western companies. Moreover, aware of its rising economic might, China sometimes allowed or denied market access to make a political or diplomatic point.[20] China's increased assertiveness in international affairs and the use of its economic prowess were seen by some as a rising threat to the existing international economic order. Concerns were further increased by China's demands for a bigger say in international institutions and the reform of existing global governance and rules,[21] which China (along with many other emerging-market economies) saw as being set in the post-WWII period and, hence, outdated.

These factors were compounded by deep suspicion towards China arising from ideological differences. *The Economist's* 2018 article, 'How the West Got China Wrong', may be a good reflection of the mainstream view of the western establishment. It argued that the west opened up to China in the hope that it would become 'more like us', with a free-market economy and political system like the western countries. However, China did not become 'one of us', but rather economically successful under a *de facto* one-party political system that does not appear to be in imminent danger of losing power. Some may find this baffling and threatening at the same time.[22] China's 'four confidences' (in the socialist path, theory, system and culture), which permeated the World Political Party Dialogues held in late 2017 after China's 19th CPC Congress, may have prompted further suspicion as to its intentions with regard to ideological competition on the world stage.[23]

China's view of the western world: from role model to flawed peer and competitor

China's view of the western world also changed. When it decided in 1992 to pursue a 'socialist market economy', China wanted to learn from the developed world about setting up market mechanisms, institutions and rules. It took advice from the 'Washington Consensus' institutions, the World Bank and the IMF, on how to push through market reforms. When China restructured its banking sector in the early 2000s, it invited large banks from the United States, the country with the most developed market economy and most sophisticated financial system, to help. Western economies, especially the United States, were seen as role models for their advanced development, mature institutions and functioning market system – all of which the majority of China's elite then thought the country should aspire to.

The global financial crisis sent shock waves throughout China as the vulnerability and flaws of the most powerful and advanced capitalist market economy were laid bare. As the US government bailed out Wall Street and main-street companies, the belief that the market knew best and that the US government did not intervene (like China), crumpled. Moreover, the tables seemed to turn; senior Chinese officials who were imploring Wall Street executives to help reform Chinese banks just a few years earlier found themselves being sought after to hold US government bonds and buy up troubled Wall Street firms.[24] This, and China's subsequent strong economic growth, led to some soul searching about the problems with the western system and the merits of China's system.[25]

After the global financial crisis, the mainstream media, both in China and abroad, seemed to emphasise how China's forceful government intervention and state-controlled economic system had been instrumental in avoiding economic disaster and dealing with the crisis. During this period, the 'Beijing Consensus' and the 'China model' became popular terms, even though they referred to different things for different people. The term 'Beijing Consensus' was first proposed as an alternative to the development model espoused by the Washington Consensus. It was said to be 'innovative' in its 'constant tinkering' with government strategy and policies to suit different situations, pursuing development objectives beyond GDP growth and seeking independence from outside pressures.[26] However, after the global financial crisis, this term and the 'China model' were used to refer to state capitalism, or strong Party control of politics and the economy.[27]

This representation de-emphasised, arguably, the most important aspect of China's development strategy thus far – a gradualist, pragmatic and adaptive approach to reform and policy. In emphasising the role of state control, it neglected the fact that China's economic success had been built on market liberalisation away from absolute state control (Chapters 2 and 3, and Figure 2.5). Moreover, China's transition was not yet complete; its development strategy was not set, but still being debated at home and continuing to evolve.[28] Nevertheless, this representation of the 'China Model' became the dominant portrayal of China's economy both at home and abroad. And with China's rapid investment expansion into Africa and other developing regions, it has been increasingly met with suspicion and seen as a challenge to the mainstream western market ideology, even western democracy itself.

Notably, China's government had been criticised at home for focusing too much and too narrowly on GDP growth at the expense of other development objectives in the years prior to the global financial crisis, and for using excessive stimulus thereafter that resulted in *guojinmintui* and significant excess capacity and bad debt. However, while economic policy was adjusted in response to the criticism, the public narrative emphasised the success of the government-led growth model and the resulting rise in China's international standing, accompanied by a rise in national confidence and pride. Many Chinese started to view the United States differently, no longer holding up the US economic system as a shining light and a perfect model, but one with deep flaws that could also fail.

China has always viewed itself as a big, important country deserving the respect of the rest of the world and a say in international affairs. However, this had not been the case for around 200 years and certainly not in the post-WWII global economic order. In the first 30 years after 1978, China concentrated mainly on domestic developments to escape poverty and kept a low profile in international affairs, following Deng Xiaoping's 'hide the shine', or 'taoguangyanghui' (韬光养晦) policy.

After the global financial crisis, there was a major shift in attitude. There was a broad realisation that China had done things right in its economic development under the CPC (although the specifics were debatable), that its large market was a big draw for foreign companies and investors, and that the market mechanism could not address some of the country's central domestic challenges. Such conclusions, plus China's rising economic power, led to increased confidence that the country could demand better terms in international trade, that the student of the west had something to teach its teachers, and that its own path of combining the market with the state was the right model for China and could provide a good alternative for others. This narrative has become the dominant one, both in China and abroad, in the past decade, with economic policies increasingly seen through a political lens.

Beyond trade friction: rule follower to rule disrupter?

China very much wanted to be included in the international economic order represented by institutions like the IMF and World Bank, which it joined in 1980. It formally applied to join the GATT in 1986 and finally joined its successor organisation, the WTO, in 2001 after 15 years of negotiation. Despite some strong domestic opposition, Beijing's reform-oriented leaders pushed hard for the country to join and be accepted by the existing world economic order. One of the most under-appreciated and arguably most important benefits of WTO entry for China was the streamlining and realignment of domestic rules and regulations to ensure consistency with WTO requirements.[29] An important reason for China's willing acceptance of what were seen as stringent rules and conditions was to incentivise domestic reform, and to use those rules to break down protective barriers between different regions within the country.[30] After WTO entry, China saw its trade being governed – and disciplined – by international rules. Anti-dumping charges against it increased significantly, for example. Indeed, China's WTO agreement had special provisions and safeguards on dumping to protect its trading partners many years after WTO entry.[31]

Over time, China learned to navigate WTO rules and use legal channels. Despite lingering restrictions, including special safeguards that gave its trading partners the right to impose quotas or tariffs, China's export growth accelerated with WTO membership. Reduced uncertainty and access to a greater market certainly helped, but it was also partly due to the country's success in moving beyond the traditional labour-intensive exports of textiles and apparel, and the rapid development of electronic processing exports. China's lack of exchange-rate appreciation throughout much of the 2000s, when its exports and trade surplus surged, may have also helped and was seen as an unfair trade practice,[32] frustrating some trading partners, especially the United States.

The renminbi was fixed against the US dollar when China's bilateral surplus with the United States surged from USD 28 billion in 2001 to USD 114 billion in 2005, while its total trade surplus rose from USD 23 billion to USD 102 billion.[33] To prevent the RMB from appreciating, the PBC bought US dollars from exporters and invested them back into US Treasuries (Chapter 5). In multiple rounds of strategic economic dialogue, the United States pressed China to change its policy, either by allowing nominal appreciation or through structural adjustment. China let its currency appreciate by about 12% against the dollar between mid-2005 and the end of 2007, but the real effective exchange rate against a basket of trading partner currencies only appreciated by about 6%. Its trade surplus with the United States, meanwhile, ballooned to USD 163 billion, while its overall trade surplus burgeoned to USD 262 billion.

China's real exchange rate did appreciate by more than 20% between 2007 and 2012 – and another 15% by 2017 – as the country reduced energy subsidies and increased the minimum wage and labour protection. Its overall trade surplus declined from 8.5% of GDP in 2007 to 3.0% in 2011 and was below 4% between 2017 and 2021. Its bilateral surplus with the US in USD terms continued to rise nonstop – to USD 202 billion in 2011 and to more than USD 300 billion in 2017 before the US–China trade war broke out. The trade surplus with the United States is largely due to global supply-chain developments and China's role as a key downstream producer of consumer goods, especially electronics. Nevertheless, because of the persistently large bilateral imbalance and the various grievances of US companies (more below), recent US administrations have not acknowledged that China has made the structural adjustments they had previously advocated.

While the causes of the trade surplus and the role of the exchange rate (and degree of RMB undervaluation) are debatable,[34] complaints that Chinese firms, mainly SOEs, benefited unfairly from low-cost funding and preferential treatment are harder to dispute. In this regard, the preferential treatment of SOEs did not seem to benefit China's exports much, as the

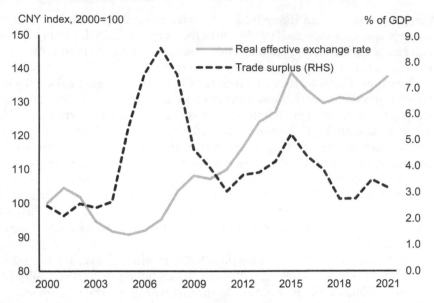

Figure 11.4 The real exchange rate and the trade surplus, 2000–2021.

Source: NBS, China Customs, SAFE, Author estimates.

SOE share of exports had dropped from two-thirds in the mid-1990s to 11% by 2012 and 8% by 2021. It may have prevented more imports, though.[35] In addition, western companies were increasingly unhappy with China's joint-venture arrangements involving technology transfers to local partners, even if many companies had voluntarily entered into such arrangements at the onset.[36] For the United States, China's flawed record on intellectual property (IP) protection had always been an issue. Microsoft, for example, estimated that it had collected only a fraction of the Chinese user fees it was due for its software.[37]

Although many issues existed well before China's WTO entry, their persistence afterwards as the economy and exports grew had a larger impact on world trade and the global economy, and were seen as more disruptive. Also, perhaps surprisingly to both Chinese and western observers, who had expected WTO entry to boost China's private economy and weaken state ownership, China's SOE profitability improved (though state-owned firms were still less profitable than private ones) and the role of the state did not visibly diminish. Indeed, the state has played a more prominent role since the global financial crisis and in recent years. China's slow opening of certain sectors, including financial services until 2019, has likely frustrated its trading partners further. Such long-standing frustrations may be one reason why they have discounted the more recent, significant areas of liberalisation.

China's rapid increase in overseas investment is also seen as another disruptive force by many in the west. The drive of Chinese companies to acquire technology, brands and resources abroad, including in Europe and the United States, had already caused alarm before the global financial crisis, partly because many of them were SOEs with easy access to finance. The failed attempt of the China National Offshore Oil Corporation (CNOOC) to buy US oil company Unocal, for instance, aroused US concern about national security. It also made Chinese companies more aware of the political sensitivities of their acquisitions in developed countries. This led to more investment in Africa (see box below) and other parts of the world that were more welcoming. China's investment and lending in Africa, meanwhile, disturbed the conventional channels of foreign investment and aid there, as well as the role of international institutions. Some African countries in financial trouble or receiving help from the United States and Europe found the conditions attached to such help less palatable once there were alternative loans and investment available from China.

Moreover, China has begun to set up international institutions in which it has a bigger role since 2015. China and other emerging economies have tried for decades to gain greater representation in the IMF and the World Bank, but their efforts have been blunted by strong resistance from developed countries, especially the United States, which does not want to give up its *de facto* vetoing power.[38] European countries, which have declined in relative economic size, have also not wanted to relinquish their outsized say. Frustrated by the slow progress and the monopolisation of leadership by the United States (World Bank), Europe (IMF) and Japan (Asia Development Bank), China has sought alternatives by co-creating new international institutions with other major emerging economies.

The Asia Infrastructure Investment Bank (AIIB) was launched in December 2015 after the United States failed to persuade its key Asian allies to stay away. With a starting capital of USD 100 billion, it aimed to scale up 'financing for sustainable development' and improve global economic governance.[39] The New Development Bank, first proposed by India at the 2012 BRICS (Brazil, Russia, India, China, and South Africa) summit, was also launched in 2015, headquartered in Shanghai, to 'support public or private projects through loans, guarantees and equity participation' and other financial instruments. By setting up these new institutions, China was no longer just a passive receiver of international rules drawn up by western countries a long time ago, but actively helping to set new rules in the international arena.

Box: China's investment in Africa and the Belt and Road Initiative

China became Africa's largest trading partner around the year 2000, and Chinese investment in Africa started to take off soon after that. China's FDI into Africa grew from USD 70 million in 2003 to USD 4.2 billion in 2020, or over 10% of total FDI in the continent that year.[40] For all the hype, China's total FDI in Africa only accounted for around 4.4% of Africa's total stock of FDI as of 2018, less than that of the United States, France and the Netherlands.[41] China's investment in

Africa has often been characterised as government driven and resource focused. And, indeed, Chinese companies have been attracted by Africa's natural resources, with more than a quarter of China's investment in Africa going to the mining sector – including energy and resources. This has often involved state-to-state deals, sometimes in countries with weak governance and high political risk.[42]

However, Chinese companies have also been attracted to Africa's large markets and cheap labour, as well as the opportunity for tariff-free exports to the United States.[43] Most Chinese firms operating in Africa's manufacturing and agriculture sectors are private, receiving little help from the government,[44] and have tended to home in on skills-rich countries such as Ethiopia and Egypt. Over the past decade, most of China's FDI has gone into construction, including infrastructure, and Africa has eclipsed Asia as the largest market for Chinese overseas construction contracts.

China's involvement in Africa has been controversial and come under fire from western governments and the mainstream media.[45] However, independent studies have found the picture to be more mixed. Researchers have found that though Chinese firms often employ a lower share of the local workforce than other foreign firms, the localisation rate has increased significantly over the past ten years.[46] China's investment has created substantial local job opportunities and contributed to faster growth in Africa, including by building infrastructure.[47]

One big criticism of China's engagement in Africa has been the large amounts of debt extended to the continent, especially some highly indebted countries. According to SAIS-CARI estimates, the Chinese government and state entities signed loan commitments worth USD 153 billion with African governments and SOEs between 2000 and 2019.[48] However, China has scaled back its lending commitments since 2016 (2013 if Angola's refinancing is excluded) and is moving away from highly indebted countries and towards economically stronger borrowers, while resource-backed lending has declined.[49] China joined the G20 debt-service suspension initiative in 2020.[50]

China's One Belt, One Road initiative, or BRI, was first proposed in 2013. It encompasses infrastructure development in the Silk Road Economic Belt, or countries along a 'belt' of road and railway transportation routes, and the '21st century maritime silk road'. Together, the BRI spans some 90 countries in East Africa, South and Southeast Asia, central Asia and the Middle East, Eastern and Central Europe and Oceania. The original plan mainly revolved around infrastructural cooperation, but it has expanded into policy coordination, trade and financial connectivity, and connectivity among people.[51] The

main official objectives are to expand trade and infrastructural connections to help generate inclusive and mutually beneficial growth.
However, commentators within and outside of China have often
attributed other goals or intentions to the plan, from exporting excess
capacity to expanding geopolitical influence, and even accelerating
RMB internationalisation.[52]

China's ascent of the technology ladder and its naked ambition to become
a technology leader have also sparked tension and met with suspicion. The
most high-profile example may be China's telecom equipment giant,
Huawei. Established in 1987 and initially focused on manufacturing phone
switches, Huawei sold mainly to small cities and rural areas in China before
expanding to developing countries. Helped by economies of scale, consistently large investments in R&D, and the acquisition of foreign technology,
the company has become one of the largest telecom equipment producers
globally over the past decade. In a field traditionally dominated by US and
European giants, Huawei has become an industry leader, with the most
advanced 5G technology in the world.

Somewhat alarming to the west has been China's plan to advance its
technological ambition through the high-tech MIC 2025 programme
(Chapter 4). China sees climbing the technology ladder as critical to sustaining development, fearing that it will be left behind by global technology
advances, especially as the country's comparative advantage of cheap labour
diminishes with its ageing population. China is also keen to do away with
its heavy reliance on imports of advanced technology and equipment, which
makes it vulnerable to changes in foreign policy and commercial interests.
Externally, China's plan is seen as a threat to existing western firms, who see
China's government subsidies and state aid as unfair competition and a
disruption to the global economic order (though the United States and other
countries actively engage in the practice). More recently, western governments have also played up national security concerns about Chinese firms.

Another source of western anxiety about China is perhaps its rapid rise
in digital technology and big data. A combination of factors – including its
wide penetration of the mobile network, massive amount of available data,
traditionally lax regulations (which have been tightened, Chapter 10) and
innovative entrepreneurs – has led to rapid growth in e-commerce, mobile
payments, car/cab hailing and other online services. These developments,
and the widespread installation of business and government surveillance
equipment, have also provided rich data sources for the development of
artificial intelligence (AI).

Such developments anywhere would have led to debate and concern
about privacy and the influence of tech companies and big data on social
governance. In the case of China, there is the added concern from the west
that it would enhance the control of the one-party political system. Western

concern over the latter has intensified in recent years as China has emphasised the key role of the CPC in economic affairs and tightened rules on internet companies, education and the media. Many believe China to be deviating from its market-oriented development strategy of the past, while China's leadership has stressed security considerations.

China's clumsiness in dealing with the world

Rising concerns about a directional shift in Chinese policy may have been a significant factor behind the sharp deterioration in US–China relations since 2017. Chinese official media have blamed the sudden shift in America's China policy on US domestic political considerations and the country's desire to suppress China's development.[53] While that may be true, it came on top of an already long list of grievances from the United States (and some other trading partners) about China's effective delays in opening up certain domestic sectors, as promised under the WTO,[54] its weak IP protection and its subsidies to SOEs.

Moreover, there have been increased concerns in recent years about the stagnation or backtracking of market-oriented reforms in China, in particular, the increased CPC presence in private and foreign companies.[55] In China, there does indeed seem to have been an undercurrent against market forces and private ownership, especially in mid-2018, when calls for the private sector to 'exit' the stage[56] were not rebutted officially for some time. President Xi's speech in November 2018 assured firms of the government's 'unwavering' support for the private sector, but confidence remained fragile.

While former US President Donald Trump's desire to disassemble political and international relations norms may have helped to galvanise anti-China forces around the administration, China seems to have been late in understanding the sea change in US perceptions and attitudes and proved inexpert in telling its side of the story in trade disputes and on economic policy. This is perhaps because China is relatively new to the international arena, having traditionally been inward looking and focused on domestic issues.

During the 1970s and 1980s, China, as a poor country transitioning towards a market economy, was mainly learning from western economies. With greater power comes greater responsibility, but China did not have experience in exercising that power or responsibility. It had always positioned itself as a weak and poor developing country and continued to see itself that way, especially compared with the United States. As China has become the world's second-largest economy and a powerful international force, however, it has often exercised its economic might, especially vis-à-vis its smaller neighbours. There is, thus, an apparent inconsistency in a self-professed developing country using its sizeable economic power to punish or reward smaller countries.

China's awkwardness on the international stage is evident in the fact that most official speeches – even those held abroad by the foreign ministry and officials – continue to target the domestic audience. Also, China's official media tend to report predominantly positive news on China, focusing on its achievements, with limited coverage of its problems, emphasising what the government has done to help achieve the successful outcome. Such reporting may exaggerate the role of the government in economic affairs and provide insufficient information for trading partners and foreign observers to understand China's strategy and policy intent.

Moreover, while reporting on China's technological progress and prowess may be largely factual and can boost domestic confidence, it may also exaggerate China's actual strength in many technological fields and its threat to the dominant positions still held by advanced economies. China's government is traditionally unused to explaining policies to the public or the market. This can often lead to misinterpretation and misunderstandings, with unwanted consequences. A good example is the regulatory tightening of the internet sector in 2021.

China's policymakers rightly focus on domestic issues when making economic or social decisions, but the government often does not seem sufficiently aware of its impact on the rest of the world and is not as accustomed as more developed economies to explaining its policy intentions. One example is the BRI. While there are clear synergies in China's increased investment in and trade with the economies along the Belt and Road, the government has allowed too many other interpretations from various domestic quarters to populate the airwaves. Claims about exporting or dumping excess capacity (which is not material) or exerting geopolitical influence on strategically important regions (which is hard to prove or disprove) have abounded, sometimes with what would appear to be official or quasi-official backing. It would seem that the relevant agencies did not think to communicate or work more closely with partner countries in this regard, something that could have forestalled the negative international perceptions of and backlash against China's outreach strategy.

Future scenarios

How might China's relations with the world evolve? China's government tries to project an outlook of the country's peaceful rise within a 'community of shared future for the mankind'.[57] It has repeatedly tried to assure the United States and other western powers that China would never be a hegemony and does not want to export the Chinese model or challenge the western ideology.[58] So far, China's assurances have not meaningfully allayed suspicions and fears from neighbouring countries or western powers. In just a few years, the world's main concern about China seems to have shifted from potential economic implosion to disruption of the existing global order through the expansion of its economic and political sphere of influence. The recent US–China trade war has worsened relations between China and the western world, rallying US (and other) security and ideological hawks on one hand and stoking nationalist sentiment in China on the other. The COVID-19 pandemic, the Russian invasion of Ukraine and concerns about supply-chain security have added further fuel to the fire. This has led the west, especially the United States, to reformulate strategies aimed at suppressing, containing or defeating China on multiple fronts.[59]

With mistrust and tensions so high, it seems difficult to contemplate a future in which China integrates further into a more open and inclusive global economy, and where major powers focus their energy on cooperating with each other to combat global challenges. In *Destined for War*, Graham Alison warns of the United States and China falling into a 'Thucydides trap', referencing how the rise of Athens and the fear of the rise in Sparta led to the Peloponnesian war.[60] Many seem to share this worry about a potential conflict or confrontation. Others predict a renewed Cold War in which China establishes a separate but parallel sphere of influence, decoupled from the west.[61] Some observers and scholars have disputed such predictions, however, pointing out that China has not historically been expansionist, that the military spending and capability gaps between China and the United States are substantial – far larger than those between the United States and the Soviet Union during the Cold War – and that China is still very much focused on developing its domestic economy, which is key to the 'great rejuvenation'.[62] Nevertheless, many China observers and scholars worry about the continued deterioration of US–China relations and the risks associated with it.

Fu Ying, China's former deputy minister of foreign affairs, has proposed that the US–China relationship could develop into cooperative competition, or 'coopetition', 'maintaining necessary, mutually beneficial cooperation while managing unavoidable but benign competition'.[63] Some in the US academic and diplomatic community seem to agree that the United States should find ways to co-exist with China.[64] Political scientist Joseph Nye has noted that, 'our strategy should regard our China relationship as a cooperative rivalry where we pay heed to both aspects of the term'.[65] The Biden administration's China strategy, while not well articulated, seems to attempt to compartmentalise different aspects of relations with China – confronting and containing China in areas of security, technology and ideology, competing economically and on trade, and cooperating on the challenges of climate change. This strategy seems to be finding support among several major European countries as well, as they toughen their stance on China from a security perspective and in other non-economic areas, and amend their policies on trade and investment, while welcoming China's efforts on decarbonisation.

Meanwhile, there are forces driving the decoupling of China from the rest of the world, which have only been enhanced by Russia's invasion of Ukraine. In the United States and other western economies, these forces have led to greater restrictions on China's access to advanced technology and Chinese companies' access to western markets,[66] restrictions on Chinese investment, and increased subsidies and political pressure on companies to produce in domestic markets or trusted friendly countries.[67] The United States has also tightened restrictions on Chinese students and scholars attending schools in the United States or collaborating with US academics, as well as on US investment in Chinese companies (including pressure on government pension funds, the blacklisting of Chinese public companies and rules to force the delisting of Chinese companies from the US stock market).[68]

In China, some interpret the government's strategy of 'dual circulation', which emphasises 'internal circulation',[69] as a mandate to exclude foreign participation and foreign technology and decouple from the outside world. In addition, China's concerns about national security, especially in the areas of data and the internet, have increased substantially, leading to increased emphasis on and incentives for technological self-reliance. That said, China's outward orientation seems to have continued, as evidenced by its very active pursuit of new free trade and investment agreements recently – its signing of the Regional Comprehensive Economic Partnership (RCEP), its negotiation of the EU-China Comprehensive Agreement on Investment (CAI) (even though this is now on hold), and its application to join the Trans-Pacific Partnership (TPP).

Many have pointed out that decoupling China from the world economy would be very costly and that a complete decoupling might be impossible, in any case, due to the now strong interdependence of China and the rest of the world. As Ryan Hass of the Brookings Institute puts it: 'The dense webs formed by trade, financial, scientific, and academic links between the United States and China will make it difficult' for either side to inflict harm on the other without hurting itself.[70] Joseph Nye wrote that, 'even if breaking apart economic interdependence were possible, we cannot decouple the ecological interdependence that obeys the laws of biology and physics, not politics'.[71] In fact, the supply-chain adjustments brought by political pressures of decoupling (rather than economic costs) may be reversing some of the disinflationary benefit experienced in developed economies in the previous two decades.

Nevertheless, though it would be painful for companies and is not economically efficient, some decoupling is still likely to occur as politics trump economics, and geopolitical uncertainty and political pressure force firms and institutions to make painful adjustments. Macro data until 2022 do not show obvious decoupling, as trade linkages between China and the rest of the world increased during the COVID-19 pandemic (partly due to a temporary shift from services to goods in global consumption and supply issues in other economies), and FDI inflows into China remained strong in 2020 and 2021.

However, even as Chinese exporters struggled to fill orders from the rest of the world in 2021 amid supply disruptions elsewhere, a UBS Evidence Lab survey found that exporters continued to contemplate shifting some production overseas to reduce risk.[72] The US's 'Build Back Better' plan uses tax policies, subsidies and the Buy America Executive Order to persuade US companies to move back to the United States,[73] and this is likely to be enhanced by the America Compete Act 2022. US Congress has more bills in the pipeline to try to reduce links with China.[74] Meanwhile, many countries and companies have been caught in a difficult situation, having to choose sides. The decoupling pressures have likely increased in 2022 after Russia's invasion of Ukraine and amid COVID-19 related production disruptions in China.

The external environment and the different China strategies of the major western economies will undoubtedly affect the future of China's global relationship. One cannot emphasise enough, however, that the various domestic forces and domestic challenges shaping China are likely to be the most important ones forging China's future in the world. Key domestic stakeholders include the Communist Party, the SOE sector, the urban middle class, the migrant population, private entrepreneurs and local government officials. One needs to consider the demands and motivations of various domestic stakeholders in tandem with the CPC and the government's key domestic policy objectives when predicting the country's international behaviour and strategy.

Like people all over the world, the Chinese people want a better life for themselves and their children. The CPC has promised to deliver the 'great rejuvenation of the Chinese nation', further defined as turning China into 'a modern socialist country' by 2050.[75] Modern is defined as 'prosperous, strong, democratic, culturally advanced, harmonious and beautiful'.[76] The CPC believes that the main social contradiction in China exists between people's growing demand for a better life and the country's uneven and insufficient development, while President Xi considers popular support to be the Party's most important goal.[77] Thus, the CPC has defined its implicit social contract over the coming decades as 'better satisfying people's increasing demand on multiple fronts', facilitating 'comprehensive development and common prosperity'.[78] In other words, the top domestic priority of China's government will be continued economic development and much more – better governance, social harmony (vastly reduced inequality), environmental protection and ecological balance to satisfy the growing demands of the population.

To succeed in these objectives and honour the social contract, the CPC and the government must overcome immense challenges on multiple fronts and navigate complicated and dynamic interests from key stakeholders at home. To achieve sustainable economic development, China must deal with an ageing population, over-investment in some sectors, high debt levels, inefficient SOEs, resource and energy constraints, the country's lack of core advanced technology and the need to become more innovative.

SOE reform has faced and is likely to continue facing substantial resistance, as many continue to believe that SOEs are the bedrock of China's socialist economy. Better governance requires greater participation by the people and more transparency and accountability of government. Uneven regional development, rural-urban disparities and the unequal rights and access to public services of migrant workers in urban areas are all important factors undermining social harmony. Addressing these issues will likely lead to a redistribution of benefits among different interest groups.

Tackling environmental and climate-change challenges will require major adjustments to China's industrial, transport and energy structures. While the process will create new investment opportunities, it is also likely to lead to the destruction of some existing capital, affecting the lives of millions of people and the quality of billions of dollars of assets. As the government focuses on overcoming these challenges to mould China into 'a modern socialist economy', it wants a 'peaceful and calm international environment'.[79] China has and will continue to become more assertive in international affairs, especially on what it considers to be issues of sovereignty or matters involving territorial integrity. However, this does not mean that China will necessarily be expansionary like other great powers have been.

Notes

1 IMF and UNCTAD data.
2 See Reuters (2020).
3 See Wang et al. (2017b).
4 See World Bank and WTO (2019).
5 MOFCOM data.
6 Ministry of Education data.
7 FDI inflows as a share of GDP peaked in 1993 at more than 6%. See UNCTAD (2022).
8 See Zweig and Bi (2005) and Downs and Evans (2006).
9 See Reuters (2011), French (2014) and Lyman (2005).
10 See Prasad et al. (2003).
11 SDR is the notional currency unit used by the IMF. The RMB became part of the SDR basket in 2015. See IMF (2015).
12 See the US-China Economic and Security Review Commission (2022).
13 China Securities Journal (2005).
14 Data from the Chinese Association of Automobile Manufacturers.
15 See World Bank (2001).
16 World Bank Indicators.
17 See Acemoglu et al. (2016) and Caliendo et al. (2017).
18 See Hicks and Devaraj (2017) and Brynjolfsson and McAfee (2014).
19 See Wang et al. (2018).
20 For example, China tolerated a nationalistic boycott of Japanese firms and products after Japan moved to nationalise the disputed Diaoyu Island in 2012, then retailer Lotte after South Korea agreed to install the THAAD US anti-missile system in 2017.
21 For example, increased quotas and voting rights at the IMF and World Bank.
22 See The Economist (2018a).
23 See The Diplomat (2017).
24 See Paulson (2015), Leonhardt (2009) and China Briefing (2008).
25 See China People's Daily (2010) and Liu, H. (刘鹤) (2013).
26 See Ramo (2004) and Leonard (2006).
27 See The Economist (2009) and Bell (2015).
28 See Zhang (2012b), Chen (2010) and Tao (2016).
29 According to China's Ministry of Commerce, the country cleaned up over 2000 central-government and more than 190,000 local-government rules and regulations after joining the WTO.
30 See Long (2011).

31 Member countries could continue to use 'non-market economy' status in anti-dumping investigations against China for 15 years after its WTO entry and 'transitional product-specific safeguards' against imports from China for 12 years after.
32 See Bergsten (2003) and Goldstein and Lardy (2008).
33 China Customs data.
34 See Mundell (2004), Wang (2004) and Wang and Hu (2010).
35 See Lardy (2014) and China Statistical Yearbooks (various years).
36 See Office of the United States Trade Representative (2018) and Reuters (2018).
37 See Financial Times (2012).
38 For example, major decisions require 85% of the vote. The US has *de facto* veto power, as it alone has more than 17% of the vote.
39 See AIIB (n.d.).
40 UNCTAD and SAIS data.
41 Estimate based on UNCTAD, García-Herrero and Xu (2019) and SAIS data.
42 See Chen, Dollar and Tang (2016).
43 See Financial Times (2019) and Sun (2017).
44 See Park (2021).
45 See French (2014) and Reuters (2011).
46 See Oya and Schaefer (2019), Tang (2016) and Kernen and Lam (2014).
47 See Abekah-Koomson and Chinweokwu (2020), McKinsey & Co. (2017) and Sun (2017).
48 See Boston University Global Development Policy Center (n.d.).
49 See Acker and Brautigam (2021).
50 See Financial Times (2021b).
51 See Xinhua News (2017).
52 See Chu (2020) and Zhang et al. (2016).
53 See, for example, China People's Daily (2018).
54 Especially in the financial services, automobile and energy sectors.
55 See Lardy (2019) and Rudd and Rosen (2020).
56 Wu (2018).
57 Xi (2015).
58 See Xinhua News Agency (2021b) and Nye (2020a).
59 See The White House (2021c) and Rogin (2022).
60 See Allison (2017).
61 See Dupont (2020).
62 See Etzioni (2017), French (2017) and Krulak and Friedman (2021).
63 See Fu (2019).
64 See Kissinger (2012) and Xinhua News Agency (2021).
65 See Nye (2020a).
66 For example, the ban on Huawei from 5G market and the export of parts to Huawei.
67 See Whalen (2021).
68 See SEC (2020), USTR (2022) and US Congress (2022).
69 Dual circulation refers to a two-track approach to economic development, relying on both internal and external circulation. External circulation refers to economic connectivity with the world economy. Internal circulation emphasises the expansion of domestic demand and improvements in productivity and self-lsufficiency in the supply chain and technology.
70 See Hass (2021).
71 See Nye (2020b).
72 See Zhang and Wang (2021).
73 See The White House (2021a, 2021b).

74　See Politico (2022).
75　See Xi (2017).
76　See Xi (2017).
77　See People's Daily (2015).
78　Ibid.
79　See Xi (2014).

12 Can China sustain its economic development?

In the previous chapters, we learned how China's economy is a dynamic system that has been shaped by various key stakeholders, including the CPC, local governments, farmers (and migrant workers), SOEs, the elites and, increasingly, the growing urban middle class. The CPC and the Chinese government have proved pragmatic over the years in adapting economic policy to changing tides in both the international and domestic arenas, as well as in addressing the evolving demands of the population. The political structure and the changes in policy have also had long-term impacts on different groups of the population. Incentive structures, including the tax system and local-government finances, have helped shape many industries, the current urban and rural landscape, and the public welfare system.

Forged by these changing forces, China's economy today is full of opportunities, challenges and contradictions. The economy has grown big, but the country is still relatively poor; its average income per capita is only one-fifth of that of the United States. China's big coastal cities have modern infrastructure, yet inland regions and swathes of the west are far less developed. Some industries are advanced, while others depend on imports for core parts and components. The state seems to be everywhere, intervening in economic activity, but is often absent in areas where it is needed, such as social protection. There is a large and vibrant private sector, but it is not yet on a level playing field with SOEs and its role is often called into question. Chinese firms have become increasingly innovative, but imitation is still cheaper and the norm, especially amid inadequate IP protection. While about 200 million people have disposable income of more than US$ 15,000 a year, another 200 million live on less than US$ 3.20 a day. The population is ageing rapidly, but the average retirement age is less than 55. The list goes on.

Is China facing a middle-income trap?

What, then, are the biggest hurdles to China's sustainable development into an advanced economy? Most economists and China observers would agree that the primary challenges include its ageing population, high and rising debt levels, inefficient SOEs, an omnipresent state that may crowd out the private sector and stymies innovation, and increasing emphasis on Party

DOI: 10.4324/9781003310938-13

control, which may be at odds with the goal of a more inclusive modern society and a vibrant market economy. Many may not appreciate China's deep social challenges. Not only is inequality of income high, but so too is inequality of education, job opportunity, housing and access to basic public services and social welfare. A key reason for the deep social divide in Chinese society is the administrative and legal separation between the urban and rural population, and the segmented and segregated governance structure.

China also faces the challenge of technological advancement, much like the United States and other developed markets have before. With technological progress, automation and the resulting supply-chain adjustments, hundreds of millions of workers could soon find themselves out of work or marginalised by algorithms, which could sow the seeds of further inequality and social division. China also faces a somewhat different technology hurdle: to continue to climb the global value chain, it needs to master or develop more advanced technologies, but the rise in geopolitical tensions has prompted the United States and other advanced nations to restrict China's access to such technologies, something that is unlikely to change in the coming years.

The biggest challenge China faces is perhaps not these specific issues that need to be addressed, but the likelihood that various groups with vested interests might block the reforms necessary to address them, entrenching the problems longer term. The 'interest groups' opposed to SOE reform might include, for instance, SOE cadres, SOE workers and government agencies with interests tied to SOEs. China's elite and private company owners might resist plans to improve social protection and public services, as these could push up the cost of doing business and taxes. Local governments might be reluctant to exit direct investments and other business operations for fear of losing economic power and control. Urban residents might resent and obstruct measures that would give equal treatment to migrant workers and their families, as this could dilute their own access and welfare. How, then, can China's government build consensus, bring about compromise and move forward with reforms and policies that are beneficial to most people in the long term? This is perhaps the single biggest challenge, especially when these interest groups are not all clearly or well represented in politics and there is little open debate.

Do these challenges mean China is facing a middle-income trap? Indeed, many worry that China may fall, or has already fallen, into such a trap.[1] Such concerns arose after the country's growth rate fell from an average of 10% a year between 1980 and 2010 (and 11.4% in the 2006–2010 period) to 7.6% in 2011–2015 and again to 6.2% in 2016–2020. The 'middle-income trap' is a concept introduced by Gill and Kharas (2007) to describe economies that are being squeezed between low-wage competitors and rich-country innovators.[2] They noted that while some middle-income economies, such as South Korea and Singapore, graduated to the high-income echelon, some previously fast-growing middle-income economies, such as Brazil, stagnated for a prolonged period.

The term 'middle-income trap' quickly became very popular among policymakers and development specialists, even though there is no one clear definition of the term.[3] Gill and Kharas (2007) and Ohno (2009) explored how policy and institutional change must adapt in middle-income countries to facilitate sustained growth and enable them to move up the value chain to avoid stagnation. Spence (2011) defined it based on empirical evidence that few middle-income countries in recent decades have managed to achieve a certain per capita level of GDP. Eichengreen et al. (2012) found that middle-income countries seemed more likely to experience a sustained slowdown in growth. Still others defined the 'trap' as the lack of convergence of middle-income countries with the United States after a prolonged period.[4]

Given the differences in definition, it is no surprise that the debate continues to rage as to whether China has entered, or will enter, a 'middle-income trap'. Definitions and measurements aside, however, the fundamental concern and debate over China has centred on whether the country can successfully transition from its previous growth model, which relied heavily on cheap labour, high investment and exports, as external and domestic circumstances change. Can China overcome the challenges of an ageing population, become more innovative and move up the value chain, improve human capital and reform institutions to generate sustained productivity growth? How should Chinese policymakers address social inequality and prevent populistic policy swings that could lead to macroeconomic and financial instability as seen in some Latin American countries?[5] Moreover, China also faces a challenge that few other successful middle-income economy has faced to date, namely, resource and environmental constraints.

Such concerns and considerations were behind the formulation of the 12th Five-Year Plan (2011–2015) and subsequent economic strategies. As detailed in official documents,[6] to avoid being stagnant and trapped in the middle-income phase, China's policymakers believed that the country should (1) expand domestic demand as exports slowed, necessitating income growth through job creation, continued urbanisation and various institutional reforms; (2) move up the value chain, requiring an improvement in human capital through better and more equal access to education, increased R&D spending and industrial policy to facilitate technological upgrades (MIC 2025, for example); and (3) improve income distribution through 'common prosperity' policies, key among them the improved government provision of public services and improvements in social protection. There have been more iterations and updates of the development strategy since, but the focus on developing the domestic market, moving up the technological ladder, strengthening education and common prosperity has not changed. More recently, the government has also emphasised green development in the face of increasing resource and environmental constraints, as well as the need to address the problems of an ageing population.

More than ten years after it first confronted the possibility of the middle-income trap, China is now on the verge of entering the high-income ranks,

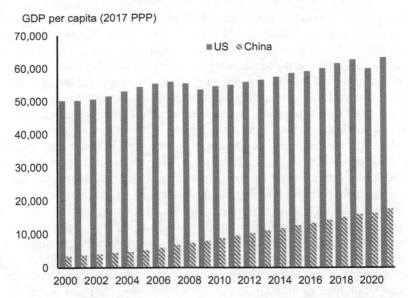

GDP per capita (2017 PPP)

Figure 12.1 GDP per capita compared to the United States, 2000–2021.
Source: World Bank.

as defined by the World Bank. The World Bank classifies nations with a per capita GDP of more than US$ 12,693 as high-income countries as of July 2021, and China's per capita GDP grew from about US$ 4000 in 2010 to US$ 12,616 in 2021 (or about US$ 10,000 in 2010 PPP terms). Of course, in relative terms, China's GDP per capita in purchasing power parity terms was just over a quarter of the US level.

Nonetheless, the concern of the Chinese authorities, China observers and investors remains: can China continue to grow and catch up with developed economies in the face of mounting challenges? The challenges have increased in recent years. The external environment has become more hostile and access to advanced technology more restricted. What are China's policy options and what is the government planning to do?

How can China sustain its economic development?

Economists and development specialists seem to agree that China needs to find alternative drivers of growth to those that spawned its earlier success (the mobilisation of high savings, cheap labour and cheap resources, and a reliance on export and property-led urbanisation). To this end, China's policymakers have emphasised the expansion of domestic demand in various strategy formulations – the latest being 'dual circulation' centred on 'internal circulation'.[7] This shows a recognition of the worsening external environment.

To support domestic demand, especially consumption demand, the government's policy plans include facilitating income growth (especially labour income growth), improving income distribution (a bigger middle class and better social protection) and adjusting the domestic supply structure to better satisfy domestic demand. To generate sustained employment and labour income growth, the government has emphasised the need to support SME development, also through more and cheaper credit, lower taxes and barriers to entry, and less red tape.[8] Improving income distribution and expanding the middle class are the focus of the government's increased drive to promote 'common prosperity', which includes more equal public service provision, the expansion of pension and healthcare insurance coverage, an intensification of anti-monopoly regulation and gradual adjustments to the tax system.

There is also consensus on the significance of moving up the value chain and climbing the technological ladder to secure China's future development.[9] Since 2018, there has been even more government emphasis on mastering core advanced technologies and becoming more self-reliant, as the US–China trade war has exposed the country's vulnerability on the technological front. To this end, China needs to increase investment in education to improve its human capital, increase R&D spending to bring about technological progress and improve intellectual property rights protection to foster innovation. China's government has targeted higher educational spending as a share of GDP for the past few Five-Year Plans, while R&D spending has climbed steadily. There have been greater efforts to improve intellectual property rights protection over the past few years,[10] though most would agree that much more needs to be done.

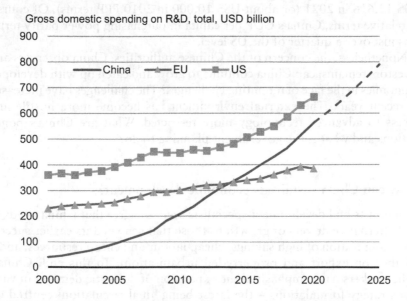

Figure 12.2 The rapid rise of R&D spending.

Source: OECD, author's calculations Forecast is from China's 14th Five-Year Plan.

In analysing why some upper-middle-income economies have failed to move up the value chain, some economists have pointed to the importance of manufacturing and policies that facilitate the 'mastering' of technology.[11] On the former, China has developed its manufacturing capacity and capabilities in recent decades, which has helped to absorb the labour transfer from agriculture and increase overall productivity. While the share of manufacturing has declined since 2012 as services have become more important, the 14th Five-Year Plan targets a relatively stable manufacturing share while pushing for more upgrades.

On policies to facilitate the mastering of technology, China's industrial policy is generally frowned upon by mainstream economists and heavily criticised by both liberal economists in China and western governments (Chapter 4).[12] China's own experience has shown that policies such as domestic content requirements, technology transfers in foreign joint ventures and a gradual introduction of competition may have helped the country increase its domestic ability to produce more sophisticated manufacturing products, in contrast to countries such as Thailand and Indonesia.[13] The MIC 2025 strategy was designed to help China master more advanced technologies, though it has vanished from official statements after strong objections and sanctions from the United States. In addition, there is domestic debate as to the efficacy of government subsidies in promoting innovation and technological progress. Scepticism aside, however, the government's determination and plans to use various incentives to facilitate technological upgrades and innovation remain.

Another source of sustained productivity growth is the more efficient allocation of productive resources. China's market-oriented reforms in the 1980s and 1990s unleashed a period of rapid productivity gains. The government has, therefore, emphasised the need to deepen reform, especially factor market reforms.[14] These involve labour market, land and capital market reforms (including the *hukou* and related benefit systems, which distort the labour market), rural land reform and measures to improve the urban land supply mechanism, and reforms to enable the better functioning of the capital market and more equal access to credit for the private sector. Reforming the SOEs is also a key part of improving resource allocation, though progress has focused mainly on imposing discipline on decision making and cost control.[15]

China's government is keen to get two other important aspects right that are not prominent in 'middle-income trap' literature: macroeconomic stability and social stability. When China's senior policymakers and scholars looked to Latin America and some Asian economies for lessons to learn, one common thread they picked up was how much a financial crisis could set back a country's income level. This could result from a sharp decline in GDP, asset losses in debt restructuring and/or significant currency depreciation.[16] If the debt crises in Latin America seemed hard for China to relate to, given the region's vastly different economic policies, the lessons from the Asian financial crisis may have been more salient, as these were economies that China sought to emulate in the early years. China has made 'no systemic financial crisis' the absolute bottom line of its macroeconomic policymaking – and this was only reinforced by the global financial crisis. Another lesson learned from Latin America, in particular, was the importance of social harmony and stability. Policymakers in China observed that income inequality contributed to populism and polarised politics, leading to irresponsible, unsustainable, wild policy swings and macro instability, entrenching deep social divides.[17] They were alarmed by the sharp rise in inequality and public protests at the beginning of the 21st century in China and have since prioritised maintaining social stability and addressing social issues through policy change.

Specific policies on maintaining macroeconomic stability have included modest monetary stimulus in response to the COVID-19 pandemic, tighter regulations on shadow banking and measures to contain and reduce leverage in LGFVs, the excess-capacity and property sectors since 2015. Concerns about macro and financial stability were also behind the government's flawed attempt to stabilise the stock market in 2015, and the re-tightening of capital controls and exchange-rate management following the 2015 RMB reform. Concerns about inequality and social stability have been key factors behind the government's 'common prosperity' policies. Policies aimed at addressing environmental issues, food and drug safety problems, work safety issues, social media and internet regulations have also arisen from concerns surrounding social stability.

Controlling China's debt problem will be important to macroeconomic stability and sustained long-term growth. Despite success in containing leverage in 2017–2018, debt risks increased after the COVID-pandemic and as the debt-to-GDP ratio increased sharply in 2020. Concerns about debt have been further heightened since the second half of 2021, when debt payment problems at China's largest property developers led to worries about the financial system. As discussed in Chapter 7, China's total property-exposed debt is substantial. Moreover, a severe property downturn would likely lead to a hard economic landing, sparking debt issues in property-related industrial sectors and for local-government finances. However, as discussed in Chapter 9, the government is likely to be pragmatic in its property and deleveraging policies and in dealing with any subsequent bad debt and liquidity issues.

Indeed, since end 2021, the government has started to ease credit and property policies to help stabilise the situation. Property policies saw a major turn-around in late 2022 when the government eased financing to property developers from all channels. Any debt restructuring will likely be gradual, and regulatory forbearance and the central bank's liquidity provision will help banks repair their balance sheets and limit the credit squeeze that typically accompanies a debt crisis. Remember that a high saving rate, majority state ownership of banks and a closed capital account should help China manage the debt challenge in the coming years. This also means that controls on capital outflows are unlikely to be removed anytime soon and that interest rates are unlikely to move meaningfully higher, even with further interest-rate liberalisation. In other words, while China may face the problems of a debt overhang, such as low returns on investment, it can still maintain a relatively stable macroeconomic and financial environment.

The rapidly ageing population is another major challenge on China's path to becoming a high-income country. This is something that most other economies that transitioned to high-income status did not have to face until they were much richer. China's population is set to peak this decade, while its working-age population (15- to 59-year-olds) started to decline in 2011. On current trends, the working-age population is likely to decline by another 50 million or so between 2020 and 2030. Some experts are worried that China will get old before it gets rich.[18] But will getting old prevent China from getting rich? China's own experience of the 2010s showed real GDP growing by close to 7% a year even as the working-age population shrank by 40 million,[19] helped by the continued labour transfer from rural areas. This decade, there are fewer rural people left to move to cities – agricultural employment was only 23.6% of total employment in 2020. What's more, the ageing of the agricultural workforce may also prevent further migration to urban areas; the average age of migrant workers rose to 41.4 years in 2020.

One way to facilitate rural-urban migration is to further relax the *hukou* system to facilitate whole-family migration and to reduce the exit of older migrants from the labour force.[20] Another way of mitigating the decline in the working-age population would be to extend China's retirement age, which the government has said it will gradually do. If the current effective retirement age of less than 54 years can be extended by three years by 2030, another 40 million people can be added to the labour force. Thus, the

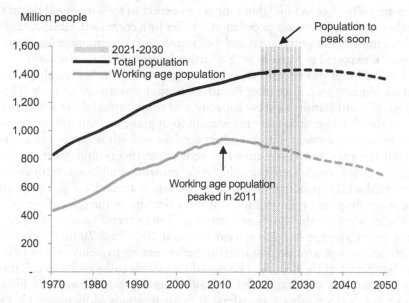

Figure 12.3 Population and working-age population 1970–2050.

Source: NBS, UNPD, author's estimates.

ageing population should not be a major constraint on the quantity of labour supply in the coming decade.

China has changed its population policy to encourage more births, although the efficacy of this policy is unclear, particularly as most other East Asian economies have low birth rates as well. In any case, any impact of such a policy on the labour supply will take at least 15 years to materialise. Meanwhile, China must (and plans to, as reflected in the 14th Five-Year Plan) improve its human capital by increasing the average length of education of its labour force and expanding vocational training. Importantly, the government needs to address systematic inequality and improve the education of millions of rural children, as discussed in Chapter 6.

How much can China grow over the next decade?

As China confronts the challenges ahead, by how much can its economy grow in 2021–2030?

The most common way to estimate trend or potential growth is with a simple growth model, using the Cobb–Douglas production function, $Y = AL^{\beta}K^{\alpha}$, where L is the labour input, K is the capital input, A is total factor productivity (TFP), and α and β are the output elasticities of capital and labour, respectively. First, we separate China's economy into the agricultural and non-agricultural sectors. Agriculture can be assumed to grow at a low single-digit rate as technology and productivity improve, independent of the labour input. The further transfer of surplus rural labour to non-farming sectors should not affect agricultural output, as has been the case in the past four decades. For the non-agricultural economy, labour input can expect to see a marginal rise as the decline in the working-age population is offset by a continued, albeit declining, labour transfer from rural areas and the extension of the retirement age. Human capital is expected to increase with a further improvement in education.

Capital input should still have room to grow, as China's capital stock per capita remains low, even after decades of rapid investment growth (Figure 12.4). Notwithstanding excess capacity and some capital destruction in the years ahead, China still needs investment to upgrade its manufacturing technology and equipment, build modern services and infrastructure (including digital infrastructure), and invest in renewable energy and green technology.[21] As for total factor productivity growth, continued reforms and increased R&D spending should help stabilise it around 1.5% a year after the sharp drop that followed the first three decades of the reform period.[22]

Under a reasonable baseline scenario, China's trend growth is likely to slow to an average 4–4.5% a year between 2021 and 2030.[23] Growth is likely to average around 5% initially before easing to below 4% a year in the latter part of the decade. The slowdown seems to be inevitable. Labour input growth is slowing in the face of an ageing population and limited scope for further labour transfers. It is increasingly difficult to channel investment to productive areas, as industries face excess capacity at home and competition from abroad. More restricted access to advanced

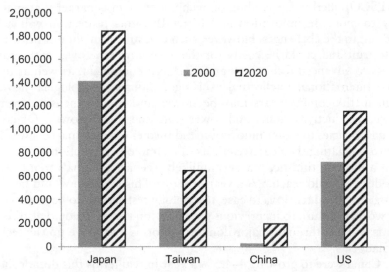

Figure 12.4 The capital stock per capita is still relatively low.

Source: CEIC and author's estimates.

technology is likely to damp productivity growth. And the remaining reforms to improve the efficiency of resource allocation (and TFP) are arguably more difficult than before as interest groups resist changes to the *hukou* system, SOE restructuring and land reform.

In a more pessimistic scenario, China's trend growth may only average about 3% this decade, reduced by a sharply different domestic business and policy climate and/or tougher external environment. On the domestic front, the 3-year long zero-COVID policy, which has led to a sharp and lasting reduction in human and business interaction, and a change in priorities to security over economic development, may have caused substantial damage to business confidence and investment, and could weaken innovation, and spur a decline in or withdrawal of FDI. It could also lead to a generally more restrictive regulatory environment and aid the decoupling of China's economy and supply chain from the rest of the world. In sum, this would lead to slower capital accumulation and productivity gains and, hence, trend growth.

On the external front, technology restrictions and decoupling measures from the advanced economies may intensify. As China relies heavily on imports from the United States and other major developed economies for core components in many sectors, difficulties in accessing these could disrupt industrial production and slow China's productivity and trend GDP growth. Tighter restrictions will also trigger more Chinese investment in R&D and technology. In the long run, such investment is likely to lead to increased domestic capabilities and sustained technological upgrades, eventually establishing China's own technological ecosystem substitute imports.

China's large talent pool (4.4 million R&D personnel, according to UNESCO), increased spending on technology, a vast market that makes it easy to monetise innovation and better IP rights protection will help it respond to the challenges. However, such investment might not bear immediate fruit and could be costly for the economy. Moreover, with reduced access to advanced technology and high-tech equipment, as well as diminished international intellectual exchange, China's technological advancement in the coming years may be slower and more expensive, meaning slower productivity gains and lower potential GDP growth. Of course, China's policies to foster innovation and further open its markets would be key to mitigating the negative effects of technology restrictions.

In a more optimistic, but very unlikely, scenario, China's trend growth this decade could reach 5% a year or more. This scenario would need current geopolitical tensions to ease, technology restrictions to be reversed and the world to return to its previous globalisation trend. It would also require China to push through major domestic reforms and move up the technology ladder.

If China were to grow by 4–4.5% a year in real terms this decade, it may still account for at least 30% of global growth. China's nominal GDP may reach US$ 30 trillion in 2030, assuming no change in the RMB exchange rate against the US dollar.[24] The number of Chinese people with annual disposable income greater than US$ 10,000 (a household disposable income greater than US$ 30,000) could rise to 680 million by 2030, more than doubling from 2020.[25] Such a rise in income levels and the government's renewed emphasis on 'internal circulation' and common prosperity should continue to support the economy's rebalancing towards consumption and services. Consumption as a share of GDP could rise by about 5 percentage points by 2030[26] from current levels, while the share of services could rise to 60% from 56% in 2020.[27]

Alongside this rebalancing towards consumption, China's economy is set to see structural changes in three technological aspects. First, digitalisation. Companies are transforming their business models with digital services to match changes in consumer behaviour, for example, with online retail, smart education, automated restaurants and biometric payments. Despite tighter regulations on internet businesses, the accelerated growth in consumer reliance on digital services since the COVID-19 pandemic is likely to continue. This will lead to greater demand for and reliance on big data, 5G, the internet of things (IoT) and artificial intelligence (AI), while additional investment in related 'new infrastructure' should enable further business transformation and the evolution of consumer behaviour.

Second, automation and technological upgrades. Over the past two decades, by investing in and importing machinery and equipment, and through foreign direct investment and integration into the competitive global market, China has gradually moved up the manufacturing value chain. It is catching up with automation too: Chinese companies installed 168,000 industrial robots in 2020, compared with Japan's 38,700 and the US's

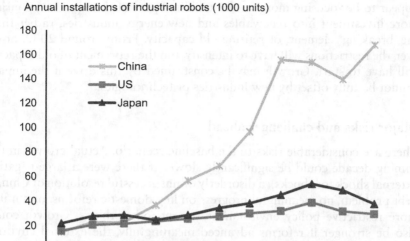

Figure 12.5 Annual industrial robot installations in China, the United States and Japan.
Source: World Robotics 2021.

30,800, according to the International Federation of Robotics.[28] Automation is also moving from factory applications into the service sector, including restaurants, healthcare and logistics.

Third, the development of green technology. China's 2060 goal of carbon neutrality and 2030 peak emission target are expected to lead to a higher share of non-fossil energy in total energy consumption, the electrification of energy use (especially in transport), and development and deployment of other energy-saving technologies in construction, materials, manufacturing and transport.

The decarbonisation drive may not necessarily restrict China's potential growth in the very long term. It is true that as environmental rules tighten and costs rise, not only will investment in traditional, energy-intensive production and the fossil-fuel sectors decline, but the existing capital stock in these sectors will also depreciate rapidly. This shift in the real economy will also impact the values of financial assets and potentially lead to greater financial-sector risk and higher funding costs for all. In addition, supply restrictions in the carbon-intensive industries could push up overall costs in the economy and constrain economic growth.

However, China's decarbonisation policies are likely to focus on increasing investment in renewable energy, upgrading industrial plants and power grids, building more public transport networks and advancing new low-energy, low-emission materials and technologies. The net outcome will depend on how aggressively China restricts traditional sectors, how high it will let carbon prices rise and how rapidly and successfully the green technology breakthrough happens. Over the next few years, the government would appear to be focusing more on the 'building' part of the equation, pouring more investment into renewables and new-energy industries, rather than the 'breaking' element, or retiring old capacity. From around 2030, however, the restrictions will have to intensify and the retirement of old capacity will have to start. Growth may be constrained by this drive if the impact cannot be fully offset by new industries or technologies.

Major risks and challenges ahead

There are considerable risks to the baseline scenario. Actual growth in the coming decade could be significantly slower if there were a large negative external shock (or shocks), a disorderly or unsuccessful resolution of China's debt problem, no meaningful progress on key domestic reforms, or a much more restrictive policy environment, among other things. Growth could also be stronger if reforms advanced meaningfully, the external environment improved, and China's technological advances surpass expectations.

China still has more policy levers to pull than most other major economies to offset future economic shocks. Having learned from past lessons, Chinese policymakers limited the size of fiscal and monetary stimulus in 2020 and 2021. Such restraint leaves policy room for the future. Despite the sharp increase in 2020, China's overall government debt was about 85% of GDP as of end 2021 – largely manageable, though it has likely increased in 2022. On the monetary policy front, the PBC has been modest in its balance-sheet expansion compared with many other central banks. China has no immediate need to undertake outright quantitative easing or to directly monetise fiscal deficit.

One of the biggest risks to China's outlook in the coming years is rising geopolitical tension, especially the worsening of US–China relations. The latter has already led to higher tariffs on China's exports to the United States and more restrictions on access to technology for Chinese companies. Investment-related restrictions and political pressure on other countries to decouple from China are also increasing. These developments and heightened uncertainty are likely to weaken confidence and business investment in general, even though data up to 2021 show continued strong FDI inflows. A further fanning of geopolitical risk, especially a confrontation with the United States, could lead to turmoil in China's financial markets, as well as globally, and disrupt China's plan to become a high-income country.

However, the greater damage from geopolitical tension could be how it might change the course of China's domestic policy and development strategy. Such damage from a more hostile external environment could arise from a more inward-looking government and more nationalistic public that turns away from certain policies and strategies because they embrace 'western' norms or ideals. These could include market orientation, openness to foreign competition and ideas, private entrepreneurship, greater public participation and debate, international exchange of ideas and academic research, and diversification and inclusivity of beliefs and expression (the latter two are important for fostering innovation).

The key challenges are domestic

Notwithstanding external risks, the future of China's development critically depends on addressing key domestic challenges. If China can continue to combine a deepening of reforms to foster productivity growth with enhanced social protection, policies to open up the economy and further integrate globally, and foster competition and innovation, its long-term outlook should remain solid. In this regard, fundamental questions remain about the future of the state versus the market, the balancing of social equality and efficiency, dealing with the impact of technological advancement and big data, and remaining open (both to the outside world and in society to allow for different ideas and minority views, for example) while pursuing its own development path.

The role of the state versus the market

How will the role of the state versus the market evolve? After many years of trying, China seems to have embarked on a major realignment over the past couple of years. The objectives and principles behind this adjustment seem sensible: to rectify the lack of a proper government presence in market supervision, public service provision and social protection, and to reduce the role of government in allocating resources and direct economic operations.[29] There have been more visible changes on the former.

It is clear that the state will continue to increase its presence in providing public goods and improving social welfare, such as basic education and healthcare, environmental protection, labour protection, pensions and health insurance. It will also increase market regulatory and supervisory functions, including setting and enforcing rules and standards on food and drug safety, consumer protection and market competition. However, when it comes to reducing the government's role in some areas, including local governments' direct investment activities and levelling the playing field on market entry and resource access for the private sector, progress has been more limited. There have been only limited advances on capital market, *hukou* and land reforms, falling far short of the government's objective to let the market play a decisive role in allocating productive factors.

Most notably, China's SOE reform has largely stagnated over the past decade. Despite the calls of the 18th Third Plenum in 2013 and a framework SOE reform plan in 2015, there has been little concrete progress. SOE reform from 2015 to 2017 focused more on controlling costs and improving management accountability. The installation of a modern enterprise governance structure has happened in tandem with increased Party control at enterprise level. The 'mixed ownership' reform, which some hoped would lead to the diversification of ownership structures through increased private participation, has not proved meaningful, as it has increased the cross-shareholdings of SOEs, while private shareholders have often become passive financiers.

The divestment of SOEs, meanwhile, has frequently been equated with the loss of state assets. The 2020–2022 'three-year action plan' for SOE reform[30] seems to focus more on SOEs playing a leading role in achieving the government's multiple economic and social objectives, from innovation to social protection. Also, with tighter controls on data, privacy and content, private companies may face more government restrictions than before in new strategic industries involving big data and advanced technologies, in addition to restrictions in traditional state-dominated sectors, such as energy and finance, on the grounds of economic and national security. Data are now also considered a future productive factor that will face more government control.

The lack of meaningful progress on reducing the state's role in investment and resource allocation amid an increase in state control elsewhere could be troubling. First, while SOE profits have increased thanks to better cost controls and spending discipline, they are still low compared with private profits (Figure 12.6). Can SOEs remain competitive and productive without robust competition from the private sector and rigorous market discipline? If the allocation of productive factors cannot be more meaningfully determined by market forces, can TFP gains sustain growth in future to deliver reasonable economic growth?

In addition, the lopsided adjustment of the state's role versus the market may give the impression that China is backtracking from the idea of a market-oriented economy and reforms in general. Indeed, left-leaning domestic commentators have not shied away from fanning such beliefs and praising the system of state ownership, state control and central planning.[31] Such displays of nostalgia for the old system are sometimes interpreted as a sign

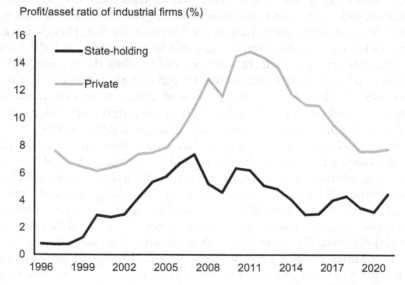

Figure 12.6 SOE profitability still lags behind the private sector.

Source: NBS, author's calculations.

of the senior leadership changing its economic thinking, undermining business confidence and private investment.[32] This is perhaps one reason why senior leaders have repeatedly stressed their unwavering support for private ownership and market orientation.[33] However, without material progress on SOE-related reforms, confidence in the private sector and the market may not be easily restored.

Social equality and economic efficiency

Another key question is how China might balance improving social equality with retaining economic efficiency.[34] While the economic literature has demonstrated that inequality hurts growth in the long run, and that equality and efficiency can go hand in hand,[35] some redistribution policies can scupper economic incentives and hurt efficiency.[36] It is understandable that China's government wishes to reduce inequality for the sake of social harmony and sustainable growth, but the scope and scale of the redistributive policies are not yet clear. Some in China have attributed many of the ills of society to its market orientation and private ownership and have called for an 'exit' of private enterprises and a radical redistribution,[37] or a return to the government allocation of income and assets, including housing.

So far, China's senior leadership has continued to follow a more gradual and moderate approach, emphasising the importance of sustained income growth, the improvement of public services and social welfare over radical redistribution. The government has already promised it will not 'rob the rich to help the poor',[38] as this would probably lead to the suppression of investment, lower growth and, ultimately, poor welfare for all. This means that radical tax increases and the feared renationalisation of certain private businesses are highly unlikely. However, the moderate approach might be derailed by populist and radical elements within the CPC and society at large, given the severity of inequality and the public's frustration with the limited progress on reducing it over the past decade.

Ideally, China would gradually transition to a more equal society with less 'wild west' capitalism, better social provision and protection, and a narrower social divide, while retaining a vibrant market-oriented economy. But even a moderate redistribution effort is likely to face strong resistance from powerful and vocal interest groups. For example, improving social welfare and labour protection would incur greater costs for business owners. Income tax reform would mean higher taxes for high-income individuals, including business owners. And *hukou* and land reform would affect local-government interests.

One way to mitigate both the potential disruption and resistance to policy change is to ensure a reasonable pace and better 'primary distribution' of economic growth. A reasonable pace of growth means that the economic pie is still growing, while better primary distribution means a steady increase (or at least no decline) in the labour share of income. To ensure the economy maintains reasonable growth, policies need to support the private sector, tax rates should not be too high (and necessary tax reforms should be gradual), returns to capital should incentivise continued investment, and the effective labour supply should continue to increase through *hukou*, pension, education and labour-market reforms.

To improve primary income distribution, policies should facilitate a shift in the growth model to ensure job creation. In this regard, the state should contribute more to social welfare and labour protection to mitigate the rise in costs for small businesses. Given the poor state of local-government finances, the improvement in social welfare will need to be gradual to ensure fiscal sustainability in the long run and to avoid over-promising. It would also be more feasible to build better schools and hospitals in rural areas and lower-tier cities and gradually remove restrictions on access in urban areas, as the sudden abolition of all restrictions could pit the urban middle class and elite against the migrant population and lead to social unrest.

Technology, big data and the rise of the digital economy

China's next stage of development is set to be profoundly shaped by technological progress, the proliferation of social media and the rise of big data. Technological advancement is necessary for China to move up the value chain and sustain its economic development, but the experience of the United States and other advanced economies has shown that it can displace workers and contribute to polarisation and wage inequality.[39] Without policy responses to train and redeploy people displaced by machines and algorithms, technological progress could lead to a thinning of the middle class and a worsening of the social divide. Companies will have to adapt or fail, while employees will have to adjust, or face being replaced. The rise of e-commerce and online meal delivery, for example, has created millions of new jobs and enabled the creation of thousands of small businesses, but has also displaced small offline shops and restaurants, as well as the people they employed. In addition, the tech giants consider the new gig-economy jobs created in place of the old ones – such as delivery drivers – to be self-employment, providing no benefits, little protection and no future advancement or career to speak of.

The rise of the digital economy and big data also poses big social and governance questions that the government must address. For example, at what cost to privacy should consumer convenience come? To what extent should companies be allowed to target various consumer groups and differentiate (or discriminate) between different groups of people, especially when it comes to information and healthcare services? How much should big data and algorithms be allowed to shape social organisation and governance?

Academic research has shown that the internet and social media have had a profound impact on politics worldwide, eroding trust in governments and polarising views and policies.[40] What has happened in the United States and elsewhere in recent years shows how social media or a manipulation thereof has influenced elections, deepened the social divide and worsened polarisation. Such developments have not only threatened and weakened the proper functioning of western democracy,[41] but can also pose a threat to China's governance. Recent regulatory tightening on internet companies, big data and content companies reflects in part the Chinese government's concern over these issues.

The mainstream western media have framed the tightening as a crackdown on the technology sector, capitalism or private businesses,[42] but the underlying governance issues and social choices are more universal. It is unclear to what extent China's approach will be appropriate for the new, digital economy and society. Can the government remain a neutral party and distribute digital resources fairly while respecting individual rights? Could over-regulation lead to more hidden ways to bypass rules, especially when more activities are done virtually? To what extent can government institutions be free of the influence of algorithms? More importantly, will over-regulation stymie entrepreneurship and innovation?

Charting its own course

As China tries to deal with these challenges and sustain its development in the coming decades, there are no clear models for it to follow. It very much wants to chart its own course, too. A clear difference to other advanced economies is its insistence on maintaining the 'socialist' regime led by the CPC. Of course, China can draw lessons from its own transition over the past four decades. The external and domestic challenges it faced in the late 1970s and, again, after 1989 seemed almost insurmountable at the time, and the ideological debate was fierce. The economic difficulties it had to overcome in the late 1990s were arguably greater than now. But China stayed the course, undertaking further reforms, opening and developing the economy, and maintaining macroeconomic and social stability. To this end, the government's traditionally pragmatic and adaptive approach certainly helped. Will it be able to preserve that pragmaticism in an increasingly ideologically charged and polarized world? Will there be a sufficiently robust self-correcting mechanism to help it in future trials and tribulations?

It may be China's decarbonisation drive that helps it establish a working channel with the main western powers, enabling them to come together over their shared interests, as neither can achieve their climate goals without the other. Outside of potential collaboration on major global issues such as climate change, however, China's relationship with the west is likely to remain fraught, with a rising China becoming increasingly assertive and influential in global affairs and much of the western world wary of its rise due to its size and ideology. Having open channels of communication and collaboration is critical if China and the other major powers are to avoid potentially dangerous misunderstandings and manage conflicts.

Notes

1 See Cai (2012), Woo (2012) and Eichengreen et al. (2012).
2 See Gill and Kharas (2007).
3 See Glawe and Wagner (2017) and Gill and Kharas (2015).
4 See Im and Rosenblatt (2013).
5 See Liu (2010).
6 The 12th to the 14th Five-Year Plans.
7 The 14th Five-Year plan.
8 As discussed in Chapters 4, 5 and 10, the government has scaled back government approval processes, reduced fees and taxes, and increased funding access for SMEs.
9 See Garrett (2004), Spence (2011) and China's 12th to the 14th Five-Year Plans.
10 For example, amendments have been made to intellectual property rights law and a special court has been established, with more cases being heard.
11 See Rodrick (2013), Kuijs (2017) and Kim and Park (2017).
12 See USTR (2021).
13 See Gill and Kharas (2007) and Kee and Tang (2016).
14 The 3rd Plenum of the 18th CPC Congress (2013).
15 See Wang (2014, 2015).
16 See Liu (2006, 2010).
17 See Liu (2006).
18 See Deloitte (2017) and The Economist (2018b).
19 Data from the 6th and 7th censuses.
20 See Cai (2021).
21 See Tsinghua University (2021).
22 See World Bank and DRC of the State Council (2019) and Zhu et al. (2019). Kuijs (2019) estimates that TFP growth picked up after 2017.
23 Author's estimate.
24 Author's estimates.
25 Author's estimate.
26 Consumption as a share of GDP fell sharply from 55.8% in 2019 to 52.4% in 2021 due to the COVID-19 pandemic and a lack of government support for consumption. Private consumption also fell by 3 percentage points to 36.1%.
27 Author's estimate.
28 See International Federation of Robotics (2021).
29 See Xi (2017) and the 14th Five-Year Plan.
30 See CPC Deepening Reform Committee (2020).
31 Private internet companies with vast amounts of data have often promoted the view of Big Data helping to achieve the central plan, perhaps out of their own commercial interest.
32 For example, 2018 saw private investment plummet amid calls for the private sector to 'exit' the stage (Wu 2018).
33 See Xi (2018), Li (2020) and Liu (2021).
34 See Okun (1975).
35 See Berg et al. (2012), Easterly (2007) and Ostry et al. (2014).
36 See, for example, Benabou (2002).
37 See, for example, Wu (2018).
38 See Han (2021) and Liu (2021).
39 See Brynjolfsson and McAfee (2014), Autor et al. (2003), Goos and Manning (2007), Michaels et al. (2014) and Acemoglu and Restrepo (2020).
40 See Guriev et al. (2021) and Evangelista and Bruno (2019).
41 See Barrett (2021), Beauchamp (2019) and Edsall (2021).
42 See for example the Economist (2021), Yang et al. (2021) and Financial Times (2021a).

Appendix A
Availability and reliability of China's economic statistics

Every China economist has had to confront the question of data quality. Are China's economic data reliable? Does the government fudge the numbers? If the data are highly problematic, how can anyone truly understand what's going on? Are there good alternatives to official economic data? These are just some of the perennial questions on Chinese data.

As the second-largest economy in the world, China's development matters a great deal to companies and investors around the world. It is natural for people to expect China to be as easily monitored as other large economies, such as the United States and the eurozone. China, however, is still a developing country. It has been undergoing major transformations and has not yet completed its transition from a planned economy to a market one. All of this means that China's economic statistics are not as reliable or detailed as those in developed economies. On the plus side, China's statistics have been improving both in terms of quantity and quality, and are generally better than those of most developing countries. Despite the many problems of official data, they are generally adequate for understanding broad economic trends and economic cycles. Moreover, China observers can rely on an increasingly rich set of sectoral and private-sector data and surveys, as well as the important export and import data of partner countries to supplement the official Chinese data. Private alternative estimates to official GDP come with their own flaws and biases and are not necessarily more reliable.

Issues with GDP data

The key statistics problems in China include non-typical practices in terms of statistical methodology, deliberate data alteration and falsification at local levels, frequent changes or suspension of data coverage, and a lack of coverage and transparency in some areas.

Regarding China's GDP and related national accounts data, one of the main data issues stems from the central role given to the production-side approach. It sums up value-added by sector, unlike the expenditure-side approach prioritised by most developed economies, which adds up investment, consumption, government spending and net exports. China uses the production-side GDP method because it already had an extensive bottom-up data reporting system on the production side, which tracked the input and output of different sectors and was used to manage the planned economy. This system can provide GDP estimates quickly, but the original reporting system tends to miss new enterprises and sectors that did not exist before. While the economic census conducted every five years since 2004 has helped update economic classifications, the reporting-based GDP estimate (compared with the survey-based expenditure approach) still does not track the ups and downs of economic cycles very well. This is because new and small businesses and new modes of activity (which may be missing in old economic classifications) tend to grow faster in boom times and fare worse during a downturn than the established entities that report their data. This may partly explain the relative smoothness of China's GDP data.

There is another methodological issue that may also contribute to the smoothness of GDP. Production-side GDP comprises the value-added of the agriculture, industrial, construction and services sectors. Analysing quarterly industrial value-added, we discover that the implied deflator for industrial value-added is identical to PPI, which measures factory-gate output prices. This practice tends to exaggerate price effects and, hence, to overestimate real industrial value-added growth when the PPI falls sharply in downturns and to underestimate it when PPI grows strongly in upswings.

The more serious criticism of China's GDP data pertains to deliberate falsification by local governments. There is a common saying in China to describe the phenomenon: that data make officials and officials make up data ('官出数字, 数字出官', or 'guanchushuju, shujuchuguan'). For example, between 2000 and 2010, national GDP was consistently 7–8% smaller than the sum of local GDPs. There is a technical component to the inconsistency – since there are no customs between provinces, it is difficult to estimate what output or value-added was 'exported' to other regions and what has been 'imported' for local use, especially on the services side. More importantly, however, since local officials have been promoted mainly on their economic performance (especially GDP and investment), they have often pressurised local statistical staff to report higher growth numbers. The NBS is aware of the problems with local data and makes various adjustments for them. It also uses data collected by separate survey teams to supplement bottom-up data reporting.[1] The government has recently implemented reforms to increase the independence and quality of economic data at the local level. However, the fact that the NBS is not independent from the government will likely always lead to some concerns on data reliability.

While China does publish expenditure-side GDP and component data, they only come out annually, with a long delay, and only in nominal terms. The NBS does collect relevant information for estimating quarterly GDP by expenditure, but has not published such data (with the exception of quarterly contributions to GDP growth). This is apparently because the expenditure data come out more slowly and estimates are usually subject to significant revision, which may be considered unhelpful by some officials.

Issues with investment and consumption data

While China does not publish the quarterly expenditure components of investment (fixed capital formation) and consumption, it does publish monthly fixed asset investment (FAI) and retail sales numbers, though the former only in nominal terms. These two proxy figures have caused endless confusion and headaches for China observers. For example, after the global financial crisis, people often asked how it was possible that China's GDP was only growing at 9–10% per annum with FAI growth of over 30% and retail sales growth of more than 15%. One obvious explanation is, of course, that GDP growth was in real terms, while the other two were in nominal terms. But the discrepancy goes far beyond this.

There are a few problems with using FAI as a proxy for fixed investment in GDP. First, the monthly FAI is an aggregate fixed investment *spending* reported by enterprises (above-scale ones) in nominal terms, which also includes secondary land and asset transactions. It is a different concept to GDP-consistent fixed investment (or fixed capital formation), which measures additions to the economy's capital stock. In addition, FAI growth data seem to have an upward bias. We have found that the divergence between the levels of FAI and fixed capital formation increased up to 2016; since 2017, it has declined sharply due to FAI methodology changes and unexplained adjustments by the NBS (Figure A.1).

Until a few years ago, the upward bias may have been only partly due to methodological issues (such as using the approximate progress of planned investment rather than, as has happened since 2017, estimates of actual

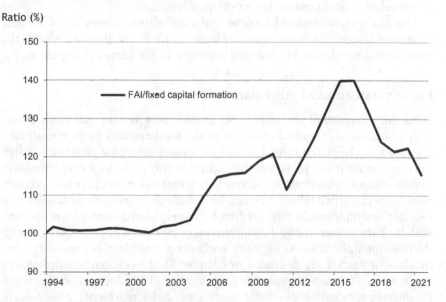

Ratio (%)

Figure A.1 FAI data increasingly diverged from fixed capital formation until 2016.

Source: NBS, author's calculations.

spending). As FAI has been used as a key indicator for assessing the performance of local government officials, it has likely often been artificially inflated, given the influence that local officials have had on the data. The significant inflation of FAI data was revealed by a central government inspection team to Liaoning province, and the governor openly acknowledged the practice in 2017,[2] prompting the methodology change in FAI estimates.

Another issue with FAI, and many other data, is that when the NBS changes data coverage and methodology periodically, historical data are often not adjusted. As a result, data series have multiple structural breaks, making analysis of developments over time extra challenging.

The lack of quarterly data on fixed capital formation also means it is difficult to gauge inventory changes in the economy. These often play a crucial role in the economic cycle. Although China does report monthly inventories in the industrial sector, they are reported in nominal terms and have limited coverage.

The retail sales number is also conceptually different to private consumption. While this is true in other countries too, it reduces the utility of retail sales data in the absence of quarterly consumption data. Retail sales exclude most services (but include some catering). In contrast, China's retail sales do include some sales to government institutions, as well as some investment goods, which reduces its value as a private consumption proxy. As services gain greater weight in the household consumption basket, the divergence between retail sales and consumption has increased. Also, during the COVID-19 pandemic, mobility restrictions severely hampered the consumption of certain services, so retail sales may underestimate the weakness of household consumption during the pandemic.

The quarterly household income and expenditure survey gives a fuller picture of household consumption. However, there are also issues with the underreporting of both income and spending in the survey (Chapter 8).

Labour statistics and other data issues

While the government generally ranks employment as a top economic objective, China's labour statistics are one of the weakest links in its overall economic data. The government has had an annual target for gross new urban job creation for many years, but this indicator only provides a rough measure of new urban employment. Its biggest flaw is that it does not take into account exits from the urban labour market, be it through retirement or layoffs. The monthly unemployment rate used to be the registered unemployment rate, with both the numerator and denominator comprising people registered with the relevant authorities. As migrant workers operated largely outside the formal labour market (as discussed in Chapter 6), the original unemployment rate was insufficient to capture the true situation. The adoption of a surveyed (or investigative) unemployment rate since 2018 represents a significant improvement, but still fails to fully capture the unemployment picture, such as in the case of migrant workers on the move. Consequently, the notable jump in the unemployment rate in March and April 2022 may still underestimate the true unemployment situation under COVID restrictions.

China's wage data are also relatively scant with inadequate coverage. Average wages are available by sector and by region but are published only annually. The quarterly household survey also has per capita wage-type income data. But there are no monthly wage data, let alone hourly earnings, which could give a timelier indication of labour-market or earnings developments.

Aside from issues with regard to specific indicators, China's economic data are often subject to large-scale revisions and discontinuations of coverage. The revisions are largely due to frequent improvements in and updates of statistical methods and coverage, which help enhance the understanding of China's economy. As noted, though, the NBS frequently does not revise historical data accordingly (e.g., the 2010 FAI adjustment) or adjust other data that are obviously linked (e.g., GDP and fixed capital formation that are linked to FAI), making it difficult to undertake historical analysis. The sudden discontinuation of certain data can also inconvenience analysts and prompt suspicion of deliberate concealment, even if this is not the case.

Another issue is the short history of many of the data series. This is because China only started to transition from an agricultural and centrally planned economy 40-some years ago, and many sectors and markets have not existed for that long. New data have become increasingly available, due to changes in either the economic structure or statistical methodology. For example, China's stock market only came into existence after 1990, the NBS manufacturing purchasing managers index (PMI) began in 2004–2005, and money markets and market interest rates have less than 20 years of history. Moreover, there are numerous structural breaks in the data due to changes in coverage or historical revisions. For example, the large one-off transfer of banks' bad loans to AMCs in 1999 broke the continuity of bank lending data, while the large debt swap of 2015–2016 distorted TSF credit numbers until the PBC adjusted the data coverage a few years later (Chapters 5 and 9).

This all means that one cannot expect to pull data from a database and run regressions in a straightforward way or acquire meaningful results as one does with, say, US data. Careful data adjustments need to be made.

How does one track China's economic development?

The many issues notwithstanding, most researchers have found China's data sufficient to provide a reasonable picture of economic development.[3] Over time, China's economic data have improved significantly across the board. Recent research by staff from the San Francisco Federal Reserve Board found that China's official statistics had improved in data quality and methodology and were of higher quality than the data of many other developing countries.[4] With regard to the national accounts, China switched from producing agricultural and industrial total output to producing standard value-added national accounts from 1993, and has steadily improved its GDP data estimates by adopting international practices and using periodic economic censuses.[5] The production-based GDP estimates come out quickly and are supplemented by annual GDP by expenditure and national income data, the latter linked to flow-of-funds data. China also has extensive input–output tables to enrich understanding of overall economic linkages, thanks to its legacy of economic plans.

China's centrally planned system has also left the country with a legacy of unusually rich sectoral data, especially all things related to industrial production. For example, if investors find that the monthly industrial production (value-added) does not give a sufficiently quick or satisfactory picture of industrial activity, they can monitor steel production and steel mill operation rates, coal production, electricity consumption, automobile sales, railway freight turnover and port throughput (and, more recently, full-load truck freight transport). Some of these numbers are available daily, weekly or every ten days. There are also detailed price and inventory data available from industrial associations, useful for cross-checking the actual demand and supply situation in key industrial sectors. To track property construction – a powerful driver of China's economic cycle over the past 20 years – one can make use of the official monthly data on property sales, new starts, completions, floor space under construction, property development investment and land sales. There are also daily property sales data for 30 large cities.

The availability of abundant physical activity data to track production and industry is in sharp contrast to the lack of detailed data on consumption/services. The detailed physical activity and commodities data can give a very good sense of the industrial part of the economy (especially heavy industry), but they should be used with caution when inferring the state of the whole economy. Physical activity momentum tends to exaggerate the overall economic cycle, as consumption and services are generally more stable than heavy industry. During the height of the COVID pandemic, however, physical activity indicators may have underestimated the severity of the economic downturn, as contact-intensive services and consumption were hit hardest.

As mentioned, employment and wage data are slow and not sufficiently sensitive to actual developments. Until a few years ago, one could use data from urban job centres to estimate the ratio of the number of jobs and jobseekers across different regions to gauge labour market conditions. However, as recruitment and job searches have increasingly moved online, the use of labour centres appears to have declined, making the data less informative. One good set of labour-market indicators is the quarterly migrant labour survey, with its information on changes in the number of migrant workers and their average wages. As migrant employment and wages are particularly sensitive to changes in the economic cycle, they can provide insight on how marginal labour demand and supply are moving.

Digitalisation has helped to enrich data availability in recent years. For example, during the COVID-19 lockdowns of 2020, and again in 2022, one could track daily transport congestion and people movement indicators across dozens of cities, follow passenger turnover on railways (mainly

Number of job opennings/number of job seekers

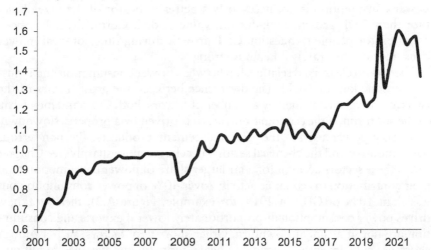

Figure A.2 The labour demand/supply ratio in labour centres has become less informative.

Source: NBS, Author estimates.

around the Chinese New Year) and subways, and monitor the waiting time of ships at ports to get a better idea of economic activity in China. These, along with movie-theatre ticket sales and tourism income, help piece together a rough picture of services and the consumption situation.

Economic activity data can also be corroborated or verified by a host of monetary and credit data, which are generally timely and much less susceptible to falsification. The government's fiscal data, such as tax revenue, are now also available monthly. Financial data, including equity- and bond-market transactions, interbank activities and market interest rates, are available daily. On the trade front, reported exports and imports can be easily verified by trading-partner data.

No good alternatives for official data

In a bid to overcome problems in the official statistics, many have tried to come up with alternative data to assess economic growth in China. Some of the popular ones over the years included electricity consumption and the Li Keqiang index. Researchers have also tried to use alternative methods of estimating China's true GDP growth.

Electricity consumption

Many analysts considered power consumption a more reliable indicator for tracking China's real pace of economic growth and industrial production in the 2000s and during the 2015–2016 downturn. However, when there are large and uneven fluctuations in (industrial) activity across different sectors, power consumption is not necessarily a better indicator of the overall picture than GDP growth or industrial value added. Curiously, it has been common for people to question GDP growth during times of weak power consumption, but rarely when it is strong.

There is no clear fixed relationship between power consumption and industrial production (or GDP). The divergence between the growth rates of the two can often be explained by a number of factors, both short and long term. In the short run, if the economic downturn is driven by a property slowdown, the heavy power users – the steel and cement producers, the non-ferrous metal industry and the chemical sector – decelerate more sharply (see Chapter 7). As these sectors account for a far larger share of power consumption than their contribution to economic activity (over 40% of power consumption but less than 10% of GDP in 2019, for example. Figure A.3), their weakness drives power consumption disproportionately lower if exports and consumption are not in a similar downturn. Other short-term factors, such as power shortages/cuts, inventory changes in heavy industry and weather conditions, can also impact power consumption. In the long run, the increase in services relative to industry in the economy and energy-efficiency gains at factories will reduce the sensitivity of electricity usage to the economy. In the future, the electrification of transport may increase the sensitivity again.

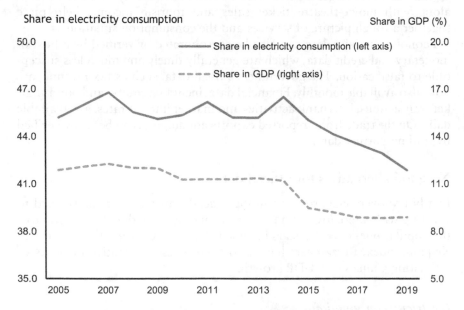

Figure A.3 Five heavy industrial sectors consume electricity disproportionally.

Source: NBS, China Electricity Council, author's estimates.

Note: The five sectors included here are ferrous metals, non-ferrous metals, non-metal minerals, chemicals, and electricity and heating.

Li Keqiang index

The Li Keqiang index is an economic measurement index created by *The Economist* in 2010 using the growth rates in power consumption, railway freight volume and bank loans.[6] It was so named because Mr. Li reportedly said in 2007, when he was party secretary of Liaoning province, that he trusted these three numbers more than the official provincial data. It became a popular alternative to China's official GDP number for investors when Mr. Li was vice premier, in charge of economic affairs, and subsequently premier.

Liaoning province is China's old industrial centre specialising in coal, steel and heavy machinery. Power consumption captures heavy-industry sector activity relatively well, as a few such sectors consume almost half the total. Also, around 2007, half of China's railway freight was used for coal transport, which slows more when the energy-intensive heavy industrial sector slows. As shown in Chapters 5 and 7, China's credit cycle was highly correlated with the property construction cycle, which is closely linked to the steel and coal sectors. Therefore, it made perfect sense that Mr. Li focused on the three indicators to track real economic activity in Liaoning. However, as with electricity consumption, while the Li Keqiang index was good for monitoring commodity-intensive sectors, it did not provide a representative picture of the overall economy, especially as services became increasingly important.

Alternative estimates of GDP growth

In addition to power consumption and the Li Keqiang index, some market analysts have come up with their own alternative estimates of GDP using private data. However, while there are some good private data for specific sectors or activities, they are generally not sufficiently comprehensive, nor do they have a big enough sample size, to provide a credible estimate of GDP. In addition, these alternative estimates often do not have enough history or consistency to cover multiple economic cycles.

There have also been serious works by academics to adjust the official GDP growth estimates to get a 'truer' picture.[7] Rawski (2001) pointed out what he considered the gross inconsistency between the 24.7% cumulative official GDP growth rate and a 12.8% cumulative decline in energy consumption between 1997 and 2000.[8] He suggested that the actual GDP growth in that period might have been less than one-third of the official figure. Wu (2014) examined multiple methodological issues in China's national accounting and offered an alternative estimate to China's GDP growth.[9] One of the key assumptions in the alternative estimates was that labour productivity growth in China's services sector should have been close to zero (or 1% a year), as in developed countries, instead of the much higher rate implied from official statistics. A more recent paper by Chen et al. (2019) offered revisions to official estimates of GDP by employing government tax data, concluding that China's GDP growth between 2010 and 2016 was notably lower than the official estimates.

These research papers all identified some key problems in China's official statistics and made laudable attempts to get to a better picture of the economy. The alternative data they used or assumptions they made in the modifications were often problematic in their own way, however. For example, China's energy statistics were even more of an issue than the economic data during the 1997–2000 period due to major organisational changes (including the sudden closure of the ministry of coal) and local governments' desire to meet official targets for capacity reduction. Energy consumption turned out to be significantly underreported during that period, and coal consumption in 2000 was later revised up by 13.3%.[10] In addition, there was a downturn in heavy industry during that time, which means one cannot assume the same fixed energy elasticity of GDP growth. Therefore, the overestimation in GDP growth in 1997–2000 was probably not nearly as dramatic as the original energy consumption data suggested.

The assumption of 0–1% growth in services productivity in China seems also unrealistic for anyone who has lived through China's transformation from a command economy of SOE-provided services to one flourishing with private firms. SOE-operated restaurants and shops typically opened for a few hours a day in the old days, with the most frequent reply to customer requests being '没有', or 'don't have', without even checking. Private businesses, in contrast, stayed open all hours and sourced goods from all over the country to meet customer needs. It is not at all surprising that services productivity growth (per employee) was substantially higher than the average in developed economies during China's transition period. The use of value-added tax and corporate tax to re-estimate GDP would involve making vast assumptions about the complicated tax code and tax policy changes that would be hard to verify and justify. In addition, assumed long-term relationships between sets of data are likely to miss the cyclicality of the economy.

In conclusion, while the official GDP statistics clearly have many flaws, it is difficult to construct a good alternative. The official data, supplemented by sectoral and financial statistics, surveys and partner-country data, are adequate to give a reasonable picture of China's economic development and long-term trends.

Notes

1 See Xu (2019).
2 See China People's Daily (2017).
3 See, for example, EIU (2021).
4 See Fernald et al. (2021).
5 See Xu (2016).
6 See The Economist (2010).
7 See Chen (2011) for a literature review.
8 See Rawski (2001).
9 See Wu (2014).
10 See Natural Resource Defense Council (2014).

Bibliography

21st Century Business Herald (2012). "People from Beijing protest against the college entrance examination in different places: seriously affecting the rights and interests of local residents." *21st Century Business Herald*, 19 October. Available from: https://news.sciencenet.cn/htmlnews/2012/10/270690.shtm.

21st Century Business Herald (2020). "Three red-lines new rules imminent, developers worry about inability to borrow." "'三条红线' 融资新规箭在弦上 房企' 债' 不动许多愁."*21st Century Business Herald*, 29 August. Available from: http://www.21jingji.com/2020/8-29/0OMDEzODFfMTU4Njc0OQ.html.

Abekah-Koomson, I. and Chinweokwu, N.E. (2020). "China-Africa investments and economic growth in Africa." In: N. Edomah (ed.) *Regional Development in Africa*. IntechOpen, London. Available from: https://www.intechopen.com/chapters/72768.

Acemoglu, D., Autor, D., Dorn, D., Hanson, G.H. and Price, B. (2016). "Import competition and the great US employment sag of the 2000s." *Journal of Labor Economics*, 34(S1)(Part 2): S141–S198.

Acemoglu, D. and Restrepo, P. (2020). "Robots and jobs: evidence from US labor markets." *Journal of Political Economy*, 128(6). Available from: https://doi.org/10.1086/705716.

Acker, K. and Brautigam, D. (2021). "Twenty years of data on China's Africa lending." *Briefing Paper* No. 4, China Africa Research Initiative. Baltimore, MD: SAIS, Johns Hopkins University.

AIIB (2022). "Asian Infrastructure Investment Bank" [website]. Beijing. Available at: https://www.aiib.org/en/about-aiib/index.html.

All-China Women's Federation (2013). "Survey report on left-behind and urban floating children in our country." "我国农村留守儿童、城乡流动儿童状况研究报告." 10 May. Available from: http://www.reformdata.org/2013/0510/22228.shtml.

Allison, G. (2017). *Destined for War: Can America and China Escape Thucydides's Trap?* Boston, MA: Houghton Mifflin Harcourt.

Anderson, J. (2007). *China Monetary Policy Handbook* (1st ed.). Hong Kong: UBS Investment Research.

Andreas, J. and Zhan, S. (2015). "Hukou and land: market reform and rural displacement in China." *Journal of Peasant Studies*, 43(4): 798–827.

Attane, I. (2002). China's family planning policy: an overview of its past and future. *Studies in Family Planning*, 33(1): 103–113. Available from: http://www.jstor.org/stable/2696336.

Autor, D., Levy, F. and Murnane, R. (2003). "The skill content of recent technologi-
    cal change: an empirical exploration." *Quarterly Journal of Economics*, 118(4).
    Available from: https://doi.org/10.1162/003355303322552801.
Bahl, R. and Martinez-Vazquez, J. (2006). "Fiscal federalism and economic reform
    in China." In: Wallack, J. and Srinivasan, T.N. (*eds.*) *Federalism and Economic
    Reform: International Perspectives*. Cambridge: Cambridge University Press, pp.
    249–300.
Bank of International Settlement (BIS) (2016). "BIS quarterly review: international
    banking and financial market developments" [online]. Available from: https://
    www.bis.org/publ/qtrpdf/r_qt1609.pdf.
Bank of International Settlement (BIS) (2022). "Credit to the non-financial sector
    data" [online]. Available from: https://www.bis.org/statistics/totcredit.htm.
Barrett, P., Hendrix, J. and Sims, G. (2021). "How tech platforms fuel U.S. political
    polarization and what government can do about it" [online]. Blog. Washington,
    DC: Brookings Institute. https://www.brookings.edu/blog/techtank/2021/09/27/.
Beauchamp, Z. (2019). "Social media is rotting democracy from within" [online].
    Vox, 22 January. Available from: https://www.vox.com/policy-and-politics/2019/
    1/22/18177076/social-media-facebook-far-right-authoritarian-populism.
Bell, D. (2015). *The China Model: Political Meritocracy and the Limits of Democracy*.
    Princeton, NJ: Princeton University Press.
Benabou, R. (2002). "Tax and education policy in a heterogeneous-agent economy:
    what levels of redistribution maximize growth and efficiency?" *Econometrica*,
    70(2): 481–517.
Berg, A., Ostry, J.D. and Zettelmeyer, J. (2012). "What makes growth sustained?"
    Journal of Development Economics, 98(2): 149–166.
Bergsten, C.F. (2003). "The correction of the dollar and foreign intervention in the
    currency markets." Testimony before the Committee on Small Business, US House
    of Representatives, 25 June.
Bernanke, B.S. (2005). "The global saving glut and the US current account deficit."
    Saendridge Lecture, Virginia Association of Economists, 14 April.
Bernanke, B.S., Bertaut, C., Pounder DeMarco, L. and Kamin, S.B. (2011).
    "International capital flows and the returns to safe assets in the United States,
    2003–2007." *Banque de France Financial Stability Review*, 15: 13–26.
Block, F. and Keller, M. (eds.) (2011). *State of Innovation: the U.S. Government's
    Role in Technology Development*. New York: Paradigm Press.
Boston University Global Development Policy Center (n.d.). "Chinese Loans to
    Africa (CLA) database" [online]. Boston, MA. Available from: https://www.
    bu.edu/gdp/chinese-loans-to-africa-database/.
Brynjolfsson, E. and McAfee, A. (2014). *The Second Machine Age: Work, Progress and
    Prosperity in a Time of Brilliant Technologies*. New York: W.W. Norton & Company.
Cai, F. (2012). "Is there a 'middle-income trap'? Theories, experiences and relevance
    to China." *China & World Economy*, 20(1): 49–61. Available from: https://doi.
    org/10.1111/j.1749-124X.2012.01272.x.
Cai, F. (2021). *Understanding China's Economy – The Turning Point and
    Transformational Path of a Big Country*. Singapore: Springer Singapore.
Cai, H. (2014). "China's consumption is significantly underestimated" [online]. *Sina Finance*,
    15 June. Available from: http://finance.sina.com.cn/zl/china/20140615/221619417142.
    shtml.
Cai, M. (2016). "Land for welfare in China." *Land Use Policy*, 55: 1–12.

Cai, Y. (2003). "Collective ownership or cadres' ownership? The non-agricultural use of farmland in China." *China Quarterly*, 166: 662–680.

Cai, Y.S. (2006). *State and Laid-Off Workers in Reform China. The Silence and Collective Action of the Retrenched*. London and New York: Routledge.

Cai, F. and Yang, T. (2000). "The political economy of rural-urban income gap." "城乡收入差距的政治经济学." *Social Science in China*, (4). Available from: https://en.cnki.com.cn/Article_en/CJFDTOTAL-ZSHK200004001.htm.

Caixin (2012). "Interview with Governor Zhou Xiaochuan." 17 November.

Caixin (2014). "Chasing low-end population from Beijing is damaging." 17 February. Available from: https://topics.caixin.com/2014-02-17/100644934.html.

Calhoun, G. (2021). "The US still dominates in semiconductors; China is vulnerable (Pt.2)." *Forbes*. 11 October 2021.

Caliendo, L., Dvorkin, M. and Paro, F. (2017). "Trade and labor market dynamics: general equilibrium analysis of the China trade shock." *Working Paper* 2015-009D (revised). St. Louis, MO: Federal Reserve Bank of St. Louis.

Carney, J. (2009). "Jim Chanos: China is headed for a huge crash" [online]. *Business Insider*, 11 November 2009. Available from: https://www.businessinsider.com/jim-chanos-china-is-headed-for-a-huge-crash-2009-11?r=US&IR=T.

Cartier, C. (2001). "'Zone fever', the arable land debate, and real estate speculation: China's evolving land use regime and its geographical contradictions." *Journal of Contemporary China*, 10(28): 445–469.

Cassidy, J. (2015). "China's long Minsky Moment." *The New Yorker*, 13 August. Available from: https://www.newyorker.com/news/john-cassidy/chinas-long-minsky-moment.

Chamon, M.D. and Prasad, E. (2010). "Why are saving rates of urban households in China rising?" *American Economic Journal: Macroeconomics*, 2(1): 93–130.

Chan, K.W. (2019). "China's Hukou system at 60." In: R. Yep, J. Wang and Johnson, T. (eds.) *Handbook on Urban Development in China*. Cheltenham: Edward Elgar Publishing, pp. 59–79.

Chang, G. (2001). *The Coming Collapse of China*. New York: Random House.

Chen, B. and Lin, Y. (2013). "Development strategy, urbanization and China's rural-urban income gap." "发展战略、城市化与中国城乡收入差距." *Social Science in China*, (4): 81–103.

Chen, B., Lu, M. and Zhong, N. (2015). "How urban segregation distorts Chinese migrants' consumption?" *World Development*, 70: 133–146. Available from: https://doi.org/10.1016/j.worlddev.2014.11.019.

Chen, S.Y. (2011). "Estimates on China's industrial statistics by sector: 1980-2008." *China Economic Quarterly*, 10(3). Available from: http://nsd.pku.edu.cn/attachments/d065b6745d234f0e81fa077945ef8f83.pdf.

Chen, X.F. (2018). Why do migrant households consume so little? *China Economic Review*, 49: 197–209. Available from: https://doi.org/10.1016/j.chieco.2017.11.005.

Chen, X.W. (2014). *Chinese Economists on Economic Reform*. New York: Routledge.

Chen, W., Chen, X., Hsieh, C.-T. and Song, Z. (2019). "A forensic examination of China's national accounts." *NBER Working Paper* 25754. Cambridge, MA: National Bureau of Economic Research. Available from: https://www.nber.org/system/files/working_papers/w25754/w25754.pdf.

Chen, W., Dollar, D. and Tang, H. (2016). "Why is China investing in Africa? Evidence from the firm level." *Brookings Working Paper* 2016/06. Washington, DC: Brookings Institute.

Chen, Z.W. (2010). *China Model Never Exists*. 没有中国模式这回事. Taipei: Eight Flags Culture Publishing House.

Cheng, G. and Chen, X.W. (2006). "Rural collective land cannot directly enter the market." "农村集体用地不能直接进入市场." *China Youth Daily*. 23 February.

China Banking Regulatory Commission (2016). "Consumer finance companies are showing preliminary impact on boosting consumption" [online]. 15 December. Beijing. Available from: http://www.gov.cn/xinwen/2016-12/15/content_5148633. htm.

China Banking Regulatory Commission (2017). "Guidance on banking sector risk prevention." Document No. 6. Beijing. Available from: https://www.cbirc.gov.cn/ cn/view/pages/ItemDetail.html?docId=140120&itemId=928&generaltype=0.

China Banking Regulatory Commission Office (2017). "Notice on special management of banking sector regulatory, idle circulation and related party arbitrage." Document No. 46. Beijing. Available from: https://www.waizi.org.cn/law/18867. html.

China Banking and Insurance Regulatory Commission (2018). "Guidance on regulating asset management businesses of financial institutions." Beijing. Available from: http://www.gov.cn/zhengce/zhengceku/2018-12/31/content_5433072.htm.

China Banking and Insurance Regulatory Commission (2022a). "Main monitoring indicators of banking and insurance sectors in Q4 2021." "2021 年四季度银行业保险业主要监管指标数据情况." Beijing. Available from: https://www.cbirc.gov. cn/cn/view/pages/ItemDetail.html?docId=1037852&itemId=915&generaltype=0.

China Banking and Insurance Regulatory Commission (2022b). "Circular of the China Banking and Insurance Regulatory Commission and the People's Bank of China on strengthening financial services for new citizens." Beijing. Available from: http://www.gov.cn/zhengce/zhengceku/2022-03/06/content_5677508.htm.

China Briefing (2008). "CIC in talks to buy 49% of Morgan Stanley." *China Briefing*, 21 September. Available from: https://www.china-briefing.com/news/cic-in-talks-to-buy-49-of-morgan-stanley/.

China Center for Disease Prevention and Control (CDC) (2011). "National infectious disease and emergency public health event online direct reporting system program." "国家传染病与突发公共卫生事件网络直报信息系统建设项目." 王陇德等, 26 April. Beijing.

China Economic Daily (2019). "China household wealth survey." "中国家庭财富调查报告" [online]. 30 October. Available from: http://www.ce.cn/cysc/fdc/ fc/201910/30/t20191030_33470849.shtml.

China Economic Net (2013). "Central Bank: bank liquidity is in overall adequate level" [online]. 17 June. Available from: http://finance.ce.cn/rolling/201306/25/ t20130625_17133299.shtml.

China Economic Weekly (2014). "No breakthrough in Wenzhou's financial reform, problems with private bank financing remain" [online]. 9 April. Available from: http://politics.people.com.cn/n/2014/0409/c70731-24857616.html.

China Economic Weekly (2017). "The Central Environmental Inspector is very powerful: from 2016 to 2017, it covered the country's 31 provinces in full." "中央环保督查威力大." 6 November. Available from: http://www.ceweekly.cn/ magazine/ceweekly/2017/43/.

China Economic Weekly (2020). "Great leap forward and abandoned projects – whereto for domestic chips?" "大跃进与烂尾潮同现 - 国产芯片路在何方?" 2 November. Available from http://www.ceweekly.cn/2020/1102/318726.shtml.

China Education Daily (2014). "National college entrance exam applicants stop falling, those in different *hukou* jurisdiction rose sharply." 9 June 2014. Available from: http://edu.sina.com.cn/gaokao/2014-06-09/1231422958.shtml.

China General Administration of Customs (2022). "2021 exports value by types of trade and ownership of exporters" [online]. Available from: http://www.customs. gov.cn/customs/302249/zfxxgk/2799825/302274/302277/302276/4127665/ index.html.

China Institute for Income Distribution (n.d.). "China Household Income Project (CHIP) data" [online]. Available from: http://www.ciidbnu.org/chip/index. asp?lang=EN.

China Internet Network Information Center (2021). *Forty-Eighth Internet Network Development Statistical Report.* Beijing. Available from: https://www.cnnic.com. cn/IDR/ReportDownloads/202111/P020211119394556095096.pdf.

China Labor Bulletin (2007). "Reform of state-owned enterprises in China" [online]. 19 December. Available from: https://clb.org.hk/content/reform-state-owned-enterprises-china#10a.

China News (2003). "State Council established commanding centre for SARS control and a RMB 2 billion fund" [online]. 23 April. Available from: http://www. chinanews.com.cn/n/2003-04-23/26/297024.html.

China News (2021). "Han Wenxiu: common prosperity will rely on shared struggle, not 'rob the rich to help the poor'" [online]. 26 August. Available at: https://www. chinanews.com.cn/gn/2021/08-26/9551847.shtml.

China Photovoltaic Industry Association (2014). "2011–2012 China's PV industry development report." "2011–2012 年中国光伏产业发展报告." Beijing. Available from: http://www.chinapv.org.cn/association_news/282.html.

China Securities Journal (2005). "How to change the reality of '800 million shirts for one plane'" [online]. 21 May. Available from: http://finance.sina.com.cn/ stock/t/20050521/112273867.shtml.

China Securities Regulatory Commission (2005). "Circular of the China Securities Regulatory Commission on the pilot issue of share-trading reform." 29 April. Beijing. Available from: https://www.chinanews.com.cn/news/2005/2005-04-29/26/569170.shtml.

China United Steel Association and Greenpeace (2017). "Diagnosing 2016 China's steel capacity reduction." "问诊 2016 年中国钢铁行业去产能." Jiangyin and London. Available from: https://www.greenpeace.org.cn/wp-content/uploads/2017/02/.

Communist Party of China (CPC) Central Committee (1978). "The communique of the 11th CPC Congress 3rd plenum." Beijing. Available from: http://cpc.people. com.cn/GB/64162/64168/64563/65371/4441902.html.

CPC Central Committee (1980). "Several issues about further strengthening and enhancing the agricultural contract system." *The Reform Database* [online], 27 September. Available from: http://www.reformdata.org/1980/0927/6012.shtml.

CPC Central Committee (1982). "Minutes of the national rural work conference." *The Reform Database* [online], 1 January. Available from: http://www.reformdata. org/1982/0101/6010.shtml.

CPC Central Committee (1985). "1985 central document no. 1: ten policies for further activating the rural economy." *China Economic Net*, 24 September 2008. Available from: http://www.ce.cn/cysc/ztpd/08/ncgg/ngr/200809/24/t20080924_16903087. shtml.

CPC Central Committee (1987). *13th CPC Congress Work Report*, Beijing.

CPC Central Committee (1993). "Decision of the Central Committee of the Communist Party of China on some issues concerning the establishment of the socialist market economy." "中共中央关于建设社会主义市场经济体制若干问题的决定." Beijing. Available from: http://www.people.com.cn/item/20years/newfiles/b1080.html.

CPC Central Committee (1997). "Report of the CPC 15th National Congress." "中国共产党第十五次全国代表大会报告." Beijing. Available from: http://www.cctv.com/special/777/1/51883.html.

CPC Central Committee (2002). "CPC Central Committee decisions on important issues related to state owned enterprise reform and development." "中共中央关于国有企业改革和发展若干重大问题的决定." *China News*, 16 May. Available from: https://www.chinanews.com.cn/2002-05-16/26/186031.html.

CPC Central Committee (2007). "The CPC 17th National Congress report." Beijing. Available from: http://www.gov.cn/ldhd/2007-10/24/content_785431.htm.

CPC Central Committee (2008). "Decision on key issues on advancing rural reform and development." Beijing. Available from: http://www.gov.cn/jrzg/2008-10/19/content_1125094.htm.

CPC Central Committee (2013). "Decision of the Central Committee of the Communist Party of China on several major issues concerning comprehensively deepening the reform." 27 November 2013. Beijing. Available from: http://www.npc.gov.cn/zgrdw/npc/xinzhuanti/xxgcsbjszqhjs/2013-11/27/content_1814720.htm.

CPC Central Office and State Council Office (2017). "Opinions on deepening education system reform." "关于深化教育体制机制改革的意见." Beijing. Available from: http://www.gov.cn/zhengce/2017-09/24/content_5227267.htm.

CPC Central Office and State Council Office (2021). "Opinions on further reducing student homework and after-school tutoring burdens during mandatory education period." Beijing.

CPC Deepening Reform Committee (2020). "Discussion on SOE reform three-year action plan." Beijing. Available from: http://www.sasac.gov.cn/n4470048/n13461446/n15390485/n15390490/c15564887/content.html.

Choukhmane, T., Coeurdacier, N. and Jin, K. (2019). "The one-child policy and household saving" [online]. Available from: https://tahachoukhmane.com/wp-content/uploads/2020/07/CCJ_OneChildPolicy_231219.pdf.

Chu, Y. (2020). "China's global rise, from socialist self-reliance to embracement of economic globalization." In: I. Rossi (ed.) *Challenges of Globalization and Prospects for an Inter-civilization World Order*, pp 465–481. Cham: Springer Nature.

Cong, L., Gao, H., Ponticelli, J. and Yang, X. (2018). "Credit allocation under economic stimulus: evidence from China." *Chicago Booth Research Paper* No. 17-19. Available from: https://doi.org/10.2139/ssrn.2862101.

Cyberspace Administration of China (2021). "14th Five Year Plan on informatisation." Beijing. Available from: http://www.cac.gov.cn/2021-12/27/c_1642205314518676.htm.

Dai, Z.C. (2003). "Fifty years of implementation of China's health and epidemic prevention system and the principal of prevention." "中国卫生防疫体系及预防为主方针实施 50 年—纪念全国卫生防疫体系建立 50 周年." *China Public Health*, 19(10): 1–4.

Dell'Ariccia, G., Igan, D., Laeven, L., Tong, T., Bakker, B. and Vandenbussche, J. (2012). "Policies for macrofinancial stability: how to deal with credit booms." *IMF Staff Discussion Notes* 12/06. Washington, DC: International Monetary Fund. Available from: https://www.imf.org/external/pubs/ft/sdn/2012/sdn1206.pdf.

Deloitte Insights (2017). "Ageing tigers, hidden dragons." Deloitte US. Available from: https://www2.deloitte.com/content/dam/insights/us/articles/4201_VOA-3_Ageing-tigers-hidden-dragons/DI_VOA3.pdf.

Deng, Y.H., O'Brien, K. and Zhang, L. (2020). "How grassroots cadres broker land taking in urbanizing China." *Journal of Peasant Studies* 47 (6): 1233–1250.

Di, N. and Li, R.D. (2018). "Rabies vaccine producer ordered to halt production." 15 July 2018, *Caixin global*. Available from: https://www.caixinglobal.com/2018-07-16/rabies-vaccine-producer-ordered-to-halt-production-101304579.html?sourceEntityId=10130345.

Ding, C. and Lichtenberg, E. (2008). "Using land to promote urban economic growth in China." College Park, MD: University of Maryland, Department of Urban Studies and National Center for Smart Growth. Available from: https://www.researchgate.net/publication/23519183_Using_Land_to_Promote_Urban_Economic_Growth_in_China.

Ding, C. and Lichtenberg, E. (2011). "Land and urban economic growth in China." *Journal of Regional Science*, 51(2): 299–317. Available from: https://papers.ssrn.com/sol3/papers.cfm?abstract_id=1818634#:~:text=Land%20to%20accommodate%20urban%20development%20in%20China%20is,economic%20growth%20in%20coastal%20areas%20but%20not%20elsewhere.

Ding, H. and He, H. (2018). "A tale of transition: an empirical analysis of economic inequality in urban China, 1986–2009." *Review of Economic Dynamics*, 29: 106–137.

Ding, Z.L., Duan, X.N., Ge, Q.S. and Zhang, Z.Q. (2010). "On the major proposals for carbon emission reduction and some related issues." *China Earth Sciences*, 53: 159–172. Available from: https://link.springer.com/article/10.1007/s11430-010-0012-4.

The Diplomat (2017). "For the first time, Chinese Communist Party to hold a world political parties dialogue." 29 November. Available from: https://thediplomat.com/2017/11/for-the-first-time-chinese-communist-party-to-hold-a-world-political-parties-dialogue/.

Dollar, D. (2007). "Poverty, inequality, and social disparities during China's economic reform." *World Bank Policy Research Working Paper* 4253. Washington, DC: World Bank. Available from: https://openknowledge.worldbank.org/handle/10986/7404.

Downs, E.S. and Evans, P.C. (2006). "Untangling China's quest for oil through state-backed financial deals." *Policy Paper*. Washington, DC: Brookings Institute.

Du, R.S. (2005). *DU Runsheng Autobiography: Chronicals of Major Decisions on China's Rural System Reform*. Beijing: Renmin Publishing House.

Du, C. and Zhu, H.P. (2016). "The paths of China's medical and health system." "中国医疗卫生体制走过的那些路." Center for Public Policy Research, Chinese Academy of Social Science. Availabe from: http://www.casscppr.org/article/yiliaogaige/fuwu/1361.html.

Duca, J.V., Muellbauer, J. and Murphy, A. (2010). "Housing markets and the financial crisis of 2007-2009: lessons for the future." *Spatial Economic Research Centre Discussion Paper* 49. London: London School of Economics. Available from: http://eprints.lse.ac.uk/33613/1/sercdp0049.pdf.

Dupont, A. (2020). "The US-China cold war has already started." *The Diplomat*, 8 July. Available from: https://thediplomat.com/2020/07/the-us-china-cold-war-has-already-started/#:~:text=The%20US-China%20Cold%20War%20Has%20Already%20Started%20The,flags%20on%20top%20of%20a%20trishaw%20in%20Beijing.

Easterly, W. (2007). "Inequality does cause underdevelopment: insights from a new instrument." *Journal of Development Economics*, 84(2): 755–776.

ECON Centre for Economic Analysis (2002). "Environmental challenges in China: determinants of success and failure." *Econ-Report* 34/2002. Commissioned by the World Bank. Oslo. Available from: https://documents1.worldbank.org/curated/pt/387031468771864566/310436360_200502760900204/additional/wdr27850.pdf.

The Economist (2009). "Beware the Beijing model." 26 May. Available from: https://www.economist.com/business/2009/05/26/beware-the-beijing-model.

The Economist (2010). "Keqiang ker-ching: how China's next prime minister keeps tabs on its economy." 9 December. Available from: https://www.economist.com/asia/2010/12/09/keqiang-ker-ching.

The Economist (2011). "Trading places." 19 December. Available from: https://www.economist.com/graphic-detail/2011/12/19/trading-places.

The Economist (2016). "Minsky's moment." 30 July. Available from: https://www.economist.com/schools-brief/2016/07/30/minskys-moment.

The Economist (2018a). "How the West got China wrong." 1 March. Available from: https://www.economist.com/leaders/2018/03/01/how-the-west-got-china-wrong.

The Economist (2018b). "China's predicament: getting old before getting rich." 14 August. Available from: https://www.economist.com/special-report/2018/08/14/chinas-predicament.

The Economist (2021). "China's attack on tech." 14 August. Available from: https://www.economist.com/weeklyedition/2021-08-14.

Economist Intelligence Unit (2021). "Recent challenges in reading China's GDP." 4 March. Available from: https://www.eiu.com/n/recent-challenges-in-reading-chinas-gdp/.

Edsall, T.B. (2021). "Democracy is weakening right in front of us." *New York Times*, 17 February. Available from: https://www.nytimes.com/2021/02/17/opinion/digital-revolution-democracy-fake-news.html.

Eichengreen, B., Park, D. and Shin, K. (2012). "When fast-growing economies slow down: international evidence and implications for china." *Asian Economic Papers*, 11(1): 42–87.

Etzioni, A. (2017). *Avoiding War with China*. Charlottesville, VA: University of Virginia Press.

European Commission (2010). *An Integrated Industrial Policy for the Globalisation Era – Putting Competitiveness and Sustainability at Centre Stage*. Brussels: European Economic and Social Committee. Available from: https://www.eesc.europa.eu/en/our-work/opinions-information-reports/opinions/industrial-policy-globalised-era-putting-competitiveness-and-sustainability-centre-stage.

European Union Chamber of Commerce in China (2017). *China Manufacturing 2025: Putting Industrial Policy Ahead of Market Forces*. Beijing. Available from: http://docs.dpaq.de/12007-european_chamber_cm2025-en.pdf.

Evangelista, R. and Bruno, F. (2019). "WhatsApp and political instability in Brazil: targeted messages and political radicalisation." *Internet Policy Review*, 8: 1–23.

Farrell, D., Gersch, D. and Stephenson, E. (2006). *The Value of China's Emerging Middle Class*. New York: McKinsey. Available from: https://www.mckinsey.com/~/media/McKinsey/Featured%20Insights/China/The%20value%20of%20emerging%20middle%20class%20in%20China/The-value-of-Chinas-emerging-middle-class.pdf.

Federal Reserve Economic Data (FRED) (2022). "Household debt service payments as a percent of disposable personal income." St. Louis, MO: St. Louis Federal Reserve Bank. Available from: https://fred.stlouisfed.org/series/TDSP.

Feng, J., He, L. and Sato, H. (2009). "Public pension and household saving: evidence from urban China." *Fukino Project Discussion Paper* No. 009. Tokyo: Hitotsubashi University. Available from: http://www.hit-u.ac.jp/ijrc/pdf/files/Fukino_DP_09_P5Y78A.pdf.

Fernald, J., Edison, H. and Loungani, P. (1999). "Was China the first domino? Assessing links between China and other Asian economies." *Journal of International Money and Finance*, 18(4): 515–535.

Fernald, J.G., Hsu, E. and Spiegel, M.M. (2021). "Is China fudging its GDP figures? Evidence from trading partner data." *Journal of International Money and Finance*, 114: 102262. Available from: https://www.sciencedirect.com/science/article/abs/pii/S0261560620302187

Fewsmith, J. and Xiang, G. (2014). "Local governance in China: incentives & tensions." *Daedalus*, 143(2): 170–183. Available from: https://www.researchgate.net/publication/275013704_Local_Governance_in_China_Incentives_Tensions.

Financial Stability Board (2011). "Shadow banking: strengthening oversight and regulation" [online]. Available from: https://www.fsb.org/wp-content/uploads/r_111027a.pdf?page_moved=1.

Financial Times (2012). "Microsoft alleges piracy in China lawsuits." 10 January. Available from: https://www.ft.com/content/f87227ac-3b89-11e1-a09a-00144feabdc0.

Financial Times (2019). "The other side of China's investment in Africa." 27 March. Available from: https://www.ft.com/content/9f5736d8-14e1-11e9-a581-4ff78404524e.

Financial Times (2021a). "China's misguided crackdown on business." 29 July. Available from: https://www.ft.com/content/fc211f0a-388e-42ce-957b-c66fb8640ce4.

Financial Times (2021b). "China cut finance pledges to Africa amid growing debt concerns." 1 December. Available from: https://www.ft.com/content/b7bd253a-766d-41b0-923e-9f6701176916.

Findlaw.cn Regulatory Library (1984). "Notice of the State Economic Reform Commission on printing and distributing the minutes of the symposium on the pilot work of urban economic system reform." Beijing. Available from: https://china.findlaw.cn/fagui/p_1/37005.html.

Fitch Ratings (2022). "China corporate bond default rate set to rise in 2022." Hong Kong and Shanghai. Available from: https://www.fitchratings.com/research/corporate-finance/china-corporate-bond-default-rate-set-to-rise-in-2022-27-01-2022.

French, H.W. (2014). "Into Africa, China's wild rush." *New York Times*, 16 May. Available from: https://www.nytimes.com/2014/05/17/opinion/into-africa-chinas-wild-rush.html.

French, H.W. (2017). *Everything under the Heavens*. New York: Alfred A. Knopf.

Fu, Y. (2019). "China and the US should prepare for an era of 'co-opetition'." *Financial Times*, 6 November. Available from: https://www.ft.com/content/beb6c052-ff00-11e9-a530-16c6c29e70ca.

Gallup. (2021). "China" [online]. Available from: https://news.gallup.com/poll/1627/china.aspx.

Gan, J. (2008). *Privatization in China: Experiences and Lessons*. Hong Kong: Hong Kong University of Science and Technology. Available from: https://english.ckgsb.edu.cn/sites/default/files/privatization_in_china.pdf.

Gan, L. (2018). "2017 urban housing vacancy analysis." *China Household Finance Survey*. Chengdu: Southwest University of Finance and Economics. Available from: https://chfs.swufe.edu.cn/_local/D/65/2B/57D2F2A832F77C8F3C1DDC4926E_ADF9EA0C_121D6C.pdf.

García-Herrero, A. and Xu, J. (2019). "China's investment in Africa: What the data really says and the implications for Europe." *Bruegel*, 22 July. Available from: https://www.bruegel.org/2019/07/chinas-investment-in-africa-what-the-data-really-says-and-the-implications-for-europe/.

Garnaut, R., Song, L. and Yao, Y. (2006). "Impact and significance of state-owned enterprise restructuring in China." *China Journal*, 55: 35–63. Available from: https://doi.org/10.2307/20066119.

Garrett, G. (2004). "Globalization's missing middle." *Foreign Affairs*, 83: 84–96. Available from: https://doi.org/10.2307/20034139.

Ge, W. (1999). "Special economic zones and the opening of the Chinese economy: some lessons for economic liberalization." *World Development*, 27(7): 1267–85.

Gallagher, M. (2013). "Social Cohesion, Urbanization, and Labor Conflict." Background paper for *Urban China: Toward Efficient, Inclusive, and Sustainable Urbanization*. Washington, DC: The World Bank.

Gill, I. and Kharas, H. (2007). *An East Asian Renaissance – Ideas for Economic Growth*. Washington, DC: World Bank.

Gill, I. and Kharas, H. (2015), "The middle-income trap turns ten." *Policy Research Working Paper* No. 7403. Washington, DC: World Bank. Available at: https://openknowledge.worldbank.org/handle/10986/22660.

Glawe, L. and Wagner, H. (2017). "The People's Republic of China in the middle-income trap?" *ADB Institute Working Paper Series*, No. 749. Tokyo. Available from: https://www.adb.org/publications/prc-middle-income-trap.

Goldstein, M. and Lardy, N.R. (2008). *Debating China's Exchange Rate Policy*. Washington, DC: Peterson Institute for International Economics.

Goos, A. and Manning, A. (2007). "Lousy and lovely jobs: the rising polarization of work in Britain." *Review of Economics and Statistics*, 89(1): 118–133. Available from: https://doi.org/10.1162/rest.89.1.118.

Government of the People's Republic of China (2001). *The 10th Five Year Plan of National Economic and Social Development*. Beijing. Available from: http://www.gov.cn/gongbao/content/2001/content_60699.htm.

Government of the People's Republic of China (2006). *The 11th Five Year Plan of National Economic and Social Development*. Beijing. Available from: http://www.gov.cn/gongbao/content/2006/content_268766.htm.

Government of the People's Republic of China (2011). *The 12th Five Year Plan of National Economic and Social Development*. Beijing. Available from: http://www.gov.cn/2011lh/content_1825838.htm.

Government of the People's Republic of China (2016). *The 13th Five Year Plan of National Economic and Social Development*. Beijing. Available from: http://www.gov.cn/xinwen/2016-03/17/content_5054992.htm.

Government of the People's Republic of China (2021). *The 14th Five Year Plan of National Economic and Social Development*. Beijing. Available from: http://www.gov.cn/xinwen/2021-03/13/content_5592681.htm.

Groves, T., Hong, Y., McMillan, J. and Naughton, B. (1994). "Autonomy and incentives in Chinese state enterprise." *Quarterly Journal of Economics*, 109(1): 183–209.

The Guardian (2010). "Twitter gaffe: US embassy announces 'crazy bad' Beijing air pollution." 19 November. Available from: https://www.theguardian.com/environment/blog/2010/nov/19/crazy-bad-beijing-air-pollution.

Guriev, S., Melnikov, N. and Zhuravskaya, E. (2021). "3G internet and confidence in government." *Quarterly Journal of Economics*, 136(4): 2533–2613.

Han, J. (2008). *Thirty Years of China's Economic Reform: Volume on Rural Economy.* "中国经济改革三十年: 农村经济卷." Chongqing: Chongqing University Press.

Han, W.X. (2021). "Common prosperity needs striving together, not 'robbing the rich to help the poor'." 26 August, *China News.* Available from: https://www. chinanews.com.cn/gn/2021/08-26/9551847.shtml

Hass, R. (2021). *The 'New Normal' in US-China Relations: Hardening Competition and Deep Interdependence.* Washington, DC: Brookings Institute.

He, D., Wang, H. and Yu, X. (2015). "Interest rate determination in China: past, present, and future." *International Journal of Central Banking.* Available from: https://www.ijcb.org/journal/ijcb15q5a7.pdf.

He, H., Huang, F., Liu, Z. and Zhu, D. (2018). "Breaking the 'iron rice bowl': evidence of precautionary savings from the Chinese state-owned enterprises reform." *Journal of Monetary Economics*, 94: 94–113. Available from: https://www. sciencedirect.com/science/article/abs/pii/S0304393217301654.

He, J.D. and Yu, X.L. (2003). "How was the urban-rural dual society formed?" *Book Room* [online]. Chinese University of Hong Kong. Available from: http:// ww2.usc.cuhk.edu.hk/PaperCollection/Details.aspx?id=2299.

Hessler, P. (2010). *Country Driving: A Journey through China from Farm to Factory.* London: HarperCollins.

Hicks, M. and Devaraj, S. (2017). *The Myth and the Reality of Manufacturing in America.* Muncie, IN: Ball State University, Center for Business and Economic Research.

Ho, P. (2005). *Institutions in Transition: Land Ownership, Property Rights, and Social Conflict in China.* Studies on Contemporary China. Oxford: Oxford University Press.

Hsieh, C.T. and Song, Z. (2015). "Grasp the large, let go of the small: the transformation of the state sector in China." *NBER Working Paper* No. 21006. Available from: https://www.nber.org/papers/w21006.

Hu, H. and Wang, T. (2011). "All about social housing." Hong Kong: UBS Investment Research.

Hua, S., Cai, Q., Ji, Z. and Dong, S. (2020). "Study of China's infectious disease control early warning mechanism – revelation from the early stage Covid-19 control." "华生 蔡倩 汲铮 董申. "中国传染病防控预警机制探究 ——来自新冠病毒疫情早期防控中的启示." 武汉大学董辅初经济社会发展研究院." Wuhan: Wuhan University Dongfuren Economic and Social Development Institute [online].

Huang, Y., Ge, T.T. and Wang, C. (2020). "Monetary policy framework and transmission mechanisms." In: M. Amstad, G. Sun and W. Xiong (eds.) *The Handbook of China's Financial System*, pp 38–62. Princeton, NJ: Princeton University Press.

Huang, Z. (2013). "Re-understanding Chinese workers – historical evolution of labor laws and current informal economy." "重新认识中国劳动人民——劳动法规的历史演变与当前的非正规经济." *Open Times.* No. 5. Guangzhou. Available from http://ww2.usc.cuhk.edu.hk/PaperCollection/Details.aspx?id=9190.

Huaxi Metro Daily (2020). "SARS experience: response standards and adjustments in China's response to emergency public health events." "非典经验: 中国对突发公共卫生事件的应对标准与变化." 8 March. Available from: http://www.chinanews.com/gn/2020/03-08/9117490.shtml.

Im, F.G. and Rosenblatt, D. (2013). "Middle-income traps: a conceptual and empirical survey." *Journal of International Commerce, Economies and Policy*, 6(3): 1–39.

International Federation of Robotics (2021). *World Robotics Report 2021.* Frankfurt am Main. Available from: https://ifr.org/ifr-press-releases/news/robot-sales-rise-again.

International Monetary Fund (IMF) (2004). "People's Republic of China Article IV consultation—staff report." *IMF Country Report* No. 04/351. Washington, DC. Available from: https://www.imf.org/en/Publications/CR/Issues/2016/12/31/Peoples-Republic-of-China-Staff-Report-for-the-2004-Article-IV-Consultation-17828.

IMF (2012). "The liberalization and management of capital flows: an institutional view." *Policy Paper*. Washington, DC. Available from: https://www.imf.org/en/Publications/Policy-Papers/Issues/2016/12/31/The-Liberalization-and-Management-of-Capital-Flows-An-Institutional-View-PP4720.

IMF (2015). "Press release: IMF executive board completes the 2015 review of SDR valuation." *IMF Press Release*. Washington, DC. Available from: https://www.imf.org/en/News/Articles/2015/09/14/01/49/pr15543.

IMF (2016). "People's Republic of China: staff report for the 2016 Article IV consultation." *IMF Country Report* No. 16/270. Washington, DC. Available from: https://www.imf.org/external/pubs/ft/scr/2016/cr16270.pdf.

IMF (2017). "People's Republic of China: financial system stability assessment-press release and statement by the executive director for People's Republic of China." *IMF Country Report* No. 17/358. Washington, DC. Available from: https://www.imf.org/en/Publications/CR/Issues/2017/12/07/people-republic-of-china-financial-system-stability-assessment-45445.

IMF (2022). "People's Republic of China: staff report for the 2021 Article IV consultation." *IMF Country Report* No. 22/21. Washington, DC. Available from: https://www.imf.org/en/Publications/CR/Issues/2022/01/26/Peoples-Republic-of-China-2021-Article-IV-Consultation-Press-Release-Staff-Report-and-512248.

Jefferson, G. (2016, rev. March 2017). "State-owned enterprise in China: reform, performance, and prospects." *Working Paper* 109R. Waltham, MA: Brandeis University, Department of Economics and International Business School.

Jiang, F.T. and Li, X.P. (2010). "Direct market intervention and competition hinderance, direction and fundamental flaws of China's industrial policy." "直接干预市场与限制竞争:中国产业政策的取向与根本缺陷." *China's Industrial Economics*, 09: 26–36.

Johnson, C. (1982). *MITI and the Japanese Miracle: The Growth of Industrial Policy, 1925–1975*. Stanford, CA: Stanford University Press.

Johnson, Z. and Zühr, R. (2021). "A new era? Trends in China's financing for international development cooperation." *Donor Tracker* [online], 10 May. Available from: https://donortracker.org/insights/new-era-trends-chinas-financing-international-development-cooperation.

Karacadag, C. (2003). "Financial system soundness and reform." In: W. Tseng and M. Rodlauer (eds.) *China: Competing in the Global Economy*. Washington, DC: International Monetary Fund. Available from: https://doi.org/10.5089/9781589061781.071.

Kee, H.L. and Tang, H. (2016). "Domestic value added in exports: theory and firm evidence from China." *American Economic Review*, 106(6): 1402–1436.

Kernen, A. and Lam, K.N. (2014). "Workforce localization among Chinese state-owned enterprises (SOEs) in Ghana." *Journal of Contemporary China*, 23(90): 1053–1072.

Kim, J. and Park, J. (2017). "The role of total factor productivity growth in middle-income countries." *ADB Economics Working Paper Series* No. 527. Manila: Asian Development Bank.

Kissinger, H.A. (2012). "The future of U.S.-Chinese relations: conflict is a choice, not a necessity." *Foreign Affairs*, 91(2). Available from: http://www.jstor.org/stable/23217220.

Kling, A. (2011). "The new commanding heights." 5 July. Washington, DC: Cato Institute. Available from: https://www.cato.org/commentary/new-commanding-heights.

Koopman, R., Wang, Z. and Wei, S.-J. (2012). "Estimating domestic content in exports when processing trade is pervasive." *Journal of Development Economics*, 99: 178–189.

Kornai, J. (1986). *Economics of Shortage* (Chinese version). New York: Economic Science Publishing.

Krugman, P. (1994). "The myth of Asia's miracle." *Foreign Affairs*, 73(6): 62–78.

Krulak, C.C. and Friedman, A. (2021). "The US and China are not destined for war." *Project Syndicate*, 24 August. Available from: https://www.chinausfocus.com/foreign-policy/the-us-and-china-are-not-destined-for-war.

Kuijs, L. (2005). "Investment and saving in China." *Policy Research Working Paper* No. 3633. Washington, DC: World Bank. Available from: https://openknowledge.worldbank.org/handle/10986/8319.

Kuijs, L. (2017). "Trend growth in Ems will continue to vary widely." *Emerging Market Research Briefing*, 22 May. Oxford: Oxford Economics.

Kuijs, L. (2019). "Long-term growth to remain solid, barring decoupling." *China Research Briefing*, 15 February. Oxford: Oxford Economics.

Kuijs, L. and Wang, T. (2006). "China's pattern of growth: moving to sustainability and reducing inequality." *World Bank Policy Research Working Paper* No. 3767. Washington, DC: World Bank. Available from: https://papers.ssrn.com/sol3/papers.cfm?abstract_id=849385.

Kung, J.K. and Liu, S.Y. (1997). "Farmers' preferences regarding ownership and land tenure in post-Mao China: unexpected evidence from eight counties." *China Journal*, 38: 33–64.

Lam, D. (2011). "How the world survived the population bomb: lessons from 50 years of extraordinary demographic history." *Demography*, 48: 1231–1262.

Lam, J., Wang, T., Zhang, N., Yan, M., Leung, M., Han, T. and Chen, C. (2020). "UBS Evidence Lab inside: China housing survey – stabilising purchase intentions." Hong Kong, UBS Investment Research.

Lardy, N.R. (1983). *Agriculture in China's Modern Economic Development.* Cambridge: Cambridge University Press.

Lardy, N.R. (1992). *Foreign Trade and Economic Reform in China, 1978–1990.* Cambridge: Cambridge University Press.

Lardy, N.R. (1998). *China's Unfinished Economic Revolution.* Washington, DC: Brookings Institute Press.

Lardy, N.R. (2008). "Financial repression in China." *Working Paper* No. PB08-8. Washington, DC: Peterson Institute for International Economics.

Lardy, N.R. (2014). *Markets over Mao.* Washington, DC: Peterson Institute of International Economics.

Lardy, N.R. (2019). *The State Strikes Back: The End of Economic Reform in China?* Washington, DC: Peterson Institute of International Economics.

Legal Daily (2012). "Guangxi plans to ban gender-testing and abortion after 14 weeks." 27 April. Available from: http://www.scio.gov.cn/zhzc/8/4/Document/1151186/1151186.htm.

Leonard, A. (2006). "No consensus on the Beijing consensus." *Salon*, 15 September. Available from: https://www.salon.com/2006/09/15/beijing_consensus/.

Leonhardt, D. (2009). "The China puzzle (will China still bank roll us?)." *New York Times*, 13 May. Available from: https://www.nytimes.com/2009/05/17/magazine/17china-t.html.

Li, B. (2018). *Formulating the Dual Pillar Framework of Monetary Policy and Macroprudential Policy.* 构建货币政策和宏观审慎政策的双支柱调控框架. Beijing: China Finance Publishing.

Li, H., Hong, G.Z. and Huang, L.X. (2013). "The mystery of China's land finance growth: the reform of the tax-sharing system and the strategy of land finance growth." "中国土地财政增长之谜 ——分税制改革、土地财政增长的策略性." *China Economic Quarterly*, 12(4). Available from: http://ww2.usc.cuhk.edu.hk/PaperCollection/webmanager/wkfiles/2012/9322_1_paper.pdf.

Li, H.B., Loyalka, P., Rozelle, S. and Wu, B. (2017). "Human capital and China's future growth." *Journal of Economic Perspectives*, 31(1): 25–48). Available from: https://www.aeaweb.org/articles?id=10.1257/jep.31.1.25.

Li, K.Q. (2016). *Government Work Report to the National People's Congress*. Beijing. Available from: http://www.gov.cn/guowuyuan/2016-03/17/content_5054901.htm.

Li, K.Q. (2019). *Government Work Report to the National People's Congress*. Beijing. Available from: http://www.gov.cn/zhuanti/2019qglh/2019lhzfgzbg/index.htm.

Li, K.Q. (2022). *Government Work Report to the National People's Congress*. Beijing. Available from: http://www.gov.cn/zhuanti/2022lhzfgzbg/index.htm.

Li, K.Q. (2020a). "What is the deep meaning of Li KeQiang's reiteration of the "two unwavering" implications?" 19 September. Beijing. Available from: http://www.gov.cn/guowuyuan/2020-09/19/content_5544580.htm.

Li, L., Jiang, Y. and Chen, Q.L. (2008). "A review of China's health care reform after the reform and open policy in 1978." *China Health Economics*, 27(2): 5–9.

Li, L.M. (2014). "Thoughts on 60 years' of public health in new China." "新中国公共卫生60年的思考." *China Public Health Management*, 30(3): 311–315.

Li, S. and Luo, C.L. (2007). "Re-estimate of China's rural-urban Income Gap." "中国城乡居民收入差距的重新估计." *Peking University Journal*, 2: 111–120.

Li, T. (2020b). "Ten years ago, 1% of migrant workers had the possibility of buying a house, and now 19%-20%." *Sina Finance*, 10 December. Available from: https://finance.sina.com.cn/hy/hyjz/2020-12-10/doc-iiznezxs6171760.shtml.

Lin, J.Y.F. (1988). "The household responsibility system in China's agricultural reform: a theoretical and empirical study." *Economic Development and Cultural Change*, 36(3): 199–224.

Lin, J.Y.F. (1992). "Rural reforms and agricultural growth in China." *American Economic Review*, 82(1): 34–51. Available from: http://www.jstor.org/stable/2117601.

Lin, J.Y.F. (2012). *New Structural Economics: A Framework for Rethinking Development and Policy.* Washington, DC: World Bank. Available from: https://openknowledge.worldbank.org/handle/10986/2232.

Lin, J.Y.F. and Liu, Z. (2000). "Fiscal decentralization and economic growth in China." *Economic Development and Cultural Change*, 49(1): 1–21. Available from: https://www.jstor.org/stable/10.1086/452488.

Lin, J.Y.F. and Monga, C. (2010). "Growth identification and facilitation: the role of the state in the dynamics of structural change." *Policy Research Working Paper* No. 5313. Washington, DC: World Bank.

Lin, J.Y.F., Zhang, J., Wang, Y. and Kou, Z. (eds.) (2018). *Industrial Policy: Review, Reflection and Outlook.* 产业政策:总结、反思与展望. Beijing: Peking University Press.

Liu, H. (2006). "Key challenges of and lessons from Latin American economies." "拉美经济的主要挑战和经验教训." 比较. *Comparative Studies*. Available from: http://www.50forum.org.cn/home/article/detail/id/2424.html.

Liu, H. (2010). "Special interview: discussion on new policies." "刘鹤专访:谈新国策." *New Century* (Weekly), *Caixin Media*. No. 43. 1 November. Available from: https://magazine.caixin.com/2010-10-30/100193833.html.

Liu, H. (2013). *Comparative Study of the Two Global Crises*. 两次全球大危机的比较研究. Beijing: China Economics Publishing.

Liu, H. (2021). "High quality growth must be achieved." *People's Daily*, 24 November. Available from: http://www.gov.cn/guowuyuan/2021-11/24/content_5652964.htm.

Liu, P. (2005a). "Guarantee laws: unlock the deadlock of borrowing difficulties." *Sina Finance*, 12 November. Available from: http://finance.sina.com.cn/review/observe/20051112/17192114456.shtml.

Liu, S.Y. (2005b). "Land policy and urban spatial expansion financing." Presentation at a workshop organized by the Development Research Centre of the People's Republic of China, Beijing, 16 January.

Liu, S.Y. (2018a). *The Land System and China's Development*. 土地制度与中国发展. Beijing: China Renmin University Press.

Liu, Y. (2018b). "Impacts of land finance on urban sprawl in China: the case of Chongqing." *Land Use Policy*, 72: 420–432.

Liu, H., Yang, F. and Xu, Y. (2013). "Analysis of China's urban housing situation based on the 2010 population census." "基于 2010 年人口普查数据的中国城镇住房状况分析." *Journal of Tsinghua University* 6(28). Available from: http://www.cre.tsinghua.edu.cn/__local/D/76/10/CB684020FF0E3CF431B58628135_BAD0F781_D1AEE.pdf?e=.pdfz.

Liu, R., Feng, Z., Yang, Y. and You, Z. (2010). "China's population collection pattern based on population density." "基于人口集聚度的中国人口集疏格局." *Progress in Geography*, 29(10): 1171–1177.

Liu, S.Y., Carter, M.R. and Yang, Y. (1998). "Dimensions and diversity of property rights in rural China: dilemmas on the road to further reform." *World Development*, 26(10): 1789–1806.

Livi-Bacci, M. (2001). *A Concise History of World Population* (3rd ed.). Cambridge, MA: Blackwell.

Long, Y.T. (2011). "China's WTO entry is a win-win, forcing domestic reform and opening." *Sina Finance*, 09 December. Available from: http://finance.sina.com.cn/g/20111209/132110965917.shtml.

Lou, J.W. (2014). *Rethinking Intergovermental Fiscal Relations in China*. 中国政府间财政关系再思考. Beijing: China Finance and Economics Publishing.

Lou, J.W. (2015). *Deepening Fiscal and Tax System Reform*. 深化财税体制改革. Beijing: People's Publishing House.

Lu, M. and Chen, Z. (2004). "Urbanization, pro-urban economic policy and rural-urban income gap." "城市化、城市倾向的经济政策与城乡收入差距." 经济研究. *Economic Research*, 7: 50–58.

Lu, M., H. Ou, and Chen, B. (2014). "Rationality or bubble? An empirical study on urbanization, migration and housing prices." *The Journal of World Economy* 1: 30–54.

Lu, X.Y. and Wang, X.Q. (1981). "The origin and future development of package production to households: an investigation report on the problem of package production to households in gansu province." 陆学艺、王小强. "包产到户的由来和今后的发展." Reformdata.org, 15 November. Available from: http://www.reformdata.org/1980/1115/15758.shtml.

Lu, Z., Long, W., Pang, X. and Li, R. (2022). "The impact of childhood migration on rural migrants' adult income." "童年迁移经历对农村流动人口成年时期收入的影响." *China Rural Survey*, 1: 1–17.

Luo, H. and Cao, B. (2011). "China environmental regulatory framework overview." Program report No. 1. Beijing: EU-China and PRCEE, Ministry of Environmental Protection. Available from: https://www.clientearth.cn/media/pithp0su/2011-07-01-china-environmental-regulatory-framework-overview-ext-cn.pdf.

Luo, Y. and Harrison, T.M. (2019). "How citizen journalists impact the agendas of traditional media and the government policymaking process in China." *Global Media and China*, 4(1). Available from: https://doi.org/10.1177/2059436419835771.

Lyman, P.N. (2005). *China's Rising Role in Africa*. New York: Council on Foreign Relations.

Ma, J. (ed.) (1991). *Contemporary Chinese Township and Village Enterprises*. 当代中国的乡镇企业. Beijing, Contemporary China Publishing House, p. 55.

Ma, J. (2007). "Environmental governance urgently needs social consensus: public participation in curbing power rent-seeking." "环境治理亟待社会共识 公众参与遏制权力寻租." *China Dialogue*, 1 March. Beijing: China Public Environment Policy Institute. Available from: http://www.chinadialogue.net/How-participation-can-help-China-s-ailing-environment.

Maddison, A. (2001). *The World Economy, Volume 1: A Millennial Perspective*. Paris: Organisation for Economic Co-operation and Development.

Maddison, A. (2003). *The World Economy, Volume 2: Historical Statistics*. Paris: Organisation for Economic Co-operation and Development.

Maddison, A. (2007). "Chinese economic performance in the long run, 960-2030 AD, second edition, revised and updated." Paris: Organisation for Economic Co-operation and Development. Available from: https://doi.org/10.1787/9789264037632-en

Maliszewski, W., Arslanalp, S., Caparusso, J., Garrido, J., Guo, S., Kang, J. (2016). "Resolving China's corporate debt problem." *Working Paper* 16/203. Washington, DC: International Monetary Fund. Available from: https://www.imf.org/en/Publications/WP/Issues/2016/12/31/Resolving-Chinas-Corporate-Debt-Problem-44337.

McGregor, J. (2005). *One Billion Customers: Lessons from the Front Lines of Doing Business in China*. New York: Free Press.

McGregor, R. (2012). *The Party: The Secret World of China's Communist Rulers*. London: Harper Collins.

McKinsey & Co. (2017). *Dance of the Lions and Dragons – How Are Africa and China Engaging, and How Will the Partnership Evolve?* Available from: https://www.mckinsey.com/~/media/McKinsey/Featured%20Insights/Middle%20East%20and%20Africa/The%20closest%20look%20yet%20at%20Chinese%20economic%20engagement%20in%20Africa/Dance-of-the-lions-and-dragons.ashx.

Meza, E. (2014). "IRENA: PV prices have declined 80% since 2008." *PV Magazine*, 11 September.

Michaels, G., Natraj, A. and Van Reenen, J. (2014). "Has ICT polarized skill demand? Evidence from eleven countries over 25 years." *Review of Economics and Statistics*, 96(1): 60–77.

Ministry of Commerce (2019). "China retail sales industry development report 2018/19." Beijing. Available from: http://images.mofcom.gov.cn/ltfzs/201909/20190920083807922.pdf.

Ministry of Commerce (2021). "China has fulfilled its WTO commitment." Beijing. Available from: http://www.gov.cn/xinwen/2021-10/29/content_5647515.htm.

Ministry of Commerce (2022). "Ministry of Commerce briefing on internet sales market and other development." Beijing. Available from: http://www.gov.cn/xinwen/2022-01/27/content_5670877.htm.

Ministry of Construction (1994). "Urban economic housing construction and management measures." "城镇经济适用住房建设管理办法." Beijing.

Ministry of Construction (1999). "Notice of the Ministry of Construction on further promoting the reform of existing public housing." "建设部关于进一步推进现有公有住房改革的通知." Beijing.

Ministry of Construction (2007). "Management measures of economic housing." Beijing. Available from: http://www.gov.cn/zwgk/2007-12/01/content_822414.htm.

Ministry of Ecology and Environment (2014). "2013 China environmental conditions report." Beijing. Available from: https://www.mee.gov.cn/hjzl/sthjzk/zghjzkgb/201605/P020160526564151497131.pdf.

Ministry of Ecology and Environment (2018). "End-period evaluation report on the implementation of 'Air pollution control action plan'." Beijing. Available from: https://www.mee.gov.cn/gkml/sthjbgw/stbgth/201806/t20180601_442262.htm.

Ministry of Ecology and Environment (2020). "Press conference on ecological and environmental protection during the 13th Five Year Plan." Beijing. Available from: https://www.mee.gov.cn/xxgk2018/xxgk/xxgk15/202010/t20201021_804298.html.

Ministry of Ecology and Environment and National Bureau of Statistics (2006). "China green national account research report 2004." Beijing. Available from: https://www.mee.gov.cn/gkml/sthjbgw/qt/200910/t20091023_180018.htm.

Ministry of Finance (1984). "Report on adopting the second-phase profit-to-tax reform in state-owned enterprises." Beijing. Available from: http://www.reformdata.org/1984/0918/7497.shtml.

Ministry of Finance (2017). "Notice on further regulating local debt raising." Beijing. Available from: http://www.gov.cn/xinwen/2017-05/03/content_5190675.htm.

Ministry of Finance (2018). "Notice on local debt management." Beijing. Available from: http://www.gov.cn/xinwen/2018-03/27/content_5277661.htm.

Ministry of Finance (2022). "Report on the implementation of 2021 central and local government budget and budget proposal for 2022." Beijing. Available from: http://www.gov.cn/xinwen/2022-03/13/content_5678838.htm.

Ministry of Finance and the National Healthcare Security Administration (2019). "Notice on doing 2019 urban-rural basic health insurance work." Beijing. Available from: http://www.gov.cn/zhengce/zhengceku/2019-10/12/content_5438753.htm.

Ministry of Human Resources and Social Security (2006). *China Labour Statistical Yearbook 2006*. Beijing, China Statistics Press. Available from: http://www.mohrss.gov.cn/SYrlzyhshbzb/zwgk/szrs/tjsj/201206/t20120627_67038.html

Ministry of Industry and Information Technology (2008). "Special 11th Five-Year Plan for the integrated circuit industry." http://cn.chinagate.cn/economics/2008-01/10/content_9509554_4.htm.

Ministry of Industry and Information Technology (2009). "Urgent notice on curbing excessive steel capacity increase." Beijing. Available from: http://www.gov.cn/zwgk/2009-05/14/content_1314437.htm.

Ministry of Industry and Information Technology (2014). "National plan for advancing IC industry development." Beijing. Available from: http://www.cac.gov.cn/2014-06/26/c_1111325916.htm.

Ministry of Industry and Information Technology (2015). "Implementation guidelines on high end manufacturing innovation project." "高端装备创新工程实施指南." Beijing. Available from: https://wap.miit.gov.cn/cms_files/filemanager/oldfile/miit/n973401/n1234620/n1234623/c5542102/part/5542110.pdf.

Modigliani, F. and Cao, S.L. (2004). "The Chinese saving puzzle and the life-cycle hypothesis." *Journal of Economic Literature*, 42: 145–170.

Morduch, J. (1995). "Income smoothing and consumption smoothing." *Journal of Economic Perspectives*, 9(3): 103–114.

Mundell, R. (2004). "China's exchange rate: the case for the status quo." Paper presented at an *IMF seminar on China's foreign exchange system*, Dalian, China, May 26–27.

Nabar, M. and Tovar, C. (2017). "Renminbi internationalization." In: R. Lam, M. Rodlauer and A. Schipke (eds.) *Modernizing China*. Washington, DC: International Monetary Fund. Available from: https://doi.org/10.5089/9781513539942.071.

National Audit Office (2013). "Audit report on 2012 urban social housing projects." "2012 年城镇保障性安居工程跟踪审计结果." Report No. 29. Beijing. Available from: http://www.gov.cn/zwgk/2013-08/09/content_2464030.htm.

National Bureau of Statistics (1988). "Statistics report on national economy and social development of 1987." Beijing. Available from: http://www.stats.gov.cn/tjsj/tjgb/ndtjgb/qgndtjgb/200203/t20020331_30000.html.

National Bureau of Statistics (1999a). "50 years of new China series: the thriving industrial economy." *New China Fifty Years Report Series*, No. 4. Beijing. Available from: http://www.stats.gov.cn/ztjc/ztfx/xzg50nxlfxbg/200206/t20020605_35962.html.

National Bureau of Statistics (1999b). "The rise of TVEs." *New China Fifty Years Report Series*, No. 6. Beijing. Available from: http://www.stats.gov.cn/ztjc/ztfx/xzg50nxlfxbg/200206/t20020605_35964.html.

National Bureau of Statistics (2011). "Tabulations of the 2010 population census" [online]. Beijing. Available from: http://www.stats.gov.cn/tjsj/pcsj/rkpc/6rp/indexch.htm.

National Bureau of Statistics (2017). "Energy production in 2016" [online]. Beijing. Available from: http://www.stats.gov.cn/tjsj/zxfb/201702/t20170228_1467575.html.

National Bureau of Statistics (2018a). *China Economic Census Yearbook 2018*. Beijing.

National Bureau of Statistics (2018b). "The development, deficiency and challenges of China's merchandise trade." "我国货物贸易的发展、不足与挑战." 统计科学研究所宏观经济预测分析小组. Beijing. Available from: http://www.stats.gov.cn/tjzs/tjsj/tjcb/dysj/201810/t20181012_1627392.html.

National Bureau of Statistics (2019a). "Bulletins of the fourth economic census" [online]. Beijing. Available from: http://www.stats.gov.cn/tjsj/tjgb/jjpcgb/.

National Bureau of Statistics (2019b). "National account calculations" [online]. Beijing. Available from: http://www.stats.gov.cn/tjsj/zbjs/201912/t20191202_1713058.html.

National Bureau of Statistics (2021a). *The 7th Population Census*. Beijing. Available from: http://www.stats.gov.cn/tjsj/pcsj/rkpc/d7c/202111/P020211126523667366751.pdf.

National Bureau of Statistics (2021b). "2018 input-output tables of China." Beijing: China Statistics Press. Available from: https://data.stats.gov.cn/ifnormal.htm?u=/files/html/quickSearch/trcc/trcc01.html&h=740.

National Bureau of Statistics (2022a). "Frequently asked questions and answers" [online]. Beijing. Available from: http://www.stats.gov.cn/tjzs/cjwtjd/.

National Bureau of Statistics (2022b). "Migrant worker monitoring survey report 2021" [online]. Beijing. Available from: http://www.stats.gov.cn/tjsj/zxfb/202204/t20220429_1830126.html.

National Bureau of Statistics (2022c). *China Population Census Yearbook 2020.* Beijing: China Statistics Press. Available from: http://www.stats.gov.cn/tjsj/pcsj/rkpc/7rp/indexch.htm.

National Development and Reform Commission (1991). "People's Republic of China economic and social development 10-year plan and the 8th Five Year Plan." "中华人民共和国国民经济和社会发展十年规划和第八个五年计划纲要." Beijing.

National Development and Reform Commission and the United Nations Population Fund (2014). *Providing Public Services for Regular Urban Residents.* Research report. Beijing. Available from: https://china.unfpa.org/zh-Hans/publications.

National People's Congress of the People's Republic of China. (2018). *Constitution of the People's Republic of China.* Beijing. Available from: http://www.npc.gov.cn/npc/c505/201803/e87e5cd7c1ce46ef866f4ec8e2d709ea.shtml.

National People's Congress of the People's Republic of China (1980). "Guangdong special economic zone ordinance." Beijing.

National People's Congress of the People's Republic of China. (1995). *The People's Bank of China Law.* Beijing. Available from: http://www.gov.cn/gongbao/shuju/1995/gwyb199510.pdf.

National People's Congress of the People's Republic of China (1998). *Land Administration Law of the People's Republic of China (1998).* 中华人民共和国土地管理法 (1998 年). Beijing.

National People's Congress of the People's Republic of China (2011). "Press conference on NPC standing committee's special hearing of social housing situations." "全国人大常委会专题询问保障性住房情况发布会." Beijing. Available from: http://www.scio.gov.cn/xwfbh/rdzxxwfbh/xwfbh/wjb44184/Document/1691981/1691981.htm.

National People's Congress of the People's Republic of China (2015). "Director general of the State Administration for Industry and Commerce answers questions on business administration reform." Beijing. Available from: http://www.npc.gov.cn/zgrdw/npc/zhibo/zzzb30/node_27354.htm.

National People's Congress of the People's Republic of China (2021). "The establishment and improvement of the socialist legal system with Chinese characteristics." "中国特色社会主义法律体系的形成和完善." Beijing.

National People's Congress of People's Republic of China. (2021). "General report on state-owned assets management by the State Council." Beijing. Available from: http://www.npc.gov.cn/npc/c30834/202110/c63f586559e84bc0ae85fa752d358f0c.shtml.

National Reform Commission (1984). "Minutes of the work conference on urban economic system reform pilot program." Beijing. Available from: https://china.findlaw.cn/fagui/p_1/37005.html.

Natural Resource Defense Council (2014). "Recommendations for China energy statistics." Beijing. Available from: http://www.nrdc.cn/information/informationinfo?id=122&cook=1.

Naughton, B. (2021). *The Rise of China's Industrial Policy, 1978–2020.* Mexico City: Centro de Estudios China-México, Universidad Nacional Autónoma de México. https://dusselpeters.com/CECHIMEX/Naughton2021_Industrial_Policy_in_China_CECHIMEX.pdf.

Nie, H. and Jiang, M. (2011). "Government-enterprise collusion and mining disasters, evidence from China's provincial panel data." "政企合谋与矿难，来自中国省级面板数据的证据." *Economic Research*, 6: 146–156.

Nielsen (2019). *Report on the Indebtedness of Young People in China*. Beijing. Available from: https://vicsdf.com/doc/loXhBhDzd8V4e5xguKUHew.

Nove, A. (1969). *Economic History of the USSR*. London: Allen Lane.

Nye Jr., J. (2020a). "A strategy for China." In: *Domestic & International (Dis) Order: A Strategic Response*. Washington, DC: Aspen Institute. https://www.aspeninstitute.org/wp-content/uploads/2020/11/Chapter-5_Nye_A-Strategy-for-China.pdf.

Nye Jr., J. (2020b). "Power and Interdependence with China." *Washington Quarterly*, Spring 2020.

O'Brien, K.J. and Li, L. (1999). "Selective policy implementation in rural China." *Comparative Politics*, 31: 167–186.

Ohno, K. (2009). "Avoiding the middle-income trap: renovating industrial policy formulation in Vietnam." *ASEAN Economic Bulletin*, 26(1): 25–43. Available from: http://www.jstor.org/stable/41317017.

Oi, J.C. (1992). "Fiscal reform and the economic foundations of local state corporatism in China." *World Politics*, 45: 99–126.

Okun, A.M. (1975). *Equality and Efficiency: The Big Trade-Off*. Washington, DC: Brookings Institution Press.

Organisation for Economic Co-operation and Development (OECD) (2000). "Main determinants and impacts of foreign direct investment on China's economy." *OECD Working Papers on International Investment*, 2000/04. Paris: OECD Publishing. Available from: https://doi.org/10.1787/321677880185.

Ostry, J.D., Berg, A. and Tsangarides, C.G. (2014). "Redistribution, inequality and growth." *IMF Staff Discussion Paper* SDN/14/02. Washington, DC: International Monetary Fund.

Oya, C. and Schaefer, F. (2019). *Chinese Firms and Employment Dynamics in Africa: A Comparative Analysis*. London: IDCEA Research.

Page, J. (2011). "Land dispute in China town sparks revolt." *Wall Street Journal*, 15 December.

Park, Y.J. (2021). "Chinese investment in Africa involves more than megaprojects." *Washington Post*, 21 April.

Paulson Jr., H.M. (2015). *Dealing with China*. New York: Grand Central Publishing.

People's Bank of China (PBC) (1993). "Notice of the People's Bank of China on operational issues of implemneting the 'State Council's notice on further reforming the foreign exchange management system'." Beijing. Available from: http://www.elinklaw.com/zsglmobile/lawView.aspx?id=33637.

People's Bank of China (PBC) (2005). "Measures for short-term bill management." Beijing. Available from: http://www.pbc.gov.cn/tiaofasi/144941/144957/2817096/index.html.

People's Bank of China (PBC) (2012). "The 12th Five Year Plan for financial sector development and reform." Beijing. Available from: http://www.pbc.gov.cn/goutongjiaoliu/113456/113469/2863578/index.html.

People's Bank of China (PBC) (2015a). "Updated transcript of the mid-price quotation briefing of the RMB/USD exchange rate." 完善人民币兑美元汇率中间价报价吹风会文字实录." 13 August. Available from: http://m.safe.gov.cn/safe/2015/0813/4617.html.

People's Bank of China (PBC) (2015b). "Central bank releases for the first time stock data on the scale of social financing, which reached RMB 122.86 trillion at the end of 2014." 10 February. Available from: http://www.gov.cn/xinwen/2015-02/10/content_2817538.htm.

People's Bank of China (PBC) (2016). *RMB Internationalization Report*. Beijing.

People's Bank of China (PBC) (2017). *China Financial Stability Report 2017.* Beijing. Available from: https://www.gov.cn/xinwen/2017-07/06/5208092/files/572fec1a7b41440295c62fe548ad56fd.pdf.

People's Bank of China (PBC) (2019). "China monetary policy report, quarter four, 2018." Beijing. Available from: http://www.pbc.gov.cn/en/resource/cms/2019/03/2019032115562784220.pdf.

People's Bank of China (PBC) (2020). "Draft amendments for comments to the 'People's Bank of China Law'." Beijing. Available from: http://www.gov.cn/zhengce/zhengceku/2020-10/24/content_5553847.htm.

People's Bank of China (2022). "Green finance help carbon emission peak and net zero." Beijing. Available from: http://www.pbc.gov.cn/goutongjiaoliu/113456/113469/4500507/index.html.

PBC Department of Investigation and Statistics (2020). "2019 Chinese urban households balance sheet survey." "2019 年中国城镇居民家庭资产负债情况调查." 中国金融微信号. Beijing. Available from: http://www.xinhuanet.com/2020-04/25/c_1125902781.htm.

People's Daily (2010). "China's answer in the face of international financial crisis" [online]. 5 January. Available from: http://www.gov.cn/jrzg/2010-01/05/content_1503824.htm.

People's Daily (2013). "Smog affected 600 million Chinese" [online]. 22 July. Available from: http://news.cntv.cn/2013/07/22/ARTI1374451738503165.shtml.

People's Daily (2015). "Xi Jinping: people's heart is the most important politics." 10 June. Available from: http://politics.people.com.cn/BIG5/n/2015/0610/c1001-27128818.html.

People's Daily (2017). "Governor said Liaoning resisted pressure and squeezed 'water' out of data." 17 January. Available from: http://politics.people.com.cn/n1/2017/0117/c1001-29030885.html.

People's Daily. (2018). "What's the essence of the U.S. provoking the trade war? [online]." 10 August. Available from: http://opinion.people.com.cn/n1/2018/0810/c1003-30220231.html.

People's Daily (2019). "Current year shantytown starts exceeded 3 million units" [online]. 14 December. Available from: http://cpc.people.com.cn/BIG5/n1/2019/1214/c419242-31506038.html.

People's Daily (2021a). "At the end of last year, the national railway operated 146,000 kilometers of track" [online]. 26 September. Available from: http://www.gov.cn/xinwen/2021-09/26/content_5639361.htm.

People's Daily (2021b). "China's operating highspeed railway lines exceed 40,000 kilometres." 31 December. Available from: https://3w.huanqiu.com/a/54dc9a/46CwRl3gMIz?agt=56.

Perkins, D.H. (1988). "Reforming China's economic system." *Journal of Economic Literature*, 26(2): 601–645. Available from: http://www.jstor.org/stable/2726364.

Pesek, W. (2015). "Welcome to China's dangerous year." *Barron's*, 29 December. Available from: https://www.barrons.com/articles/welcome-to-chinas-dangerous-year-1451353372.

Pew Research Center (2021). *Pew Global Attitudes Survey 2021.* Washington, DC. Available from: https://www.pewresearch.org/global/database/indicator/24.

Phoenix News (2020). "A brief introduction to the distribution of coal resources in China" [online]. 13 March. Available from: https://ishare.ifeng.com/c/s/7uoKmDUE6Y9.

Piketty, T., Li, Y.. and Zucman, G. (2017). "Capital accumulation, private property and rising inequality in China, 1978-2015." *NBER working Paper* 23368. Cambridge, MA: National Bureau of Economic Research. Available from: https://www.nber.org/papers/w23368.

Politico (2022). "'We're in an economic war:' White House, Congress weigh new oversight of U.S. investments in China." 19 February. Available from: https://www.politico.com/news/2022/02/19/china-investments-economy-us-congress-00008745.

Prasad, E.S., Rogoff, K., Wei, S.J. and Kose, M.A. (2003). "Effects of financial globalization on developing countries: some empirical evidence." *IMF Occasional Paper* No. 220. Washington, DC: International Monetary Fund.

Pritchett, L. and Summers, L.H. (2014). "Adiaphora meets regression to the mean." *NBER Working Paper* 20573. Cambridge, MA: National Bureau of Economic Research. Available from: http://www.nber.org/papers/w20573.

Prud'homme, D. and von Zedtwitz, M. (2018). "The changing face of innovation in China." *MIT Sloan Management Review*, 59(4): 24–32.

Qin, H. (2019). "Future housing system has been established, four types of housing supply." *Huaxia Times*, 1 January. Available from: https://www.163.com/dy/article/E4F5G0O60512D03F.html.

Qu, J.D., Zhou, F.Z. and Ying, X. (2009). "From overall control to technical governance." "渠敬东 周飞舟 应 星. "从总体支配到技术治理"." *Social Science in China* (6). Available from: http://www.shehui.pku.edu.cn/upload/editor/file/20180309/20180309153425_1558.pdf.

Qin, B., Strömberg, D. and Wu, Y. (2017). "Why does China allow freer social media? Protests versus surveillance and propaganda." *Journal of Economic Perspectives*, 31(1): 117–40. https://doi.org/10.1257/jep.31.1.117.

Qin, F., Ouyang, J. and Li, G. (2020). "Fully release education dividend, mitigating the depletion of demographic dividend." *Guangming Daily*, 16 November 2020. http://theory.people.com.cn/n1/2020/1116/c40531-31931756.html.

Ramo, J.C. (2004). *The Beijing Consensus*. London: Foreign Policy Centre. Available from: https://fpc.org.uk/publications/the-beijing-consensus/.

Rawski, T. (2001). "What is happening to China's GDP statistics?" *China Economic Review*, 12(4). Available from: https://doi.org/10.1016/S1043-951X(01)00062-1.

Reinhart, C.M. and Rogoff, K.S. (2009). *This Time Is Different: Eight Centuries of Financial Folly*. Princeton, NJ: Princeton University Press,

Reinhart, C.M. and Rogoff, K.S. (2013). "Banking crises: an equal opportunity menace." *Journal of Banking & Finance*, 37(11): 4557–4573. Available from: https://www.sciencedirect.com/science/article/abs/pii/S0378426613001362.

Reuters (2011). "Clinton warns against 'new colonialism' in Africa." 11 June. Available from: https://www.reuters.com/article/us-clinton-africa-idUSTRE75A0RI20110611.

Reuters (2016). "Unpaid and angry, some Chinese workers ditch holidays to protest." 4 February. Available from: https://www.reuters.com/article/us-lunar-newyear-china-insight-idUSKCN0VD2ZJ.

Reuters (2018). "EU expands WTO case against Chinese technology transfers." 20 December. Available from: https://www.reuters.com/article/us-eu-china-wto-idUSKCN1OJ1AP.

Reuters (2020). "China's 2019 annual crude imports set record for 17th year." 14 January. Available from: https://www.reuters.com/article/us-china-economy-trade-crude-idUKKBN1ZD0CI.

Rodrik, D. (2004). "Industrial policy for the twenty-first century." *CEPR Discussion Paper*, No. 4767. London: Centre for Economic Policy Research. Available from: https://cepr.org/active/publications/discussion_papers/dp.php?dpno=4767.

Rodrik, D. (2010). "The return of industrial policy." *Project Syndicate*, 12 April. Available from: https://www.project-syndicate.org/commentary/the-return-of-industrial-policy-2010-04.

Rodrick, D. (2013). "Unconditional convergence in manufacturing." *Quarterly Journal of Economics*, (128)1: 165–204. Available from: https://drodrik.scholar. harvard.edu/publications/unconditional-convergence-manufacturing.

Rogin, J. (2022). "Biden doesn't want to change China. He wants to beat it." *Washington Post*, 10 February. Available from: https://www.washingtonpost. com/opinions/2022/02/10/biden-china-strategy-competition/.

Rogoff, K. and Yang, Y. (2021). "Has China's housing production peaked?" *China and the World Economy*, 21(1): 1–31.

Rounds, Z. and Huang, H. (2017). "We are not so different: a comparative study of employment relations at Chinese and American firms in Kenya." *SAIS-CARI Working Paper* No. 2017/10. Washington, DC: SAIS-CARI, Johns Hopkins University.

Rozelle, S. and Hell, N. (2020). *Invisible China: How the Urban Divide Threatens China's Rise*. Chicago, IL: University of Chicago Press.

Rudd, K. and Rosen, D. (2020). "China backslides on economic reform." *Wall Street Journal*, 22 September. Available from: https://www.wsj.com/articles/ china-backslides-on-economic-reform-11600813771.

Rumbaugh, T. and Blancher, N. (2004). "China: international trade and WTO accession." *IMF Working Paper* 04/36. Washington, DC: International Monetary Fund.

SAIS-CARI (2019). "SAIS-CARI China in Africa database" [online]. Washington, DC: China-Africa Research Initiative, Johns Hopkins School for Advanced International Studies SAIS-CARI. Available from: https://www.sais-cari.org/data.

Schularick, M. and Taylor, A. (2012). "Credit booms gone bust: monetary policy, leverage cycles and financial crises, 1870–2008." *American Economic Review*, 102(2): 1029–1061.

Securities and Exchange Commission (SEC) (2020). *Holding Foreign Companies Accountable Act (HFCAA)*. Washington, DC. Available from: https://www.sec.gov/hfcaa.

Shen, J. (2007). *Labour Disputes and Their Resolution in China*. Oxford: Chandos Publishing.

Shen, X. (2015). "Private Chinese investment in Africa: myths and realities." *Development Policy Review*, 33(1): 83–106.

Shi, F.Q. (2010). "Comments on Dr. Wang Xiaolu's 'grey income and national income distribution'." National Bureau of Statistics [online], 25 August. Available from: http://www.stats.gov.cn/ztjc/ztfx/grdd/201008/t20100825_59069.html.

Shih, V.C. (2010). "China's 8000 credit risks." *Wall Street Journal*, 10 February. Available from: https://www.wsj.com/articles/SB10001424052748703427704575052062978995460.

Shih, V.C. (2011). "China needs a credit crunch." *Wall Street Journal*, 29 June.

Shiina, Y. (2012). "Defining and measuring the shadow banking system." 28 August. Basle: Financial Stability Board, Bank for International Settlements. Available from: https://www.bis.org/ifc/events/6ifcconf/shiina.pdf.

Shroff, A. (2020). "'Made in China 2025' disappears in name only." *Indo-Pacific Defense Forum*, 23 March. Available from: https://ipdefenseforum.com/2020/03/made-in-china-2025-disappears-in-name-only.

Sina Finance (2018). "Guo Shuqing: half of bank lending should go to private enterprises in 3 years." *Sina Finance*, 8 November. Available from: https://finance.sina.com.cn/money/bank/bank_hydt/2018-11-08/doc-ihnprhzw4576911.shtml.

Spence, M. (2011). *The Next Convergence: The Future of Economic Growth in a Multispeed World*. New York: Farrar, Straus and Giroux.

State Administration for Market Regulation (2021). "Press conference on enhancing business registration service and better business environment." Beijing. Available from: http://www.gov.cn/xinwen/2021-04/29/content_5603688.htm.

State Council (1980). "Temporary stimulations on adopting a "layered lump-sum contract system by revenue and expenditure categories" fiscal management system." "国务院关于实行'划分收支、分级包干'财政管理体制的暂行规定." Notice No. 33. Beijing.

State Council (1984). "Temporary rules on further expanding SOE autonomy." "关于进一步扩大国营企业自主权的暂行规定." Beijing: China Reform database.

State Council (1985). "Notice on implementing the provisions on the financial management system of "division of taxes, verification of income and expenditure, and hierarchical contracts"." "关于实行"划分税种、核定收支、分级包干"财政管理体制的规定的通知." Beijing.

State Council (1987). "Report on the national economy and social development plan." Beijing. Available from: http://www.gov.cn/gongbao/shuju/1987/gwyb198709.pdf.

State Council (1988). "Requirements on some issues of accelerating and deepening foreign trade system reform." "国务院关于加快和深化对外贸易体制改革若干问题的规定." Notice No. 12. Beijing.

State Council (1989). "State Council decision on current key industrial policy points." Document No. 29. Beijing. Available from: http://www.gov.cn/zhengce/content/2011-09/07/content_1453.htm.

State Council (1992). "Rules on switching operating system of fully owned state industrial enterprises." "全民所有制工业企业转换经营机制条例." Ordinance No. 103. Beijing.

State Council (1993a). "Decision on implementing tax sharing fiscal management system." "关于实行分税制财政管理体制的决定." Notice No. 85. Beijing.

State Council (1993b). "Notice on further reform foreign exchange management system." "国务院关于进一步改革外汇管理体制的通知." Notice No. 89. Beijing.

State Council (1994a). "Notice on deepening reform of grain purchase and sales system." "国务院关于深化粮食购销体制改革的通知." Notice No. 32. Beijing.

State Council (1994b). "Decisions on deepening urban housing reform." "关于深化城镇住房制度改革的决定." Notice No. 43. Beijing. Available from: http://cpc.people.com.cn/BIG5/n1/2019/1214/c419242-31506038.html.

State Council (1994c). "National industrial policy outline of the 1990s." Beijing. Available from: http://www.gov.cn/gongbao/shuju/1994/gwyb199412.pdf.

State Council (1998). "Notice on further accelerating urban housing system reform and housing construction." "国务院关于进一步深化城镇住房制度改革加快住房建设的通知." Notice No. 23. Beijing.

State Council (2000). "Notice on some policies on encouraging software and IC industry development." Document No. 23. Beijing. Available from: http://www.gov.cn/gongbao/content/2000/content_60310.htm.

State Council (2003). "Notification on fostering continuous healthy development of the property market." Beijing. Available from: http://www.gov.cn/gongbao/content/2003/content_62364.htm.

State Council (2004). "Decision on deepening reform and tightening land management." Beijing. Available from: http://www.gov.cn/gongbao/content/2004/content_63043.htm.

State Council (2005). "Interim stipulations on industrial structural adjustments." Document No. 40. Beijing. Available from: http://www.gov.cn/zwgk/2005-12/21/content_133214.htm.

State Council (2006). "National medium and long-term science and technology development plan 2006-2020." "国家中长期科学和技术发展规划纲要 (2006-2020 年)." Beijing. Available from: http://www.gov.cn/gongbao/content/2006/content_240244.htm.

State Council (2009). "Steel industry adjustment and rejuvenation plan." Beijing. Available from: http://www.gov.cn/zwgk/2009-03/20/content_1264318.htm.

State Council (2010). "Decision on accelerating the development of strategic new (emerging) industries." Document No. 32. Beijing. Available from: http://www.gov.cn/zwgk/2010-10/18/content_1724848.htm.

State Council (2011). "Policies on further encouraging the development of software and integrated circuit industries." Document No. 4. Beijing. Available from: http://www.gov.cn/zwgk/2011-02/09/content_1800432.htm.

State Council (2013a). "Plan for State Council organizational reform and functional change." Beijing. Available from: http://www.gov.cn/2013lh/content_2354443.htm.

State Council (2013b). "Action plan on prevention and control of air pollution." Document No. 37. Beijing. Available from: http://www.gov.cn/zwgk/2013-09/12/content_2486773.htm.

State Council (2014). "National new urbanization plan 2014-2020." "国家新型城镇化规划 (2014-2020 年)." Beijing. Available from: http://www.gov.cn/gongbao/content/2014/content_2644805.htm.

State Council (2015). "Made in China 2025." Beijing. Available from: http://www.gov.cn/zhengce/content/2015-05/19/content_9784.htm.

State Council (2016). "National 13th Five Year Plan on strategic new industry development." Document No. 67. Beijing. Available from: http://www.gov.cn/zhengce/content/2016-12/19/content_5150090.htm.

State Council (2018). "Explanations about State Council organization reform." *Guowuyuan*, 14 March. Beijing.

State Council (2019). "Temporary regulation on the procedure of major executive decisions." "重大行政决定程序暂行条例." State Council Order No. 713. Beijing. Available from: http://www.gov.cn/zhengce/content/2019-05/08/content_5389670.htm.

State Council (2020). "Some policies to foster IC and software industry development in the new era." Document No. 8. Beijing. Available from: http://www.gov.cn/zhengce/content/2020-08/04/content_5532370.htm.

State Council (2021). "The 14th Five Year Plan on digital economy development." Document No. 29. Beijing. Available from: http://www.gov.cn/zhengce/content/2022-01/12/content_5667817.htm.

State Council Information Office (2001). "State Planning Commission reduces price approval items, liberalises most prices of goods and services previously set by the central government." "国家计委减少价格审批项目放开大多数原由中央政府制定的商品和服务价格." Beijing. Available from: http://www.scio.gov.cn/xwfbh/xwbfbh/wqfbh/2001/0711/Document/327684/327684.htm.

State Council Information Office (2003). "Minutes of the April 20 press conference." Beijing. Available from: http://www.china.com.cn/zhibo/2003-04/20/content_8784515.htm.

State Council Information Office (2021). "China's policy and action in combating climate change (white paper)." Beijing. Available from: http://www.scio.gov.cn/zfbps/32832/Document/1715491/1715491.htm.

State Council Office (2008). "Guidelines on key areas of high-tech industries with current development priorities." Beijing. Available from: http://www.gov.cn/ztzl/kjfzgh/content_883675.htm.

State Council Research Office (2006). "Reporting on the problems of Chinese farmer-turned workers." *Reform Magazine*, 5. Available from: http://rdbk1.ynlib.cn:6251/qw/Paper/311037.

State Economic and Trade Commission, Ministry of Finance, Ministry of Science and Technology, and State Taxation Administration (2002). *National Industrial Technology Policies*. SETC Document No. 444. Beijing. Available from: http://www.chinatax.gov.cn/chinatax/n810341/n810765/n812203/200204/c1209100/content.html.

State Environmental Protection Administration – Policy Research Center for Environment and Economy (2001). *New Countermeasures for Air Pollution Control in China – Final Report*. Beijing.

State Information Centre (2021). "Current situation of new strategic industries and suggestions for the 14th FYP period." Beijing.

State Tax Administration (2019a). "Answers to media questions on 'General plan for lowering social insurance contribution'." Beijing. Available from: http://www.chinatax.gov.cn/chinatax/n810341/c101340/c101373/c101374/c5006343/content.html.

State Tax Administration (2019b). "Notice on tax cut and tax waiver for small and micro-sized enterprises." Beijing. Available from: http://www.chinatax.gov.cn/n810219/n810744/n4016641/n4016661/c4023833/content.html.

Sun, G.F. (2011). *First Row – Close Range Thinking of China's Financial Reform.* 第一排——中国金融改革的近距离思考. Beijing: China Economic Publishing House.

Sun, G.F. (2019). "China's shadow banking: bank's shadow and traditional shadow banking." *BIS Working Paper* No. 822. Basel: Bank for International Settlements. Available from: https://www.bis.org/publ/work822.pdf.

Sun, I.Y. (2017). *The Next Factory of the World: How Chinese Investment Is Reshaping Africa*. Brighton, MA: Harvard Business Review Press.

Sun, L. (2002). "New trends of China's social structural evolution since the mid-1990s." *Modern China Studies*, 2002(3). https://www.modernchinastudies.org/us/issues/past-issues/78-mcs-2002-issue-3/1243-90.html.

Sun, Y. and Du, D. (2010). "Determinants of industrial innovation in China: evidence from its recent economic census." *Technovation*, 30(9–10): 540–550. Available from: https://doi.org/10.1016/j.technovation.2010.05.003.

Tan, M., Li, X., Xie, H. and Lu, C. (2005). "Urban land expansion and arable land loss in China – a case study of Beijing-Tianjin-Hebei region." *Land Use Policy*, 22: 187–196.

Tang, J. (2011). "Review and reflection of land expropriation reform." "征地制度改革的回顾与思考." *Chinese Land Science*, 25(11). Available from: https://m.aisixiang.com/data/47834.html

Tang, X. (2016). "Does Chinese employment benefit Africans? Investigating Chinese enterprises and their operations in Africa." *African Studies Quarterly*, 16(3–4): 107–128.

Tang, Y. and Côté, I. (2021). How large-scale land protests succeed in China. *Journal of Chinese Political Science*, 26: 333–352.

Tao, R. (2012). "Difficulties of China's growth model." In: Tsinghua-Brookings Research Center (ed.) *China in the Next Five Years: Opportunities and Challenges*. Available from: https://www.brookings.edu/wp-content/uploads/2016/06/2-Preface-Tao-Ran.pdf.

Tao, R. (2016). "The dilemma of China's growth model." Tsinghua-Brookings Public Policy Research Centre. Available from: https://www.brookings.edu/wp-content/uploads/2016/06/2-Preface-Tao-Ran.pdf

Tao, R., Su, F., Liu, M. and Cao, G.Z. (2010). "Land leasing and local public finance in China's regional development: evidence from prefecture-level cities." *Urban Studies*, 47(10): 2217–2236.

Tao, R., Yuan, F. and Cao, G.Z. (2007). "Regional competition, land transfer and local fiscal effects: an analysis based on the panel data of China's prefectural cities from 1999 to 2003." *World Economy*, 10: 15–27.

Tian, G.Q. (2016). "Debating industrial policy: limited government vs active government." "争议产业政策:有限政府，有为政府." *Caijing*, 5 November.

Time Magazine (2003). "Beijing's SARS attack." *Time Magazine*, 8 April. Available from: http://content.time.com/time/subscriber/article/0,33009,441615,00.html.

Tsinghua University (2021). "Summary report of 'study on China's long-term low carbon development strategy and transition path'." Available from https://www.efchina.org/Reports-zh/report-lceg-20210711-zh.

Tsui, K.Y. (2011). "China's infrastructure investment boom and local debt crisis." *Eurasian Geography and Economics*, 52(5): 686–711.

UNCTAD (2022). "World Investment Report 2022." Available from https://worldinvestmentreport.unctad.org/world-investment-report-2022/.

UNCTADStat (n.d.). "United Nations Conference on Trade and Development (UNCTAD) statistics" [online]. Available from: https://unctadstat.unctad.org/EN/#.

United Nations, Department of Economic and Social Affairs, Population Division (2022). *World Population Prospect 2022*. Available from: https://population.un.org/wpp/

U.S.-China Economic and Security Review Commission (2022). "China companies listed on major U.S. stock exchanges" [online]. 31 March. Washington, DC. Available from: https://www.uscc.gov/research/chinese-companies-listed-major-us-stock-exchanges.

US Congress (2022). *H.R. 4521 – America COMPETES Act of 2022*. Washington, DC. Available from: https://www.congress.gov/bill/117th-congress/house-bill/4521.

US State Department (2021). *US-China Joint Glasgow Declaration on Enhancing Climate Action*. Washington, DC. Available from: https://www.state.gov/u-s-china-joint-glasgow-declaration.

Office of the United States Trade Representative (USTR) (2018). *Report on Findings of the Investigation into China's Acts, Policies, and Practices Related to Technology Transfer, Intellectual Property, and Innovation Under Section 301 of the Trade Act of 1974*. Washington, DC. Available from: https://ustr.gov/sites/default/files/Section%20301%20FINAL.PDF.

USTR (2021). *U.S. Statement on Trade Policy Review of China, October 2021*. Washington, DC.

USTR (2022). *Fact Sheet: USTR Releases 2022 President's Trade Policy Agenda and 2021 Annual Report*. Washington, DC. Available from: https://ustr.gov/sites/default/files/USTR%20Trade%20Policy%20Agenda-Annual%20Report%20Fact%20Sheet.pdf.

Vagliasindi, M. and Gorgulu, N. (2021). "What have we learned about the effectiveness of infrastructure investment as a fiscal stimulus?" *Policy Research Working Paper* 9796. Washington, DC: World Bank.

Vendryes, T. (2010). "Land rights in rural China since 1978: reforms, successes, and shortcomings." *China Perspective*, 4: 87–99.

Wang, C. (2012). "History of the Chinese family planning program: 1970–2010." *Contraception*, 85(6): 563–569. https://doi.org/10.1016/j.contraception.2011.10.013.

Wang, F.L. (2005). *Organizing through Division and Exclusion: China's Hukou System*. Stanford, CA: Stanford University Press.

Wang, J. (1988). "Choosing the right long-term development strategy – thoughts about an economic development strategy with great international circulation." "选择正确的长期发展战略——关于国际大循环经济发展战略的构想." *Economic Daily.* 5 January.

Wang, J. (2013a). "The economic impact of special economic zones: evidence from Chinese municipalities." *Journal of Development Economics*, 101: 133–147.

Wang, S. (2013b). The success and failure of China's SEZs, debate in the mid-1980s. *21ˢᵗ Century*, 139. Available from: https://www.cuhk.edu.hk/ics/21c/media/articles/c139-201212054.pdf.

Wang, T. (2004). "Exchange rate dynamics." In: E. Prasad (ed.) *China's Growth and Integration into the World Economy*, pp 21–28. Washington, DC: International Monetary Fund.

Wang, T. (2009). *Where Are We with the Stimulus Package?* Hong Kong: UBS Investment Research.

Wang, T. (2011a). *China Monetary Policy Handbook* (2nd ed.). Hong Kong: UBS Investment Research.

Wang, T. (2011b). "Bubble or no bubble? The great Chinese property debate." Hong Kong: UBS Investment Research.

Wang, T. (2011c). "Is Wenzhou China's first domino?" Hong Kong: UBS Investment Research.

Wang, J.J. (2014). "Vertical government power and governance: analysis of China's government-society relations." "纵向政府权力结构与社会治理:中国"政府与社会" 关系的一个分析路径." *Zhejiang Social Sciences*, 9. Available from: http://rdbk1.ynlib.cn:6251/qk/Paper/570011.

Wang, T. (2014a). "PSL: form or substance?" Hong Kong: UBS Investment Research.

Wang, T. (2014b). "China's evolving monetary policy framework." In: K. Guo and A. Schipke (eds.) *New Issues in Monetary Policy: International Experience and Relevance for China.* Joint conference by the People's Bank of China and the IMF. Beijing. Available from: https://www.imf.org/external/np/seminars/eng/2014/pbc/pdf/Book070214.pdf.

Wang, T. (2015). "Something positive about the SOE reform plan." Hong Kong: UBS Investment Research.

Wang, T. (2016). "Dealing with China's debt challenge." In: M. Ai and A. Schipke (eds.) *Strengthening the International Monetary System and International Experience in Resolving Debt Problems.* Joint conference by the People's Bank of China and the IMF. Beijing. Available from: https://www.imf.org/external/np/seminars/eng/2016/pbc/pdf/ebooken.pdf.

Wang, T. (2020). "Monetary policy instruments." In: M. Amstad, G.F. Sun and W. Xiong (eds.) *The Handbook of China's Financial System*, pp 63–86. Princeton, NJ. Princeton University Press.

Wang, J.S. (2010). "A study on the attitudes toward immigrants by urban residents with regional disparities based on the 2005 national comprehensive social survey data." *Chinese Journal of Sociology*, 30(6): 156–174.

Wang, X.L. (2010a). "Urbanization path and city scale in China: an economic analysis." 经济研究. *Economic Research*, 10: 20–32.

Wang, X.L. (2010b). "Gray income and the household income gap." Beijing: National Economic Research Institute.

Wang, F. and Mason, A. (2004). "The demographic factor in China's transition." Paper prepared for the *"China's Economic Transition: Origins, Mechanism, and Consequences" conference*, Pittsburgh, PA, 4–7 November 2004.

Wang, G. and Lin, N. (2019). "70 years of China's foreign exchange market development: history and experience." 经济学动态. *Economic Perspectives*, 10: 3–10.

Wang, H. and Wheeler, D. (2000). *Endogenous Enforcement and Effectiveness of China's Pollution Levy System*. Policy Research Working Paper 2336. Washington, DC: World Bank.

Wang, T. and Hu, H. (2010). "How undervalued is the RMB?" Hong Kong: UBS Investment Research.

Wang, T., Hu, H. and Weng, D. (2012). *What to expect from Chinese consumers in the next decade?* Hong Kong: UBS Investment Research.

Wang, T. and Zhong, J. (2016). "What are the real problems with China's debt?" Hong Kong: UBS Investment Research.

Wang, W. and Wang, T. (2008). "50 years of the Hukou system." "户籍制度 50 年." *Population Research*, 132(1): 43–50.

Wang, Y. and Han, Z. (2015). "The crisis and opportunity of China's development." "产业发展的危与机." *Sina Finance*, 26 February. Available from: http://finance.sina.com.cn/money/bond/20150226/154421599167.shtml.

Wang, Y. and Hua, X. (2017). "Detailed content of 'active government' in new structural economics – and reply to Tian Guoqiang's criticism." "详论新结构经济学中" 有为政府" 的内涵——兼对田国强教授批评的回复." *Economic Review*, 3: 17–30.

Wang, T., Chen, L. and Zhang, N. (2017c). "Deleveraging by supervisory tightening in China?" Hong Kong: UBS Investment Research.

Wang, T., Chen, L. and Zhang, N. (2017d). "China de-leveraging: where are we?" Hong Kong: UBS Investment Research.

Wang, L., Wang, Z., Ma, Q. et al. (2019). The development and reform of public health in China from 1949 to 2019. *Global Health*, 15. Available from: https://doi.org/10.1186/s12992-019-0486-6.

Wang, T., Zhang, N., Bedford, J. and Zhong, J. (2016a). "China's 'missing' shadow credit." Hong Kong: UBS Investment Research.

Wang, T., Zhang, N., Zhong, J. and Luo, Y. (2016b). "How did China manage a big turnaround?" Hong Kong: UBS Investment Research.

Wang, T., Zhang, N. and Yan, M. (2021). "Can consumer credit drive consumption rebound?" Hong Kong: UBS Investment Research.

Wang, T., Zhang, N., Zhong, J., Kwok, D. and Chen, L. (2017a). "Understanding China (part IV): the perpetual property bubble debate." Hong Kong: UBS Investment Research.

Wang, T., Zhang, N., Zhong, J., Lam, J. and Yan, M. (2022). *Could the property downturn be China's Minsky moment?* Hong Kong: UBS Investment Research.

Wang, T., Zhong, J., Peng, C., Yan, M., Liu, W., Liu, J., Gong, P., Lam, J., Chen, X. and Chen, B. (2020). "Consumer behavior and intention after Covid-19: UBS Evidence Lab pulsecheck consumer survey." Hong Kong: UBS Investment Research.

Wang, Z., Wei, S.-J., Yu, X. and Zhu, K. (2017b). "Measures of participation in global value chains and global business cycles." *NBER Working Paper* 23222. Cambridge, MA: National Bureau of Economic Research.

Wang, Z., Wei, S.-J., Yu, X. and Zhu, K. (2018). "Re-examining the effects of trading with China on local labor markets: a supply chain perspective." *NBER Working Paper* No. 24886. Cambridge, MA: National Bureau of Economic Research. Available from: https://ssrn.com/abstract=3236693.

Wei, G.Q., Cui, G.F. and Song, Y.B. (2016). "Jing-Jin-Ji control of coal-burning experience." "京津冀各地散煤治理经验探析." *Environmental Protection*, 6: 28–30.

Wei, S.-J. and Zhang, X. (2011). "The competitive saving motive: evidence from rising sex ratios and savings rates in China." *Journal of Political Economy*, 119(3): 511–564. Available from: https://doi.org/10.1086/660887.

Wen, J.B. (2007). *Work Report of the Government*. Beijing: Central Government of the People's Republic of China. Available from: http://www.gov.cn/test/2009-03/16/content_1260188.htm.

Wen, J.B. (2009). *Work Report of the Government*. Beijing: Central Government of the People's Republic of China. Available from: http://www.gov.cn/test/2009-03/16/content_1260221.htm.

Whalley, J. and Zhang, S. (2004). "Inequality change in China and (Hukou) labour mobility restrictions." *NBER Working Paper* No. 10683. Cambridge, MA: National Bureau of Economic Research.

Whalen, J. (2021). "Countries lavish subsidies and perks on semiconductor manufacturers as a global chip war heats up." 14 June, The Washington Post. Available from: https://www.washingtonpost.com/technology/2021/06/14/global-subsidies-semiconductors-shortage/

White, G. (ed.) (1988). *Developmental States in East Asia*. London: Macmillan Press.

White, G. (ed.) (1991). *The Chinese State in the Era of Economic Reform*. London: Macmillan Press.

The White House (2014). "U.S.-China joint announcement on climate change." Washington, DC. Available from: https://obamawhitehouse.archives.gov/the-press-office/2014/11/11/us-china-joint-announcement-climate-change.

The White House (2021a). "FACT SHEET: Biden-Harris Administration announces supply chain disruptions task force to address short-term supply chain disconti-nuities." Washington, DC. Available from: https://www.whitehouse.gov/briefing-room/statements-releases/2021/06/08/.

The White House (2021b). "White House executive order on ensuring the future is made in all of America by all of America's workers." Press release, 25 January.

The White House (2021c). "Interim national security strategic guidance." Washington, DC.

White House Office of Trade and Manufacturing Policy (2018). "Office of trade & manufacturing policy report: "how China's economic aggression threatens the technologies and intellectual property of the United States and the world"." Press release, 19 June. Washington, DC. Available from: https://trumpwhitehouse.archives.gov/briefings-statements/office-trade-manufacturing-policy-report-chinas-economic-aggression-threatens-technologies-intellectual-property-united-states-world/.

Whiting, S.H. (2010). "Fiscal reform and land public finance." In: J. Man and Y.H. Hong (eds.) *China's Local Public Finance in Transition*. Cambridge, MA: Lincoln Institute of Land Policy, pp. 125–144.

Williamson, J. (1990). "What Washington means by policy reform." In: Williamson, J. (eds.) *Latin American adjustment: how much has happened*. Washington, DC: Institute of International Economics, pp. 5–20.

Williamson, J. (2002). *Did the Washington consensus fail?* Washington, DC: Petersn Institute of International Economics. Available from: https://www.piie.com/commentary/speeches-papers/did-washington-consensus-fail.

Williamson, J. (2004). "The strange history of the Washington consensus." *Journal of Post Keynesian Economics*, 27(2): 195–206. Available from: http://www.jstor.org/stable/4538920.

Wolf, M. (2018). "China's debt threat: time to rein in the lending boom." *Financial Times*, 25 July. Available from: https://www.ft.com/content/0c7ecae2-8cfb-11e8-bb8f-a6a2f7bca546.

Wong, C. (2013). "Paying for urbanization in China: challenges of municipal finance in the twenty-first century." In: R.W. Bahl, J.F. Linn and D. Wetzel (eds.) *Financing Metropolitan Governments in Developing Countries*, pp 273–308. Cambridge, MA: Lincoln Institute of Land Policy.

Woo, W. (2012). "China meets the middle-income trap: the large potholes in the road to catching-up." *Journal of Chinese Economic and Business Studies*, 10(4): 313–336.

World Bank (1983). *China: Socialist Economic Development*. Washington DC.

World Bank (1993). *The East Asian Miracle*. Washington, DC.

World Bank (2001). *China, Air, Land, and Water, Environmental Priorities for a New Millennium*. Washington DC.

World Bank (2003). *China – Promoting Growth with Equity: Country Economic Memorandum*. Washington, DC. Available from: https://openknowledge.worldbank.org/handle/10986/14643.

World Bank (2007). *Cost of Pollution in China: Economic Estimates of Physical Damages*. Washington, DC: World Bank Environmental and Social Development Unit, East Asia & Pacific Region. Available from: https://data.worldbank.org/indicator/IC.BUS.EASE.XQ.

World Bank Indicators (2020). "Ease of doing business rankings" [database]. Washington, DC. Available from: https://data.worldbank.org/indicator/IC.BUS.EASE.XQ.

World Bank Indicators (2000–2018). "CO_2 emission data" [database]. Washington, DC. Available from: https://data.worldbank.org/indicator/EN.ATM.CO2E.KT?locations=CN.

World Bank and Development Research Center (DRC) of the State Council, the People's Republic of China (2014). *Urban China: Toward Efficient, Inclusive, and Sustainable Urbanization*. Washington, DC: The World Bank.

World Bank and Development Research Center of the State Council, the People's Republic of China (2019). *Innovative China: New Drivers of Growth*. Washington, DC: World Bank. Available from: https://openknowledge.worldbank.org/handle/10986/32351.

World Bank and World Trade Organization (2019) *Global Value Chain Development Report 2019: Technological Innovation, Supply Chain Trade, and Workers in a Globalized World*. Washington, DC: World Bank Group. Available from: http://documents.worldbank.org/curated/en/384161555079173489/Global-Value-Chain-Development-Report-2019-Technological-Innovation-Supply-Chain-Trade-and-Workers-in-a-Globalized-World.

Wu, C.P. (1986). "Theoretical explanations for the birth rate decline in China." 邬沧萍。中国生育率下降的理论解释. *Population Research*, 10(1): 10–16.

Wu, L. (2002). "Analysis of China's urbanization process 1978-2000." "1978–2000年中国城市化进程研究." *Research in Chinese Economic History*, 3: 73–82.

Wu, H.X. (2014). "China's growth and productivity performance debate revisited." The Conference Board EPWP 14–01. New York. Available from: https://www.conference-board.org/pdf_free/workingpapers/EPWP1401.pdf.

Wu, Q. (2009). "China's public health: historical evolution, current state and future challenges." "中国公共卫生的历史沿革、现状与未来挑战." 中国医疗卫生发展报告. *China Medical and Health Development Report*, 5.

Wu, X.P. (2018). 12 September 2018 [online]. Available from: http://redchinacn.org/portal.php?mod=view&aid=36799.

Wu, T., Zhao, H. and Ou, X. (2014). "Vehicle ownership analysis based on GDP per capita in China: 1963–2050." *Sustainability*, 6(8): 4877–4899. Available from: https://www.mdpi.com/2071-1050/6/8/4877.

Wu, Z. (2013). "China's money shortage: short-term pain better than long-term pain." *New York Times Chinese website*, 26 June. Available from: https://cn.nytimes.com/china/20130628/cc28crunch/zh-hant/.

Xi, J.P. (2014). *Xi Jinping on the Governance of China*. 习近平谈治国理政. Beijing: Foreign Languages Publishing House, pp. 265–266.

Xi, J.P. (2015). "Speech at the United Nations development summit." *Xinhua News Agency*, 27 September. Available from: http://www.xinhuanet.com/world/2015-09/27/c_1116687809.htm.

Xi, J.P. (2017). "Report of the party's 19th national congress plenary session." *Xinhua News Agency*, 27 October. Available from: http://www.gov.cn/zhuanti/2017-10/27/content_5234876.htm.

Xi, J.P. (2018). "Speech at the private enterprise forum." *Xinhua News Agency*, 1 November. Available from: http://www.gov.cn/xinwen/2018-11/01/content_5336616.htm.

Xi, J.P. (2020). "Speech at the meeting to coordinate works on Covid-19 control and social economic development." *Xinhua News Agency*, 24 February. Available from: http://www.gov.cn/xinwen/2020-02/24/content_5482502.htm.

Xi, J.P. (2021). "Speech at the centennial celebration of the Communist Party of China." Available from: http://www.gov.cn/xinwen/2021-07/01/content_5621847.htm

Xiao, G. (2004). "People's Republic of China's round-tripping FDI: scale, causes and implications." *ADB Institute Discussion Paper* No. 7. Tokyo: Asian Development Bank Institute. Available from: https://www.adb.org/sites/default/files/publication/156758/adbi-dp7.pdf.

Xinhua News Agency (2017). "China's ambassador to the UN: BRI helping to achieve sustainable development goal." *Xinhua News Agency*, 13 April. Available from: https://www.financialnews.com.cn/gc/201704/t20170413_115877.html.

Xinhua News Agency (2018). "Major progress on illegal vaccine production of Changsheng Biology." *Xinhua News Agency*, 27 July. Available from: http://www.xinhuanet.com/politics/2018-07/27/c_1123187880.htm.

Xinhua News Agency (2020). "Investigation report of the circumstances related to Doctor Li Wenliang as exposed by the public (The National Inspection Commission)." Available from: http://www.xinhuanet.com/2020-03/19/c_1125737457.htm.

Xinhua News Agency (2021a). "Xi Jinping held video conference with US President Biden." *Xinhua News Agency*, 16 November. Available from: http://www.gov.cn/xinwen/2021-11/16/content_5651232.htm.

Xinhua News Agency (2021b). "U.S., China should seek way to coexist, cooperate." *Xinhua News Agency*, 11 November.

Xinhua News Agency (2022). "Liu He presided over a meeting of the financial commission of the State Council to study the current situation." *Xinhua News Agency*, 16 March. Available from: http://www.gov.cn/guowuyuan/2022-03/16/content_5679356.htm.

Xu, D. (ed.) (1988). *Contemporary Chinese Population*. 当代中国人口. Beijing: China Social Science Publishing, pp. 294–295.

Xu, R.J. (2006). "The waves of educated-youth returning to cities." "许人俊. "知青返城浪潮起落纪实"." *China Reform Database*, 15 March. Available from: http://www.reformdata.org/2006/0315/8097.shtml.

Xu, X.C. (2016). "The right way to look at China's GDP growth." National Bureau of Statistics website. Available from: http://www.stats.gov.cn/tjsj/sjjd/201601/t20160121_1307412.html.

Xu, X.C. (2019). "Accurately understanding China's current gross domestic product." *Statistical Research*, 36(5). Available from: 10.19343/j.cnki.11-1302/c.2019.05.001.

Xue, L. and Liu, B. (2013). "Taking stock 10 years after SARS: changes in public governance system." "盘点 "非典" 十年:公共治理体系变革." *Study Times*. 17 June. Available from: http://theory.people.com.cn/n/2013/0617/c49154-21866221.html.

Yan, M., Wang, T., Peng, C., Ye, A., Lam, J., Liu, J. and Zhou, A. (2020). "China consumer credit: UBS Evidence Lab Inside – is the fever of consumer credit cooling?" Hong Kong: UBS Investment Research.

Yang, D. (2021). "From education industrialization to non-profit orientation of education." 从教育产业化到教育的非营利化. *Tencent News*, 17 November. Available from: https://new.qq.com/omn/20211117/20211117A04X9H00.html.

Yang, S. and Wen, T.J. (2010). "Economic volatility, fiscal system evolution and land resource capitalization – empirical analysis on issues related to 'three encirclements' since reform." "经济波动、财税体制变迁与土地资源资本化——对中国改革开放以来 "三次圈地" 相关问题的实证分析." *World of Management*, 4: pp. 32–41.

Yang, D., Zhang, J. and Zhou, S. (2011). "Why are saving rates so high in China?" *IZA Discussion Paper* No. 5465. Bonn: Forschungsinstitut zur Zukunft der Arbeit. Available from: https://ftp.iza.org/dp5465.pdf.

Yang, J., Zhai, K. and Webb, Q. (2021). "China's corporate crackdown is just getting started." *Wall Street Journal*, 5 August. Available from: https://www.wsj.com/articles/china-corporate-crackdown-tech-markets-investors-11628182971.

Ye, L. and Wu, A.M. (2014). "Urbanization, land development and land financing: evidence from Chinese cities." *Journal of Urban Affairs*, 36(s1): 354–368. Available at from: https://ssrn.com/abstract=2690998.

Yeung, Y., Lee, J. and Kee, G. (2009). "China's special economic zones at 30." *Eurasian Geography and Economics*, 50(2): 222–240.

Young, A. (1995). "The tyranny of numbers: confronting the statistical realities of the east Asian growth experience." *Quarterly Journal of Economics*, 110(3): 641–680.

Yu, J. and Wang, Y. (2019). "The development of China's photovoltaic industry and the new opportunities of the "Belt and Road initiative"." "中国光伏产业的发展与"一带一路"的新机遇." *New Structural Economics Working Paper* C2019007. Beijing: Peking University, China Centre for Economic Research.

Yu, J.R. (2009). "Major types and basic characteristics of group events in today's China." "当前中国群体性事件的主要类型及其基本特征." *Journal of China University of Political Science and Law*, 6: 114–120.

Yu, Y.D. (2002). "The dynamic growth path of M2-GDP." "M2-GDP 的动态增长路径." *World Economy*, 12: 3–12.

Yuan, G.M. (袁钢明) (2007). "China's steel industry – developing amid macroeconomic changes." "中国钢铁工业—在宏观经济变动中发展." Japan Institute for Asian Economic Research. Available from: https://www.ide.go.jp/library/English/Publish/Reports/Jrp/pdf/143_2.pdf.

Zang, L. and Zhang, Y. (2019). "Understanding 40 years of change in China's governance framework: theoretical interpretation based on local-central government relations." "理解中国治理机制 40 年变迁:基于中央与地方关系的学理再诠释." *Social Science*, 4. Available from: http://cohd.cau.edu.cn/module/download/downfile.jsp?classid=0&filename=a49038a9f12141ecac47b7f0ea6e52fd.pdf.

Zeng, D.Z. (2010). *Building Engines for Growth and Competitiveness in China: Experience with Special Economic Zones & Industrial Clusters*. Washington, DC: World Bank.

Zeng, Y. (1992). *Family Dynamics in China: A Life Table Analysis*. Madison: University of Wisconsin Press.

Zhang, A.H. (2022). "Agility over stability: China's great reversal in regulating the platform economy." *Harvard International Law Journal*, 63(2). Available from: http://doi.org/10.2139/ssrn.3892642.

Zhang, F., Yu, M. and Yu, J. (2016). "One belt and one road and RMB internationalization." "一带一路和人民币国际化。." *CCER Discussion Paper* C2016003. Bejing. http://nsd.pku.edu.cn/cbw/tlg1/2016a/250356.htm.

Zhang, K. and Li, C. (2021). "Adjustments of administrative regions in 70 years of new China: process, characteristics and outlook." "新中国 70 年区划调整的历程、特征和展望." *Social Science Journal*, 1. Available from: http://www.cre.org.cn/xs/zueshudongtai/16287.html.

Zhang, L. (2012a). "Economic migration and urban citizenship in China: the role of points systems." *Population and Development Review*, 38(3): 503–533.

Zhang, L. and Li, T. (2012). "Barriers to the acquisition of urban Hukou in Chinese cities." *Environment and Planning A*, 44: 2883–2900.

Zhang, L.M., Brooks, R., Ding, D., Ding, H., He, H., Lu, J. and Mano, R. (2018). "China's high savings: drivers, prospects, and policies." *IMF Working Paper*, WP/18/277. Washington, DC: International Monetary Fund.

Zhang, N. and Wang, T. (2017a). "New estimates of China's 'missing' shadow credit." Hong Kong: UBS Investment Research.

Zhang, N. and Wang, T. (2017b). "How do subsidies matter for the property market?" Hong Kong: UBS Investment Research.

Zhang, N. and Wang, T. (2021). "UBS CFO survey: stronger capex intentions, higher credit costs and continued supply chain shift." Hong Kong: UBS Investment Research.

Zhang, W.Y. (2012b). *What Changed China: Overview and Path of China's Reform*. 什么改变中国: 中国改革的全景和路径. 中信出版社. Beijing: CITIC Press.

Zhang, W.Y. (2016). "Why I am against industrial policy – debate with Yifu Lin." "我为什么反对产业政策——与林毅夫辩." *CCER Bulletin*, 62(1306). Available from: https://www.ccer.pku.edu.cn/yjcg/jb/243026.htm.

Zhang, Y.W. and Liu, T.X. (2015). *The Transformation of China's Industrial Policies*. 张永伟、刘涛雄. "中国产业政策转型研究 ——从产业政策迈向竞争与创新政策"." Beijing: Center for Industrial Development and Environmental Governance, Tsinghua University.

Zhang, X.C., Xu, Z. and Qin, D. (2013). "Private lending rates and private capital outlet: the case of Wenzhou." "民间借贷利率与民间资本的出路:温州案例." *Journal of Financial Research*, 3(393): 1–14.

Zhao, R.W. (1992). "Some special phenomena in income distribution during China's transition period." "中国转型期中收入分配的一些特殊现象." *Economic Research*, 1: 53–63.

Zhao, R.W. and Li, S. (1997). "The widening of China's income disparity and reasons." "中国居民收入差距的扩大及其原因." *Economic Research*, 9: 19–28.

Zheng, M.L. (2017). "Whoever does not reform must step down." *Ta Kung Pao*, 17 February. Available from: http://news.takungpao.com/mainland/focus/2017-02/3422196.html?pc.

Zheng, S., Sun, W., Wu, J. and Yun, W. (2014). "Infrastructure investment, land leasing and real estate price: a unique financing and investment channel for urban development in Chinese cities." *Economic Research Journal*, 8: 75–81.

Zheng, Y.N. (2014). *Technology Empowerment: China's Internet, State and Society*. 技术赋权: 中国的互联网, 国家与社会. Shanghai: Oriental Publishing House.

Zheng, Y.N. and Wu, G.G. (1994). "On central-local relations – the axis of China's system transition." "论中央—地方关系——中国制度转型中的一个轴心问题." *Modern China Studies*, 6. Available from: https://www.modernchinastudies.org/us/issues/past-issues/51-mcs-1994-issue-6.html

Zhong, K.B. (2007). "Coal mine safety: challenges facing government supervision in the transitional period." "煤矿安全:转型期中国政府监管面临的挑战." *Guangdong Social Sciences*, 1. Available from: http://rdbk1.ynlib.cn:6251/qk/Paper/334450

Zhong, R. (2020). "Behind China's chip fever: investment bubble and abandoned projects." "中国"芯片热"背后:投资泡沫、项目烂尾." *New York Times China*, 28 December. Available from: https://cn.nytimes.com/technology/20201228/china-semiconductors/.

Zhou, L.A. (2007). "Study on Chinese local officials' promotion championship model." "中国地方官员的晋升锦标赛模式研究." *Economic Research*, 7: 36–50.

Zhou, L.A. (2008). *Local Governments in Transition: Officials' Incentives and Governance*. 转型中的地方政府:官员激励与治理. 格致出版社. Shanghai: Grace Press.

Zhou, Q.R. (2004). "Rural land rights and land requisition system – important options facing China's urbanization." "农地产权与征地制度———中国城市化面临的重大选择." *China Economic Quarterly*, 4(1): 193–210.

Zhou, Q.R. (2010). *What China Has Done Right – The Unfolding of Deng's Drama*. 中国做对了什么? Beijing: Peking University Press.

Zhou, X.C. (2016). "Individuals increasing mortgage borrowing has the right logic." *China Daily*, 26 February.

Zhou, X.G. (2011). "The authoritarian system and effective governance: systemic logic in contemporary China's governance." "权威体制与有效治理: 当代中国国家治理的制度逻辑." 开放时代. *Open Times*, 10: 67–85.

Zhu, L. and He, W. (2018). "40 years of rural poverty reduction amid industrialisation and urbanisation." "工业化城市化进程中的乡村减贫 40 年." *Labour Economics Research*, 4: 3–31.

Zhu, L.J. (2003). "The Hukou system of the People's Republic of China: a critical appraisal under international standards of internal movement and residence." *Chinese Journal of International Law*, 2(2): 519–565.

Zhu, M., Zhang, L.M. and Peng, D. (2019). "China's productivity convergence and growth potential." *IMF Working Paper* WP/19/263. Washington, DC: International Monetary Fund.

Zhu, S.Y. (2000). "Research of reform issues in China's urbanization." "中国农村城镇化进程中的改革问题研究." *China Rural Survey*, 6: 2–24.

Zou, Y. (2016). "Current situation of excess capacity and policy suggestions on capacity reduction." Beijing: State Information Center. Available from: http://www.sic.gov.cn/News/455/7349.htm.

Zweig, D. and Bi, J. (2005). "China's global hunt for energy." *Foreign Affairs*, 84(5). Available from: https://doi.org/10.2307/20031703.

Index